COUNTERPOINT

COUNTERPOINT

A Translation of KONTRAPUNKT
by HEINRICH SCHENKER

Volume II
of *New Musical Theories and Fantasies*

Book I
Cantus Firmus and
Two-Voice Counterpoint

Translated by John Rothgeb and Jürgen Thym

EDITED BY JOHN ROTHGEB

SCHIRMER BOOKS
A Division of Macmillan, Inc. New York

Collier Macmillan Publishers London

Copyright 1910 by J.C. Cotta'sche Buchhandlung Nachfolger

The English language edition has been authorized by Universal Edition A.G.

Copyright © 1987 by Schirmer Books
  A Division of Macmillan, Inc.

Schirmer Books
A Division of Macmillan, Inc.
866 Third Avenue, New York, N. Y. 10022

Collier Macmillan Canada, Inc.

Library of Congress Catalog Card Number: 86-18645

Printed in the United States of America

printing number
1 2 3 4 5 6 7 8 9 10

Library of Congress Cataloging-in-Publication Data

Schenker, Heinrich, 1868–1935.
  Counterpoint: a translation of Kontrapunkt.

  "Volume II of New musical theories and fantasies."
  Bibliography: p.
  Contents: bk. 1. Cantus firmus and two-voice counter-
point—bk. 2. Counterpoint in three and more voices,
Bridges to free composition.
  1. Counterpoint. I. Rothgeb, John. II. Title.
MT55.S2413   1987   781.4'2   86-18645
ISBN 0-02-873220-0 (set)
ISBN 0-02-873221-9 (v. 1)
ISBN 0-02-873222-7 (v. 2)

To the Memory of My Father

Contents

PART TWO.   TWO-VOICE COUNTERPOINT

Chapter 1.   The First Species: Note Against Note   110

Preface to the English Translation

Kontrapunkt, published here for the first time in English translation, is the second installment of Schenker's magnum opus, *Neue musikalische Theorien und Phantasien* (see Appendix A). Standing chronologically between *Harmonielehre* and *Der freie Satz,* it presents a systematic treatment of voice-leading principles that is in many respects fundamental to a full understanding of both the earlier and the later work.

The irreducible core of *Kontrapunkt* is a set of prescriptions and restrictions (*Ge-* and *Verbote*) for writing exercises in the five species of counterpoint originated by Fux, as well as several combinations of the species which are here explored systematically for the first time. Thus the treatise belongs, on the one hand, to a well established tradition. What is most strikingly unique about Schenker's *Kontrapunkt,* on the other hand, is that his prescriptions and restrictions (which do not differ significantly from those of Fux and several later teachers) are derived not from the compositional practice of a particular period, but from a connected and systematic set of direct observations of the effects that necessarily accompany each of the basic ways of combining tones both simultaneously and in succession. These observations locate the effects of each basic tonal configuration on one or more of several continua: for example, from good to poor, from simple to complex, from more to less natural, and from more to less comprehensible. Thus similar motion to perfect intervals (to cite a perennial issue of contrapuntal theory) is observed to be *poor,* and the thoroughness with which Schenker specifies the reasons underlying this observed quality (and those that underlie others as well) is another unique aspect of his treatment of the subject. The occurrence of dissonance as a passing tone is characterized by simplicity and naturalness; the dissonant neighboring note, although retaining the favorable attribute of movement by step, is less simple and less natural, for reasons that are likewise specified.

Beyond absolute prescription and restriction, such observations may lead to preferences or tendencies, or may determine which subsequent species or textural situation may provide resources sufficient to counteract the poor effect of a given voice-leading procedure, and may thus define the conditions under which an initially proscribed configuration can become acceptable. Direct progression to a perfect consonance by nonparallel similar motion, for example, remains prohibited throughout two-voice counterpoint, but is admitted under appropriate mitigating circumstances in counterpoint of three or more voices. Such circumstances, together with the fuller texture established by the presence of three voices, provide "motivations and counterforces" able to adequately reduce or suppress effects that are in themselves "always poor" (p. 141).

Schenker's purpose, then, is by no means to provide an ordinary textbook for writing counterpoint in any particular historical style. Although the writing of exercises, and the concomitant acquisition of skill in leading voices, is indispensable for thorough assimilation of Schenker's text, the goal of the exercises is not chiefly to prepare the student for actual composition, but to train the musical ear. Indeed, it was Schenker's view that the process of learning to hear properly was itself an art, and the study of counterpoint an indispensable ingredient in its cultivation. But to function properly in that capacity, contrapuntal study first had to be "thoroughly separated from composition if the ideal and practical verities of both are to be fully developed" (p. 10). This is a theme followed through so consistently and with such compelling logic throughout Schenker's text as to require no additional elucidation here.

The two volumes of *Kontrapunkt* were published in 1910 and 1922, respectively. The period during which Schenker was writing them saw political, social, and artistic changes of the most consequential type, especially in Central and Eastern Europe. In the last decades of the nineteenth and the first decade of the twentieth century it became obvious that the Austro-Hungarian monarchy was increasingly unable to provide a political framework that could control the many forces threatening the empire—specifically, mass movements of nationalism, socialism, and more urgent demands for democracy. Adamant in his rejection of both communism and Western-style democracy as ideologies exalting the masses (and thus the lowest common denominator), Schenker was convinced that Art could thrive only in an environment that did not succumb to the popular (and thus leveling) trends of the times. He believed that genius—the single source of high Art—could flourish only in an elitist, aristocratic culture, however flawed the particular aristocracy might be; and in observing the world around him he realized with bitterness that such cultures were doomed by forces both from within and from without.

Against such a backdrop, it is perhaps understandable that Schenker's political and social arch-conservatism found expression in his musical publications, including the two volumes at hand. Especially his fanatical Germanic nationalism—a posture radically tempered, incidentally, by events of the period from 1933 to the end of his life—has caused subsequent editors of his works to expunge passages that were considered at best irrelevant and at worst offensive. Our own editorial policy in this respect has been shaped by our distaste for censorship in any form; our text is, therefore, unabridged. We urge the reader to recognize that however much Schenker may have regarded his musical precepts as an integral part of a unified world-view, they are, in fact, not at all logically dependent on any of his extramusical speculations. Indeed, no broader philosophical context is necessary—or even relevant—to their understanding.

We thank Professor Saul Levin for assistance with a passage from Fux's Latin text. Professor Allen Forte read portions of the translation and made valuable suggestions, as did Professor Charles Burkhart. Irene Schreier Scott furnished a perceptive critique of our draft of Schenker's Preface, and also provided access to a copy of *Kontrapunkt* annotated by Oswald Jonas. Professor Marilyn Gaddis Rose and the associates of the Translation Research and Instruction Program at the State University of New York at Binghamton furnished sound advice about the treatment of certain section-headings. The alert proof-readers who deserve thanks are David Raymond and Tamara Levitz. Finally, we acknowledge with gratitude the expert production supervision provided by Michael Sander of Schirmer Books.

JOHN ROTHGEB
Binghamton, N.Y., 1986

TECHNICAL NOTE

We have retained the somewhat unusual typographical feature of the German original wherein certain passages of text are set in a smaller type size. A few of the passages in question—especially in the Introduction—are of the nature of digressions that partly follow through on a train of thought subordinate to the main text; the large majority, however, present quotations from earlier theorists, together with critiques of their views.

In many cases a style of punctuation similar to Schenker's own has been used. While this may give the text a slightly archaic appearance, it often helps to clarify the meaning.

The original musical examples contained a multitude of misprints of all kinds. These have been corrected without comment. Examples quoted by Schenker from earlier treatises were almost all printed in open score in the original sources; we have followed the orthography of Schenker's German edition in our use of condensed scores. In most cases, designations of vocal ranges for pre-existing counterpoint exercises have been added by Schenker.

Author's Preface

We stand before a Herculaneum and Pompeii of music! All musical culture is buried; the very tonal material—that foundation of music which artists, transcending the spare clue provided by the overtone series, created anew in all respects from within themselves—is demolished. The most marvelous and, one might say, "created" of the arts, that art which, among all arts, caused the severest birth-pangs and thus was the last bequeathed to us—the youngest of the arts, *music*—is lost!

Mankind, to be sure, is completely unaware of this deplorable state of affairs; people continue to intoxicate themselves with grand slogans, with pompous catchwords. They speak emphatically of the "twentieth century" and of "progress"; they ecstatically praise the *Zeitgeist* and the "modern," and see an abundance of "geniuses" on all sides: "genius"-composers, "genius"-conductors, "genius"-performers. All without the slightest notion of how little such ecstacy can be reconciled with the talk that soon follows once again about "sterility" of the present, about "stagnancy of production," and even about waning artistic potency. Heaven knows how the world manages to rhyme "rise" with "fall"!

But the puzzle and contradiction is easily solved, since in reality only the decline is a sad fact, while truly positive, artistic forces are almost completely lacking.

I plan to discuss more precisely in a later volume the decline and its causes. The seriousness of the task to which I introduce the reader in the volume at hand, however, demands that I deal with these circumstances even here, if in a brief and perfunctory manner.

First of all, it is necessary to speak here about the external factors that caused the decline of our art, and among them, about the performing musician in particular.

No master's authority has ever been able to convince those who merely perform music that it is little, far too little, to do nothing more than learn to play the violin, a wind instrument, keyboard, or to conduct. If the masters so sternly censured performers' activity when it was inartistic and lacking in depth and schooling, if they vented their scorn often with truly prophetic rage, performers only savored more fully the adulation of the world, which pampered them with wealth and honors as "artists." Why bother oneself about music, if one had a family, money, and a position?

Performers disregard the fact that notational symbols really hide more than they make explicit, and that, strictly speaking, even today they are hardly more than neumes behind which another world opens wide and deep—a true *beyond*, like the very soul of art. They always play, to express it more clearly, only on a *single* surface, so to speak—merely in a planimetric way—where they should play in several dimensions, as though in a stereometric way. They play away as if only to get to know the work, where they ought to get to know the work first in order to be able to play it at all. What it means to know a piece thoroughly—this, unfortunately, they do not know.

The damage suffered by music through this artistic opportunism and ignorance, through the complete lack of responsibility on the part of performing musicians, can be grasped only by considering how much—one could almost say, how organically—music is dependent on performance. A comparison with other arts is instructive. After Rembrandt completed a painting, nobody had any further power over it; only the role of the observer was left for others. The painting suffers no injury if one observer rambles fatuously about it; it reaps no benefit if another enjoys it more intelligently: the picture is complete and remains the same for all eternity. Works of music, however, have a different and sadder fate. For most people, a symphony by Beethoven has to be performed by an orchestra and a conductor or in the form of a piano reduction for two or four hands. But what the *performers* play—is it really the symphony by Beethoven? Are the different performances all good, do they all do justice to the work? If not, which rendition is the Beethoven symphony? Where is it? Where is the authentic shape as Beethoven himself conceived it? But what if one had to say that *none* of the known renditions even approximates what is to be expressed? That, indeed, is the truth of the matter! Inferior instinct and (often) complete lack of secure knowledge on the part of today's performing musicians are the reasons that the masterworks—how bitter a truth!—have not been heard in our time in their authentic shape. Their content is not yet known (I will prove this, as promised earlier, in as much detail as possible on another occasion); and, for that reason, performances often sound as though a Japanese or Chinese were to pick up a text by Goethe without sufficient knowledge of the German language. Now it becomes clear why people today feel the constant need to "progress" and why it is incessantly claimed that Classical composers have been "surpassed." If one knows the works of the masters only in a limited fashion—then, of course, one may see in (for example) Richard Strauss an innovation and improvement over Beethoven. But I say: perform the masterworks of J.S. Bach, Haydn, Mozart and Beethoven as they really are; they will always surpass with ease the works of today's and tomorrow's "surpassers."

The "dilettante" may be singled out as another factor [in the decline of music].

Vanity and the desire to be entertained drive him to art, but he stubbornly insists that such an impulse be viewed as "artistic instinct" and held in high esteem. A serious organic relation to art remains foreign to him forever; but he arrogantly demands that his relation to art be recognized as the only correct one. He simply proclaims that art exists "for" him—for whom else? and why?—; that exactly his instincts, because they are still uncorrupted, would be the best guides for art; and that his perception, because it is unbiased, would lead to the most correct judgement. In short, he acts as master of the situation, generously promotes Bach, Mozart, and Beethoven, and proudly manufactures "festivals," "jubilees," and the like. It is no use to explain to him that art exists not for him but for its own sake, like everything in the world: sun and earth, animals and flowers; that Bach, when writing the *Well-Tempered Clavier,* certainly was concerned only with the nature of the motives and gave no thought to the dilettante; that compositions (which seemingly belong to a transcendental world) often have a far longer life than human generations, and that, therefore, they have to be understood almost as animate creatures, just as human beings themselves. Today's dilettante does not grasp any of this.

But what is the reason for his arrogant self-deception? We live in an era in which all values in human relationships are turned exactly upside down, by reason of false, unworthy sentimentality: those who need to be led become leaders; the woman assumes the man's role; the child is pampered as an "individuality" and excused from work before even having learned to work; workers who represent mere instruments in human form consider themselves producers. No wonder the relation of the dilettante to art has also been evaluated falsely and wrongly. Today even the simplest things are not understood: that everything in the world has its place and is necessary, to be sure, but that it does not follow merely from this necessity that everything is of equal value. That despite their mutual dependency—in terms of necessity of existence, they remain equal!—the man ranks above the woman, the producer is superior to the merchant or the laborer, the head prevails over the foot, the coachman is more than the wheel of the wagon he steers, the genius means more than the people who represent merely the soil from which he springs. But how is the dilettante to grasp that he does have value inasmuch as he is a receptacle for art, but never more than just this—thus his is a function of only minor relevance!

In an era so confused in its spiritual and social outlook, it is therefore very difficult to get across to the dilettante that the uncorrupted instincts of which he is so proud have no value whatever for art itself as long as they remain untrained, unrefined, and unable to move on the same level as the artistic instincts of the masters, who alone have true artistic instincts in the first place. Just having perceptions is trivial in itself; if any value is to be ascribed to perception, the latter must first be of a certain quality. The dilettante's perception cannot serve as a standard for judging a work, since he has not yet learned how really to hear it. All this he does not grasp nor comprehend. It is a thought foreign to him that the true measure of culture is not represented by enjoyment but solely by the creation of an art-work. Does not a newly created work of art have greater significance than the enjoyment of a whole nation? What is accomplished by the dilettante's stubborn and arrogant insistence on his perception and his opinion?

But what really annoys us about the dilettante and may devalue his character even more (if that is possible) is that he no longer *wants* anything from art. When he claims that art is "for" him, he does so only because of frivolous laziness, since such an attitude simply spares him the difficulty of having to come to terms with art itself. If an artist tried to state his opinion on matters of banking, politics, the army, or jurisprudence to a banker, politician, general, or lawyer he would soon be told that he simply lacked all qualifications to hold such opinions, and that more was required than just dilettantish impressions. On the other hand, the "dilettante" in the field of art insists on the notion that art has to come to him; he ventures to criticize Bach and Brahms for having composed works with which his primitive ability to enjoy cannot cope; he dares to demand of artists that they adjust art to his taste and judgment, although he surely does not benefit from it at all! This much is clear: the average person is afraid of any effort, in life as well as in art. Provided in all respects with spiritual and material gifts by his superiors, he spends his miserable life with a few trifles of religious, moral, and artistic principles. All the more ungrateful and conceited, he bustles about on earth, thinking himself nothing less than the final purpose of all creations of God and the geniuses among men. The average man goes about his business exactly this way also in art, and he wants to have it the same there too. Taking—taking without effort, and pretending unashamedly that this alone is an achievement equivalent to creation! That the dilettante cynically transforms his innate fear of exertion into a demand on art—that is the most revolting and disgusting aspect of his character!

Such is the dilettante, today's master of art! Ever the beneficiary, he still has no notion, sadly enough, of how completely he is occupied throughout his life with the destruction of the very thing he so imperfectly enjoys. Just imagine: he has but one avenue of approach to the musical art-work—that of habituation. All he can do is adjust himself to an art-work or not. No wonder that when this frail bridge collapses, habit finally becomes blunted and complete estrangement and indifference take its place. Often it is simply this way: if a dilettante has listened only a few times to a symphony by, for example, Beethoven, and thus has become accustomed to it, immediately he makes so bold as to claim impudently that he knows the symphony very well, and then he asks—this dilettante!—for something else, something new, always something else *and* new: in short he wants what is called "progress." For his sake, Beethoven, whose worth is virtually obliterated precisely by estrangement and emaciation, is put aside and one steps "forward" to something allegedly new and better; in other words, this dilettante, like a child, is given a doll, which he soon throws away only to ask for a new one. That is how wretchedly lazy and destructive the dilettante is; that is how the great music-loving public relates to that redeeming force called art! It is no different with art than with mankind in general: outside the realm of art, the tragic fate of mankind is always to hunger and long for a redeemer; and although countless redeemers have walked the face of the earth, the great human community has not known what to do with them; the more mankind destroyed their accomplishments, the more loudly it cried out for another redeemer. Alas, what a curse hangs over the average person: to be forced to take, without even being *able* to take!

Now we turn to the remaining factors [in the decline of music]; we turn to music itself. The composer may be first in order of discussion.

Today it is the fashion to talk about an "excess of technique," an excess that allegedly stifles the composer. If we could only gain clarity about what this slogan really means! Is technique not the fulfillment on the part of the artist of those demands which the subject matter itself, far above the artist, imposes on him? In pursuit of such fulfillment, is not technique then a necessary, good, and—so to speak—healthy thing? Is not the technique of a work comparable to the health of a body whose organs fulfill all the functions nature demands of them? If we mean technique in its authentic and true significance, how can we speak logically of an "excess of technique"? Does anyone ever speak seriously of an excess of health? How could this be more than simply health itself? And by the same token, how can an excess of technique—so long as it is understood in its true significance—mean more than only technique? Just consider this: musical technique not only has not been detrimental to our masters; it has, on the contrary, enabled them to give us works such as the B-Minor Mass, the St. Matthew Passion, *Don Giovanni,* and the Ninth Symphony. Why should having musical technique today produce such an adverse effect, if it is indeed true that what today's composers have really is *technique?* It is easy to see that the slogan contains a contradiction: the two words, "excess" and "technique," cannot be joined, if the latter is correctly understood. If the term "technique" has to be associated on logical grounds with an inferior way of organizing tones, then I ask: what is the point of the slogan, which intended in the first place to express praise and recognition of today's composers through the very word "technique"? What kind of praise remains if "technique" is no longer used in a positive sense? Now we get to the heart of the matter: the slogan obviously wants to indicate criticism with its first little word "excess," but praise with its second word "technique." It wants to have both criticism and praise simultaneously, but is unable to express either. This is a true reflection of today's immature mode of thought and feeling. It is high time to abandon this nonsense, to save "technique" from its stifling embrace with "excess" and to represent it only as something true and positive. With this in mind, I say on the contrary: today's composers suffer not from an "excess of technique," as is commonly believed, but rather from too little of it.

Indeed, we no longer have *any* technique! Today's generation even lacks the ability just to understand the existing technique of the masters, which would be required as the first step toward any kind of progress. In comparison with works of our masters, today's compositions have to be considered musically too simple, even *far* too simple and too primitive! Despite heaviest orchestration, despite noisy and pompous gestures, despite "polyphony" and "cacophony," the proudest products of Richard Strauss are inferior—in terms of true musical spirit and authentic inner complexity of texture, form, and articulation—to a string quartet by Haydn, in which external grace hides the inner complexity, just as color and fragrance of a flower render mysterious to humans the undiscovered, great miracles of creation.

The difficult art of synthesis—truly the only source of all musical laws—has become too difficult for the weak nerves of today's musicians. For that reason, they simply abandon the necessity for synthesis and rather escape to the convenient surrogates of program music, music drama, and similar things.

At difficult passages in their works, one sees them always at a loss, specifically at a loss for technical means, which our predecessors had long since mastered. In view of this, is it not justified to say that today's compositions should be dated back by at least two or three centuries?

And furthermore, today's works in part indulge again, as did compositions from the era of vocal polyphony, in empty sonorities (*leere Klänge*)—that is, in a technique which many centuries ago had to be abandoned because it hindered the generation of [musical] content. What difference does it make that in the past those sonorities were triads, and today are mostly seventh-chords? Emptiness is their principal common denominator. Imagination, wealth of ideas and, above all, a determined pursuit of [musical] content, of course, are needed for composing out those sounds; but exactly these virtues and skills are lacking in today's composers. They try to make up for these shortcomings by stuffing their sounds with the excelsior of passing tones. Indeed, passing tones are the sum and substance of today's pompously flaunted technique. If composers could at least demonstrate a greater mastery of this art! But even here a secure instinct and reliable aural skills are lacking: the passing sounds are usually wrongly constructed, so that disorderly and inadvertently comical discords are generated instead of forthright conflicts between several voices. The present era, which is guilty of using this latest non-technique for the first time in the history of our art, was also the one to find a suitable name for it: generally it is called "cacophony."

The lack of technique, which, as I have said, caused our generation to regress artistically by centuries, also explains finally why today's musicians produce so little. Compare the works of our masters with those of today's authors: what a difference in quantity alone, to say nothing of quality. On the one hand, J.S. Bach, Haydn, Mozart, Beethoven, Schubert, Schumann, Mendelssohn, Brahms—such abundance! On the other hand, Strauss, Pfitzner, Humperdinck, Mahler, Reger—such poverty! How little even in quantity the latter write in comparison with those masters who are often denounced as cerebral artists—for example, Beethoven and Brahms. It is only the uproar of the daily newspapers, which always report how Mr. A. is "working on a symphony" or Mr. B. is "composing an opera," only the offensiveness of countless reviews of performances, that evoke the image of an increased productivity of contemporary artists. Close your ears and simply read their list of works and the sad truth becomes obvious.

One can go further still: lack of technique penetrates artists to the core. When an artist has reached his fortieth year, he becomes listless, at odds with art, at odds with life. He does not know what to do; there is no longer a goal for him; all powers decline. He lacks an organic continuity in pursuing a clear goal in life; he ages and dies. . . . Wherever one looks today, a burial ground of artists! . . . And all because the artist neglected in his youth to base his art on a sound foundation that could revitalize him time and time again even in later years. How different, on the other hand, are our masters! Just see how, as a true artist, each of them—to paraphrase a line from the Song of Solomon—"ascends like a column of smoke," increasing the content of his life and art until the end, ever richer, ever more perfect. This is the blessing of what I would like to call technique.

Obviously I cannot be expected to say anything more positive about the present state of *theory*. The volume at hand contains enough to lament from this area; more will be provided in later studies.

A few remarks concerning the methods alone. Unfortunately, theory—leaving aside completely the falsity of its content—always pays attention to the average talent alone and therefore is concerned only with a minimum of instruction itself. It never reaches out to encompass also what the masters themselves considered valuable as experience, to say nothing of the high and highest ideals contained in their works. The sad results of such activity are not difficult to imagine: theory always lets only the average proliferate, and thus inflicts mortal injury on art, which can never live on the sterile and self-suffocating average.

Add to this the incompetent treatment of the most important questions. One is content to say, for instance, "we have major and minor," and so forth. But what does the word "have" mean in this context? What is the student to make of it? Obviously not more than the theorist himself meant by it. And this is sufficient for both. The enormous damage of such a teaching method can be measured only by one who knows that the great human community always accepts what it believes rather than what it should learn to comprehend. Any error is welcome so long as it is presented only in such a way that the intellectual mechanisms are reduced to a minimum. If somebody dares to oppose that method with a different one and sets about explaining what our major and minor systems really are, the result will often be just this: the student will at best admit that he has not completely understood the new explanation; he really "understood" the former explanation of major and minor much better! I readily acknowledge that I never understood Richter's *Harmonielehre*, for example—neither the words in the text nor the notes of the musical examples; nevertheless, thousands of students and teachers claim to have understood that book very well, and, so they say, also to have benefited from working through it. Of course, one should never query them about details; but even the fact that they do not know what to say about it does not disturb their conviction that they have understood it very well. They manage to understand what they do not know and to know what they do not understand. This is the core of the matter: for the world, understanding is simply believing—that is, accepting without effort. Heaven knows how many things the world has "understood" since the creation of the earth without really understanding anything, but only believing! This is the reason for its inclination toward error, which it had only to believe, and for its disinclination toward truth, which—alas!—requires understanding. And therefore, as we see every day, the world follows the cleric rather than Christ, the rabbi rather than Moses, and Bülow rather than Beethoven.

In view of this disposition of mankind, it immediately becomes clear how easy it is for *teachers* and *editors* in music. The truth is what they say it is; and exactly what they say will continue to be believed (excuse me: "understood"). What a dark force: the teacher and editor in music! How they undercut art in their way, and how much more damaging and damnable their activity the less they can be excused simply on grounds of bad faith. How thoroughly young people are misled in schools, conservatories, academies, and the like; how many crimes are committed there against music; how completely everything is institutionalized in a way that leads away from music rather than towards it. Volumes of protest, scorn, and anger could and should be devoted to all of these matters.

The auxiliary disciplines connected with music are no less distressing. Which *history of music* has been able thus far to offer what it should above all offer: a real history of musical technique? Which work has at least pointed toward this goal, not to mention worked out the thesis that the principal idea in the evolution of musical technique has been the composing out of sounds?!

Do we have studies today which, in terms of specific musical content, could compare to the *monographs* of Marpurg, C.P.E. Bach, Quantz, and others? Name just one biography that has done justice to the musical content of an artist's work in specific artistic respects to the same degree that it has done justice to the external data of his life.

What is the use, in musical histories, monographs, and biographies, of focusing chiefly on only the extraneous events, when they can never help us understand the art-work itself? Why lavish such care on discussion of the so-called *Zeitgeist*—often invoked, it has become a real nuisance and plague in our literature during the course of the last decades—when that other, more important, care that should be devoted to the works themselves is lacking? Why all this idle talk, when it is nothing but a cover-up for the incompetence of the author, whose specific musical knowledge obviously does not suffice to clarify the content of the compositions themselves? The question should be posed: is it really the *Zeitgeist* that is responsible for the production of compositions, or is it, rather, artistic technique that generates them? If it is true, as is commonly believed and written, that the *Zeitgeist* is the main factor in the creation of works, then we could assume that, given the right circumstances, Beethoven could have written a work like his Ninth Symphony even before Haydn's first symphony. But is such an assumption correct? How great the times of Alexander the Great, Hannibal, Caesar, and Luther! But why did those times not produce a *Don Giovanni* or a *German Requiem?* Alas, how overdue an understanding that environmental influences entrench themselves, so to speak, in the works of composers only in terms of the compositional technique that exists at the particular historical moment, and that, therefore, only technique is of primary importance. How right and fair it would be to pay attention to the evolution of compositional technique instead of rambling on about the *Zeitgeist!* But this is the heart of the matter: the decline of our art manifests itself in the fact that all forces fail today to come to grips with music in purely artistic terms. One need only glance at the many—far too many—concert guides, program books, and analyses to grasp the terrifying and unbelievable situation. The authors of such books are able to read—just simply to read!—the works of our great masters no better than the performers. Even if it still remains to substantiate all this later in greater detail, I cannot now be silent about the fact that the masterworks of music literature are completely misrepresented in those concert guides. The more the authors of such analyses assure us that the structure of a specific work is clear to them and easy to comprehend, the more the opposite is true—namely, that they know nothing whatever about it. What Kretzschmar, Riemann, Grove, and the rest write about, for example, Beethoven's symphonies is simply wrong and untrue. A thousand times untrue!

That is where we have finally arrived in our art today. Do not be deceived: the life of art, too, has its agony, as does a person who is not blessed with the mercy of a sudden death. Thus I can say that music basically has been moribund for decades—despite Schumann, Mendelssohn, and Brahms—until it finally fell victim to the pervasive vandalism of our time.

In view of these circumstances, our first task must be a real excavation before we can even begin work that will allow us to proceed (I do not say: "progress"!). And in this spirit I invite all true friends of music to examine with me the principles of voice leading. I hope they gain with me the conviction that these principles constitute an inalienable, organic part of all theory and will retain their validity as long as music itself dwells among humans.

But now let us turn to the subject matter of the volume at hand.

All musical technique is derived from two basic ingredients: voice leading and the progression of scale degrees. Of the two, *voice leading* is the earlier and more original element.

The first instincts for voice leading may have originated during the earliest epoch of monophony:[1] in the succession of pitches of a horizontal line, avenues had to be taken that led to the fifth and third (see *Harmony,* §76f.[2]).

When composers later ventured into setting several voices against each other simultaneously, instincts increased with goals. Indeed, the era of vocal polyphony brought forth technical accomplishments and, subsequently, theoretical insights that remained valuable and fundamental for voice leading for all eternity.

The *consonance* was recognized as the first and only true prerequisite of all polyphony. In comparison to the a priori nature of consonance, the *dissonance* was discovered to be only a derivative phenomenon; whether as a passing tone in the horizontal dimension or as a prepared dissonant syncopation in the vertical dimension, the dissonance always needs the consonance as its prerequisite. Furthermore, it was gradually perceived that similar motion presented a danger for the effect of perfect intervals. The effect was altogether poor in composition for only two voices, but receded more or less into the background as more voices appeared. From that perception resulted, on the one hand, the ban on *parallel* or *nonparallel similar motion* in two-voice writing and, on the other hand, an acknowledgement (through the admission of at least nonparallel similar motion in writing for three or more voices) of the paralyzing force of polyphony.[3] The essence of a well-constructed, fluent *melody* was recognized as consisting in a happy medium between ascending and descending melodic forces. And so forth.

In the long run, vocal technique proved unable to increase content. Moreover, the sounds produced by polyphony strove for a solution suited specifically to them. (See *Harmony,* p. 163ff.)

The vocal era came to an end. Composers learned in the next stage—and this is the most significant revolution in the field of musical technique!—to fertilize the sonority itself in a new way. The sonority was, in a sense, "set free" by a longer series of tones, whose multiplicity in succession is grasped precisely through the sonority's unity. The sonority was *composed out,* and thereby was represented through the horizontal line. And thus the first step was taken on the way to the final goal of producing a longer succession of sonorities, each with its own multitude, according to a new principle special to those sonorities alone.

Who knows whether the recitative, discovered by the Italians, in which—according to the usual definition—a single chord presumably merely "supports" a larger number of tones, did not actually have a different mission in technical terms—specifically, to revive artistic awareness of the interrelation between the chord and a longer succession of tones born of it?

When, subsequently, two voices written according to the same principle of composing out were superimposed, the result was a situation completely different from any that could have been observed previously in two voices. Now the lower voice as well as the upper had passing tones of its own which, located between the harmonic tones of a single sound, proved to be true passing tones by nature.[4] These passing tones in the lowest voices, however, had to have a peculiar influence on voice leading, as soon as more than merely two voices were involved. Since even within a polyphonic context these tones could not deny their innate passing character, composers had to grant for the first time the status of simple passing tones even to inherently dissonant seventh-chords and consequently give them a freer treatment—that is, exempt them from the need of preparation or of being resolved in just one way. Add to this chromatic progressions in their multi-faceted application in simple passing tones, in the preparation of dissonances, and the like; add to this greater liberties in the movement of voices in general, especially because of the characters of the instruments (thus in the field of instrumental music): the result was a type of voice leading which, in comparison to the earlier vocal-contrapuntal era, appeared to exhibit many technical innovations. This was the voice leading of *thoroughbass.*

During the vocal era, the principles of vocal voice leading were taught repeatedly in treatises, but all treatises were superseded in significance finally by a work from the eighteenth century—thus in a sense a posthumous work—the famous *Gradus ad parnassum* by J.J. Fux from the year 1725 (see Introduction, p. 2). Similarly, the theory of the voice leading of thoroughbass has been discussed repeatedly in important works, but it certainly received its best and final form in C.P.E. Bach's "Theory of Accompaniment" (the second part of his *Versuch über die wahre Art, das Clavier zu spielen*).[5] Marpurg could remark about this work (in his *Anhang über den Rameau- und Kirnbergerschen Grundbass*):[6] "Meanwhile the most perfect work has appeared concerning the practice of thoroughbass; after this work . . . no realistic person will consider trying his powers on this subject matter."

In the two main treatises just mentioned, the theory of voice leading alone was presented; thus [it appears] in completely pure form at least in that no notion of scale degree is intermixed with it—not even in the matter of doubling of intervals, for example. Fux had no idea whatever of scale degrees, while C.P.E. Bach, who was well aware of the new theory, was deterred by a fortunate artistic instinct from mixing those two heterogeneous disciplines.

Besides the advantage of a pure representation of voice leading, those two authors held an edge in the method with which they set forth their theory. They knew that in order to show the effect of voice leading it was not sufficient to convince the student merely through words or to indicate the effect with only a few tones; rather, they tried to illustrate the circumstances preceding and following, as they appear, of course, only in a somewhat larger context. Therefore, they constructed their exercises with an unbelievable instinct and gave them a scope adequate to demonstrate various problems of voice leading as convincingly as possible. Indeed, not all that must be said about (for example) melodic fluency can be represented by only three or four tones. By the same token, only a few tones cannot really show whether a combination of intervals is good or whether certain progressions have a bad effect. Beyond that, one must know, for example, whether the pitches are conceived as vocal or instrumental, since the mode of performance is not without consequence. In this sense, Fux's *cantus firmus*—more details about it in the Introduction—and the more or less extensive succession of sounds used by C.P.E. Bach as the foundation for his demonstrations, really cannot be prized highly enough from a methodological standpoint.

In contrast to these obvious advantages in presenting the theory of voice leading, unfortunately in Fux as well as in C.P.E. Bach there are also errors that sully not only the method but also the content of the theory itself.

Fux tended to oppose the widespread blossoming of instrumental music. He based his theory of voice leading on a purely vocal foundation, not so much because he was convinced of the value of the method as such but because he wanted to turn the new generation of artists away from instrumental music, which he considered harmful, and to reconvert them to vocal music as allegedly the one and only redeeming technique. What damage Fux's theory suffered in its details will be shown step by step in the present work. We shall be concerned here only with the principal fault. By elevating voice leading to the rank of a binding theory of composition—specifically, one based exclusively on a purely vocal foundation—he unfortunately closed the door to instrumental music from the outset. He was thus unable to show the most important aspect: the fact that all voice leading remains in the final analysis one and the same, even if it appears in a new guise in instrumental music because of the different circumstances present there.

On the other hand, the thoroughbass theory of Bach was faulty because, unfortunately, problems are shown there not in their origin but in an already advanced state. Thoroughbass shows us prolongations of archetypes (*Urformen*),[7] without first having familiarized the reader with the latter in any way. It was impossible to recognize and avoid this mistake, because thoroughbass had above all to serve a practical purpose. If the best musicians of that time made an important stylistic distinction between thoroughbass and truly artistic accompaniment, the conceptual confusion of the two was nevertheless a widespread error. It was caused by the fact that thoroughbass functioned as a didactic tool at least for learning the art of accompaniment; the execution of thoroughbass in four parts unfortunately became the highest attainable form of accompaniment for less talented musicians. Of necessity, people believed that realization of the figures of thoroughbass in continuous four-part texture already constituted artistic accompaniment.

Both the voice leading theory of thoroughbass and Fux's vocal voice-leading theory caused similar damage—the former because of its dedication to the practical purpose of accompaniment, the latter because of its dedication to free composition on a vocal basis.

The result then is: Fux as well as C.P.E. Bach fall short of demonstrating a quasi-absolute unified voice-leading theory encompassing both vocal and instrumental composition. In Fux's theory, what is missing is the "future," so to speak—the prolongations—, while Bach's theory lacks the "past"—the archetypes (*Urformen*).

The most fateful confusion in the theory of voice leading was to come, however, from a completely different direction.

Almost at the same time Fux published his work, Rameau came out in France with a new theory of chord functions, with the theory of tonic, dominant, and subdominant as main chords to which all other chords can be reduced.[8] It was he who created the theory of *scale degree*, that theory which in musical technique, as mentioned above, represents the complement of voice leading. That Fux and Rameau presented their theories almost simultaneously—the theory of voice leading and the theory of scale degree—may perhaps be interpreted as a hint by fate to understand and to treat the two disciplines independently of each other. However, it happened differently. What was a blessing in Fux's case, namely the wealth of centuries of experience from a past epoch he needed only to tap, was for the most part non-existent in Rameau's case. The latter stood only at the beginning of the great instrumental era; he did not even know the works of his contemporary J.S. Bach, and, of course, he was not able to predict how later masters such as C.P.E. Bach, Haydn, Mozart, Beethoven, and their like would compose. In other words, he had no idea whatever of those grand structures that originated in the transformation of a series of sonorities into a widely expanded succession of tones, often involving chords of a passing character, while the sonorities themselves progressed according to certain psychological principles. Who knows whether Rameau would not have conceived his theories differently had he known all those technical developments experience brought about later on. The paucity of the material from which he could draw experience may be cited as the reason that originally his notion of the scale degree and the number of degrees was too limited. What he calls scale degree (fundamental bass) is only to a very small extent also a source of [musical] content. Nor does he specify the true laws according to which the scale degrees move; he still fails to recognize that only *several* sounds of the thoroughbass taken together can perhaps claim the significance of a scale degree; that in order to penetrate to the essence of the scale degree, it is not sufficient to reduce individual phenomena of the thoroughbass merely to their respective fundamental basses and regard the succession of the latter as identical to the succession of scale degrees. He commits the same error, however, in the opposite direction as well. From a succession of fundamental basses he develops an upper voice, a melody, with the express pretense of demonstrating principles of voice leading with it as well. Thus scale degree and voice leading get into an overly close proximity for Rameau, and he is prevented from achieving complete clarity about the nature of both. He does not see that the paths that scale degrees must traverse cannot be dictated by principles of voice leading, and that, conversely, to use scale degrees in demonstrating voice leading is approximately the same as adding apples and oranges. And thus he becomes the first to add to the two above-mentioned methods of teaching voice leading a third and most deficient one, that of combining voice leading and fundamental bass and explaining each in terms of the other. This alone was an error of a gravity that had not previously been equalled, but the error was compounded in that Rameau most often illustrated his theories with all too brief examples. A succession of only two sonorities frequently has to serve to demonstrate a problem concerning the theory of scale degrees and voice leading. What a mountain of errors!

After composers had begun to write down everything to be asked of the performer, thus finally abandoning thoroughbass practice, a substitute had to be provided for new generations for purposes of teaching and composing. In part the substitute was offered under the rubric "counterpoint" à la Fux; in part it was offered in the form of that theory which deduced voice leading from scale degrees. Thus Rameau's theories, especially as they were later expanded by Kirnberger and Marpurg in Germany, gained their place alongside counterpoint. From that time on, two disciplines have existed for young people who want to study music: voice leading is taught in "counterpoint," while the theory of scale degrees is allegedly presented in so-called "harmony." The latter, however, includes, as we already know, all those flaws that inhere in Rameau's theory as a result of its amalgamation with voice leading, and which have subsequently become even more dubious. The triumph of this fatefully disorienting method, which explains sufficiently neither scale degree nor voice leading, increased the damage ad infinitum; again and again, successions of two chords are used to demonstrate problems of scale degrees and voice leading simultaneously.

Whenever I see in works of theorists of the latter provenance how all the zeal of their claims concerning scale degree and voice leading (for example, the theory of doublings and the controversies involving parallel and nonparallel similar motion) founders on the poor construction of their examples, I am reminded of a playroom and a doll house. It is well known how children play with dolls; one time the doll represents this or that friend, another time it is an aunt—in short: the doll represents whatever they need for their games. They talk to the doll and even receive an answer—of course, always the answer they themselves utter.... The theorists of harmony with their tonal dolls are no different. The tonal doll may represent this or that succession of scale degrees, this or that voice leading—in short: whatever they need, the tonal doll is always agreeable. At the present time, when Riemann has gratuitously warmed over the theories of Rameau once again and drawn the last possible consequences from them, the "tonal-doll theory"—if I may use such a term—celebrates real orgies. A new confusing world of "leading tones" and "doublings" is fabricated—a world of which the true theory of voice leading and scale degrees can know nothing.

My own intention, therefore, was to cleanse the theory of voice leading of all the impurities it suffered from the three methods mentioned above (the vocal method of Fux and his predecessors, the thoroughbass method of C.P.E. Bach and his predecessors, and finally the method of Rameau and his successors who mixed scale degree and voice leading). The theory of voice leading is to be presented here as a discipline unified in itself; that is, I shall show how, after being worked out first of all on a purely vocal basis and then revealing its presence in the technique of the thoroughbass, in chorales, and finally in free composition, it everywhere maintains its inner unity. For example, the question of doubling will be treated in counterpoint as well as in free composition only from the standpoint of voice leading; it will be completely separated from scale degrees.

As my readers know, I have already presented the theory of scale degrees in *Harmony*, without adding any voice-leading theory. It now becomes clear why I used there as musical illustrations not mere tonal dolls but quotations from musical literature. This was not caused by the vanity of testing my wit in solving difficult passages of free composition; it was rather an integral part of my method, which assumes that the nature and origin of a scale degree can be demonstrated only by illumination of all forces that the scale degree encompasses. And again, it is interest in complete clarity of the discipline rather than vanity that compels me to say here that my theory is the first that points to the *scale degree as the generator of [musical] content*. One need only compare Sechter's work, for instance, with my own to recognize that the practical artistic purpose of generating and increasing content is better served by the psychology of scale degree progression as I present it, and that my theory presents viewpoints on issues of chromaticism and alteration which are far more pure, unified, and compelling.

The scale degree exists in our perception only as triad; that is, whenever we expect a scale degree, we expect it first of all only as triad, not as a seventh-chord. In this sense, the seventh is absolutely not an a priori element of our perception comparable to the fifth and the third; it is rather an event a posteriori, which we understand best of all with reference to the function associated with it; that is, we understand it in retrospect as a passing tone, or a means of chromaticization, or the like. For this reason I always discussed scale degrees only as triads and not as seventh-chords in the first section of *Harmony,* where I explained the foundation of the [major and minor] systems (cf. especially §78). Furthermore, the fact that a pedal point can appear on the fundamental, fifth, or third of a sound, but never on its seventh, is additional evidence that only the triad is and remains an a priori scale degree. How much light this sheds on that age-old insight of the first contrapuntal epoch, which— even in the realm of polyphony generated without scale degree—generally distinguished consonance and dissonance in the same way.

Moreover, scale-degree progression, as a purely abstract expression of motion, is a matter so completely different from the concrete progression of the bass voice that one may even write parallel octaves against the bass in those places where its motion happens to coincide exactly with the path of the harmonic progression; this reflects the extent to which the obbligato character of the bass is obliterated whenever its primary duty is to express the scale-degree progression.[9]

Finally, I may be permitted to report to the reader the success of the first volume. From reviews, letters, and communications, I was able to conclude that especially that part of the work which dealt with the reputation of the church modes received the greatest applause and the most unreserved approval of musicians. Since there is nothing I strive for more ardently than [to ensure] reliability of the teacher, I am glad to have provided many teachers with a secure position on this matter, which is important not only for historical reasons. Generally, the content [of my book] was often called "inspired," but it was doubted whether my theory could have any practical value in this form. I feel justified in saying that it is far more *practical* to show a student of art whence he should derive his content (admittedly leaving aside that primal source, inspiration) than to let him merely play with musical dolls—which in any case is only an idle, though costly, activity. If the student has first of all learned the art of voice leading, he may turn to the world of scale-degree progressions in order to see what they are; how they yield [musical] content; how they relate to the [overall] structure; how much scale-degree progression is used up by one musical idea, how much by another; and how one can use scale degrees in an economical way and still construct a wide-ranging musical thought, and the like. I readily admit that I failed to do full justice in the first volume to many issues; but I had to be content, since the goal I envisioned remained so distant.

COUNTERPOINT

Introduction

Art provides its own laws and marshals time.—Goethe

The most common opinions—those accepted by everybody—often are the ones that should be investigated most carefully.—Lichtenberg

Scaling of even the highest peak begins in the valley.—Japanese proverb

"Nothing is more terrifying than a teacher who knows no more than the students are to know. Whoever wants to teach others may conceal the best of his knowledge, but must never be a dabbler." More than to any other field, this maxim of Goethe's applies to instruction in counterpoint.

It is high time at last to gain clarity about what the theory of counterpoint ought to accomplish. First of all, the teacher has to learn to distinguish between counterpoint and free composition and to justify the prescriptions and restrictions (*Ge- und Verbote*) he provides, so as to be able to explain forthrightly to the student the apparent contradictions between the theory of counterpoint and one or another voice-leading procedure in (for example) Beethoven. Once and for all, the response—as fatuous as it is barbaric—with which many a teacher dismisses his inquisitive students must finally be abandoned: "Yes, when you are a Beethoven, you too may write that way." Doesn't the teacher realize how poorly such an answer serves as an explanation? Doesn't he realize that the moral slap in the face he believes himself to have dispensed to his student is on the contrary, to a far greater degree, only a slap in his own face?

But for the fact that sheer lack of talent—because it really cannot be otherwise—unfortunately must enjoy full immunity forever, the teacher would have to be reprimanded for his impudence in giving the impression that Beethoven had composed *poorly!* No, it is a thousandfold lie: Beethoven never composed poorly, and has no need of indulgence from a teacher who is not able to hear. Despite such egregious arrogance, however, a few mitigating circumstances may be cited in defense of the teacher. For counterpoint, from its inception to the present, has been misunderstood as hardly any other field. The misconceptions that have accompanied its evolution can even be clearly distinguished both chronologically and substantively.

I. The Fundamental Error of the Older School of Counterpoint

When the principles of voice leading began to be deduced from the earliest compositional experiences, it was overlooked that they could not be applied to composition itself in an absolute fashion. They had a limited application, only to the theory of voice leading—like grammatical rules, for example, that first of all represent nothing but a basis for the simplest articulation of thoughts. How great the distance even in language from the first principles concerning subject, predicate, object, and the like, and from a simple sentence based only on these elements, to the proud, free architecture of an actual work of art in language! In music, however, this great gulf has simply been overlooked and the contrapuntal rules elevated immediately to the status of rules of composition—that is, to principles that would be binding in free composition as well.

This absolute and invariable *identification of counterpoint and theory of composition* must thus be considered the original and fundamental error that our time has unfortunately inherited.

The origin of this error, to be sure, is an understandable and excusable deception. We can assume that the reason for this deception was that in the earliest period of vocal polyphony, even compositions themselves were probably similar in appearance to exercises in modern treatises (see my *Harmony*, pp. 163-174). There were as yet no unfolded harmonies; there was no true length, and no scale degrees or modulations; and the multifaceted techniques of a later period, too, involving articulation and synthesis, were unthinkable. Provided with only a small stock of technical devices (for example, characteristic techniques to initiate and link thematic shapes, and canon and other imitative procedures), composers still meandered along the text from passage to passage and from cadence to cadence, while the compositional genre—already a kind of free composition—did not differ significantly from a type born of voice leading alone. Today, admittedly, it is difficult—even impossible—to determine the extent to which free composition, on the other hand, was influenced by erroneous theory, because there has always been an interaction between theory and practice, no matter whether the theory was correct or not. Counterpoint and theory of composition at that time were an undifferentiated mass—perhaps not dissimilar to that old theology in which the seeds of all disciplines of knowledge and art were placed under the aegis of a deity.

It would lead too far afield to document in detail the above mentioned errors of the theorists. In the course of the discussion I will have ample opportunity to point them out with quotations from the older treatises themselves. As convincing examples one may cite, for example, J.J. *Fux's* Preface to his *Gradus ad Parnassum* (translated into German by Lorenz Mizler),[1] which, incidentally, is still the most excellent work on counterpoint; or the Introduction to *Theorie des Kontrapunktes und der Fuge* by Luigi *Cherubini*.[2]

Here I want to comment at least on what J.G. *Albrechtsberger* says in his *Gründliche Anweisung zur Composition*[3] (Chapter 6, p. 17):

Strict composition is a type of music written for voices alone without any instrumental accompaniment. It is subject to more rules than free composition, because a singer cannot find his notes as easily as an instrumentalist. It is often performed in churches and chapels (hence the term *stilo alla capella*) with the accompaniment of an organ, sometimes also with violins and oboes moving in unison with the soprano, or a few trombones. . . . But when the instruments are not used—as is the custom during Lent in court chapels—no dissonant leaps are allowed (except for diminished fourths and fifths if they are duly and promptly resolved). It is also forbidden to leap from or to a dissonance. Hidden fifths, octaves, and unisons are forbidden altogether in two-voice counterpoint in the five species used in exercises above or below a simple melody (a chorale or cantus firmus). In three-voice counterpoint some are permitted; in four-voice counterpoint, even more are allowed.

(Notice how suddenly he speaks without scruple in the last sentence of "exercises" and "species," after having just described [strict] counterpoint with reference to a capella works only.)

In the first species . . . no dissonant chord is allowed; . . . in the second and third species, dissonances are permitted only as regular passing tones, except for a certain type of changing-tone figure. "Cast-out" notes (*notae abjectae*) are never permitted in strict composition . . . ; furthermore, all tied dissonances, which find their place in the fourth species, must be prepared by a consonance in strict composition and must be resolved, descending rather than ascending, to the nearest consonance a whole- or half-step below. Finally, chromatic and enharmonic progressions are not allowed here.

(All these remarks by Albrechtsberger, however, refer only to "exercises" in the five species, as is clearly evident; and it is strange that he did not bother to make the slightest distinction between the "exercises" as such and the actual a capella compositions mentioned in the beginning, even though we can certainly assume that he himself knew that "exercises" and finished works of art are by no means identical!)

Hence, the first five species belong to strict composition

("Hence"?!—Read once more the first sentences of this quotation, which dealt with entirely different matters, and try to resolve this contradiction if possible!)

as they are presented here and in Fux's treatise. . . . Strict composition encompasses the imitative style used in churches, the rigorous and serious counterpoint with or without chorale; furthermore, simple and double fugues, and finally the canon. In short: strict composition encompasses all contrapuntal, a capella compositions for voices, especially those works without the accompaniment of instruments.

(Didn't Albrechtsberger suddenly forget here the "exercises" he discussed in such detail before?!)

In strict composition, two notes of the same letter-name, such as *c - c* or *d - d,* are not permitted in succession in a single measure in any of the five species of counterpoint. This rule, however, has two exceptions: the first in the fifth species . . . ; the other one in vocal pieces, when one note can be turned into two for the sake of short syllables. . . .

(Observe his use, regarding the problem of repeated notes, of the term "exception," to which we will return later.)

Free composition is the genre in which a dissonant chord can occasionally be sounded without preparation on any part of the bar in all five species, in imitative genres, contrapuntal pieces, and fugues; but the dissonance must

> always be properly and naturally resolved. . . . In free composition, one is seldom restricted to any one of the five species.

("Seldom"? No, never! Incidentally, one is never so restricted even in a capella works!)

> All note-values can be used for the principal voice as well as for the accompanying voices. . . . Free composition occurs in all three styles, namely, church, chamber, and theater style; for example, in masses, graduals, offertories, psalms, and hymns accompanied by the organ, and in fugues where many dissonances are attacked without preparation, and tied dissonances can even be resolved upward as suspensions. . . . Today one can hear and find a thousand examples of free composition for twenty in the strict style.

(Of course! Every composition already represents in itself a *free* and never a strict composition!!)

> However, since neither type of composition can achieve the highest possible degree of purity without the principles of counterpoint, it is advisable to begin to learn [composition] with strict two-voice counterpoint.

Even though in the final analysis no real justification is provided for this last sentence, we may perhaps consider it a ray of light amidst the whole chaotic assemblage of notions.

Failure to justify the contrapuntal prescriptions and restrictions, however, is a characteristic shortcoming of almost all the theory presented by the older theorists, and we may perhaps regard only Fux, founder of the discipline, as the teacher who at least took the greatest care in investigating the problems. How could one expect a compelling justification of the various doctrines when counterpoint and composition were erroneously lumped together in the first place? Wasn't that simply impossible, since no one knew whether the doctrines should apply only to exercises or even to composition as well?

But later the first misconception of the older theorists was to become dubious in yet another respect. That happened at a time when instrumental music became predominant and the problem of length was solved—at first only on the basis of monothematicism—in the closed form of the fugue. Because of the misconception that the theory of counterpoint was also a theory of composition, the older theorists made fugal theory a direct appendage to contrapuntal theory; as a consequence, the character of the fugue as an independent form of composition had to suffer because of its proximity to the theory of voice leading. Since that time, counterpoint and fugue remained inseparably linked in textbooks. The unfortunate confusion that resulted from this linkage is almost incredible: the fugue alone was viewed as the highest, perhaps the exclusive goal of contrapuntal theory; moreover, it was thought that only the fugue *contained* counterpoint, while in other genres (such as the sonata or the symphony) counterpoint was absent so long as a movement did not sound "fugal" in some way; and that only a writer of fugues should be considered a master of counterpoint, and even then only *when* he wrote them, and so on and on. It was not recognized that the fugue is really an autonomous form in itself—as autonomous as, for example, a rondo, or a three- or four-part form. Also ignored was the fact that any musical product—even a waltz or march, to say nothing of a sonata or intermezzo—had to incorporate counterpoint precisely as a relationship of at least two voices [*Free Composition (FrC.)*, §71]. Thus, people went so far as to consider counterpoint and fugue almost identical. (For A.B. Marx, who had a greater talent for aesthetics than for the specifics of music, counterpoint became amalgamated with polyphony to such an extent that he always used term "polyphony" rather than "counterpoint" in his books!) More and more this misconception prevailed, and finally people even thought of anything fugal as an actual fugue regardless of whether the piece was a self-contained organism or not.

Several composers, for example Mozart, in the last movement of his String Quartet in G major [K. 387], and also Beethoven, in the last movement of his String Quartet op. 59 no. 3, used the fugal style only in the first-theme sections of movements otherwise written in cyclical (sonata) form—just as J.S. Bach, for example, often began preludes or gigues of his suites with fugal passages. Ignorance quickly interpreted the cyclical form of these movements as fugues. Don't musicians up to this hour talk idiotically about "the Jupiter Symphony with the closing fugue," even though the fugal technique first appears only in a modulatory passage (!) connecting the principal theme-group with the secondary section, and later emerges only in a similarly subordinate function without being able to prevent the musical discourse from manifesting itself as anything but a real sonata form?!! Don't they deny themselves the pleasure of perceiving Mozart's genius simply by deflating such inspired use of fugal technique within a larger structure to the value of a mere fugue? If the possibility of such an occurrence (as in the last movement of the symphony just mentioned) were simply denied to be an instance of sonata form, how easily could musicians then be led to believe that all sonatas in general are alike and also that all fugues are no less alike? Or consider Beethoven's Piano Sonata opus 110: such an ingenious linkage between the third (Adagio) and fourth movements (a true fugue), in that the first half of the Adagio is followed by the first half of the fugue, while the second half of the Adagio is finally succeeded by the modulatory and concluding parts of the fugue! But what did our theorists and virtuosos make of it? They all see only the fugue, but their own modest artistic instinct unfortunately does not suffice to penetrate further into the realm of Beethoven's artistic fantasy. Faulty response to their achievements has not, however, prevented our masters from using their fugal technique as innovatively as we witness it in the examples just mentioned. On the other hand, we see lesser talents, who enjoy exploiting the ignorance of the musical public by showing off their fugal technique to gain respect. In full knowledge that only a few individuals can really judge the quality of fugal techniques, they write either only a few fugal measures or even whole fugues, and then are immediately awarded, according to plan, the honorary title "master of counterpoint"; for only the fugue is considered counterpoint by the musical public! Need I mention names? Recently a childish piano paraphrase using waltz motives of Johann Strauss, and really having little to do with art (a paraphrase similar to that produced *en masse* by conductors of military bands using two, three, or even four well-known motives simultaneously) has been introduced with the snobbish and arrogant title "Contrapuntal Paraphrase."

II.   Compounding of the Error by the Modern School of Counterpoint

The stress created by the initial misconception necessarily became un-
bearable in the long run, when it was time to come to grips with the powerful
creations of our classical composers—a magnificent world appearing almost out
of the blue, with new types of developments, scale-degree progressions,
modulatory plans, and forms. Add to this the works of Schubert, Schumann,
Wagner, Brahms, and others. Like it or not, the pressing need finally arose to
resolve once and for all the contradiction between, on the one hand, the ways
those masters set their tones according to new psychic forces, and, on the
other hand, the former theory—especially contrapuntal theory—which made the
discrepancy between the two worlds (practice and theory) really appear too
wide and great.

However, even under these pressing circumstances the more correct path
was not found, since people preferred, apparently completely unconsciously,
to continue on the path of the old misconception, especially since externally
the path still appeared new and correct. The strategy of the more recent
theorists remained the same as that of the older ones: counterpoint was
considered, as before, also a theory of composition! How should and could
any difference at all be found? For if even Fux, for example, derived his
principles only from the vocal compositions of earlier periods in order to make
them useful—as he thought necessary—to compositions of the "strict style," the
more recent theorists preferred to base their contrapuntal doctrines on the
music of classical and post-classical composers (that is, on modern harmonic
and formal shapes), again to serve the needs—as they also thought necessary—of
modern compositions. That vocal music in the one case, and instrumental
music in the other, served as point of departure—is this distinction more
important than the similarity that in both cases (and herein lies the complete
identity of older and modern schools!) only the composition, the *actual
composition,* is the real point of departure, the source of contrapuntal doctrines
as well as their ultimate goal?

The fact that more recent theorists, in accordance with modern music,
have changed the function of the former cantus firmus is of only minor
relevance in comparison to the fateful opinion, held then as well as now, that
the first voice-leading exercises are to be immediately connected with free
composition—vocal for the older school, instrumental for the newer.

This more recent and modern misconception of viewing counterpoint and composition as identical can be found, for example, in *Lehrbuch des Kontrapunktes,* by
E.F. *Richter,*[4] pp. 15-16:

> In contrast to the earlier method, our point of departure is counterpoint in four
> instead of two voices; for we attach greater significance to harmonic progression
> as the foundation of music in general: harmony is no longer the accidental result
> of a partly quite mechanical contrapuntal procedure, but appears as an element

that provides the melodic progression with direction. How the greater significance (in comparison to former approaches) of the harmonic progression or direction in counterpoint is manifested will be shown by a small example by Bach [example follows]. Despite all the contrapuntal independence of the voices in this well-known example, the following simple harmonic progression is nevertheless decisive [illustration follows]. If we compare this rich succession of harmonies, regulated in meter as well as in rhythm, with any composition from an earlier period . . . the directive force of harmony is clear in the former, while the unregulated succession in the latter is only an accidental result of voice leading. Herein lies the essential difference between modern and early music, and thus also counterpoint and its treatment, and we have to take this into account, at least in part, while learning counterpoint, however simple our beginning will be.

The last sentence alone contains all false conclusions and other misconceptions of the author in their most concise and thus also most synoptic version. Because classical music has true logic in its harmonies, does it follow that contrapuntal exercises (the author simply says "thus") have to incorporate this logic? On the other hand, what motivates the author to keep the "beginning" only "simple," if it is true, as he says, that counterpoint and modern composition should and must move into close proximity? According to this theory, the student would have to "select the harmonies with care so that they can establish a firm and secure foundation" (p. 17) and to use four-voice counterpoint as a point of departure in order to arrive finally at two-voice counterpoint as an extract, so to speak, of the former. All this has the sole purpose of familiarizing the student even in contrapuntal exercises with the logic and progression of harmonies appropriate to modern works of art—in other words, it is meant to pave the way for modern music, and to do so even at the level of the exercises themselves. (Incidentally, we know that the same author, conversely, also applied the voice leading of counterpoint in exercises of harmony. See *Harmony*, §§90–92.) Nowhere and never, however, is he aware that he aims for a goal that is illogical from the outset; it will, in fact, remain illogical and thus unattainable for all time.

Hugo *Riemann* almost goes even further (if that is possible); he remarks in his *Lehrbuch des Kontrapunkts*,[5] Chapter 1, §1:

Nothing can be faultier, therefore, than asking the student to produce a large number of countermelodies, as different from each other as possible, to a given cantus firmus, each of them interpreting the cantus firmus harmonically in a different way. On the contrary, the student ought to be encouraged to arrive through repeated improvements and refinements at just one countermelody which he considers correct and natural; and finally, to produce one really good and perfect countermelody (instead of many melodies of equal—that is, inferior—value), and to elevate it from the realm of mere naturalness and correctness to the level of art and beauty.

And clearer still:

The task cannot be to invent another melody against a given voice (specifically, the cantus firmus) in such a way that the new melody appears without significance and content in comparison with the given one. [Riemann adds in a footnote: "Thus without any doubt the principal concern of an aspiring composer must be that he learn to understand correctly his own melodic ideas and to give them an effective polyphonic treatment that completely brings out their individual character."] On the contrary, the goal must be to enhance the significance of the cantus firmus through the countermelody. The counterpoint ought to interpret the cantus firmus. One should study in this connection, for example, the fugues of J.S. Bach; not even in the modulatory transition passages does the theme receive a meaning different from that given to it immediately by the first counter-subject. A theme would have to appear without character if it were to be interpreted at one time in one way, at another time in a different way. We will see soon enough to what extent the meaning can be specialized in its details, but the core, the firm scaffold, must remain fixed.

In this light, Riemann does not feel at all deterred from giving, for example, the following melody as an exercise:

Example 1

It hardly can be expressed more glaringly than with these words that counterpoint [as Riemann conceives it] has to amount to composition, understood in the most delicate sense of the word. Observe that the student has to learn here to express the little melody only in its best and most artistic form. But how could the theorist overlook the fact that the melody, posited at the outset merely as an exercise, is actually much too small and limited to be anywhere nearly equal to the artistic demands simultaneously imposed on it? Doesn't the expression with which a composer provides his melody in a real composition depend also on circumstances other than merely the few tones it contains? Is it really irrelevant in practice whether the melody occurs—in the case of the sonata form, for example—at the beginning or as part of the secondary group, or the development, or at the end, or—in the case of a different form—whether the melody appears for the first, second, or third time? Who, on learning the theme from Beethoven's String Quartet op. 59 no. 1 for the first time, would expect, after so many difficult contrapuntal treatments in the course of the movement, to hear the theme in the coda in yet another, very peculiar—one might say, Russian nationalistic—contrapuntal treatment? Who would expect just *such* a contrapuntal treatment? If it is clear that there are a thousand special circumstances that force the composer to provide his melody with one type of expression or another, then what can it mean to search for just one such definite expression for a melody which has no such circumstances and thus remains without any particular affective orientation? Disregarding the fact that even the greatest among the great masters still have to struggle to define the expression of their own ideas (how beautifully Lichtenberg formulates this: "The idea still has too much leeway in its expression; I have pointed with the blunt end of a stick, where I should have used the point of a needle"); disregarding also that it is least inappropriate to require the very beginner to find immediately a best expression, which in reality is unthinkable and unattainable because of the lack of suitable prerequisites; disregarding all this, I ask only: wouldn't anyone who requires such unnatural things from the beginner by analogy also have to consider it possible that, for example, those splendid sentences with which instruction in French or English grammar normally begins could immediately carry a definite expression—an expression as definite as only eminent actors provide for sentences from *Faust* and the like? What can sentences like the following signify for an actor: "This room has three windows"; or "On the desk are several books, a pencil, and a notebook"; and what kind of expression could or should he select for them! And by analogy, what kind of expression should a student select as the best and only one for the exercise-melody quoted above? Doesn't the garish theory of Riemann demonstrate most clearly the gulf that truly separates "exercise" and real composition, a gulf that cannot be bridged and must by nature remain forever?

S.W. *Dehn's* grotesque statement in his *Lehre vom Kontrapunkt*[6] also belongs to this category; he declines, with the following words, to give his students more detailed instruction concerning construction of the basic [cantus-firmus] melody: "One is a melodist by the grace of God." Such an overestimation of the role of the cantus firmus, if the grace of God is invoked even in this case as the last resort that cannot be appealed! How great Dehn's misconception was about the real function of contrapuntal doctrine, if he was able to arrive at this overestimation at all! Perhaps the least that should be said in response is "God helps those who help themselves!" For nothing is so simple and useful as to instruct students in writing a cantus firmus, and in few things can we so easily do without God's help as in this enterprise.

But even Heinrich *Bellermann*—see the Preface to his book[7]—misunderstands the true function of counterpoint when he writes:

> Even those who want to devote their energies in the freest of fashions to [music for] the theatre or the concert hall will benefit by acquiring skill in voice leading. Consider, for example, an opera composer who wants to write an aria in which an obbligato instrument is to accompany the voice or in which the violins are to be used for flowing passages—how easily such things will come to him if he has grown accustomed from the outset of his studies not to string chords together but to write obbligato voices. With how great assurance he will compose his ensemble pieces and finales if he is able to write a fugue easily.

Is counterpoint able by itself to provide such benefits to the students? No, this is utopian; because, as I have said before, a huge chasm gapes between the exercises of counterpoint and the demands of true composition.

Need I discuss in detail how, because they suffer from the basic misconception that results from confusing counterpoint and composition, more recent contrapuntal theorists must have as many difficulties in justifying their doctrine as the older ones? That is all too obvious. Even from the modern theorists we receive doctrines that either appear unfounded or are justified only in extremely vague terms. And, incidentally, even the misunderstanding of the fugue as the alleged touchstone of counterpoint remains almost exactly the same with them as with the theorists discussed earlier.

It is more important, however, to affirm that forcing contrapuntal exercises to approximate composition, as the modern school does, has worsened much more than improved the situation of contrapuntal doctrine. That is clear simply from the fact that, on the one hand, the exercises of the modern theorists are really no longer true exercises and that, on the other hand, the explanation of free art-works by precepts of contrapuntal theory [alone] remains as elusive today as ever. The intended unification of counterpoint and free composition has resulted in exactly the opposite: the two are farther apart now than ever! The true nature of things cannot be trifled with: what does not belong together by nature will not and cannot be welded together by any effort or trick.

III.   Clearing Up the Misconception

From the preceding discussion, the reader himself may well have discerned the only path that can lead us out of this unfortunate misconception: counterpoint must somehow be thoroughly separated from composition if the ideal and practical verities of both are to be fully developed.

To this end, it will be my first task (a) at the outset to draw the boundaries between the *pure theory of voice leading* and *free composition.* Yet precisely such a clear-cut discrimination between the "exercise" and the free work of art makes all the more imperative a second task, namely (b) to reveal the *connection between counterpoint* (which may be considered the first musico-grammatical exercises) *and the actual work of art*—to show the nature and foundation of this connection. For there is indeed a relationship between counterpoint and composition, although it is far from being one of complete identity, and is therefore completely different from what has been supposed by theorists of both the old and the new schools.

Concerning (a): In respect to the first task, that is, the thoroughgoing distinction between counterpoint and pure compositional theory, the following matters should be discussed:

1.   The purpose of counterpoint, rather than to teach a specific style of composition, is to lead the ear of the serious student of music for the first time into the infinite world of fundamental musical problems.

Constantly, at every opportunity, the student's ear must be alerted to the psychological effects associated with intervals in music; how the second differs from the fifth and the sixth, and related matters; or how one is to interpret and treat situations in which two, three, or four voices produce an effect by working together or, better still, in contrast to one another. The musical instinct must be enlightened about the effect associated with each of the three types of motion of the voices. The following, therefore, may be considered the principal goal of contrapuntal study: investigation of the possible configurations of the voices and the treatment of each, wherein at the same time the most painstaking effort must be exerted always to make manifest to the ear (in respect to both configuration and treatment) the gradation from the most natural and simple to the more advanced and less simple.

It should be obvious that such a training of the ear for artistic purposes, whether creative–artistic or re-creative–artistic, is indispensable. Even the ear of a Mozart and a Beethoven required an introductory study of this kind, as is clearly demonstrated by the errors that appear often enough in their earliest lesson-books. This postulate, by the way, also lies in the nature of the subject itself; for counterpoint is an experiential art, which is founded on the hardest-won and also the subtlest perceptions of composers and teachers of many centuries, from the very discovery of polyphonic composition. How, then, can any individual be excused from recapitulating the experiences of so many generations, if he is to avoid the same mistakes that earlier epochs had learned to avoid through one or another device of art? Here one sees again the fact, already familiar from organic nature, that it is indispensable to pass through an embryonic stage of development!

2. According to this interpretation, counterpoint must restrict itself only to the topography of a modest and naturally simple exercise, which might be compared to a small practice stage—and that is precisely what the cantus firmus is—in order to demonstrate the nature of the problems and their solutions. It should not aspire to be more than a preliminary school for actual composition. In no case, however, should such an exercise and its treatment be regarded as a complete compositional product.

The use of the cantus firmus as the basis of contrapuntal experiments, incidentally, is very much the same as, for example, the use of plaster casts, plaster ornaments, and stylized forms for instruction in drawing, instead of a living model. The beginner in drawing, too, must avoid the complexities and imponderables of a model from nature.

3. The formulation of the problems, as well as their solution, is to be founded exclusively upon the vocal element, and not on an instrumental-mechanical technique. At the beginning of the period of contrapuntal music, it was the human voice—and indeed only the human voice—which taught the first discriminations between the true and correct, and the false and unnatural. Because of its limited compass (scarcely more than one and a half octaves on the average), and because of the necessary participation of the emotional faculty in the production of the intervals, the human voice is able to reveal in the most dependable way the true magnitudes of the various reaches. For this reason, it is most perfectly qualified to serve as a guide and judge over all matters of voice leading, today as well as centuries ago.

How comparatively easy it is to play, for example, a sixth on the piano or any other mechanical instrument, and how quickly the ear can become disoriented by the fact that the hand and the instrument do not make the larger reaches far more difficult than the smaller! To know what [for example] a sixth is in reality, we must ask only the human voice. Consider, too, the reasons the Church may have had, in the first period of vocal polyphony, for forbidding certain intervals altogether, or allowing some only in the ascending direction, others only descending (cf. Bellermann, Chapter VIII). Clearly the Church, with perfectly correct instinct, learned from the first experiments that the human voice is subject to a law—if I may adapt a concept from economics—of psychological inflation: that which, like the intervals of the human singing voice, is in such short supply and is so difficult to come by, must be viewed as a precious commodity. The small instrument of the singing voice cannot allow its few intervals—those rare valuables—to be so abused as the keys of a piano. Even in simple speech, we hear the organic-mechanical interconnection between intervals and content. All the more so in stylized art song! Far from characterizing the oldest compositional rules as unimportant and arbitrary caprices, then, I recommend rather that they be considered welcome contributions to the history of our understanding of voice leading [in particular], and of the nature of the singing voice in general. Because the human larynx is unchanging, it is still correct and important even today to make the distinctions [among intervals] that the Church once found necessary. The Church derived her conclusions as though from the resultant of two interacting sources of influence: the need for a service of the most neutral character, and the nature of the singer's instrument. To be sure, at that time the ecclesiastical rules were, understandably, also rules of composition; but in the present day, when it is necessary (as I have stated at the beginning of this chapter) to distinguish clearly between composition and that preliminary school represented by strict counterpoint, we must use the eternally valid nucleus of those rules for strict counterpoint, even if we no longer view them as applicable to composition.

4. Contrapuntal theory addresses the problems of voice leading by presenting them in the form of prescriptions and restrictions. That is, we experience one aspect of tonal activity in that counterpoint disallows one thing or another, while we experience a different aspect in that it prescribes a particular procedure. (This will be seen more clearly later on.) For the present, however, only this, which must be noted well: one should not be deceived by the large number of prohibitions; even though contrapuntal theory establishes many prohibitions, it is certain that far more is allowed. Even in the real world of written exercises, there is far more freedom than restriction! (Just as in life generally there is more freedom than restriction, and it is merely their own folly when people who stare and gape only at the prohibitions succumb to the illusion that the opposite is true.)

At the same time, all of the contrapuntal rules must be supported by good reasons. This, certainly, is the most difficult matter; and because of the difficulty, it is fully understandable that until now most theorists have avoided providing a basis for counterpoint. If even religion has had to cope with the fact that mankind asks "why," isn't it all the more understandable that contrapuntal theory, which in fact has long enjoyed almost the reputation of a musical religion, would meet the same fate? If this task had been addressed earlier—I have already pointed out that this was thwarted mostly by the incessant conflation of counterpoint and composition-theory—much that is deplorable in the current state of affairs would surely have been avoided.

Concerning (b): Regarding the second task, its execution in the course of the work itself will most clearly reveal the method to be used. For the present, I shall content myself with a reference to the previously cited analogy with the art of language. In my opinion, we can safely proceed with free composition in much the same way that we do when we ask, for example, why the sentence construction in *Faust* is freely organized as follows:

> Habe nun, ach! Philosophie,
> Juristerei und Medizin,

Und, leider! auch Theologie
Durchaus studiert, mit heissem Bemühn!

(I have—alas!—studied philosophy,
law and medicine as well,
and—unfortunately!—theology too,
thoroughly, with zealous application!)

and not in the way that one would have to teach a beginner to express the same thoughts. Aren't the reasons behind Goethe's use of the above construction just these, for example: considerations of verse (prosody, rhyme), and Faust's vexation, which psychologically motivates him to revolutionize and freely alter the normal ordering of the sentence components; also his zeal, which makes that vexation truly credible, and so forth? If we imagine these psychic forces to be absent, we see immediately that without them it would be childish, indeed impossible, to use the same construction. The first essays and exercises of the student are differentiated from the real art works of language precisely in that in the former, the psychic compulsion toward freer formations is lacking, and indeed must be lacking! But does Goethe's sentence, just because of this freer construction, constitute an offense against German grammar altogether? Who can miss the fact that this sentence, in spite of all kinds of departures from normal organization, basically manifests only prolongations[8] of the most ordinary grammatical laws? In a similar way, the new forces that accompany free composition in music form an apparently new order; yet those who have true understanding see the fundamental contrapuntal principles profoundly and mystically at work in the background. The phenomena of free composition, then, are invariably to be understood only as the prolongations of those principles.

The end result of my new approach to contrapuntal study is that my teaching resembles that of the older theorists more closely than that of the more recent ones—and this fact truly fills me with pride! What I have particularly in common with the older teachers is that, here and there, our exercises are similar in character. The very essential distinction which sets me apart from them is that I regard counterpoint and its exercises purely as voice-leading lessons, while they—initially, perhaps, as a consequence of the character of their own compositions, but later even in opposition to it—viewed those exercises as actual compositions. As a result, they thoroughly intermixed the principles of counterpoint and those of composition, so that finally the precepts became unusable for both counterpoint and composition alike. When the more recent theorists, striving for a closer connection to modern music, abandoned the cantus firmus, they lost the natural foundation of the first, simple exercises. And yet, at the same time, they failed to achieve the freedom of true melody, because of the lack of necessary extension, and because of the thousandfold variety of presuppositions that inhere in the small configurations replacing the cantus firmus. The exercise-constructs were on the one hand too complex for exercises, which are supposed merely to introduce basic problems of voice leading; on the other hand, they were too limited for a genuine compositional study. Such exercises, in essence without character, can never securely point the student in the right direction.

We recall that in many respects the views of, for example, C.P.E. Bach, as he set them down in his theoretical work, cannot be surpassed. And (to cite an example from painting) according to important painters, [Albrecht] Dürer's theories have lasting validity.

IV. The Nature and Value of Contrapuntal Theory According to the Present Method

Contrapuntal theory, which is nothing but a theory of voice leading, demonstrates tonal laws and tonal effects in their absolute sense. Only contrapuntal theory is able to do so, and therefore it should do so. This is its greatest value and, at the same time, its significance for all eternity!

It teaches the most characteristic effect of tones—one might say, the proprieties of their movement—and with utmost certainty liberates the student of art from the delusion that tones must signify something external and objective in addition to their absolute effect.

In this study, the beginning artist learns that tones, organized in such and such a way, produce one particular effect and none other, whether he wishes it or not. One can predict this effect: it *must* follow! Thus tones cannot produce any desired effect just because of the wish of the individual who sets them, for nobody has power over tones in the sense that he is able to demand from them something contrary to their nature. Even tones must do what they must do! This knowledge is to be gained only in contrapuntal theory, and it is the most precious treasure an artist can gain.

The artist learns to humble himself before the absolute character of tonal life. Indeed, only with reference to the standard of the absolute in music does he learn to seek out certain goals and attain them. He comes to know the effects that the tones must produce under one set of circumstances or another, and, in a spirit of modesty—the true hallmark of every great man—and freedom, he can only choose or not choose a given effect. At the same time, he is protected from the disappointment of intending a particular effect while the tones bring forth a completely different one. For the tones are always independent of the composer's mood, and are able to produce their effects only in keeping with the preconditions attendant on them in the individual case. In the study of counterpoint, the student can acquire the foundation for his first insight and conviction that there actually is a connection between the artist's intention with regard to tones and the effects they produce—a marvelous connection, of which dilletantism has no notion. In the best of cases—and this applies precisely to geniuses, and only to them—intention (that is, prediction of effect) and effect correspond perfectly; but in the great majority of cases the tones, acting entirely on their own and, so to speak, behind the back of the composer, produce an effect completely different from that intended.

If we wanted to characterize the principal error of "modern" music most objectively, we could define it with reference to what has just been said as follows: the composers of the present day have lost all authority over the secrets of tones. It happens, unfortunately, as would be necessary according to the presuppositions of tones, that composers intend something far better than they achieve! With Richard Strauss, Pfitzner, Mahler, and even Reger—with Tchaikowsky, Elgar, and all the rest, it is always the same: they no longer know which effects they can and should seek, and they understand still less how to achieve the effects that should be sought. All is chance and good luck—or (sometimes) bad luck!

The absolute character of the world of tone, as one discovers it for the first time in the study of counterpoint, means that music is emancipated from every external obligation, whether it be [the expression of] words, the stage, or the narrative aspect of any kind of program. The self-referential nature of tones obliges the composer to adapt himself to their inner life, and to relegate to a lower place any other purpose that may have been associated with music. This means that the consideration of a secondary purpose must never become the principal aim; the tones themselves, through (mostly unintentional) bad effects, would have to protest against any such secondary purpose. (Incidentally, in the case of mistaken notions of this kind—and as is well known, they are the order of the day—the bad absolute effects one encounters provide the professional with his most effective weapon against the false pronouncements and opinions of the composers themselves, as well as their apologists.)

Finally, the study of counterpoint is also the best way to put an end to those false notions concerning the nature of music usually entertained by philosophers, poets, and others. Having only scant understanding of the absolute character of the world of tone—even E.T.A. Hoffmann is by no means an exception—they are forced to introduce very dubious elements into their conceptions and definitions. For example, consider Schopenhauer, who asserts that "the composer reveals the innermost essence of the world and expresses the most profound wisdom in a language which his rational faculty does not understand." If we but supplement such vague opinions with the organic, the unique-absolute qualities of the tonal world, we have nothing less of wonder or mystery! But we understand all the better why music, resting in its special tonal processes and released, by virtue of its inborn world of motivic association, from any need to establish connection with the external world, manifests that character which has been observed but little understood by philosophers and aestheticians; [and we understand] why music seems so detached from the world, or, as Schopenhauer puts it, expresses "an innate universality, along with the most definite precision." This "definite precision" that so amazes the philosopher is nothing but the inherent effect of tones, the self-sufficient character of motives, of which unfortunately he has no notion. And, seen from another perspective, the autonomy of tones is at the same time nothing but music's "innate universality." Thus Schopenhauer's conclusions, that music "represents the innermost core preceding all creativity, or the heart of things," unfortunately comes into conflict with music itself. We see that despite many correct presentiments, the philosopher finally fails because of lack of clarity. Music is not "the heart of things"; on the contrary, music has little or nothing to do with "things." Tones mean nothing but themselves; they are as living beings with their own social laws.

If the philosopher, using counterpoint as a point of departure, could only have formed an idea of the absolute nature of music, it might have then been so much easier for him to understand the ultimate mystery of the world, its absolute nature, and perceive the dream of the creator of the world as a similarly absolute phenomenon!

V.   Synopsis of the Present Work

In accordance with the discussion above, my contrapuntal theory will present only that which really belongs to the theory of voice leading in its strictest sense.   .

From the outset I eliminate fugal theory as well as all procedures related to that form (including canon and double counterpoint) which properly have their place in the theory of [musical] form.

Thus I plan to treat the topic of the cantus firmus, then counterpoint in two, three, four, and more voices using the familiar five species, and finally, as a newly added subject matter, the bridges to free composition.

In the course of the discussion, I will justify each prescription and restriction and elaborate on how the application of [these rules] more or less changes in the context of free composition. By this procedure I believe I shall be able to contribute best toward eliminating that unfortunate confusion of counterpoint and composition as well as its sad consequences.

PART ONE

The Cantus Firmus as the Foundation of Contrapuntal Studies

Chapter 1

Conditions and Limitations of the Cantus Firmus in General

§1. *The construction of the cantus firmus as determined by its purpose*

Since contrapuntal theory has to treat the relationship between at least two voices, we must deal first of all—before we enter into the actual theory of correct relationships—with the foundation itself, that is, with the principal voice [the cantus firmus] as the given precondition of the added voice.

For even the construction of the principal voice must take into account certain observations and artistic rules such as have been derived instinctively in a way most logically suited to their purpose. If the latter consists in studying problems of voice leading alone, then everything must be avoided in the cantus firmus that would give it an individual character—that is, turn it into a kind of real melody in the sense of free composition.

Thus first of all we must prevent *groups of several tones* from establishing such *units based on rhythm or harmony* as are precisely the lifeblood of free melody. In other words: we must aim for a complete equilibrium of the tones in relation to each other, in contrast to the predominance of individual, independent fragments characterized by rhythmic variety and a harmonic common denominator.

§2. *Rhythmic equilibrium in the cantus firmus*

All rhythmic variety must therefore be avoided in the cantus firmus; rhythm must make its contribution to equilibrium by presenting the cantus firmus note for note in equal durational values with complete neutrality. It does not matter which values serve as the basis—whether only a breve ⊟ is used throughout or a semibreve **o** (that is, today's whole-note), or a dotted whole-note **o.** in triple meter, or even half-notes ♩. In the following presentation we will use only the whole-note and, more rarely, triple meter.

As far as rhythm is concerned, no note enjoys any particular weight or preference, and this is the reason for the invariably rigid rhythmic appearance of the cantus firmus. Another (historical) reason for the rhythmic neutrality can be found in *Harmony,* pp. 154ff., especially the Note on p. 163.

I have already discussed in the introduction how this rhythmic appearance, demanded solely by the mechanics of exercises, led to the illusion that they constituted a special and allegedly still valid genre of composition, namely "strict composition."

The misconception just mentioned may be considered the reason *Fux, Albrechtsberger, Cherubini,* and *Dehn,* for example, always view cantus firmus and chorale as synonymous in their theoretical works. They place their exercises now under one rubric, now under the other, without troubling themselves to give the student any instruction at all about the cantus firmus itself. In reality, there is a considerable difference between an authentic artistic chorale and the cantus firmus of even their own exercises, as will be shown later on. Therefore, I considered it necessary to emphasize this peculiarity [here], since it led to even more unfortunate consequences, because the above-mentioned masters often gave the impression of teaching real composition while actually presenting mere voice-leading problems.

Although *Bellermann* hardly digresses from the great model of Fux, he is, so far as I know, the only contrapuntal theorist who discusses the cantus firmus in a special and very worthwhile chapter (p. 99ff., "Von der Melodie"); he deals with actual chorale-writing as a four-voice setting (p. 268ff., and p. 418ff.) only after completing the discussion of strict four-voice counterpoint. As meritorious as Bellermann's discussion of melody is overall, one can only regret that he does not entirely enlighten us on the problem that emerges here for the first time of rhythm in contrapuntal exercises. Without clear awareness or better reasoning, he simply writes (p. 99):

Since it suffices for our purpose to invent melodies that appear graceful in their intonation—that is, in their harmonic relationships, which are to be discussed here in theory and practice—we disregard entirely the sung word for the time being and, moreover, *limit rhythm to its simplest relationships.* For that reason we want to establish melodies that progress from tone to tone in whole notes (or in two-beat values).

That is all [he says]; as we see, it is too superficial to serve as a really good explanation.

§3. *Equilibrium among tones also in the harmonic aspect*

In order to prevent units from being established in the cantus firmus on the basis of harmony, one must avoid successions of pitches that would protrude sharply as arpeggiation or figuration of a single chord no matter whether consonant or dissonant.

The same restriction applies also to other configurations such as may result, for example, from surrounding one single tone with its neighboring notes, and related procedures.

In view of the unlimited abundance of potential dangers, contrapuntal theory does as much as it ought to do—that is, it does enough—if it calls the student's attention to these problems and leaves it up to him to avoid those dangers of unit-formation (cf. Chapter 2, §§6 and 18).

It would therefore be poor to write [a cantus firmus] as follows:

Example 2

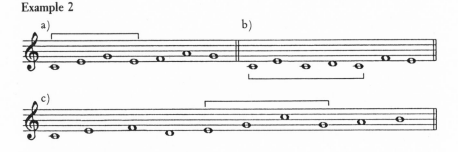

Bellermann writes (p. 99):

Furthermore, the aspiring composer must guard against grouping two, three, or four single bars (whole notes) together and thereby emphasizing certain tones of the melody through position and stress (as happens all too easily and often inadvertently). This must be avoided because rhythmic subdivisions often help smooth out certain harmonic harshnesses and infelicities that are quite noticeable when all tones of the melody have the same durational values.

§4. *Restriction on length as well*

The restriction on length stands in a natural relationship to the rhythmic restriction. Why should anyone extend a melody that clings to such rhythmic equilibrium and which inevitably would, therefore, in the long run be in a certain sense aesthetically *unsatisfactory?* Why extend such a melody, when it is only an exercise? Would it not be better, for the purpose of investigating the greatest variety of problems, to take a second or third melody, which, because of differences in construction, would provide an opportunity to gain new voice-leading experience? That alone is the reason the cantus firmus was never extended beyond fifteen or sixteen bars—a limitation by correct instinct.

Although I arrive at the same conclusions as the other authors, I would like to emphasize the difference in explanation, because it appears to me urgently necessary finally to pave the way for a recognition that the cantus firmus is really nothing but an exercise. This will shed proper light on the methods of teaching counterpoint.

Bellermann (p. 99f.) gives another reason for the restriction on length. His notion that the cantus firmus is a real melody, almost a type of composition—that is, more than merely a voice-leading exercise—, leads him to write: "We must make sure that the melody is a self-contained musical thought, not longer than can be comfortably grasped without the ear's getting tired and forgetting the initial tone. Such a thought, such a melody, will, therefore, consist of only 9, 10, 11, 12, 13, or at most 14 or 15 beats or bars, as the following two examples show" (two examples follow).

§5. *The question of modes*

Turning to the question of modes, I consider it insupportable to torture the student of counterpoint with the old modes while he is working on cantus-firmus exercises.

Therefore, we shall deal here only with major and minor.

It will be easier to leave aside the old modes if the reader agrees with what I said about them in *Harmony*, pp. 55ff. and 94–96. As I stated there, they were little more than well-meaning attempts at interpreting musical phenomena, attempts that went wrong in their conclusions; they were scarcely more than modest efforts to categorize horizontally conceived melodies—efforts that began as external, mnemonic aids but nevertheless had the power to influence compositional practice in an adverse way at the same time. In short, they were experiments, which were necessary in the course of history before the artistic and theoretical recognition of major and minor; but today they have become superfluous.

This question urgently needs clarification, because there are still theorists who in their honest belief use the church modes even for contrapuntal exercises (see below), and also because tendencies have emerged to include "tonal systems" even of exotic peoples in our music. This is done under the pretense of creating a new "era of exotic Romanticism" in Germany, as is boastfully proclaimed—a kind of "world music" that is supposed to suit the German character so well. Even though the intentions in all these cases seem to be so diverse, the error is one and the same, since neither the so-called church modes nor exotic scales should be considered real systems. For that reason, a detailed criticism may be permitted here which rejects the efforts just mentioned.

Anyone who wants to get a clearer idea of the true nature of the earliest Gregorian chant and the old church modes may examine for purposes of comparison (at least partial comparison), for example, the contemporary music of the Japanese, Arabs, Chinese, and Jews (disregarding, of course, the difference between Oriental and Western worlds)—that is, that music which we are used to conceiving under the rubric "exotic." In this music, precisely as in the earliest Western music, we often encounter in the melodic construction a definite degree of inadvertent irrationality and a similar absence of those harmonic nodal points, the fifth and third, which provide orientation. The horizontal line in the music of these peoples is still in a state of chaos (cf. *Harmony* p. 134), simply because sensitivity to the fifth and third has not yet matured. (Little insight into this stage of development is provided simply by invoking "heterophony.") Even the rhythm is nothing short of chaotic and unregulated, and that, of course, is the very reason a vertical dimension, polyphony, is completely lacking. Finally, a parallel exists in that the Orientals, exactly like our ancestors—and this is proof enough!—submit to the puerile preoccupation with scale systems they commit to paper simply by following the horizontal direction of the melodies. They assume, for example, a pentatonic system consisting of five degrees: *C D E · G A · C* or *C D Eb · G Ab · C;* or a hepatatonic system consisting of seven degrees: *F G A B C D E F* (Chinese), *D E F G A B C D* (Japanese), *C D Eb F♯ G Ab B C* (Gypsy), *F G A B C♯ D♯ F* (Chinese whole-tone scale), *C Db E F G Ab B C* (Indian), and so forth.

In addition, all these so-called systems, like our old church modes, can begin with any of its tones, whereby the number of systems is increased to monstrous proportions. And thus countless systems are assumed in a situation in which even one "system" in the strict sense of the word is impossible from the outset, since the all too modest tonal material is simply not differentiated enough. For that reason, the so-called systems—again exactly as in the earliest period of Western music—are of value at most only as mechanical-descriptive tools and can, of course, apply only to the horizontal dimension at that.

An attempt at polyphony—in itself perfectly conceivable—by the Japanese of today, for example, could perhaps lead to the same discovery of the harmonic principle as that made by the Westerner of centuries ago. But without such an attempt, I consider it impossible to come to terms with music. For obviously it is just the friction between horizontal and vertical dimensions that finally helped the human ear and sensibility to discover the natural principle of fifth and third, and this consequently led to the establishment of orderly relationships in melodies as well as harmonies. Thus, in music, today's Westerner has an advantage over today's Oriental as well as over the Westerner of the past—that is, the advantage of harmonic awareness with all of its beneficial consequences; to be exact, an advantage of several (eight to eleven) centuries.

It is inconceivable, on the other hand, how artists and theorists in our midst (for example, Saint-Saëns, Busoni, Bellermann, Capellen, A.J. Polak, L. Riemann, and others) can call for a return to the old church modes and exotic scales as a means of expanding our musical horizon. This certainly belongs among the most ironic and shameful characteristics of the present confusion and general lack of orientation.

Was it not disastrous enough that the Middle Ages—because of ignorance about the putative systems of antiquity, especially those of the Greeks—considered it necessary to accept them at face value?! Do we still refuse to learn anything from this bitter experience, the source of so many artistic and theoretical misconceptions for so many centuries? Such ignorance about a course of evolution that moved beyond its beginnings in such a logical way! Such ingratitude to destiny, which vouchsafed only to Western man the magnificent miracle of music as well as insight into the prescriptions of nature! And, further, such lack of awareness in respect to those heroes of music whose efforts guided us toward an understanding of what alone can form a true system! Alas, why did our great masters live and work, if today their works—built upon usable systems—can be declared *regressive* in comparison to little Chinese, Japanese, and Arabic melodies and scales (and this is exactly what happens when exotic scales are extolled under the rubric "progress")! It was none other than our masters who triumphantly elevated us long ago—even centuries ago—beyond the Chinese, Japanese, and Arabic stages, as well as that of the church modes, because they recognized the need for a compromise between horizontal and vertical harmony and thus were the first to create *diatony* [FrC., pp. 5, 11] out of the primeval chaos. Those exotic people still lack diatony, and that is the reason for the irrational character of their music.

But granted, nobody really wants intentionally to misinterpret brilliant works and the course of evolution. It is more correct, although a bitter truth, to say that only a certain inadequacy of artistic instinct on the part of artists and theorists is responsible for propagating old church modes or exotic scales. Obviously their instinct, however good it may be, is unable to come to grips with the still higher instinct of those artists who showed music its path, and to understand creativity to the fullest. Today's artists and theorists do not understand how to penetrate to the inner core of intuition in the art-works of our greatest masters. It is incomprehensible to them how the masters pursued their avenues with true clairvoyance; specifically, how they learned—in accordance with nature, on the basis of the overtone series—to project motivically the harmony of the major triad; how they accepted in an analogous, albeit artificial, way the minor triad; how they recognized the act of repeating a series of pitches as the principal force of all music of all times; how they managed to forge, from this principle alone, unalterably valid and definitive forms in the greatest possible variety; and, finally, how they acquired and passed on to us, by combining all these postulates (the major and minor triad, the creation of a series of pitches based on these sounds, the repetition of a given series of pitches, the application of harmonic principles to the horizontal and vertical dimensions in certain situations, and so on), the intuition that pitches belonging only to one and the same diatony are scale degrees—that is, producers and bearers of content.

Where artistic instinct fails, awareness is lacking: without a strong artistic instinct, there can be no real theory of art! In a theoretical textbook—I use one of the most recent ones as an example: the *Harmonielehre* by Rudolf Louis and Ludwig Thuille[1]—the nature of the major system is defined as vaguely as this (pp. 3ff.):

The *major scale* originates when a major tonic is joined by its two dominants of the same species—that is, by major chords:

Example 3

C: IV   I   V

The key is completed and exhaustively defined by the three triads: tonic, dominant, and subdominant. If we put the pitches contained in these triads into a stepwise succession (beginning with the tonic):

Example 4

C: I   V⁵   I³   IV   V   IV³   V³   I
     (IV⁵)   (I⁵)

we gain the diatonic major scale.

(For the construction of the minor system, see p. 20f.) If major is defined this way, then how we can fail to forgive musicians when, deserted by instinct and theory alike, they eagerly turn to various "systems" that never have been and never will be systems; we can even forgive them when they constantly ask, with seemingly superior (but in reality vacuously sarcastic) reflection: must there be only major and minor, today and tomorrow and forever? Why not something different and completely new—anything that occurs to us, such as C Db Eb F♯ G♯ A B C, or C D E F G Ab B C, or such systems as are allegedly represented by the old church modes or the exotic scales? Isn't it evident that the above definition fails to explain why in the major system a major triad must be joined by two other major triads; why these have to be "of the same species"; why the scale is produced simply by the rolling together (?) of these three triads; and why, on the other hand, the independence of the other four tones—those other than C, F, and G—is denied?

Shouldn't all these points first of all be *justified*? Isn't such an approach truly a *petitio principii*?[2]

How can one claim to have understood the "system" if its individual scale degrees, except for I, IV, and V, are deprived of their independence and thus of their attractive capability of assuming various functions? How much better it corresponds to the true meaning of a composition when, for example, scale degree III is understood in its different functions: (1) how, as the fourth ascending fifth (following the principle of the fifth—see *Harmony*, §§14–18), it confronts the tonic; (2) how it can also appear (following the principle of thirds—*Harmony*, §126) as the harbinger of scale-degree I, or of V, depending on whether the passage in question manifests development or inversion. But theorists, having no notion of any of this, have lately been teaching that the scale degrees II, III, VI, and VII are not really scale degrees in their own right but are assimilated by I, IV, and V, and therefore must give way to the latter. On the contrary, it is the functional versatility of the scale degree that is the basis of [compositional] practice, and this, of course, at least presupposes its independence!

And conversely, how much closer we come to the instinct of creators when we recognize that precisely the independence of scale degrees II, III, VI, and VII constitutes the psychological root of all chromaticism and all alteration (see *Harmony*, §19, and pp. 105–125). How much better this is than finding, in the appearance of the IV, V, and I functions, more than the mere *appearance* of these functions, and, on this pretext, denying the independence [of the other scale degrees] in favor of I, V, and IV—while the latter scale degrees, as foreground degrees, certainly retain their position of dominance within the system in any case.

When Schubert, for example, composes a succession VI — III — V — I (*Deutsche Tänze* op. 33 no. 3, bars 5–8 of the second part), is that really the same as when Brahms, for example, writes elsewhere ("Der Tod, das ist die kühle Nacht," op. 96 no. 1, bars 16ff.): $III^{\flat 5} — VI^{\sharp 3} — II^{\flat 5} — V^7 — I$? Does the diatonic progression by fifths beginning on III in the latter case have so little independence of purpose that theory, believing it can perhaps better be explained by assuming such things as sequence and derivations from other scale degrees, need pay it no further heed? Or does it have an independent purpose? If so, how can it be justified other than by recognizing the independent quality of the individual scale degrees, even that of III, which is in question here?

Or another example: When a composer, having presented the IV, moves to II (compare, for example, the Chopin quotation in *Harmony*, Example 123) in order to begin, so to speak, the last cycle there, must the II not be recognized again as a scale degree in its own right, simply because of the effect associated with the descending fifth II — V? Why would a composer bother to take the detour via II if the latter were not an independent scale degree but were merely a substitute for IV? And, furthermore, why would he finally even lower the II—that is, turn it into a Phrygian II, as, for example, Chopin does (*Harmony*, §50)?

Why would Brahms, for example, have led the bass in the first movement of his Symphony No. 4 (see bars 114–119) specifically through a IV — II — V progression if his purpose were not to invoke the particular force of the descending fifth from II to V?

Example 5

Doublebass

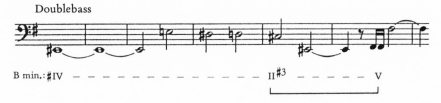

B min.: ♯IV – – – – – – – – – – – – – – – – II♯3 – – – – – – V

And would it not be wrong to deny the independence of scale degree II in the following example (given only in condensed form):

Example 6

R. Wagner, *Faust* Overture

The E in Example 6a is so strongly emphasized as the bearer of all content (which can be reduced to the simpler form outlined in Example 7) that the middle sonority, which could perhaps be interpreted as a ♯IV, is more correctly understood as a neighboring-note harmony (cf. Part 2, Chapter 2,

Example 7

below). The descending fifth $E-A$ (= $II^{\natural5}_{\natural3}-V$) in D minor stands so much in the foreground that this principal effect must not be ignored in favor of a certain speculative theory which assumes G as the root of scale-degree IV (allegedly the only scale-degree in question here) instead of II.

Need I mention further that the necessity of recognizing [the independence of] VI (to speak of this scale degree as well) would necessarily follow simply from the psychological effect of the deceptive cadence (*Harmony*, §121)? This should be clear to everyone. What would be the point of writing V — VI (usually followed by VI — (II —) V — I or something similar) if VI were merely a substitute for I or IV rather than a scale-degree in its own right? Is V — VI really no different from V — I or V — IV? Can this really be the truth? Furthermore, is II — I, for example, really the same in effect as IV — I?

Theorists removed themselves too far from art and indulge too much in speculation when they assume that descending fifths such as II — V and the like were used by composers mainly in idle "sequences" and as derivations from other scale degrees.[3] Taken together, these descending fifths often enough present the key as a whole, not an alleged sequence (see, for example, J.S. Bach's French Suite No. 1, Minuet, bars 1–8, where the scale degrees I — IV — VII — III — VI — II — V — I simply define D minor without any tendency to sequence or to modulate); or they appear—and this too, unfortunately, is still not heard properly—in the form of smaller, albeit well-defined, fragments of a key, several of which are then joined together simply by means of elision or chromatic modulation. Thus, more is certainly contained in the following examples than a mere sequence:

Example 8

Chopin, Etude in A Minor Op. 10 No. 2

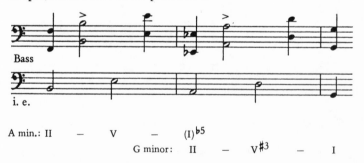

A min.: II   —   V   —   (I)$^{\flat5}$

    G minor: II   —   V$^{\sharp3}$ —   I

By the same token Chopin, for example, in his Etude in C Minor op. 10 no. 12, bars 55ff., is able to gain from an admittedly only latent background that is at first diatonically conceived:

Example 9

C minor: V   I   IV   VII   III   V   I

via the following hypothetically posited process of tonicization:

Example 10

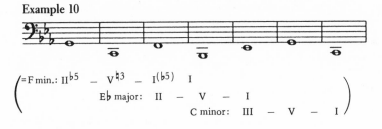

the final shape:

Example 11

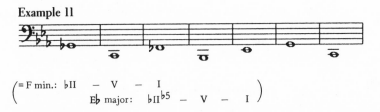

Considering that none of these passages manifests "sequential character," does it not follow necessarily that all scale-degrees—not only I, IV, and V—must be recognized as scale-degrees in their own right?

It is, of course, easier for theorists to say: "The major scale originates . . ."[4] if they then turn around and define it by going back to the finished system and merely describe it superficially in words. Such words not only deceive the author; they also immediately mislead the reader: having read them, he believes himself to have understood them, including everything that may lie behind them, so that he is never able to realize how far removed he still is from true comprehension of the most important compositional problem. Only the inevitable consequences of [pursuing] these tendencies finally expose the truly sad state of affairs. For if the uniquely true and natural system, the major system, already tested in the most magnificent works of art, were really understood inside out, down to the deepest roots of its compositional necessities, how could it be possible to write about the major and minor systems as is done today? How could such a ridiculous definition of "system" be purveyed, and the character of "systems" comparable to major and minor be ascribed to utopian scales, devoid of diatony and triadic value—devoid, that is, of any value for art?

From these inconsistencies, it is most evident how little the general perception of our time is in accord with the artistic instinct of our great masters. These inconsistencies signify for practice and in theory just this: vague nostalgia for the church modes and exotic systems, vague theoretical definitions, and the like.

The complete lack of any technique in today's composition (which necessarily had to follow as a consequence of misunderstanding or of the inability to rise to the level of what had already been accomplished); the new epoch of irrationality that has recently broken out in our art—admittedly, an irrationality different from that of music's incipience—: these are matched only too naturally by our craving for the musical-primitive irrationality of foreign peoples as well. It is the decline of our art that creates such inadvertent correspondences with the incipient art of exotic peoples!

Furthermore, disregarding all insufficiencies of instinct and knowledge as well as the common points of inadvertent irrationality—what naive presumption lies in the propaganda for other "systems."

Just imagine that there were some among today's painters who would tout the primitive drawings of the Eskimos as finished art forms to be imitated and disseminated; or imagine poets who would seriously propose to open up a new future for language by going back to the babbling of a three- or four-year-old child. How much effort was connected with language's growth to maturity, how indispensable its artifice if communication among human beings is to be preserved! And now, one hundred years after Goethe and Schiller, should the German nation, because of an unfortunate temporary depression, seek for a change to acquire again the imperfect communicative tools of a child in order to attempt a so-called spiritual renewal? By the same token, in view of the benefits of so beautifully developed an art as music, how can anyone dare to suggest that we look to musically inferior races and nations for allegedly new systems, when in fact they have no systems at all!

Let me not be misunderstood: Even the babbling of a child, the first awkward sentences, certainly have a captivating charm, as do Arabic, Japanese, and Turkish songs. But in the first case our joys are derived from the child itself and the wonderful miracle of a human being in its development; in the second, our curiosity is aroused by the foreign peoples and their peculiarities.

Skillful artists, still, have always successfully limited the problem of musical exoticism in practice. They solved it by attempting to make the original melodies of foreign peoples (often original only because of their imperfections and awkwardness) accessible to us through the refinements of our two tonal systems. They expressed the foreign character *in our major and minor*—such superiority in our art, such flexibility in our systems! And there was never any tendency to go beyond this "transposition." Think, for example, of Haydn's and Beethoven's *Schottische Lieder,* Schubert's unique *Divertissement à l'hongroise,* the Hungarian Dances by Brahms, the Slavonic Dances by Dvořák, and the Norwegian Dances by Grieg, as well as *Scheherezade* by Rimsky-Korsakov, among others. The point in all these cases was not to loosen our system in order to incorporate a foreign one, but, on the contrary, to use our major and minor systems to express the foreign element, which does justice in a certain sense to a primeval state of music but needs to be adjusted in some way to suit the needs of a more advanced art. It cannot be denied that some situations (e.g., the representation of a certain emotional state) justify even a procedure like that of, for example, Berlioz, who uses the truly Aeolian melody of the "Dies irae" in the last movement of his *Symphonie fantastique* in the alleged "old system" without alterations—that is, without significantly adjusting it to our system. (Compare, on the other hand, the treatment of the same melody by Saint-Saëns in *Danse macabre.*) Nevertheless, the other method used by the masters mentioned above is more artistic and more logical. For what can it mean when, for example, Helmholtz states in his *Lehre von den Tonempfindungen:* "We know today that we cannot use Gothic ornaments in a Greek temple; by the same token, it must also be clear to us that we cannot harmonize the music of other periods and nations, which had tonal qualities other than major and minor, according to the patterns of our major and minor harmonies."[5] Helmholtz has not sufficiently understood how much purely artistic considerations contributed to the establishment of our systems, and that melodic formulas which never were systems and thus were incapable of supporting larger musical structures should be compared neither with our systems, which have proven themselves to have just such power, nor with the architectural system of Greek temples, which has shown itself to have a similar power in respect to their own structures. What a monumental difference between the imaginary Dorian system in music and the authentic Dorian system in Greek architecture!

In the same connection, allow me to refer finally to the arrangement of German folk songs (7 volumes) by Brahms. German folk songs undoubtedly appear to have been influenced by harmonic considerations already at an earlier stage and thus rank infinitely higher than the exotic melodies. Nevertheless, I view Brahms's arrangements as essays in which our system is applied also to melodies stemming from earlier periods [of music history] and originating with people for whom the "system" was basically something unknown or at least unconscious. I know from Brahms himself that, among other things, he wanted to protest, with these arrangements, against widely disseminated editions of German folk songs and the artistic level of the treatments. For this reason, he had written a special pamphlet in which his arrangements were to serve merely as illustration of his opposing viewpoints; convinced of the uselessness of the written word, he later destroyed the polemical manuscript and decided to edit only the musical examples in the form of the independent volumes known to us.

From this it follows that if folk songs are to be brought into the realm of art, art has to prevail—even if the songs are as advanced and developed as the folk songs of the German nation. The fully developed art must take care to unveil the soul of the song with the means proper to and proven by art, so that the most intimate (and yet undeveloped) quality of the song is revealed, thus expressing with firm artistic contours the feeling for the folk song current among the people. This does not mean that compositional artifice must enter the song in the name of art. By no means! But if we compare the arrangements by Brahms with those by other editors, the proper function of real art in relation to a folk song immediately becomes clear. Once the song moves from the ethnic to the artistic realm and is about to be appropriated by art, one can no longer believe that the song has to be returned in its artistic form to the people; only the principle of art is in effect now, and it is entirely unconcerned about the people. The people have once and for all given the song over to art as a kind of "suggestion," and now art elaborates the song artistically in its own realm and with its own means, albeit with means that should not overstep the [original] suggestion by much. The German people—I mean the broadest stratum of the German people—will never want to sing their folk songs in Brahms's version, any more than the Gypsies, for example, will accept their own songs and dances in his most ingenious arrangement. But can the artist and art be blamed for this? Anyone who thinks so might consider this: the artist does not come out of the blue, but is a part of his people, and indeed its best part; whatever the artist receives he returns a thousand times, and thus earns the most sincere gratitude of his nation and of humanity. If the artist had stopped where most people inevitably must stop, how could we have acquired those blossoms [of art] that provide our enjoyment? If art had never gone beyond the folk song or the Gregorian chant, how could we have conquered polyphony, motets, sonatas, and symphonies? One should not, then, attempt to set up a dichotomy between art and the people where none exists, but should finally understand that the people, for a reason different from dichotomy, must leave off where art begins; for musical art really cannot stop after sixteen bars!

Object to Goethe because he raised the Faust of the people to a Faust in art! Growth is the fate of humans, and this despite the fact that growth may even prove fatal!

When it comes time to decide what has been beneficial and significant for the progress and creative power of the human species, what do hundreds of folk songs for lute from olden times (which lately have become so fashionable) mean, or the balalaika recitals of Russian provenance, in comparison with a fugue by J.S. Bach or a symphonic movement by Beethoven or even just the *Scheherezade* by Rimsky-Korsakov?

As a final word on this topic, I might recommend to those artists and theorists who long so much for other systems that they save their energy for more worthwhile matters. What do they ultimately get out of such efforts in word and tone? Inevitable disappointment awaits those who arrive suddenly at a result that had been achieved long ago and a thousand times better: either they grasp the necessity of learning to create melodies from harmonies and thus pay homage to the triad, and—recognizing the need to establish orderly relations among the several triads—arrive naturally at the diatony of major and minor, or they simply continue their attempts to harmonize exotic melodies. But in the Western world we have long recognized the value of the triad as well as of diatony; and as far as the harmonization of [exotic] melodies is concerned, the above-mentioned masters remain unattainable models for the Capellens, Polaks, Dittrichs, and even for Saint-Saëns and Busoni, because those masters, with their unfathomable instincts, were at home in our systems in a far deeper sense. Must there be a "world music" just because of preconception and will? Can inorganically developed whims ever really merge into organic laws? And since there could be no "German Empire of the Holy

Roman Nation," must there be a "German Music of the Japanese or Indian Nation?"

It goes without saying that among the more important authors *Fux* (p. 53) is still firmly grounded in the old church modes:

> After eliminating the variety of whole-tones and semitones, theorists abandoned the three genera of the Greeks, as I indicated above. This may be useful to remember when considering that another system replacing the Greek one was introduced, in which the three genera were reduced to two: diatonic and chromatic (see Table I, Figure 10).
>
> However, since men's insatiable desire for ever new and different things was not satisfied with just these two genera, composers have used in their compositions a combination of both, which now has been introduced everywhere. I regard such a combination of genera as acceptable, since one must go with the times. But composers should be admonished not to use this mixed genus in a capella works performed without the accompaniment of the organ; if they fail to observe this, they can be assured that they will never attain the final aim they hoped to reach, for in this style none but the diatonic genus alone can be used. I want to recommend highly to all this important rule, which extensive practice and experience have taught me.

Fux was instinctively right in demanding that exercises with a cantus firmus use only the diatonic genus; but, since he unfortunately fails to understand the fundamental difference between cantus-firmus exercises and the settings of free composition, he overshoots the goal by far in attempting to restrict even the latter to the diatonic genus. A glance at, for example, J.S. Bach's chorale settings, motets, and the like suffices, however, to show how insupportable Fux's restriction is if applied outside the realm of contrapuntal exercises themselves. Fux, of course, is to a certain extent aware of the greater freedom in [free] compositions; thus his misconception in a narrow sense consists—to express it most precisely—in singling out the free a capella compositions and mistaking them for cantus-firmus exercises. The only correct part, however, is that vocal settings—and that includes a capella compositions—must be more circumspect regarding chromaticism than instrumental settings, a notion so completely lacking among today's composers.

Albrechtsberger is entirely naive on this problem, as shown by the following remarks (p. 33):

> I have already shown in the fourth chapter that the Greeks as well as our old theorists had twelve variable modes. Their mode on *E,* which they called Phrygian, appears to have been nothing but a hybrid. It is very peculiar that Herr Kapellmeister Fux accompanies this mode in his examples with a minor third at the beginning and a major third at the end, like the other minor modes. His fame, however, is immortal, for he has served many hundreds as teacher and master. Is it his fault that many things have changed nowadays? The other five authentic modes [would have] posed no problem if they had only carried as a key signature the necessary flats and sharps, which would have enhanced their melodies. For that reason we will retain modern composers' 24 keys established in the same (fourth) chapter for all five species.

These sentences hint at the insight that the authentic modes could perhaps somehow be reduced to major and minor if only it were allowed to add the necessary sharps and flats. More important for us, however, is the result that Albrechtberger keeps to only major and minor in his exercises. *Cherubini* does the same.

All the more noteworthy is the regression of *Bellermann,* who again uses the old church modes for his exercises. He adopts this course not so much to follow his model Fux (see his Preface, p. VII: "I have followed Fux . . . in the sequence of topics to be discussed") as out of true and deep conviction. Thus it is doubly unfortunate that his conviction rests only on misconceptions. Using a somewhat incorrect basis as a point of departure, he nevertheless arrives, following his better instincts, at the principal statement: "Thus, the study of music must begin with melody," which we must certainly endorse; but then he abruptly draws from this observation the following conclusions:

> The simplest and most natural relations in art need to be studied first of all and investigated in all their aspects. In the field of harmony, which we want to examine here in particular, this is done by studying the diatonic scale, whose rich variety of forms encompasses not only our major and minor scales but also the different species of octaves (that is, the church modes and related matters). Therefore, the study of harmonic relationships is under all circumstances to be based on those epochs in which music pursued its course according to the strict laws of pure diatonicism, if students are not to be engulfed at the outset with false and erroneous opinions and conceptions.

And later, on p. XV, he states:

> All exercises in the works mentioned above [that is, the treatises of Albrechts-berger and Cherubini] limit themselves to major and minor. This procedure, however, has several disadvantages: without thorough study of the church modes we never learn to appreciate correctly the old masterworks and to understand the course of music history. Furthermore, it is of the utmost importance for correct modulation—if we want to write in a strict diatonic style—that we know how to establish a regular cadence on every degree of the diatonic scale. The correctness of this statement, I believe, will become evident only after the study as prescribed here has been completed.

This, of course, is all false in reasoning and judgment: is it the purpose of counterpoint to deal with music history and to introduce us to the old masterworks rather than to concern itself, first and foremost, with eternally valid principles of voice leading? Why should one write—just for the sake of old church modes—only in a strict diatonic scale when one can and should also write chromatically? Is the major mode not as purely diatonic as the other old church modes? And is it not possible, by strictly observing the vocal principles [of voice leading], to demonstrate the rules of voice leading in the major mode just as well as in the diatonicism of the church modes? Why then favor the latter—which, by the way, if used in counterpoint, would actually have to *mis*lead the student about the course of music history?

I have already shown in the introduction the peculiar bias of Bellermann; what necessarily led him to the errors mentioned above is only his basic misconception of the purpose of contrapuntal doctrine together with the erroneous belief in the church modes that has just been refuted.

Chapter 2

The Structure of the Cantus Firmus in Particular

Beginning

§1. Construction of the beginning

The cantus firmus reveals itself as an exercise already in the construction of its beginning: since it is to represent the most primitive state of a melody, it should begin only in the simplest and most primitive of all possible ways—specifically, with the tonic of the key. How could the brevity and the neutral rhythm of the cantus firmus justify a more individual beginning? This alone is the reason for the old rule: *The cantus firmus must always begin with the tonic of the key.*

This solution of the problem of the beginning, however, as one can see (but as has unfortunately been so thoroughly misunderstood), stems exclusively from the given limited situation and the exercise-purpose of the cantus firmus. The solution therefore always applies, conversely, only to the cantus firmus itself; it makes no claim whatever to be a universally valid principle of composition—that is, a general rule for all true art-works in free composition—to the extent that it would have to be expressly considered even an "exception," or at best a particular deed of a "strong talent," if a work of free composition should begin other than with the tonic. (Intellectually lazy teachers, with condescension that is both touching and grotesque, tend to "excuse" such peculiarities without, however, recommending them as models to the student.)

Depending on its individual emotional character and tendency, a real work of art may show a different beginning without constituting an infraction of a so-called "law of strict composition." For if different situations require different solutions—and the cantus firmus is just such a special situation—how can the solution of one situation contradict that of another? Each solution is justified on its own account: this does not negate the fact that even in free composition, in an actual compositional context, it may be considered artistically ethical *to match a simple situation only with a simple beginning—that is, a beginning*

with a tonic—instead of contradicting its simplicity with a complicated begin-
ning.

The results of regarding the rule stated above for writing mere exercises
as equally binding outside the domain of the cantus firmus is shown by an
example from free composition, the chorale "Gelobet seist du Jesu Christ"
and the three settings that follow:

Example 12

Ge - lo - bet seist du   Je - su Christ,   dass   du Mensch ge -

bo - ren bist von   ei - ner Jung - frau,   das   ist   wahr, dess

freu - et sich der   En - gel Schar.   Ky - ri - e - leis.

Example 13a

a) J. S. Bach (Riemenschneider No. 51)

Basso continuo:

Example 13a *continued*

Example 13b

b) J. S. Bach (Reimenschneider No. 160)

Example 13c

c) Bellermann, pp. 277-278

As is evident, the three arrangements cited above are obviously grounded in G major, if not actually in the "Mixolydian" system.

If we abandon all prejudice of earlier theory and use our unbiased ear to the fullest by simply following in the horizontal melodic direction (see Example 12 above) the fifths, which help to establish the content so beautifully and thereby clarify it so convincingly (cf. *Harmony*, §76), what do we really hear?

The first phrase is dominated by the fourth G — C (that is, the fifth C — G in inversion), whereby our instinct, following the tonicizing tendency of the fifth (see *Harmony*, §133), unfailingly forms at first the impression of C major. That this first impression is also correct is indeed confirmed by the following passage, which (compare the paragraphs just cited) certainly could have revealed [any] contradiction and thus have led to a correction.

In the second phrase, the ear immediately relates B to D and these two tones to G, which produces the triad G - B - D. Such natural development of the original C major toward the fifth, G, of its key area!

The third phrase immediately returns with the initial fourth $G—C$ (= $C—G$) to the key of C major, but by moving through $D—G—D$ (= $G—D$), it manages to achieve the effect of a half-cadence $(I—V)$; the latter, it should be noted, is exactly in C major. Consider this, then: while the second phrase concludes the modulation of G major with the inversion D to G, the third on the contrary unfolds the same fifth in the developing, ascending direction from G to D [*Harmony*, p. 31ff.].

The fourth and fifth phrases cadence most clearly in the tonic. This tonic, reached already at the word *Engel*, finally imbues the concluding tone G with the effect of merely a fifth of the tonic harmony. According to this natural and "quintessential" aural perception, however, the four-part setting of the chorale cited above has to be entirely different. Limiting myself to triads in root position and avoiding all inversions, passing tones, and other means of diversification (see *Harmony*, Example 50), I present in the following example a setting that strives merely to give expression to the tendency.

Example 14

(At the third fermata it would, of course, be possible to cadence in D, exactly as the settings cited above demonstrate.)

Wherein lies the difference? While I hear the chorale in major, namely C major, especially for reasons suggested by the fifths of the melody, the composers of the first three settings thought it necessary to hear it in Mixolydian. Thus we read in Bellermann (p. 120): "The entire melody is Mixolydian; the first phrase establishes an Ionian cadence on C, the second a Mixolydian on G, the third a Dorian on D, the fourth an Aeolian on A, while the fifth concludes in Mixolydian on G." The assumption of a Mixolydian system, however, is primarily based on the fact that the chorale's first and last tones are G and, furthermore, on the rule posited by contrapuntal doctrine that the first tone of the melody must also be the first tone of a system—thus, Mixolydian in this case. The internal fifth-relationships are thus rendered mute by this external feature alone; it is obvious that when it comes to salvaging the honor of an alleged system, one does not inquire much into the inner authenticity and significance of melodic progressions (Tonfolgen). Pereat cantus, vivat modus![1] evidently was the motto of the earlier theorists. Thus Bach and Bellermann force themselves—just for the sake of theory!—to begin as well as end the chorale harmonically with the triad on G. Even if we admit that under certain circumstances such constructions could perhaps be accounted for by some artistic whim or license—precisely from the standpoint of free composition, thus not at all by theory alone—, those settings still contain enough stilted and forced features imposed by the Mixolydian system on the otherwise normal melody in major. This "forced" character has not been mitigated by much, even though a J.S. Bach rushed in to support the false system with such artistic voice leading and so many [other] basic devices that make the setting beautiful. I need only point out, for example, the first fourth G — C, which, understood in Mixolydian, would have to be interpreted as the tonic's lower fifth—and this immediately at the outset of the melody! As I remarked above, however, the same fourth immediately turns into the most natural harmonic feature once the melody is heard in major, where it exactly circumscribes the tonic triad.

Moreover, how unnatural, for example, the assumption of an "Aeolian" mode in the fourth phrase: if we try something that has always been permitted, even by theory, in the Aeolian mode (Harmony, §27)—specifically, instead of the alleged Aeolian leading tone G, its raised form G♯—it immediately becomes clear that such an alteration, because it is essentially untrue, would have to conflict with the melody and corrupt the passage throughout. Indeed, both J.S. Bach and Bellermann ignore the Aeolian mode that theory assumes for the horizontal direction [of the melody in phrase 4], the former in spite of his freest approach to the setting, which would have permitted even such extravagant things. Even though both otherwise make grave concessions to theory, especially at the beginning and end of their chorale settings, in this passage they finally let their instinct prevail over theory, because the latter's demands were so unnatural. Thus, the chorale melody, interpreted as Mixolydian, seems only forced and stilted, even though, within the [otherwise] unnatural requirements imposed upon it, it has the normal tonic beginning and ending required by theory; from the standpoint of major, however, it appears completely natural—more peculiar by only a small nuance than so many other melodies in major in that it begins as well as ends with the fifth of the tonic. Now, is it not an accomplishment when a system (in this case the major system) enables a melody to return to its natural key and even permits it to appear in some respects more individual than other melodies belonging to the same system? (In this connection see also *Harmony*, p. 137, Example 107!) Isn't it more appropriate to attribute this wealth to the major system, instead of sacrificing the wealth and simply risking distortion of the kind represented by the Mixolydian mode in relation to the chorale cited above?

It is evident from this example why I have rejected the church modes in *Harmony* as well as here (see Chapter 1, §5). It can be seen here in a most convincing way how the pressures of a church mode can distort a well-invented melody rather than bringing us closer to understanding it. The merely descriptive nature of the old mode—or the merely mnemotechnical side, as I have called it before—is obvious here; originally the purpose of the mode was simply to capture theoretically the beginning and end of a given melody as well as other relationships in the course of the horizontal line. Earlier periods further divided, for similar descriptive purposes, all modes into authentic and plagal or so-called perfect, imperfect, and mixed modes just to catalog and categorize the various melodic phenomena.[2] As meritorious as such an era of gathering and describing materials certainly is for the evolution of art (since it is undoubtedly based on good will and most detailed and faithful observations), a great step forward is nevertheless taken with the discovery of our two principal systems. The latter, in contrast to the old modes, are based simultaneously on two dimensions, the horizontal and the vertical. Consequently they need no longer limit themselves merely to providing a highly detailed horizontal description; rather, by the application of harmonic criteria (even to the horizontal line—compare *Harmony*, §76), therefore precisely by virtue of their deeper penetration, they are able to reveal all the more accurately the true inner core of the melody.

The chorale cited above demonstrates, furthermore, that in contrast to the cantus firmus of our exercises, the chorale melody is already a real melody—that is, a real composition—while the cantus firmus merely serves the purpose of an exercise that need not go much beyond a minimum of artistic beauty (see below, §20 of this chapter).

How many misconceptions and artificialities could have been avoided by teachers and writers of music theory up till now if they had only learned always to distinguish clearly between a real chorale and the cantus firmus, which is intended only for exercises!

But anyone who understands the difference between the two phenomena can nevertheless comprehend the meaning of the rule given here about the beginning of the cantus firmus: the tonic beginning is required *only* by the cantus firmus, and not by a chorale, to say nothing of a larger free composition. For if the chorale has shown that as a free composition it can begin with a tone other than the tonic, this applies even more to larger compositions where the scale degrees effect almost a compulsion, and hence an even clearer justification than in the chorale. (Compare *Harmony,* Examples 23, 24, 25.) This kind of beginning, as I have said before, should in no way be considered an exception, since the contrapuntal rule under consideration was invoked to solve the problem of the beginning only for the cantus firmus. This, of course, provides in a nutshell a certain perspective on the entire problem of the beginning in general. To provide such perspectives, however—especially where very simple situations are used as a point of departure—belongs among the essential tasks of instruction in counterpoint.

We may go still further and maintain that in free composition a beginning with a tone other than the tonic (or, by analogy, a harmony other than I) may not only be useful but even absolutely necessary in certain situations. It is doubtless a serious flaw in Bruckner's symphonies, for example, that almost all themes begin with the tonic. It will be demonstrated on another occasion how this technique, in itself quite normal, of necessity completely contradicts cyclic form and, within that form, makes effects that are most stifling.

Now it becomes clear to the reader why I had on principle to criticize Fux, Albrechtsberger, and others (in the note on p. 18) for confusing chorale and cantus firmus. For most teachers, the misconception they cling to has definite disadvantages that will be mentioned later; however, it should be stated here that Fux, Albrechtsberger, Cherubini, and Bellermann fortunately use only true and solid cantus firmi for their exercises, and no actual chorales, so that at least in this respect contrapuntal doctrine suffers no damage from their confusion of chorale with cantus firmus.

In contrast, however, it is clear that I have to reject the method of *Dehn,* for example, who immediately proposes a genuine, authentic chorale melody "for longer exercises" (p. 7):

Example 15

This melody, however, implies entirely different, and so much more complicated, conditions and prerequisities that really cannot be reconciled with [contrapuntal] studies, at least not with their first stage. Just think of the beginning with the tone of the dominant, of the fermatas characteristic of the chorale melody, and of the repetition of tones—all these elements carry with them their own requirements that need to be observed independently.

Main Body

§2. *The ambitus of a tenth*

The cantus firmus must move only within the ambitus of the tenth. This framework is demanded, on the one hand, by the limited range of the human voice in general as well as, on the other hand, by the brevity of the exercise itself, which certainly would have to make any melodies of a larger ambitus appear unnatural.

Fux indirectly adheres to this strict standpoint when he states (but not until his treatment of three-voice counterpoint) on p. 93: "Furthermore, in this kind of composition it is not allowed to go beyond the limits of the five lines [of the staff] unless absolutely necessary." In this connection it is important to note that Fux uses (besides the F-clef for the bass) only the older C-clef—more precisely the c^1-clef—for soprano, alto, and tenor in his exercises. Since he (at least) *plans* to set the exercises in a vocal style throughout, he recommends that the limits of the five lines not be overstepped in order to preserve the limits of the individual vocal ranges. Incidentally, here we find Fux's good insight concerning the significance of the C-clefs confirmed in a most emphatic way: the clefs [*Schlüssel*] formerly represented indeed real keys [*Schlüssel*] to the various vocal ranges in that they tried to capture the ambitus of the voices as nearly as possible within the five lines.

To clarify this, I list the content of the four principal vocal ranges in the following clefs:[3]

Example 16

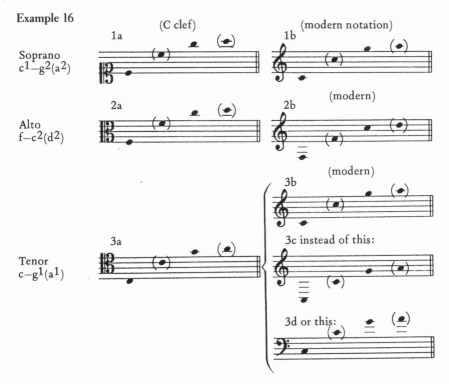

Today the C-clefs unfortunately are being abandoned more and more; they are replaced by G-clefs even for the alto and tenor, although exactly in these voices the number of ledger lines needed equals the number of staff-lines unused. (The number of ledger lines at 3c and 3d finally led to moving the content of the tenor upward by an octave!—see 3b.) Thus musicians try to unify all visual images of music even where nature herself has offered a clear differentiation of the phenomena in question. At least the sensitivity for vocal ranges is lost that way; its place is taken, certainly to the detriment of art, by an all too colorless and expressionless monotony of image—strong proof of an estrangement in understanding of the true function of clefs and their twofold relationship to vocal ranges, on the one hand, and the five-line staff, on the other. Such estrangement has already befallen wide circles and threatens to propagate itself even further. Nowadays publishers are advised to issue reprints of the old scores in uniform clefs! Such a horrendous expenditure, which really could be put to better use! And all this only for the benefit of our dear "dilettante," who is now considered the final arbiter, the ultimate goal of our art! The unwelcome and bizarre consequences to which this very indulgence by musicians of the laziness of the public has led can be seen—to quote an innocent example—in the fact that the public has long considered the range of tenor and soprano absolutely identical(!), simply because the use of the G-clef for both types of voices in the piano-vocal scores of operas seems to suggest this to them clearly, and because nobody has explained to them that, by convention, the tenor voice actually sounds an octave lower than notated.

Bellermann expressly states (p. 115ff.): "The tenth may be considered the maximum range of a melody; in the authentic octaves we arrive at it either by overstepping the boundaries of the octave by an ascending third or by moving a third below the tonic (*Grundton*), or by moving just a step above the octave and a step below the tonic. In plagal melodies we may proceed in a similar way, although in this case it is rare to go beyond the lower dominant."

§3. *The prohibition of tone-repetitions*

It is not permitted in the cantus firmus to repeat a tone even once.

First, the repetition of a tone—as is almost self-evident, incidentally—would necessarily result in the unification of the two bars; this unification, however, would necessarily be in conflict (according to Part 1, Chapter 1, §3) with the postulate of balance in the cantus firmus.

Furthermore—and this is the second reason—, a peculiar situation seems to enter the scene with the repetition of tones: involuntarily, one associates with it the image of a text, especially that of a word of two or more syllables. It is evident that such association by itself must vitiate the equilibrium of the cantus firmus.

The only exception in counterpoint to the prohibition mentioned above, the so-called *ligatura rupta* (the resolution of a syncope which incorporates an anticipation of the tone of resolution itself), will be discussed later in connection with fifth-species counterpoint (Part 2, Chapter 5, §11).

The tone-repetition to which contrapuntal doctrine responds with a prohibition—that is, only in a negative way—is therefore, by contrast, a phenomenon of free composition. In free composition there certainly is sufficient reason to emphasize the harmonic or rhythmic significance of a pitch through repetition, or to react to the requirements of a polysyllabic word, whether it be in actual vocal music or—only by association—also in instrumental music. Especially in the latter case, the performer must try to lend the words and syllables latent in the tonal repetition a personal rhetorical expression of their own by means of a kind of *declamation* of the repeated tones. For nothing is so trite as tonal repetitions in absolute music reproduced mechanically (pianists especially are the worst offenders!) without revealing any trace of the secret of the latent words.

We have just seen (Part 1, Chapter 2, §1) an example of tone-repetition in vocal composition in the chorale cited above (Example 12), and I point out that tone-repetition is one among many other distinguishing features that make the chorale, which is already a free composition, different from a cantus firmus, which is merely an exercise.

Here are some more examples from instrumental music:

Example 17
J. S. Bach, English Suite No. 6, Prélude

Example 18
Haydn, Theme and Variations in F Minor

and the finale of the E♭-major symphony by Mozart [K. 543] (with what divine eloquence it introduces the recapitulation!!):

Example 19
Mozart, Symphony No. 39, Finale
Clarinet I (concert pitch)

Violin I

Example 20

Beethoven, String Quartet Op. 130, I

Tone-repetition pervades even ornamentation (the acciaccatura, the appoggiatura, the anticipation, and the like) with a similarly rhetorical character, as the following examples show:

Example 21

J. S. Bach, English Suite No. 1, Courante I

Example 22

Chopin, Nocturne Op. 37 No. 1

Fux and *Cherubini* observe the prohibition of tone-repetition in the cantus firmus itself most strictly, but unfortunately do not discuss the matter specifically. This is regrettable, the more so since the very prohibition of tone-repetition could perhaps have most readily alerted both theorists to the difference between cantus firmus and chorale or free composition, and thereby to the true function of contrapuntal study.

Albrechtsberger, by contrast, approaches the problem in the following manner (although not until he discusses the fifth species of two-voice counterpoint). In accordance with his method, he intentionally constructs an error related to the issue in question:

Example 23

He takes this opportunity to remark (p. 67): "The error consists in setting two tones of the same pitch in succession in one single bar. . . ."[4] This, however, is not an error in vocal music where a longer note is turned into two shorter notes because of two- or three-syllable words, as in the following example:"

Example 24

Li - be - ra   nos   Do   -   mi - ne,   Do - mi - ne!

The same:

The remark "the same" [in Example 24], indicating that Albrechtsberger saw both melodies as having the same significance, suggests that he somehow already had an idea of the true reason for the prohibition of tone-repetition in the cantus firmus and contrapuntal exercises based on it. However, the awareness has not yet completely matured. First of all, he is not yet able to formulate the *reason* for the prohibition *specifically* for the cantus firmus, and, secondly, he is therefore uncertain whether tone-repetition permitted in vocal music constitutes only a license and exception or something else—that is, something that is altogether permitted and required in vocal music. (Observe the casual turn of phrase: "This, however, is not an error in vocal music," and recall the quotation from the introduction, p. 3, where he uses the term "exceptions.") One can see again here how detrimental it is that he is unable to distinguish clearly enough between "vocal music" and contrapuntal exercises. His lack of precision in differentiating [these matters] has the result that despite all [correct] presentiments he ultimately remains completely unaware that tone-repetition in the cantus firmus is prohibited without exception because of the nature of the latter, but, on the contrary, must even be required in vocal music for reasons resulting from the entirely different situation that it represents. Throughout "strict counterpoint," however, he observes the prohibition, and uses a tone-repetition only once, admittedly as a "license" (p. 152):

Example 25

However, it cannot be determined, at least not with complete certainty, whether he would have in principle permitted tone-repetition already in fugal exercises.[5]

Cherubini uses a tone-repetition in the cantus firmus in his Example 29 (p. 10). The remarks following the example—"These examples are set entirely according to the rules of strict two-voice counterpoint . . . and the melody moves always diatonically in a light and elegant fashion"—indicate that he obviously had no notion whatever of the perils of tone-repetition. Nevertheless, an inner instinct prevents him from committing the same error a second time; but it would have been his duty to shed light on this very instinct.

Bellermann, however, comments (p. 99): "In such [cantus-firmus] melodies we avoid the repetition of a tone twice or several times in succession, because such repetitions cause a stasis in the even melodic progression; furthermore, a tone repeated several times in succession assumes predominance, rhythmically, over the other tones of the melody."

In this light we can assess still more accurately the terrible pedagogical error that *Dehn* commits in his textbook when, as mentioned above, he uses for exercises not only a cantus firmus but also a real chorale, which, of course, features tone-repetitions. The student cannot but be confused when he sees in close proximity a cantus firmus without, and a chorale with, tone-repetition, both presented as exercises of allegedly equal validity without any reference whatever to the essential difference in their mechanics, including the problem of tone-repetition.

§4.   *The prohibition of chromatic progressions*

A chromatic progression is prohibited in the cantus firmus. Thus, it is not permitted to proceed as in Example 26.

Example 26

This restriction is based on the fact that the chromatic progression is itself in a certain sense already a kind of *tone-repetition* which, as mentioned above in §3, is disallowed altogether in the cantus firmus;[6] furthermore, because the altered tone—to the extent that it assumes the character of a tonal variant by the very fact of alteration—also produces the expression of a *passing tone* (in the example above, the G♯ as passing between G and A, the G♭ between G and F). This effect ties all three tones together all too closely as a unit and thus must lead to the prohibition of chromatic progressions in the cantus firmus.

In certain situations, moreover, the chromatic progression inadvertently has the detrimental effect of a *"mixture"* of keys (in the example above, A-major/minor; see *Harmony*, §38f.). Such mixture, however, is unsuited to the cantus firmus because of its drastic and forced quality, which undoubtedly protrudes most crassly in the chromatic progression; in no way can it enter into a healthy and normal relationship within the narrow scope of the cantus firmus. Furthermore, the lack of scale degrees, several kinds of contrast, and other means of differentiation prevent the two keys that are supposed to be mixed by the chromatic progression from being represented as comprehensively and clearly as in free composition; for that reason such a drastic mixture must suffer with respect to persuasiveness and precision of effect in the cantus firmus. Therefore, even for cadential purposes, the chromatic progression that would necessarily result from the direct succession of the two ascending leading tones[7] (see §23 below) is still completely prohibited in the cantus firmus:

Example 27

D $\frac{\text{min.}}{\text{maj.}}$:

    ♭VII   —   ♯VII   —   I
   (min.)   (maj.)

Mixtures can be used properly only in free composition, since the cantus firmus lacks all the necessary conditions of a purely harmonic nature that must be considered prerequisites for their use.

This may suffice concerning the prohibition of chromaticism in the cantus firmus itself.

From this the reader could conclude, on the other hand, that chromaticism might perhaps be permitted all the more readily in counterpoint for two or several voices where the increase in harmony might be able to support adequately the effect of a "mixture," or even that of *tonicization* (see *Harmony*, §136f.). However, as will be demonstrated in detail later in discussing three-voice counterpoint, even in this case the harmonies still do not have the necessary compelling urge characteristic of the harmonies suggested and supported by scale degrees in free composition. Therefore, it is not allowed in three-voice counterpoint to write, for example, the following chromatic progression:

Example 28

c. f.

Thus, the overall result is that chromaticism must be eliminated from all contrapuntal exercises, since it would disturb the intended balance of the melody by tone-repetition and passing tones; furthermore, because of the inadequacy of the tonal material itself (that is, of the cantus firmus as well as of the harmonies based on it), the potential effect of a mixture of keys or of a process of tonicization [suggested by chromaticism] could only be implied without being able to come to *full* fruition, as it does in free composition.

This finally yields the following perspective on free composition: chromaticism can be used there for the most varied purposes. For example,

(a) As passing tones:[8]

Example 29

Mozart, Rondo in A Minor K. 511

    p   *cresc.*   *p*

Example 30

Mozart, Symphony No. 39, Introduction

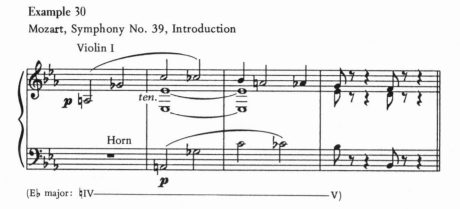

(E♭ major: ♮IV————————————————————————————V)

Example 31

J. S. Bach, English Suite No. 4, Sarabande

B♭ maj.: II   V   I ——————

(Compare also in *Harmony*, Example 88, bars 8–10, from G through G♭ to
F, etc.)

(b) As mixture: see *Harmony*, Example 77, violin I, the progression
B — B♭ — A along with G major/minor: I♮3 — ♭VI — II♭5 — V 3 — I♭3; *Har-
monielehre*, Fig. 90, bar 5 (B♭ — B♮);[9] *Harmony*, Example 81, bars 5–8
(A♯ — A — G♯ — G) along with:

$$\frac{I — V — I — \sharp IV — \natural IV — I^{\sharp3} — I^{\natural3}}{E\text{-major/minor: I}}$$

among many others.

(c) In tonicization: see *Harmony*, Example 241, bar 5 (G — G♯ in the bass)
with ♭II — ♮II♯3 — V, among others;

(d) And all kinds of other functions establishing units:

Example 32

Chopin, Mazurka Op. 17 No. 4

About the following chromatic succession, written as an intentional error (that is, for the purpose of admonition):

Example 33

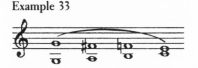

Albrechtsberger simply remarks (on pp. 30 and 32 in the context of two-voice counterpoint, first species), without providing further justification: "The error consists of the chromatic progression (or the chromatic genus) from G to E, since such semitonal progressions are allowed in this species neither ascending nor descending without the accompaniment of instruments." However, the reader may compare a similar chromatic progression on p. 147 of his book under the rubric "licenses"; this will be discussed in more detail when we get to three-voice counterpoint.

Bellermann comments (p. 103): "All augmented or diminished intervals that originate by means of chromatic alteration, such as the *small* semitone B♯ to B (and vice versa) or F to F♯ (and vice versa), are prohibited." A reason for the prohibition, however, is given neither by him nor by Albrechtsberger. For no real justification is provided in the continuation of his remarks:

> In passing we may remark here that exceptions to this rule can occasionally be found in multi-voiced compositions of good composers, even though only very rarely. Claude Goudimel, for example, uses the chromatic step G to G♯ in the motet *O crux benedicta* (bars 44 and 45). This, of course, should not be imitated in contrapuntal exercises.

Thus an "exception"—he is completely explicit! As though the motet, despite many a superficial similarity [to strict counterpoint], were not something essentially different from the contrapuntal exercise—as though it were not a free composition that presents no "exception" when it on occasion uses even a chromatic progression for its own individual reasons.

But there is worse yet, for when Bellermann disallows the chromatic progression in the cadence (not unjustifiably, as I have said, for exercises in struct counterpoint):

Example 34
    Dorian   Mixolydian

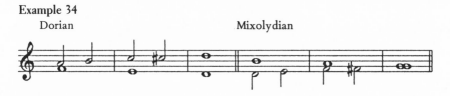

he dares to continue with the following thoughts:

> Beginners who have not yet understood the nature of the diatonic scale at times use such wrong cadences. This is not surprising in today's compositions, in which the genera (diatonic, chromatic, and enharmonic) alternate often in an irregular way. For that reason the student must be told again and again that our studies are concerned, first of all, only with strict diatonic counterpoint, from which the sixteenth-century masters never digressed (except when they intentionally wrote chromatic compositions). There are a few rare exceptions—for example, the use

of the small semitone in Claude Goudimel's motet *O crux benedicta*. . . . Cadences like those cited above, however, are entirely impossible and sound unpleasant even in free composition.

How much more beneficial it would have been for the student if Bellermann first of all had clearly understood that contrapuntàl doctrine is only a preparation for free composition, and that its function is to accustom the ear to various effects, not to apply its prescriptions and restrictions without further modification to the [completely] different situations in free composition as well. As ill-justified as it is to invoke the practices of sixteenth-century masters alone for the prohibition of chromaticism in the cantus firmus, it is equally improper to impose the same restriction (the rationale of which, by the way, is nowhere explained by Bellermann) as a rule without qualification in free composition. Such a vicious circle! On the contrary, it follows that the chromatic progression gains its right of existence in free composition to the same degree that it was unable to do so in the cantus firmus. How beautiful—just to refute Bellermann with an example—the effect of the conclusion of the first idea of the principal theme-group in Beethoven's String Quartet op. 59 no. 3 (*Allegro vivace,* bars 11-13):

Example 35

Beethoven, String Quartet Op. 59 No. 3, I

Such an unprecedented effect produced here by the chromatic progression A — B♭ — B♮ — C in the first violin! And this may suffice as proof that the chromatic progression is not only not "unpleasant" but, contrary to Bellermann's theory, can even produce a thoroughly agreeable effect.

When in the course of the same section each phrase begins with the same motive, the following parallelisms, at least, immediately furnish their own clarification:

Example 36

In the ensuing passage, however, instead of moving in a similar way to the concluding tone *C,* as in example 37:

Example 37

Beethoven, to achieve a strong directional pull toward the conclusion, immediately presents an abbreviated version of all the still missing individual components (see Example 37, c, d, and e), thus producing the chromatic progression:

Example 38

Who can deny that Beethoven, in view of the particular motivic circumstances, had the right, even the obligation, to compose the chromatic progression as daringly as he did? Furthermore, observe how Beethoven underscored the motivic connection (which in itself really cannot be misunderstood) through its harmonization, thus revealing its necessity. Just consider the harmonic succession: $C^{\flat 7} - G^{\natural 7} - C$; such apparent incoherence in the sudden juxtaposition of $C^{\flat 7}$ (functioning as V^7 of F major) and G^7 (as V^7 in C major); such logic, nevertheless, in this progression exclusively in the service of the motivic aspect! After the harmonic construction of the preceding phrases (see the content between a and b as well as between b and c [of example 36?]), wouldn't a similarly emphatic treatment of the key of F major between c and d have been necessary? Indeed, the progression $D^5 - C^{\flat 7}$, interpreted as VI — $V^{\flat 7}$ in F major, implies an elision of the I in F major, which, however—since Beethoven needed to steer toward C major as quickly as possible—, had to be reinterpreted as a IV (before V^7) of C major.

But why—and this is the central matter—should a chromatic progression that is so intrinsically necessary at this point in the composition (in spite of its cadential character) be represented as only an "exception," or as an "unpleasantry" to be condemned by theory, just because elsewhere (in the cantus firmus, for example) no necessity for such a chromatic progression would be present? It is far better, instead, to understand that each necessity carries its own rule in itself alone. This, however, should not prevent our pointing out to the student, first of all, the necessities peculiar to the cantus firmus. Only by starting from this elementary necessity can the student [finally] grasp all transformations and prolongations of the problem in free composition as well.

And how profitable it is when contrapuntal doctrine touches upon a problem of effect only through a restriction instead of a prescription! All that remains is to become aware of the reasons that reside in the cantus firmus in order to grasp the depth and breadth of the problem outside its domain as well. Contrapuntal doctrine, however, never intends to speak the last word [on a compositional issue] when it prohibits one thing or another within the framework of the cantus firmus.

§5. Only diatonic intervals are permitted

Chromatic progression having been excluded, only diatonic intervals remain for use in the cantus firmus. The rule that each interval in the cantus firmus must be diatonic, however, should not lead to the inference that, conversely, each diatonic interval is, by its own authority, permitted in the cantus firmus.

According to *Harmony*, §§58 and 60, diatonic intervals (regardless of the difference between major and minor) are:

Seconds	(major and minor)
Thirds	(major and minor)
Fourths	(perfect and augmented)
Fifths	(perfect and diminished)
Sixths	(major and minor)
Sevenths	(major and minor)
Octaves	(perfect).

Bellermann (p. 103): "Only diatonic intervals may occur in the melody." The misconceived deliberations about chromatic alteration that follow this sentence have been sufficiently discussed in §4 above.

§6. A few diatonic intervals are excluded

Even though they are diatonic, some of these diatonic intervals are excluded in the cantus firmus: the augmented fourth (tritone), its inversion, the diminished fifth, as well as both sevenths. In other words, the melody of the cantus firmus therefore must be constructed only of seconds, thirds, perfect fourths and fifths, both kinds of sixths, and the perfect octave.

The reason for this restriction is not only the dissonant character (together with its expressive consequences) of the intervals just cited, but also the difficulties of intonation attendant on them.

The latter aspect is derived from the human voice alone (see the Introduction). In contrast to all other instruments, which certainly can produce a seventh, an augmented fourth, and a diminished fifth without any difficulty, only the human voice, with its characteristic difficulties in producing those intervals—difficulties of activating the nervous system, and the like—, is able also to communicate at the same time their true psychological content. And this is all that matters in contrapuntal doctrine, which has to make the student understand, for the first time, the differences among the individual intervals.

The reader should not object that difficulty of intonation, by definition, is perhaps only too relative a concept in that, depending on better talent or increased diligence, the difficulty certainly could and would soon have to cease to be an impediment. For if, on the one hand, it remains a prudent rule always to consider only the person of average musical ability and to disregard the support of a piano or orchestra or of a second part or several other parts, the difficulty of intonation under discussion here may, on the other hand, well be attributed an absolute character for all time: there will never come a time when the human voice will be able to sing a real seventh as if it were a second. In other words: the human voice will always make it clear with the necessity of nature that the seventh is a more complex interval than, for example, the second. Better than any other instrument, the human voice reveals that the seventh, besides its dissonance (which it has in common with the second), includes the additional difficulty of a larger leap. Thus the latter is mainly responsible for the rule prohibiting the seventh in the cantus firmus, while its inversion, the second, on the other hand, is permitted. Even though the second is likewise dissonant, it signifies only the smallest span.[10]

The augmented fourth and diminished fifth, whose dissonant character already implies a difficulty of production, are further characterized by the fact that both intervals turn the natural expression of the perfect fourth and perfect fifth into a less natural one; this transmutation of expression may itself be considered another difficulty in intonation. For that reason, these intervals too are prohibited in the cantus firmus.

In addition, these intervals in the cantus firmus reveal another, even more surprising aspect. Consider the following series of tones:

Example 39

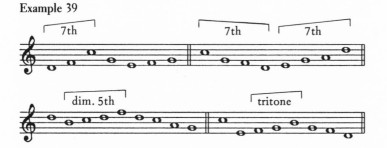

and consult the ear as to their effect: it will immediately revolt against the sevenths, diminished fifths, and augmented fourths outlined by these successions.

The reason of intonational difficulty given above obviously does not apply in these latter examples, because the intervals in question are no longer so directly produced here as they were in the first cases. A new element comes to the fore here, namely the *sum* of several *intervals*, which in our examples means sums [that yield] *dissonant* intervals; these intervals—and this is the point—are to be prohibited in the form of sums as surely as they are prohibited by the initially established rule when sounded in direct succession.

The human ear is disposed by its nature to seek out and conceive harmonic relations also in the succession of tones (see *Harmony*, §76); it seeks, as it must, fifths and thirds, in order to establish interrelationships and order of some kind among the many tones that it perceives in succession. This urge and ability of the human ear constitutes, indeed, the initial impetus of artistic evolution; only this enabled the ear finally to bring a method to the irrationality and dissonant chaos of tones.[11] I have already mentioned in *Harmony* (§76) how strengthened harmonic sensitivity later became active in the newly-invented vertical dimension (polyphony) and especially how the conception of scale degree in free composition had to result as a logical consequence from the reconciliation of the two dimensions. And, only in order to draw conclusions from this for writing the melodies under consideration [that is, cantus firmi], I take this opportunity to restate the previously cited ability of the ear to perceive intervals not only in direct succession but also in the form of sums.

As I have said, aggregates[12] of varying numbers of tones must always impress themselves upon the ear; such aggregates cannot and should not fail to appear wherever several tones occur in succession. In the following cantus firmus, for example, so beautifully constructed by the early master Fux and subsequently adopted by almost all counterpoint treatises, it is inevitable that the ear will automatically follow the motion first to the third, *F,* and then to the fifth, A:

Example 40

(Allegedly Dorian, but in fact also easily understandable simply as D minor)

so as to yield the impression of a triad, $D - F - A$, unfolded (*auseinander-gewickelt*) exactly as shown.

Such unavoidable aggregates, however, cannot and should not be subject to any restriction. The difficulty lies, rather, only with smaller and more limited aggregates, which, because they tend to form subunits, must be prohibited in all—but also in *only*—those contexts in which, by reason of various other attendant circumstances, they become too sharply defined as subunits within an otherwise prevailing condition of homogeneity.

(These remarks—only now can they be presented in proper context—about the prohibition of harmonic aggregates, whether consonant or dissonant, finally complete the train of thought begun in Part 1, Section 1, Chapter 3.)

It should be stated explicitly, however, that it is not possible to define precisely the circumstances under which such a perilous dissonant entity can arise. But anyone who has been given aural experience of just one [such] error will be able to judge correctly for himself whether, in a given instance, a dissonant aggregate actually rends the flesh of the cantus firmus with too jagged a cutting edge, or whether the tones are so felicitously ordered that the dissonant aggregate does not protrude from its surroundings in the cantus firmus.

If musicians have recognized the problem of the prohibited intervals specified above by studying the nature of the human voice, and have thereby grasped the true quality of these intervals, then they can understand all the more easily why those intervals must necessarily adjust themselves to the varying requirements of free composition as well as to the milieu of another instrument in ever different ways.

Allow me to show here, with a few examples, how the admissibility of augmented fourths, diminished fifths, and sevenths can be not only maintained but demonstrated just on the basis of the special requirements of a particular passage, so that the alleged and long-feared contradiction between contrapuntal doctrine and free composition can be eliminated without injury to either—in other words, so that neither strict counterpoint nor free composition will lose any part of its essential nature (strictness or freedom, respectively).

Example 41

J. S. Bach, Mass in B Minor, No. 1

Ky - ri - e   e - le   -   -   -   -   -   -   i - son, Ky - ri - e.

(B min.: I ——————————————— #3 IV —♮II ——————— #VII (-V) —— I)))

In this example the bracketed augmented fourth (the tritone) is adequately justified simply by the fact that the melody is accompanied. Through the accompaniment, the free counterpoint (*der freie Satz*) offers the singer's ear a rich array of harmonies whose logic is familiar to his instinct and which are therefore capable of orienting him easily with respect to the various necessary intervals, including the dissonant ones.

Moreover, the singer's melody itself is emphatically and actively involved in this familiar harmonic progression, in that it passes through and composes out the harmonies by incorporating the most variegated small configurations, according to the nature of free composition. In the example above, the melody, taken by itself, traverses the path from the tonic, *B*, to the subdominant, *E* (indeed, by way of the raised third *D#*, which supplies not only a passing but also a chromatic element), in order to continue immediately—by way of a lowered (Phrygian) ♮II, which might even be regarded as independent—to *A#*. The latter, considered alone, would represent only VII, but by virtue of kinship [*Harmony*, §108] it represents also V.

But aside from the foothold that the harmonies thus provide for the singer, here there is yet another, almost more important, circumstance that decides in favor of the admissibility of the tritone: in the context of the large configuration that grows out of the tonic scale degree, the eighth-note *G*, lying between C♯ and F♯, in reality produces more the effect of a "passing" tone (in the broader sense—cf. Part 2, Chapter 2, §5) than that of a tritone. When a passing tone occurs even in such an interval as a tritone, it becomes clear what power resides in a free composition founded on scale degrees and aiming for melodic individuality with so many resources.

If, finally, training and practice are also required of the chorister (or, for that matter, the soloist), then there can be no doubt that, in view of the many beneficial circumstances described here, he will sing that interval [of an augmented fourth] in the passage cited above with perfect accuracy.

To consider a further example, if the tritone occasionally represents the progression I—♯IV, as in a cadence:

Example 42

E maj./min.: I   ♯IV   V   —

(cf. *Harmony*, §162), then instinct for scale degrees by itself will lead the singer or player to an accurate realization of the tritone. Performers will sense that here the intent is not so much an original tritone as, rather, merely a raising of the fourth degree A, and they will easily, albeit completely unconsciously, perform the chromaticization of the IV that is so familiar to them by instinct. How could this be disallowed by contrapuntal theory—by the cantus firmus—which, indeed, within its own domain is unable to engender any sense of scale degrees?

Several features, such as can be offered only by the differentiations provided by free composition, justify the following tritone in still another way:

Example 43

Schubert, "Ihr Bild"

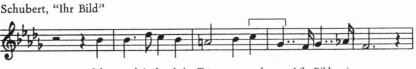

Ich   stand in dun-keln Träu - men und starrt' ihr Bild - nis an.

The "fixation"[13]—how perfectly it is painted just by the tritone! And doesn't this interval arouse in us a sensation of II of B♭ minor, C - E♭ - G♭? The latter certainly could not be ruled out, considering that V follows, although, to be sure, in the absence of an unequivocal interpretation of the tritone, the tone C could possibly also be connected directly to the F as a component of V, in which case the G♭ would have a different function, namely that of a neighboring or passing tone. But the greater the number of different effects that accumulate about the tones, the better. Such multiplicity not only does not hinder the selection of one among the various effects as the principal one: rather, it promotes it!

In the examples cited above, I was able to demonstrate the necessity of the augmented fourth as a direct succession of two tones; by the same token, it is also possible, on various grounds, to justify the delineation in free composition of a tritone as the sum of several tones. And again for the sake of the method, which is so very important [here], rather than for the examples themselves, several instances in which such tritone sums occur are shown in the following paragraphs.

To begin with a most curious example, here is a passage by Chopin:

Example 44

Chopin, Mazurka Op. 24 No. 2

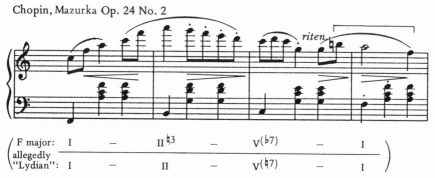

One must study the disposition of the entire first section to understand the poetic reason and thus grasp the necessity for the tritone sum bracketed above.

The first section is a three-part song form A₁ — B — A₂ and is on the whole in C major. However, in detail the disposition of keys shows a certain anomaly, which has its peculiar consequences in all parts with surprising regularity: the outer sections A₁ and A₂, in C major, intentionally derive their internal key contrast from A minor (but, instead of a real A minor, an allegedly true "Aeolian" system, avoiding the leading tone G♯ even at cadences); the middle section of the song-form, B (see Example 44), by the same token, provides a contrast to A₁ and A₂ curiously enough with the allegedly genuine "Lydian" system. This is why the composer avoided in measure 3 of our example the tone B♭, the only pitch that could have completely clarified the key of F major (especially after the chromatically altered II).

With this passage, however, Chopin by no means intends to establish the old systems as equivalent [to major and minor] and as independent; this is sufficiently clear from the refined artistry he uses in the introduction as well as the harmonization in general to provide the listener with the absolute certainty of only C major and F major (in this connection, compare in particular the ingenious conclusion of the Mazurka, which orients the listener beyond any doubt!). Thus, the passage in question simply contains a few features of artistic archaism, a highly ingenious trick, such as could befall Chopin occasionally in the midst of his fantastic improvisations. It is merely a literal quotation, a curious genre-imitation, from that golden age when people still believed in the "Lydian" system, and sang and played irrespon-

sibly, especially "nationalistic" melodies, because actually they did not know
how to play and hear better.

On the other hand, the following crude tritone:

Example 45
Wagner, *Götterdämmerung*, Act II

and these as well:

Example 46
Brahms, Trio Op. 87, Finale

are not, in spite of all their strong, similar effect (especially in the Wagner
example), again to be credited to a presumptive Lydian mode. Rather, both
cases produce only the effect of a raised IV (♯IV) in a composed-out form,
which is confirmed through the progression of scale-degrees—specifically, in
the Wagner, C-major: ♯IV (F♯) — V (G) — ♭II (D♭) — II♯³ (D) etc., and in the
Brahms, above the pedal-point on C (I): I — ♯IV — (I — ♯IV —) V (bar 4).

The following passage shows that among other things a modulation, for
example, can lead to a tritone:

Example 47
Mozart, Symphony No. 39, Andante

Violin I

A♭ maj.: I
E♭ maj.: IV ————————————————— V$^{6-5}_{4-3}$ — I

It is really the necessity inherent in the modulation that accounts for the
necessity of the tritone.

The reason one can speak of a tritone here at all is that the melodic course
of the violin up to the arrival of V takes place without accompaniment, and,

because it is completely uncovered harmonically, its effect is more striking than if it were accompanied.

The augmented fourth in the following example:

Example 48

Handel, Suites de pièces, 2nd collection, No. 1, Air with Variations, Var. I

can be explained according to the nature of keyboard writing itself (of which more will be said later). It is especially the older keyboard style which, to the extent that it made less use of fuller chordal textures (especially the kind we favor so much today), outlined its supposedly lacking harmonies so much more thoroughly and vigorously with its figuration and with all sorts of angular contours. By this means the older style produced polyphony. Why should it have presented harmonies in the form of complete chords, when it was able to express them in another way? In the preceding example we see clearly how the figuration unites within itself several strands of voice leading in the most artistic way. It stands for approximately the following setting:

Example 49

From this it follows, however, that the augmented fourth in the Handel example is merely an apparent tritone; for in reality, according to Example 49, the tone A does not go to E♭ at all, but rather to B♭, and, moreover, simultaneously engenders a line through G and F. Both of these continuations from the A, however, represent only intervals of a second.

To the extent that the augmented fourth is a part of the harmony of V, however, it is motivated, as though automatically, by the indispensability of the latter.

On the other hand, the following two extremely interesting examples may confirm that under certain circumstances even free composition shows a sensitivity to the tritone and, by preference, avoids it:

Ex-mple 50
C. P. E. Bach, Sonata in F Major, Wq. 55 No. 5

Example 51
Haydn, String Quartet Op. 52, Andante

The first example, by C.P.E. Bach, seems to me the more daring, and also the one composed with even more sensitive artistic thought. One need only attempt to use the augmented fourth in both examples to be convinced of the subtlety of judgment that led to its avoidance.

Compare, as equally striking examples, the following: C.P.E. Bach, final cadence of Rondo III (B♭) of the fourth collection of *Sonaten . . . für Kenner und Liebhaber;* or Haydn, String Quartet in E♭ op. 76 no. 6, Fantasia, bars 9 and 12 from the end, where the tritone is so conspicuously avoided and a perfect fourth is used in its place.

Having shown in the foregoing discussion how free composition can establish its exigencies, I can appropriately leave it to the student to follow similar paths in respect to the remaining prohibited diatonic intervals, the diminished fifth and the seventh. However, I may be permitted a few important further observations.

Remember that the diminished *fifth* is an integral component of scale degree V, and is without doubt sufficiently justified in free composition through the latter's necessity.

I have shown in *Harmony,* §50, how, on the other hand, the avoidance of a diminished fifth often brings about a Phrygian II, for example.

The bracketed succession in the following example:

Example 52

Bruckner, Symphony No. 1

even reduces the diminished fifth still further; it is therefore actually not an interval at all (cf. *Harmony, §55*), and is to be explained rather as an encounter between the harmonic tone *Cb* (in *D-F-Ab-Cb*) and the chromatic passing tone *F♯* (between *F* in the first half of the second bar and *G* at the second quarter of the third bar of our example). Both of these forces are heard as operating simultaneously in such a way that our succession [*Cb — F♯*], conceived accordingly, now also finds its justification.

Concerning the *seventh* in free composition, the necessary liberty in its use there is in the first place inseparable from the necessary emergence of the seventh-chord (*Vierklang*) itself, in a manner of which the theory of counterpoint remains altogether ignorant.

Thus in free composition the seventh can also be used in the context of difficult circumstances posed by a profound declamation, as is shown in the following example (note well the eloquent rests after the seventh!):

Example 53

J. S. Bach, St. Matthew Passion, Aria "Blute nur"

Droht den Pfle-ger zu er - mor   den, denn   es ist zur

Such usages of sevenths as the following, however, have to do with the nature of free composition, which delineates and combines two or more voices at the same time in its figurations (cf. Example 48).[14]

Example 54

J. S. Bach, English Suite No. 5, Gigue

Example 55

Schubert, Sonata in A Minor Op. 42, Scherzo

Example 56

Handel, Suites de pièces, 2nd collection, No. 1, Air with Variations, Var. IV

Thus in the Bach example (Example 54), the tones e^1 and b, respectively, are to be conceived as independent and sustaining, while at the same time a second voice, likewise independent, executes a chromatic passing motion—descending from e^2 to b^1 and ascending from B to e, respectively. The union of both voices causes the seventh-leaps to appear all the more natural since in fact the essential content is not the seventh-leaps but rather the passing tones moving by seconds.

In the Schubert example, e^1 (in the left hand) and g^2 (right hand) are likewise conceived as independent and sustaining, so the seventh-leaps are again only apparent, since actually only passing tones moving by seconds are present:

Example 57

The Handel example, finally, may be traced back to the following sketch in three-voice counterpoint:

Example 58

From this it follows that here, too, the seventh-leaps originate only in the transformation of a polyphonic setting into the successive pitches of a horizontal line; they bear too obviously the stamp of the progressions by seconds, precisely in keeping with their origin, to be regarded as true dissonant sevenths. Thus in order to reproduce the true sense of the passage, the performer, too, should follow only the bracketed progressions in Example 56 rather than going astray in the sevenths.

A most original seventh-usage is found in Handel's Organ Concerto in B♭ Major:

Example 59

Handel, Organ Concerto in B♭ Major

It originates in that Handel, in an obviously humorous vein, insists on changing the harmony (scale degree) only at the second eighth-note of the second bar, and up to that point does not hesitate to draw the last consequences of the foregoing, so that the main accent of the bar on the first eighth-note stands as though a latecomer to the family of scale degree I, while the second eighth-note abruptly and surprisingly takes up service in that of the new harmony, the V.

Still more important for understanding the seventh in free composition, however, is to recall a characteristic by virtue of which it occurs there more often in place of its inversion, the second, so that it loses its own import as an actual seventh at the same time.

This applies even in vocal settings, for example:

Example 60

J. S. Bach, Mass in B Minor, No. 13

Pa - trem om - ni - po - ten - tem, fac - to - rem.

The reasons for this possibility of substitution are so instructive, especially in free instrumental composition, that I cannot resist citing a few examples:

Example 61

Handel, Capriccio in G Minor

Here, the bracketed descending seventh of the bass at the end of bar 1 does at first appear to reflect only the more favorable circumstances afforded by a keyboard instrument, which reduces by far the mechanical difficulty of a seventh; but those circumstances are in fact employed to provide, instead of f^1, its lower octave f as a starting point for the next group of tones, so that the seventh $e^1 - f$ here basically represents only the second $e^1 - f^1$. Finally, under the aegis of scale-degree progression—we are, indeed, concerned here with free composition—, the f is also subject still to the earlier relationship to c on the second quarter of the first bar—that is, the relationship of a fourth: $c - f$, or a fifth: $c - F$ ($= V - I$ in F minor).

Thus we see then the following: in this example an original second is transformed into a seventh, a process that is fostered both by the increased convenience of the instrument and by the conducive effect of scale-degree progression. Without doubt, the true dissonant character of the genuine seventh is much diluted by these primary effects of second and fourth, which here flow together from different sources—that of melody and that of scale degrees. But precisely for that reason, the use of the seventh in the above passage is justified as well as needed: no veto by any contrapuntal theory can be invoked against it.

Now in the following example, the bracketed sevenths in the bass are justified not only in that they can readily be accepted as substitutes for [ascending] seconds, but also in that the d in bar 1 finds its continuation, in the manner of an independent voice (see the preceding example), in the descending progression $d — c — Bb$.

Example 62
J. S. Bach, English Suite No. 6, Prelude

Finally, not to be overlooked is their justification by the clarity of logic of the scale degrees:

$$D — G — C — F — Bb$$

which, on their own, would cause the tones c and Bb at the beginning of bars 2 and 3 to be expected, in one register or another.

Along with its obvious purpose of continuing the content in the lower octave (as in the two preceding examples), the bracketed seventh in bars 3 – 4 of Example 63, simply because it occurs in the more conspicuous soprano

Example 63
J. S. Bach, Sinfonia No. 11

range, is undoubtedly able to create its own strong effect, precisely as a seventh. It almost seems to engender a secret yearning for the singer's or violinist's portamento (or glissando)—such a wondrous intimacy is characteristic of the seventh-usage here. The same applies to the Adagio of the *Scotch* Symphony by Mendelssohn:

Example 64
Mendelssohn, Symphony No. 3, Adagio

It is not uncommon for the transformation of an initially desired second into a seventh-leap to be caused by range limitations of an instrument. Thus viola, 'cello, and double-bass, for example, of necessity invert second to seventh at the boundary of their ranges. (A familiar exception is the range-extension of the 'cello in Schumann's Piano Quartet op. 47.) Since these are perfectly ordinary occurrences in instrumental writing, it would hardly be necessary to say another word about them—especially as the ear has not the slightest difficulty in grasping the true situation—had not just such men as Liszt and Wagner, for the same reason applied backwards, seen fit to proclaim a genuine seventh of the highest, most characteristic and motivic value in a much-interpreted passage from Beethoven's Ninth Symphony (bar 138ff.) to be a merely spurious, so-to-speak "second"-ary seventh, and therefore, regarding it as an ostensibly involuntary offense on Beethoven's part, actually to "improve" it by changing it to a second.[15] I may be permitted to offer in an appendix a detailed refutation of Wagner on this point.[16]

Recently, Richard Strauss has developed almost to a mannerism the practice of inverting a second into a seventh in a melody, thus achieving surprising and strange effects. These could often be considered quite interesting if it were not for the fact that the composer's intent is often irritating.

Example 65

R. Strauss, *Ein Heldenleben*, Op. 40

Observe in bars 2–3 the bracketed seventh from c^1 to bb^1, which, of course, originates only in a second:

Example 66

Here c^1 represents a neighboring note between the two bb's of the harmony $Eb - G - Bb$. In the continuation, the bracketed sevenths $d^1 - c^2$ and $eb^1 - d^2$ stand for the seconds $d^1 - c^1$ and $eb^2 - d^2$. By contrast, and this difference should be noted here, in bars 3–4 the unbracketed seventh-resultant $f^1 - g$ has a different meaning: here the seventh is genuine; it stems from the fact that the last two sixteenths, f^1 and c^1, which are actually passing tones, are left by leap in violation of the strict rule; this serves to intensify all the more our expectation of the harmonic tones eb^1 and bb which are due, and which actually appear in the next bar:

Example 67

Similarly, for example, in *Salome* (piano score, p. 35), the same composer intentionally neglects to follow the neighboring note f^1 (see Example 68a, bar 1) immediately with its principal tone e^1, and instead, in order to increase the tension, inserts three other tones—specifically, in bar 2 the harmonic tone c^1; then in the same bar, as a neighboring note to the fifth, a^1; and finally in bar 3 the neighboring note $d^{\#7}$ (see Example 68b).

Example 68

R. Strauss, *Salome*

Finally, the following especially poignant example shows how in free composition a seventh-*resultant* may derive its justification also from factors other than the necessity [introduced by the presence there] of the seventh chord.

Example 69

J. S. Bach, Mass in B Minor, Agnus dei

How expressively the seventh-resultant $(bb^1 - c^1)$ distends itself across the change of scale-degree: $I - IV^{\natural 3}$ in G minor; it is motivated here, however, precisely by the latter.

§7. *On the exclusion from the cantus firmus of intervals resulting from mixture*

Concerning the minor system specifically, one must bear in mind that it is to be viewed from the start as a merely artificial system, one employed chiefly for motivic purposes (cf. *Harmony,* §40f.). Precisely because of this artificiality, the minor system frequently has occasion to borrow from the natural major system, particularly for cadential purposes. Therefore even in the cantus firmus—thus in the melodic realm—, if it is to be set in minor, borrowing will likewise have to be used for cadential purposes. How this mixture is to be accomplished will be shown in §23, concerning cadences.

Here it need be remarked only that, in spite of the permissible mixture, the intervals resulting from mixture are nonetheless excluded. Specifically, they are:

> the augmented second,
> the diminished fourth,
> the augmented fifth, and
> the diminished seventh.

(*See Harmonielehre,* p. 61, Tab. VI.[17])

The reasons for the exclusion of these intervals from the cantus firmus are the same as those given earlier for the seventh, augmented fourth, and diminished fifth: intonational difficulty resulting from their dissonant nature together with transmutation of expression of the basic intervals [from which the altered ones are derived].

It goes without saying, on the other hand, that free composition, for various reasons of its own, accepts these same intervals for its use.

Here, a few examples:

Example 70
Schubert, "Meeresstille"

Here the augmented second (cf. *Harmony,* $68) serves the ends of the modulation moving from $E - \dfrac{\text{major}}{\text{minor}}$ to $A - \dfrac{\text{major}}{\text{minor}}$.

In the following example it is the scale-degree progression ♭II—♯IV that is responsible for the diminished fourth in the second violin ($ab^1 - e^1$):

Example 71

Mozart, String Quintet K. 516, Menuett

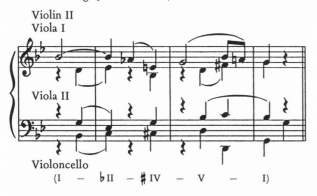

Violin II
Viola I

Viola II

Violoncello
(I – ♭II – ♯IV – V – I)

The tortuously beautiful and overpowering diminished fourths in the development of the last movement of Mozart's G-Minor Symphony (see Example 72) result from the following: Mozart, having thus far shaped the

Example 72

Mozart, Symphony No. 40, IV

Violin I

Bass

(C♯ – F♯ – C♯)

(F♯ – B – F♯)

(B – E – B)

(E – A – E)

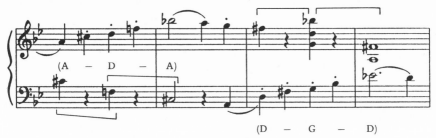

(A – D – A)

(D – G – D)

motive currently in use from one single triad or seventh-chord (as in Example 73), now for the first time, and indeed within the space of a single bar, bends it to fit two different harmonies. He thus creates the impression of an enor-

Example 73

mously vehement tearing asunder of the former whole, as though in the most frenzied mental state, so that the counterpoint in each case is forced to follow the two different harmonies and, in so doing, to produce the diminished fourth (and also the augmented fifth in the bass).[18]

Example 74

Beethoven, Symphony No. 9, I, b. 241ff.

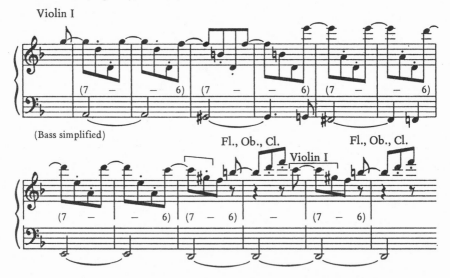

The bracketed diminished fourths in bars 9 and 11 of Example 74 are accounted for simply by the collision of the suspension (syncope) of the seventh c^3 with the tone $g\sharp^2$ as part of the harmony $G\sharp - B - D - F$, but what force here lies in the friction between the two tones!

Example 75

Wagner, *Die Walküre*, Act II

Ho - jo - to-ho!

The augmented fifth in Example 75 finds its emphatic justification in the progression of the harmonies:

$$G^{\sharp 5} \quad E^{\sharp 3} -(F-)\,C \underline{\hspace{1.5cm}} F^{\sharp} - \parallel G^{\sharp 5} - C \underline{\hspace{1.5cm}} F^{\sharp} - B$$
$$B\text{-minor: } VI^{\sharp 5} - IV^{\sharp 3} - \natural II\,(Phryg.) - V - \parallel VI - II\,(Phryg.) - V - I$$

These harmonies, as shown, can all be assigned to the key of B minor, and even constitute a circumscribed statement in this key, notwithstanding that the succession of the first two scale degrees $VI^{\sharp 5} — IV^{\sharp 3}$ moreover expresses as a secondary effect the relationship $\natural III^{\sharp 5} — I^{\sharp 3}$ in $E — \dfrac{\text{major}}{\text{minor}}$ (cf. *Harmony*, $141).

When the augmented fifth occurs as in Example 76a, on the other hand, it is an augmented fifth only apparently, and is in reality something else, something that derives from polyphony [in a single voice] (compare the remarks to Examples 48 and 56); it is explained by Example 76b.

Example 76

J. S. Bach, English Suite No. 6, Prelude

§8. *Prohibition of the diminished third and augmented sixth*

The reasons that led to the prohibition of the intervals cited in the two preceding paragraphs also prohibit, finally, the last two remaining intervals, namely the diminished third and the augmented sixth (cf. *Harmony*, §§147 and 148).

It is again evident, however, that free composition, on the other hand, can for its own reasons use these intervals in the most diverse ways:

Example 77

J. S. Bach, Mass in B Minor, No. 3

The ear immediately understands here that the diminished third, to the extent that initial consideration is restricted to the horizontal line alone, represents nothing more than a group consisting of the two neighboring notes around the tone *F♯*; instead of surrounding the main tone and being separated from one another as usual, both neighboring notes here occur in direct succession, and are interpolated between the main tone's first occurrence and its reappearance. Moreover, one must take into account the harmonization of the [melodic] succession (executed according to the prescription of the continuo), which on its own provides a strong frame of reference, and, in the last analysis, at the same time suggests the necessity of a diminished third that is actually only apparent.

The power and logic of the scale-degree progression adequately justifies the bracketed succession of two tones in bar 3 of the following example as well:

Example 78

Beethoven, Symphony No. 9, I, b. 463ff.

These tones again represent a diminished third only apparently, in that they enter into melodic proximity only through the conflict and succession of two scale degrees (♭II — V), and therefore neither aim for nor are able to express the characteristic harmonic effect of a true diminished third.

The following augmented sixth is perhaps not so much an alteration-interval as a formation based simply on passing motion:[19]

Example 79
Beethoven, Trio Op. 97, I, b. 21ff.

This is why, in spite of all its peculiarity, it is of such good effect.

§9. *Conclusions concerning the prohibited intervals*

In the cantus firmus, then, all dissonant successions except the two seconds are prohibited, regardless of whether they are of purely diatonic origin or issue from other sources (for example, mixture and similar techniques).

In *Fux* we find the following comment on p. 93 (concerning three-voice counter-point): "[*Aloys:*] What are we to think about the leap of a seventh? Remember that natural singability of the melody must be taken into account." That is all.[20]

Albrechtsberger states in rule IX on p. 23 (cf. also p. 40): "All augmented and most diminished leaps, together with the three seventh-leaps, are prohibited both descending and ascending; for example:" (there follow examples of the diminished third, the augmented second, the augmented fourth, the augmented fifth, the augmented sixth, the diminished, minor, and major sevenths, a diminished octave, and finally ninths and tenths), and at the same time he continues: "Since one may write in melodies for the four voices nothing larger than the perfect octave-leap, only the following intervals that remain are permitted:" (here examples of a minor and a major third, a perfect and a diminished fourth, a perfect and a diminished fifth, both kinds of sixths, and the perfect octave). And finally on p. 24: "The following are permitted only in free composition (*im freien Satze*) or with accompanying instruments:" (examples of sevenths follow).

Without giving any reason for doing so, Albrechtsberger thus retains also the diminished fourth and the diminished fifth for use in exercises. Accordingly he writes, for example, on p. 32:

Example 80

dim. 4th

It is, however, most regrettable that he made no effort to provide a uniform reason for the prohibition of all dissonant intervals—including, indeed, the diminished fourth and fifth—especially since, in excluding intervals larger than the octave (the ninth and tenth) he was able to cite the nature of choral writing (and thus of singing voices) as reason for the prohibition, and thereby appeared to attack the problem at its center.

Consistently applied, the criteria of differentiation that he cites—vocal writing, accompanying instruments, and free composition—would have had to suffice to prohibit the diminished fourth and fifth as well; but Albrechtsberger himself (one sees the lack of conviction) failed to understand the reason for the prohibition in sufficient depth to enable him to separate exercise from free composition clearly and thoroughly at the very outset. Thus in his theory of counterpoint there suddenly appears an element of free composition, which cannot fail to mislead the student. For why, one would have to ask, should the augmented fourth be prohibited but the diminished allowed? And likewise, why should the augmented fifth be prohibited but the diminished allowed? I assume, then, that it was merely the quest for tonality in the minor mode—the minor mode in the usual false conception, however—that led him to this irregularity, to which he surrendered the more carelessly because he had not, as noted earlier, thought the problem through adequately. He obviously felt that he should not deprive the minor mode, where the necessary raising of the leading tone produces the diminished fourth, of that interval as an—allegedly—purely diatonic one!

Cherubini teaches in rule VI (p. 7):

All movement should be diatonic or natural, in the melodic domain in particular; and conjunct motion better suits strict counterpoint than disjunct motion. Accordingly the major and minor second, major and minor third, perfect fourth, perfect fifth, minor sixth, and octave, are permitted either in ascending or descending. The augmented fourth, or tritone, diminished fifth, and major and minor seventh are expressly prohibited either in ascending or in descending.

(Compare also p. 2.)

The contrast to Albrechtsberger is striking: here the diminished fourth and diminished fifth too are prohibited. But what about the major sixth, which, mysteriously enough, is assigned neither to the permitted nor to the prohibited intervals by the above rule?

The justification of the rule follows in an "observation": "This rule is a very wise one; and the ancient masters had the more reason to observe it, because they wrote for voices alone, without accompaniment. They thus obtained an easy and correct melody where the prohibited movements would have been difficult of intonation. The rule, incidentally, is much disregarded in modern compositions." How much apparent truth in these remarks, and yet what fateful errors at the same time! Difficulty of intonation, here correctly cited as the reason for the prohibition, is not, as would have been appropriate, considered in and for itself, but only in the framework of the compositional practice of the old masters, where it can, however, no longer claim immutable validity. If it is historically correct that the earliest compositions were not too far removed from configurations that we today may describe as at least related to exercises with cantus firmus, it certainly cannot be counted as a virtue of those compositions that they were forced to take heed of intonational difficulty within the limits described above. Admittedly, given the primitive state of contrapuntal technique and the necessary concessions to vocal writing, they had no other choice. But it was surely a sign of progress when the art of composition, supported by its own multi-faceted foundations, gradually incorporated the complete roster of intervals. This was accomplished, certainly, in keeping with the limitations imposed by instrument, emotional aspect, and expression, but finally even without concern for difficulty of intonation, mastery of which the free art-work had all the more right to demand as the difficult interval rested more securely on good and necessary inner reasons. Such a crude error, then, in the final sentence of the "observation," namely in the assault on free composition! Is this rule of counterpoint—the prohibition of one or another interval—supposed to be binding also on free composition, or is it the task of contrapuntal theory merely to provide an initial approach to the problem? Is everything written after those earliest epochs to be ascribed only to "exceptions" and violations of allegedly inviolable "rules of composition"—in other words: to be regarded only as *badly written?* How insupportable, contrary to all truth and contrary to all artistic instinct, to put such ideas into the heads of students! Now we see where one ends up if one fails to comprehend the mission of contrapuntal teaching.

While the unjustified complaint against free composition in the Cherubini text is mentioned as though incidentally in passing, in *Bellermann* (p. 101ff.) it appears in a much more detailed and correspondingly more invalid formulation.

Just listen:

> In our modern music a great liberty prevails in this respect. I am speaking now not of a bad, degenerate, unconstrained modern music, but of the music of the eighteenth century, thus of men like Bach, Handel, Graun, Haydn, Mozart, who are with justification usually designated as classical composers. We find that in the melodic usage of intervals they were bound by no discernible precept, but that, guided by their taste and their refined musical instinct, they used all intervals of the diatonic scale, and not only in their vocal music for soloists (which was in large measure written for singers trained for virtuosity) but also in their choral compositions. Not only in the former, but also in the latter, they frequently overstepped the boundaries of the diatonic scale to include chromatically altered intervals. As examples I cite several themes by Handel and Graun:

Example 81

Handel, *Israel in Egypt*

Example 82

Handel, *Messiah*

Example 83

Graun, *Der Tod Jesu*

It cannot be denied that through such a free usage of intervals a profound effect, a great power of expression, is often attained. And the more recent music, which since the seventeenth century has increasingly enlisted the aid of instruments, can do such things without risk when composers proceed consciously after having acquired confidence, taste, and a mature judgment of the performance capacity of the human voice through strict studies.

And on pp. 112–113, in connection with a history of the intervals (a very informative one, incidentally), the following related ideas are set forth:

I have inserted these historical notes here in order to show that interval usage among earlier composers was not an arbitrary matter, but that they consciously and deliberately drew a boundary that was to be of the greatest importance for polyphonic a capella music. It was not the practical musicians who sought to extend these boundaries, but, notably, the theorists, who perhaps often were not sufficiently developed as practical musicians to perceive the importance of this teaching for the singability and beauty of melodies, and who occasionally indulged in various kinds of gimmickry in constructing their theories. . . . With the beginning of the seventeenth century, composers began to make freer melodic use of intervals; the academy (*die Schule*), however, to the benefit of art, continued to adhere to the stricter rules, through which developing composers gained a secure foundation in voice leading. Only since the middle of the last century, since the decadent spread of instrumental music, was the academy forsaken. The consequences are rampant capriciousness and the total failure of artistic judgment.

Unfortunately, precious little service, again, is rendered the student by these unfounded accusations. In the first place, Bellermann begins by praising the "taste" and "refined musical instinct" of our great masters, but then hints in the vaguest way that they allegedly eschewed any kind of "discernible precepts." And in the second place, with similar indecisiveness he first tries to accommodate himself to newer music ("can do such things without risk"), only once again to fulminate against the "decadent spread of instrumental music," and to praise the "academy" (?!) alone as the sanctuary of the stricter rules. Instead of such a contradictory vacillation, there was only one correct path for Bellermann in this matter: first, to learn the difference between cantus-firmus [exercises] and free composition; further, to explore the reasons the dissonant intervals named are to be absolutely prohibited in the cantus firmus; and finally—most important of all for the issue at hand—also to specify in clear language those reasons which, by contrast, necessarily permit and even demand the dissonant intervals in free composition. Only from this standpoint can it be understood, then, that even the melodic usage by our masters of the dissonant intervals, which Bellermann attributes only to "their taste and free musical instinct,"[21] agrees with rather than contradicts the "precepts" (much more correctly understood, to be sure, by the composers themselves)! Granted, as "precepts" one must not, like Bellermann, understand only those that pertain to the cantus firmus.

The precise final formulation Bellermann arrives at, however, is found on pp. 104–105 under 2:

All diatonic intervals up to and including the perfect fifth, with the sole exceptions of the tritone and the diminished fifth, may be used in melody both ascending and descending without restriction. These include the following six intervals: the large half step, the whole step, the minor third, the major third, the perfect fourth and the perfect fifth. . . .

Further, under 3:

The tritone and the diminished fifth are completely excluded from melody; and the former interval may not even be traversed by step unless the voice continues past the interval in the same direction (whether ascending or descending):

Example 84

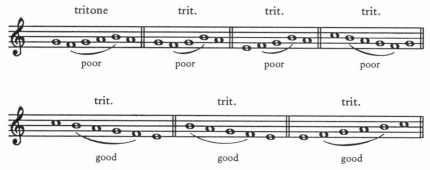

The tritone was the interval most forbidden among the early composers. In our exercises, therefore, we must treat it with very special caution and preferably avoid it altogether. Less perilous is the diminished fifth, whose stepwise traversal never has the grating stridency of the tritone. There is no objection to the following usage of the diminished fifth:

Example 85

And under 4: "The employment of all intervals larger than the perfect fifth was highly restricted, in large part even completely forbidden. We now take up these intervals in order." (But these last remarks of Bellermann's should be treated in later paragraphs that provide a better occasion.)

Finally on p. 106, under c: "The major and minor sevenths are likewise completely prohibited. Here the difficulty of intonation is above all a definitive factor, although according to our modern point of view in many cases the ascending minor seventh offers no particular difficulties."

§10.　*The permissible intervals in general*

The permissible intervals fall into two classes: the consonances and the dissonances. The consonant intervals (cf. *Harmony,* §73ff.) are

(a) the intervals that derive from the relationships 2, 3, and 5 of the overtone series, specifically:

the octave,
the fifth, and
the third,

(b) together with their inversions:

the fourth (as inversion of the fifth), and
the sixth (as inversion of the third).

The dissonant intervals are

(a) the second, and
(b) the seventh (as inversion of the second).

All of these intervals must be considered with respect to two aspects, which determine their inner nature and practical use:

1. the aspect of size, and
2. the aspect of development [represented by the ascending direction] versus inversion [represented by the descending direction].

Nature as it is manifested in the overtone series represents itself not only in the vertical direction (the harmonic principles within the triad) but also in the horizontal direction (melodic succession). Whether the octave sounds vertically or in the melodic plane, the agreeable sound and justification of both rests in like measure on the will of nature; and this is equally true of the fifth and third.

§11. Specific observations about the nature of the permissible intervals: (a) About the octave

With respect to size, the octave is, of course, the largest interval within an octave; but this fact, which would otherwise make its use in practice more difficult, is mitigated in that the octave, considered in terms of the overtone series, also has the best harmonic quality.

We further derive from the overtone series the noteworthy distinction that only the *ascending* octave manifests Nature's developmental urge as shown therein (*Harmony*, §9), while the *descending* octave on the contrary originates in the artificial process of inversion (*Harmony*, §16). For this reason the descending octave, in comparison to the ascending, causes an additional difficulty of considerable significance. The student must be fully aware of this distinction and accordingly, wherever possible, give preference to the ascending octave over the descending at least in the cantus firmus.

This explains the old prohibition of the descending octave, which *Bellermann* cites on p. 106 under d:

> The ascending octave is permitted and was often used in a highly characteristic manner, as in the following theme from Palestrina's motet "Ego sum panis vivus." [A musical example follows.] The descending octave, on the contrary, is forbidden according to the theorists; yet this is a prohibition which in practice is not infrequently violated, especially by the bass in polyphonic settings. To my knowledge, however, the descending octave was not, like the ascending one in the example, used as an essential and characteristic element of a theme. Nevertheless, in the added voices it occurs often enough, as for example in the alto of Palestrina's fourth motet "Sicut cervus desiderat," bar 13, etc.

It is surely unnecessary to point out Bellermann's faulty logic in invoking compositional practice as a chief argument in a matter of contrapuntal principle—in this case, for and against the descending octave. For it does not follow from the necessary use in free composition of both kinds of octaves that the teacher is excused from his duty to introduce to the student this distinction and the reasons behind it, especially as the distinction is prominent in compositional practice—for example:

Example 86

Mozart
String Quartet in E♭ Maj. K428, I   String Quartet in D Min. K. 421, I

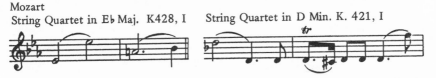

Cf. Beethoven, Leonora Overture No. 3, Op. 72, b. 144ff; also Piano Sonata Op. 106, I, b. 27ff.

§12. (b) About the fifth

The fifth, although a smaller interval than the octave, is nevertheless, by virtue of the overtone series, the *boundary interval* of the harmonic triad (*Harmony*, §11). And although in the case of the fifth, as in that of the octave, the ascending direction clearly has priority in nature, at the same time the advantage of more modest size reduces the difference in intonational difficulty between the ascending and descending directions to a greater degree with fifths than with octaves. Therefore the fifth can be used in the cantus firmus both rising and falling without restriction.

§13. (c) About the fourth

The fourth is not found in the overtone series and thus is to be regarded, both at the outset and always, merely as the *inversion of the fifth*. The following derivations exemplify the possibilities:

(a) If we begin with the tone G, instead of rising a fifth we can instead descend a fourth, which will bring us to the lower octave of the tone D:

Example 87

(b) Or, vice versa, if we set out from the tone D with the intention of falling a fifth to G, we can instead rise a fourth, and arrive at the upper octave of the G:

Example 88

Since the fourth, as inversion of the fifth, leads to the same tone as the original itself—in the first case from G to D and in the second from D to G—it, too, is to be regarded only as a *boundary interval* of the harmonic triad, indeed as a *second* boundary interval, a kind of copy of the original. We shall see later what all-important consequences are implied by this discovery of the nature of the fourth as a secondary boundary interval of the triad.

Both intervals, the fourth and the fifth, serve as boundary intervals for the same triad; nature, however, admits only *one* boundary interval for the triad. For this reason, it must be stated here that the two intervals cannot produce the same boundary-effect (present only once in any given case) for a triad with equal force; further, that a clear distinction between the two must therefore be assumed; and finally, that this distinction is to be found only through consideration of the aspect of development (the ascending direction) in the case of the fifth and the aspect of artificial inversion (the descending direction) in the case of the fourth. In this sense, one may speak of a boundary interval of *first* or of *second quality*.

In the purely melodic dimension, which is our sole consideration here, the degrading character of inversion in the case of the fourth is manifested in that the latter is achieved only by way of the fifth: it is almost as though we had to secure the tone of the fifth in our imagination first, and only afterward explicitly formulate the fourth.

Granting the primary characteristic of the fourth to be its inversional relation to the fifth, we would go too far if we emphasized in addition the difference between the ascending and the descending fourth, possibly drawing the same conclusion for practice as in the case of the octave. It is enough to observe that the ascending fourth, although it derives from the falling (and therefore less desirable) fifth, is more agreeable to the ear than the descending one just because of the ascending direction itself. This reflects the strength of the impression created by the act of ascending!

To state it briefly: the fourth can be used melodically both rising and falling without restriction. If we cannot fail to sense the latent presence of the fifth as its origin, we may nevertheless bear in mind that it is precisely the *rising* fourth that derives from the falling fifth.

If even the cantus firmus imposes no restrictions concerning the fourth, it is all the more obvious that this interval can be liberally used in free composition. Still, I should like to point out the peculiarity that the fourth, if it is used too often in succession (I refer exclusively to the melodic line), produces an altogether too inartistic and trivial effect.

It is especially in the opera style of the post-classical period that such fourth-usages are all too abundant. This is not the appropriate place to go into detail on this point, but it would be advisable for the reader to study the varieties of effect of fourth-usage—with respect to purely musical considerations, but at the same time taking into account the respective genres—by comparing, for example, the recitatives in Bach's *St. Matthew Passion* with the vocal lines in Wagner's *Tannhäuser*.

Whoever wishes to escape dilettantism might consider that along with many other ways of substituting for the fourth, especially at the beginnings of pieces, there exists the very tasteful procedure of repeating the same tone! To get a clear picture of this procedure one should refer to the beginnings of Schubert's songs "Ihr Bild," "Am Meer," and so forth. On the other hand, we should remember that the fourth is not always to be avoided: in the chorale cited above on p. 34, it was just the fourth G — C, composed as the inversion of the fifth C — G, which necessarily had to establish the key of C in a completely natural manner.

§14. (d) About the third

The third is of two types: the major third, which is a consonance born of nature, and the minor third, which, on the contrary, is merely the artificial counterpart of the major. The third is included in the content of the triad and represents, so to speak, its internal organs.

§15. (e) About the sixth

The sixth is to be regarded only as the inversion of the third. As such, it is burdened at the outset by the disadvantage that always accompanies inversion. As an inversion, then, the sixth is inferior to the third, and in addition it is affected by the further difficulty associated with large size.

It must be remembered, moreover, that the minor sixth is the inversion of the *major* third, and the major sixth, on the contrary, the inversion of the *minor* third. This accounts for the fact that the minor enjoys the advantage of easier intonation than the major.

Finally, like the fourth, the sixth is more agreeable in the ascending direction than descending.

In his treatment of first-species two-voice counterpoint, *Fux* comments on p. 72 as follows: "From [the ninth note to the tenth] you have used the leap of a major sixth, which is forbidden in the added voice, since everything must be easy to sing." (Compare Fux, p. 93.)

In the course of his presentation of the syncopated species in three-voice counterpoint, *Albrechtsberger* remarks (p. 105) that "the second error is the leap of a major sixth from D to B in the alto, which is forbidden because the note that is approached by the leap is the leading tone (*nota sensibilis*), and is difficult to sing in accurate intonation without instrumental accompaniment. The other major-sixth leaps are all allowed nowadays." I surely do Albrechtsberger no injustice if I regard the reference to the intonational difficulty of the major sixth in general as the most valuable part of this remark. Albrechtsberger accounts for this no more than Fux did. Regarding the character of the *"nota sensibilis,"* see the quotation of Albrechtsberger in Part 3, Chapter 1, §18.

Cherubini, as we saw in the quotation cited in Part 1, Chapter 2, §9, says nothing about the major sixth, but allows the minor sixth both ascending and descending. Later on, in the middle of his treatment of second-species two-voice counterpoint, rule no. 7 (p. 16), he suddenly returns to the minor sixth and describes it as more difficult of intonation than any other allowed interval. See the quotation in part 2, chapter 2, §9.

In *Bellermann* we read on p. 106, under b:

Use of the major sixth is strictly forbidden. Because it is quite consonant and stands in a relationship of 3:5, this interval is in most cases easy to sing in tune, and it is used abundantly in modern music. The old composers of the better school, however, strictly avoided it, perhaps because it impressed them as too weakly, sweetish, or passionate in effect, which would have been out of keeping with the strict simplicity of their compositions. The few examples of major sixths that can be cited, such as the tenor voice at the close of Palestrina's four-voice motet "Ego sum panis vivus" [example follows], never include this interval in the main body of the melody itself, but rather after a cadence, where [the second tone of the leap] begins a new section. We find a similar example in the Lutheran chorale melody "Mit Fried' und Freud' fahr' ich dahin." [See Example 89.]

Example 89

sanft und stil - le, wie Gott mir ver - heis - sen hat.

Such quid-pro-quo in Bellermann's discussion! Since he finds the major sixth easy to sing in tune, he is quite puzzled about the reasons for its prohibition by the strict school. How well he would like to take refuge in modern music, at least on this point, if he could reconcile it with his theoretical conscience. Yet he keeps the prohibition, just because it is hallowed by custom. About the minor sixth, he says on p. 105 under

4a: "This interval should be used only ascending [an example follows]; the descending direction scarcely occurs, even as an exception."

§16.   (f) About the second

As was mentioned before, the second represents the only horizontal dissonance that melody can use. It moves outside of the [established] triadic region, in relation to which it therefore can only produce a dissonant effect. The second is merely the fifth of the fifth, and thus lacks a direct rapport with the fundamental of the initial [implicit] triad.[22]

In size, however, the second is the smallest interval, and as we shall see later (§20), it is precisely this characteristic that contributes so much to the melodic fluency of the cantus firmus.

Use of the second in the cantus firmus is justified, moreover, by its special function in melody—a function that we can observe clearly in the Fux cantus firmus quoted on p. 54: the third tone *E*, forming a motion in seconds from *F* to *D*, represents in effect a bridge upon which the latter tones meet in a third-relationship. Attending to this resultant third, we assume a triad on *D*; but the fifth, *A*, is still missing, and thus the melody moves on. In bar 5, *G*, the fourth (and thus the lower fifth of the initial tone *D*) appears; this suggests, even before the initial third-space *D*—*F* has been fulfilled and completed, a new triad, *G*—*D*. But again, it is a second, *F* (in bar 6), which immediately cancels the impression of the new triad and leads us back into the region of the first one (*D*—*F*). When the tone *A* arrives in bar 7, however, the resultant triadic sum *D*—*F*—*A* becomes completely clear to the ear: the ear comprehends fully not only the role of the fourth, *G*, but also that of the seconds in bars 3 and 6, and also those in bars 8 and 9.

Since the second, as we have just discovered, can promote the establishment of subunits, the question now arises why it is permitted at all in the cantus firmus, which is supposed to strive for an optimally balanced condition. The answer is easy: in the first place, the second has the characteristic not only of binding together in consonant relationships (see bars 3, 8, and 10) tones that belong together—and thereby in a primitive sense fostering unity of harmony—but also, precisely because of its dissonant nature, of canceling an already established harmony (cf. bar 6), whereby unity of harmony is obliterated and destroyed. The second, then, can either promote or counteract the establishment of harmonic entities. It shares this characteristic with each of the consonant intervals, which, in succession with one another, can either establish a consonant entity or lead to a dissonant formation, as in Example 90.

Example 90

In the second place, as we observed in §6 above, unified segments are to be avoided only when they are too drastically delineated. This does not apply to that higher-level unification which, on the contrary, remains a goal worthy of attainment in any melody. Given the desirability of this larger and more comprehensive unification, then, why would the second prove less useful or more disruptive than, for example, the third, the fourth, or the others?

Finally it must be noted that just the second, because it represents the smallest intervallic entity in the horizontal direction, is best suited for gauging the remaining larger intervals, whose psychological implications can, as a result of its orienting function, be better appreciated by our ear.

§17. *Special considerations concerning the use of the permissible larger intervals*

In order to get, for example, from C to its sixth, A, a path can be chosen (see Example 91a) that uses several smaller steps such as seconds, thirds, and fourths. In view of such a possibility one can easily understand that this first method is preferable (from the standpoint of naturalness) to the other possibility, namely that of taking a direct leap to reach the sixth (see Example 91b).

Example 91

However, the fact that the larger interval can be replaced by several smaller, skillfully used intervals—a fact instinctively known not only by the composer but also by the listener—is another independent reason for the older traditional prohibition of the major sixth as well as the admonition of contrapuntal theory concerning the use of larger intervals in general. Therefore, it is completely comprehensible why the earliest church music, especially Gregorian chant, preferred the fifth as the maximum intervallic span (see Introduction, pp. 11–12); this rule, however, did not prevent the total melodic compass from exceeding the limit of the fifth under certain circumstances.

On the other hand, the leap of a minor sixth must often perform the service of opening space between the voices when they have come too close to each other. We shall discuss this later.

Turning to free composition, we see that, for example, the melody of the often-cited chorale (Example 12) finally achieves a total range of a ninth (*d* — *e¹*) even without using any intervals larger than a second, third, fourth (twice), and fifth (just once). And we see how it ascends to a major sixth (*e¹*) above the initial tone (*g*) exactly at the word *Mensch* in a most significant fashion.

Let us go one step further by investigating the vocal part of Schubert's "Doppelgänger." Even here, where the total ambitus (in the original key of *B* minor) extends from *b* to *g²* and the nature of free composition favors all manner of internal groupings, the principal intervals generating the content are again only smaller intervals, while the vocal part shows direct larger leaps only in the form of a fifth (seven times), a sixth (once), and an octave (once), the latter occurring significantly at the words *vor Schmerzensgewalt* (bars 30–32). The octave is exceeded only at the words *eig'nen Gestalt* (bar 40) with a descending ninth (*g²* — *f♯¹*), which should, however, since it is interrupted by a rest, more properly count as an apparent ninth, that is, only a second.

In general the large leap can be justified more convincingly and thus used in many more ways in free composition.[23] We already saw this when we discussed the seventh. But even larger leaps can be appropriate in free composition because of the nature of the given situation. Thus, Brahms, for example, writes a ninth in his [Alto] Rhapsody op. 53, in order to portray musically the image of *Öde* (wasteland):

Example 92
Brahms, Alto Rhapsody Op. 53

Hugo Wolf [uses a ninth] in "Der Tambour":

Example 93
Wolf, "Der Tambour"

And Wagner [uses] a tenth in *Tristan und Isolde* (score, p. 98):[24]

Example 94
Wagner, *Tristan und Isolde*, Act I

Leaps are used with an even greater justification in instrumental music. However, here the problem—already touched upon in our discussion of the seventh (p. 63f.)—emerges again: whether the leap in certain cases appears to be nothing but a substitute for a smaller interval. Thus in the last movement of Haydn's Symphony in D Major (See Example 95), the tenths in the violins must be recognized as real melodic tenths;[25] this is clear simply from the way the leaps expand beyond the octave [from within].

Example 95

Haydn, Symphony No. 104, IV, b. 295ff.

The same is true of the leaps in the bass in Beethoven's Symphony No. 3 (development section of the first movement):

Example 96

Beethoven, Symphony No. 3, I, b. 338ff.

or of the leaps of a ninth in Wagner's *Siegfried-Idyll,* which are derived in an incomparably expressive way from the thematically significant seventh:

Example 97

Wagner, *Siegfried-Idyll*

Example 98

That leaps such as those, for example, in Haydn's String Quartet in D Minor op. 76 no. 2, are authentic leaps is clear from the work's psychological quality of exuberance.

Example 99

Haydn, String Quartet Op. 76 No. 2, IV

On the other hand, the bracketed leaps of a tenth in the double-basses (Beethoven, Symphony No. 9, first movement, bar 132ff.) should more properly be interpreted as hidden thirds.

Example 100

Beethoven, Symphony No. 9, I

These very leaps conclude the second group by moving up stepwise using the diatonic basis of the *Bb* major key—see in Example 100 the scale (*Bb*) - *C* - *D* - *Eb* - *F* - *G* - *A*—until they arrive, in the continuation of this scale, again at *Bb* and lead, now in the form of real thirds, into the motive of the third (and last) group.

Example 101

Beethoven, Symphony No. 9, I

The third, disguised in the preceding tenth-leaps, appears on stage here, as is evident, clearly and most honestly as a third; this fact, however, should, I believe, induce conductors to give an expressive character already to those tenths, and this despite the *staccato* on the second sixteenth-note and the *sf* on the quarter-note. Both performance indications have nothing to do with the usual *staccatissimo* which is unfortunately so common among our doublebass players today; Beethoven used them here only to provide a contrast to the following *legato* passage of the oboe (with *portamento* expression). In other words: the tenths of Example 100, instead of being performed in a crude and unthematic way as an unimportant filler in disregard of their true thematic character, need to be infused with a stronger expression because of their real significance as thirds, which becomes obvious only later (see Example 101).[26]

Especially in the music of J.S. Bach we often find the most unusual and original substitutions of larger intervals for smaller ones. Consider, for example, the prelude cited in *Harmonielehre*, Example 372—above all, bar 6 on page 439 in particular.[27] If a harmonic reduction is made of the pianistic figurations, the content of the bar appears as in Example 102 at a.

Example 102

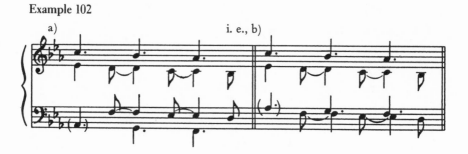

If the two lower voices are inverted, however, the same reduction leads to a different version, as at b of the same example.

The latter type at b corresponds with bar 11 on the same page,[28] with its leaps of ninths and tenths in the bass (see a in example 104):

Example 104

so that in reality—this follows from the above reasoning—behind the leaps of ninths and tenths at a in Example 104 one must assume only seconds and thirds, as at b in Example 102.

I take the liberty here of referring at last to the *portamento (porte de voix)* which is often directly associated with larger leaps, or in other cases is tacitly assumed by the composer. As is well known, the portamento, which has the function of actually filling out the large leap at least in part, is originally proper to the human voice, and the string instruments as well. The possibility of transposing this effect to keyboard instruments, however, is often doubted, even though [the possibility of] a modest imitation is granted. Of course, if only the so-called "accent"[29] is regarded as calling for portamento execution at the keyboard, then it is no surprise that the possibility is disavowed entirely. Besides the portamento that occurs in the form of an anticipation, another kind of notation appears to me to signal a real portamento on the piano—a notation derived long ago from the special characteristic of keyboard instruments. For example:[30]

Example 105

(1) J. S. Bach, English Suite No. 3, Sarabande   (2) English Suite No. 6, Allemande

Example 109

C. P. E. Bach, Sonatas for Connoisseurs and Amateurs,
5th Collection, Sonata No. 2, Largo

Example 110

Brahms, Intermezzo Op. 117 No. 2   Brahms, Trio Op. 8, I

In all these examples we see a ligature, that is, a retention of tones, which thus throws into relief the degree of tension caused by the leaps, namely an octave (Example 105, 2, bar 2, fourth quarter), a seventh (same example, 1, bar 1, second quarter), a sixth (same example, 2, bar 2, first quarter), a third (same example, 2, bar 1, fourth quarter, as well as in Examples 109[31] and 110). The ligature has the following effect: after the completed leap, the initial tone from which the leap departs sounds together with the goal of the leap; thus the interval is much more clearly presented to the ear than if the leap were to occur "naked" (that is, as a simple succession)—in other words, without simultaneous covering of the goal of the leap through continued sounding of the departure tone. To be convinced of the portamento effect in such cases, one need only omit the ligature: every ear will immediately hear the difference.

Still, the portamento produced on the piano in this way is nevertheless different from that executed by the singer or violinist, since they are not content merely to indicate the distance between the beginning and end of the interval, but traverse the space itself with a glissando. However, it would be incorrect to attribute the ligature, as is generally done, to the tonal poverty of the keyboard instrument and its constant need for filling-in. On the contrary, this notation must be understood as an original and autonomous poetic intention to present an interval in the form of a portamento [on the keyboard], even though only within the limits of an instrument which, indeed, does not permit a gliding-through of the space of the interval, but which makes it possible to mark beginning and end in its own original way through a peculiar amalgam of juxtaposition and superimposition (simultaneity) [of pitches].

It should be noted, nevertheless, that the ligature-tones do not constitute voices in the obbligato sense; this can be deduced not only from their purpose recognized above as the only correct one, but also from the fact that instead of a real ligature, which conceptually would have to imply one and the same voice, only an inauthentic and apparent ligature between two different voices is notated in the above examples. It is a ligature peculiar to the piano, and this cannot be changed: an original notation that does not create real and obbligato voices but strives, as explained, to stimulate and compel the player to achieve portamento expression.

Much closer to a real portamento of the singer or violinist is the following example by Handel:[32]

Example 111
Handel, Suite No. 5, Air, Double IV

Since the ligature falls exactly in the space of the leap—see a, bar 1, fourth and fifth eighth-notes: $f\#^1$ between a^1 and $d\#^1$—, this notation reflects exactly the principal effect of a real portamento, that is, the gliding of pitches through the space [of the leap]. As in the Bach examples, the ligature, since it connects two different voices, is again only an apparent one. (By analogy, one might consider the intervention of $g\sharp^1$ between $d\sharp^1$ and b^1 in bar 1, fifth and sixth eighth-notes, also a kind of portamento.)

No matter how we view the effect, this much is clear: we encounter here a written-out legatissimo which, in this form, is endemic to the keyboard instrument alone; in other words, an authentic and significant keyboard-specific. It goes without saying, however, that the portamento is really only a legatissimo. Therefore, it is not a mistake in performing keyboard pieces of whatever epoch (including classical and postclassical works) to use the portamento frequently, even where it is not expressly notated through ligatures (as above) but merely implied by the context of the passage.[33]

In view of a style of composition that so clearly demands expressiveness through portamento (as is evident in the passages in Example 105), it appears incomprehensible that the earliest keyboard style could have been considered expressionless; likewise, it is inconceivable that it was possible to lump the keyboard style together with the organ style of that era. Besides many other differentiating characteristics, exactly the truly keyboard-idiomatic portamento notation is convincing proof that even the earliest masters treated the [stringed] keyboard instruments differently from the organ, since they endowed the former with characteristics of an almost vocal expressiveness. But alas, how consistently today's pianists violate this principle! How they hack away at the keyboard music of Bach, Handel, and others, in public or at home, in a tempo that makes it impossible from the outset to do justice to the expression strictly required just by the notational symbols themselves. They chase and run on the piano, dust-clouds of tones rising behind the hands on the road of the keyboard, with nowhere a point of rest or a lingering, nowhere clarity or animation! It is as if J.S. Bach or Handel—those very composers—were just confused artists incapable of any kind of emotional impulse; as if only we [today] were able to discover the concept of "expression," which is supposed to be most convincingly documented by our output! Just observe: every artist or amateur will readily admit that J.S. Bach is perhaps expressive in his vocal music—in the *B*-Minor Mass or the Passions, for example; the same quality is discovered by the string player even in the works for violin; but as soon as a pianist sits down at the piano to perform a keyboard work by Bach, all life is immediately driven out of the work of art and nothing remains except a caricature of tones! Does the pianist suppose that Bach suffered a partial eclipse of his expressive capacity? Why is he not eager, like a violinist or singer who follows a good tradition (Joachim or Messchaert, for example), to rise to the full measure of Bach's art of expression? Perhaps [piano virtuosos] will finally recognize that it is not their place to represent a J.S. Bach as a keyboard-maniac just to claim for themselves a higher level of inspiration—what fatuous and idle complacency! Do today's piano virtuosos really believe that a piece by Liszt, Franck, or Grieg, for example, contains more expression than a suite, partita, or toccata by J.S. Bach? Then let them first learn to read notes and truly perceive the meaning of one or another suggestive notation; only then will they humble themselves and let Bach speak

as the great artist and human being—which should be their sole responsibility—instead of passing their own art off as the only authentic one!

Bellermann writes on p. 107 under e:

Every interval larger than the octave is, of course, excluded from the melody.
Accordingly, the intervals fall into three categories with respect to their usability
in melody:

Permitted in Both Directions	Permitted Only Ascending	Completely Prohibited
The large half-step	The minor sixth	The tritone
The whole-step	The octave	The diminished fifth
The minor third		The major sixth
The major third		The minor seventh
The perfect fourth		The major seventh
The perfect fifth		

Composers during the fifteenth and sixteenth centuries followed these laws with
greatest strictness, which may even be described as absolute; their origin, as I
stated above, can be found in the practices of Gregorian chant (which was even
more restricted in that the fifth marked the limit of the permissible intervals).
At least I know of no example of the minor sixth or octave in Gregorian chant,
so that one must assume the mensuralists added these two intervals for their
own purpose.

§18. *Several leaps in succession: (a) In different directions*

When several leaps occur in succession but in different directions, as here:

Example 112

the ear resists perceiving all of these paths at first as the most natural ones.
Rather, it wants to (and must) understand the leaps only as detours for a
shorter and more direct path that would in any case have been possible—a
path which in fact is made manifest when we see where the subsequent leap
in each case reaches its conclusion. Thus, in the above example, after the
second leap $a^1 - e^1$ has led to e^1, our ear must assume that the path d^1 to e^1
is the progression originally implied and, therefore, the simpler one. Why then
the detour via a^1, if it is certainly possible to move to e^1 more directly?
Similarly, the ear would be justified, on the other hand, in perceiving later
on precisely the tone e^1 as a detour toward the goal g^1 (approaching from a^1);

as is evident, leaps without mediation through seconds only cause difficulties of comprehension and are the reasons for many an uncertainty. Therefore, a melody constructed with such leaps has to be declared poor.

The fact that we usually perceive two leaps in different directions only as a detour, however, imbues this device, on the other hand, with a special expressive power. Since it digresses from the norm, there must have been a reason for it—and it is correct to attribute the reason to the detour of the leaps themselves. It is obvious that because of the expression connected with these leaps, they are better prohibited in the cantus firmus.

For the same reason, however, leaps in free composition, as long as they appear as substitutes for a shorter path, usually produce a more intense expression, as for example in:

Example 113

Chopin, Nocturne in F Minor Op. 55, No. 1

In that case, precisely because of their expressive quality, they are not only welcome but also required.

§19. *(b) In the same direction*

If two or more leaps occur in the same direction, disadvantages of a different kind result for the melody. They can easily lead quite beyond the appropriate range-limitation; or they establish triads or seventh-chords which are prohibited here (see Part 1, Chapter 1, §3) because of considerations of balance that must be strictly observed.

For that reason the following leaps, for example, are bad:

Example 114

Only on rare occasions does a situation occur in the cantus firmus where the continuation of the melody can absorb a dangerous aggregate of leaps and thus eliminate it for the ear.

Albrechtsberger remarks, in the context of second-species two-voice counterpoint (p. 38f.): "Three or four leaps should never in themselves result in a ninth chord or a major seventh chord, even if the added voice together with cantus firmus were to produce correct intervals. Even a minor seventh resulting from three or four leaps is rarely good. The diminished seventh, [however,] may be tolerated." There follow many examples illustrating these remarks. Concerning chords that result from leaps (where he recommends toleration of, for example, even the resultant of a diminished seventh), we find the following example:

Example 115

"tolerable"

Nevertheless, we should keep in mind that he does not discuss his rule until second-species counterpoint, in which (since four notes stand against two of the cantus firmus) a good turn of the cantus firmus may under certain circumstances eradicate a perilous seventh-resultant more easily than in the cantus firmus itself or in first-species counterpoint. This explains why, in contrast to the rule stated on p. 23 (where he disallows the diminished seventh), he tolerates such a resultant in second-species counterpoint. In my view, only the context can decide this question; in other words: if the seventh-resultant threatens to protrude too openly and drastically from its surroundings, it creates a bad effect for this very reason, and should be disallowed. Moreover, no distinction should be made between [different] sevenths, so that even the resultant of a diminished seventh, tolerated by Albrechtsberger, is [in such cases] to be viewed as disallowed.

Concerning *Cherubini,* see the sixth rule on p. 7, already cited in this chapter in §9.

§20.   *The requirement of melodic fluency*

If one wants to avoid the dangers produced by larger intervals, whether they move in the same direction or alternate directions, the easiest remedy is simply to interrupt the series of leaps—that is, to prevent a second leap from occurring by continuing with a second or an only slightly larger interval after the first leap; or one may change the direction of the second interval altogether; finally, both means can be used in combination.

Such procedures yield a kind of wave-like melodic line which as a whole represents an animated entity, and which, with its ascending and descending curves, appears balanced in all its individual component parts. This kind of line manifests what is called melodic fluency, and one may confidently state that the second (cf. §21)—as the smallest interval and agent of rescue in cases of emergency—is the primary ingredient of melodic fluency.

Melodic fluency, then, is a kind of compensating aesthetic justice vis-à-vis the overall shape, within which each individual tone is a constituent part of the whole as well as an end in itself.

If the conditions of melodic fluency are fulfilled in this way, the melody will then exude also an intrinsic melodic beauty. This will, of course, be inferior to the individual melody with its internal groupings such as one encounters in free composition; nevertheless, despite all reservations, it is at least equally far removed from unregulated chaos. In the cantus firmus we encounter a spare melodic beauty burdened with the purpose of an exercise, but a beauty nonetheless. The little organism, produced under observance of so many restrictions, still has its animation!

It is easily understandable, then, why such examples as the following attempts at a cantus firmus would have to be considered unsuccessful:

Example 116

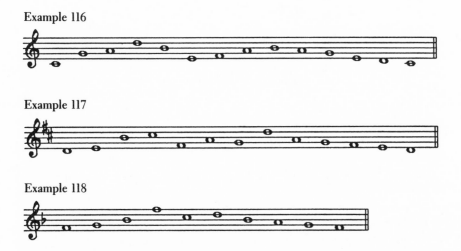

Example 117

Example 118

The principles of melodic fluency extend also to free composition. At first, [they do so] perhaps in a highly metaphysical and exemplary sense, in that even the whole of an art-work must represent nothing more than a sum of individual components that are an end in themselves as well as a means toward fulfillment of a larger purpose. Both tendencies must be balanced in a symphonic movement as a whole as well as in a modest cantus firmus that serves only as an exercise.

On a far more concrete level, however, we desire to see the requirement of melodic fluency in free composition—to mention something special and little-noticed—fulfilled also in, for example, the lines of a composition for piano or violin. Such a line may be based on the postulates of polyphony and thus may tend to express, through itself, several latent voices in a unified fashion (compare Examples 48 and 76). It may strive simply to decorate a given melodic line in an expressly monodic style—as examples may be mentioned the violin figurations set so ingeniously in the Adagio of Beethoven's Ninth Symphony (bars 43f. or 99f.), which are only a variation of the simple line of the theme, or the rhetorical *nonlegato* figures for the violins in so many Haydn symphonies. Or the line may represent only a filling voice which, nevertheless, assumes an obbligato character—for example, the line (often misunderstood) in Chopin's familiar Nocturne in F♯ Major (bars 18-24):

Example 119

Chopin, Nocturne Op. 15, No. 2

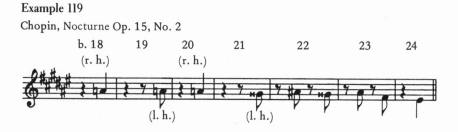

Or, finally, it may represent the most concealed result, the ultimate product of ascending and descending figurations, such as can be identified, for example, in the prelude of J.S. Bach's English Suite in *D* Minor as follows:

Example 120

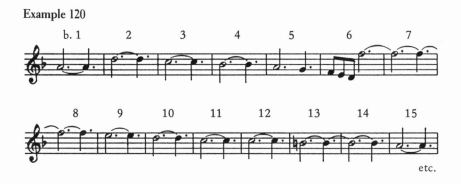

The precepts of melodic fluency are at work in all these cases and remain so no less than in the modest, simple cantus firmus itself.

In free composition, therefore, lines that are not balanced in their melodic discourse and thus do not express a unified goal will be noticed by the ear as poor. In other words, even in free composition, an excessive freedom in handling tones cannot, to say the least, always be justified. Besides many other violations of the requirements of tonality and form (which, admittedly, are more difficult to fulfill), it was left to works of the most recent literature to commit, just in the disposition of an individual melodic line, such errors as certainly may be considered proof of the decline of artistic instinct. Strangely enough, nobody was so susceptible to the danger of constructing melodic lines poorly as Anton Bruckner, who often enough could also write the most beautiful, original, and moving melodies. If there had not at all times been artists whose artistry, despite great and indeed brilliant capability, was marred by a deep-seated fissure, we would scarcely be able to understand how Bruckner above all managed to write lines such as the following:

Example 121

Bruckner, Symphony No. 1, I

Example 122

Bruckner, Symphony No. 1, I

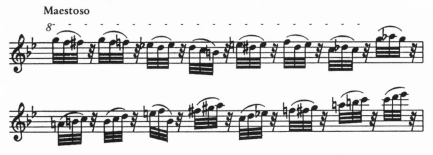

Example 123

Bruckner, Symphony No. 1, I

Example 124

Bruckner, Te deum

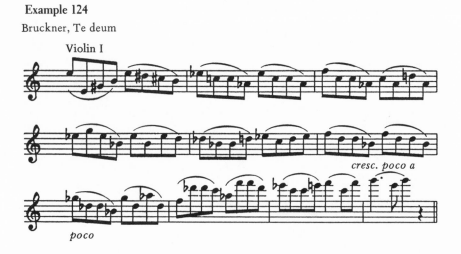

Example 125

Bruckner, Psalm 150

Example 126

Bruckner, Psalm 150

I should not be accused of wanting to do Bruckner an injustice. For I, too, know that the cited lines in most cases have merely an accompanying function and receive their true meaning from the harmonies to which they belong. But this is the core of the matter: the awkwardness of these lines results from the fact that Bruckner slavishly follows the harmonies point by point, and since the latter are so disorderly and meandering—such an abuse of third-relations, ascending or descending, with most extensive chromatic alteration!—he obviously found it difficult to span a unified contrapuntal line over harmonies that are not really unified. That is the reason for the deadly angularity in his violin and wind parts, with which he unfortunately circumscribes his harmonies all too often.

Albrechtsberger teaches on pp. 38–39 (not, indeed, until he discusses the second species—compare the note above in §19): "[Fourth,] after a large leap [by each of] two [consecutive] tones, the third should return by a leap of a fourth or third, if it is impossible to move by step."

Cherubini states on p. 2: "The motion is melodic and *fluent* when it progresses *stepwise*. It is *leapwise* when it progresses by intervals." (In addition, see rule 6 on p. 7, cited in §9.) In this definition, melodic fluency is, without doubt, conceived too narrowly. It certainly tolerates leaps too, so long as they are integrated into the whole in such a way that they do not disturb the equilibrium. Nevertheless, an irrefutable truth is contained in Cherubini's little remark, namely that it is precisely the second which is the best foundation for "melodic fluency."

Bellermann puts it this way on p. 104:

> On this occasion I note in addition that it is not good to move in two leaps of a fourth or fifth in one direction, and that in general one should avoid several leaps in the same direction. The beauty and grace of a melody consist precisely in the fact that as many steps of its range are used as possible, be they large or small, and that after a large leap upward a small leap downward is preferred, and vice versa. Nevertheless, most of this should be left to the correct musical instinct of the composer. Everybody will notice the lack of grace and elegance in the following melodies:

Example 127

whereas anybody would be happy to sing the next ones, even though in the first melody leaps of a fifth and a third occur in succession:

Example 128

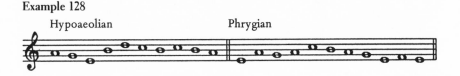

And he comments as follows on the hypo-Aeolian example:

> It cannot be denied that leaps of a fifth and a third and the like, in the same direction, may occasionally have a good effect; many an example can be found in Gregorian chant as well as in the Protestant chorale. But the beginner in composition is to be urgently advised to avoid such things entirely—specifically two leaps in one direction whose boundary tones establish the interval of a seventh, ninth, or tenth. In a descending direction such leaps most often have an even worse effect than in an ascending motion.

But we come closer to the explanation and the distinction between good and bad in all these examples by Bellermann if we seek the reasons not only in the leaps themselves but also in the other contributing factors. Thus, the example called "Ionian" by Bellermann must be considered poor not just because of the leaps and the obvious arpeggiation of the triad $C — G$ and the seventh chord $C — D$, but rather for the following reason: the leapwise motion occurs twice in succession (from c^1 to c^2 and, in reverse, from c^2 to d^1), which draws attention to its disjunct character in an unpleasant way. The Dorian example altogether lacks the third, F, for the harmonic sum of the entire cantus firmus, so that the ear is unable to decide on the motion and the meaning of the tones; and when even B and G come into the picture later on, doubt and uncertainty are clearly increased to the point of complete obscurity. On the other hand, the clarity of the triad $A - E - C$ in Bellermann's example labelled "hypo-Aeolian" is the positive reason that the intervening seventh-outline $E - B - D$ does not call attention to itself and, for that reason, is not a noticeable disturbance: the ear adds the long-expected third C to A and E, and thus unity and balance of the melody, despite the leaps, must be considered accomplished and preserved. The last example should be viewed as good without further comment.

§21.   *The prohibition of what is called "monotony"*

The repetition of a series of tones within the cantus firmus, by its very nature, calls attention to that series and, for that reason alone, highlights it as a factor disruptive to the general equilibrium of the entire melody. Such repetition is, therefore, prohibited in the cantus firmus.

Even the following fault, for example, would have to be considered in this rubric:

Example 129

Here it is not a definite series of tones that is repeated, but only the apex [of the melody], the tone A, which occurs twice, and, therefore, certainly once too often. How much better, because more unified in reaching the goal, is the following correction of the same melody:

Example 130

I have already discussed in more detail in *Harmony*, §4f., the fact that in free composition, on the other hand, it is the repetition of a series of tones that turns it into a motive; thus, that which must be considered monotony in the cantus firmus represents the essential life-principle in free composition. The various types of repetition available, both large and small, will also be shown in a different context [*FrC.*, §§251-266].

Albrechtsberger (p. 38):

> Monotony—that is, uniformity of tones or the repetition of several notes—is prohibited here; it is often encountered, however, in free composition, which is no contrapuntal exercise. But good masters use a different bass the second time, or new middle voices; they alternate instruments or *piano* and *forte* dynamic levels; or they transpose the same idea up an octave for the second occurrence. Here [in counterpoint], these devices are bad and faulty, even though the chorale is varied.

Such naiveté in all these remarks as far as free composition is concerned, even though the observation that nothing should ever be stated twice in the same way in free composition has greater validity than can be made clear in this limited context of discussion of the problem of monotony. Think only, for example, of the basic compositional principle of altering the recapitulation of a sonata movement; this principle, which has so frequently been misunderstood, has misled many an editor of classical music (even a Bülow) into faulty and all too gratuitous emendations—which, incidentally, are to be discussed in greater detail later on.

Compare, for example, in Nottebohm, *Beethovens Studien* (p. 48), the revision by Albrechtsberger (see b) of Beethoven's error (see a):

Example 131

But exactly from the standpoint of monotony, I regard his own cantus-firmus exercise in minor, cited later (§23, Exercise 7), as faulty.

§22. About modulation

The prohibition of chromatic progressions (see above, §4 in this chapter) does not prevent the melody from modulating to a related key, so long as the modulation—in the manner of a silent modulation through reinterpretation (see *Harmony*, §§64f., 97, 171f.)—results in a diatonic reinterpretation of the interval in question and otherwise remains in a natural and proper relation to the whole. Thus, in the following example, which is a variant of a cantus firmus by Fux cited in Example 40, the bracketed passage may be perceived as a turn toward *C* major if the whole melody is otherwise interpreted as being in *D* minor:

Example 132

Albrechtsberger writes a counterpoint in *C* major as follows (p. 32):

Example 133

c. f.

and remarks: "The NB above *F♯* in the alto means that the sharp has been applied deliberately, since one is allowed occasionally to move into related keys."

Compare also *Cherubini*'s cantus firmus in §23 under 9.

Cadence

§23. *About cadence formulas*

There can be no doubt that just as the first tone of the key itself [i.e., the tonic] belongs at the beginning of a cantus firmus, for the same reason that same tone belongs also at its *end;* it is equally certain that many more possible ways exist to arrive at this final goal tone.

If the concluding effect is to be reached in the smoothest and most normal way—and this alone can be the aim in the cantus firmus—then the *penultimate* tone should always be the upper or lower second [of the tonic]. If we call the two second-related tones under consideration here "leading tones"—for example, in *C* major:

Example 134

—to be exact, the *ascending* leading tone at a and the *descending* leading tone at b, then the rule for normal cadential situations can be stated as follows: *The penultimate tone must be one of the two leading tones.*

Cantus firmi in minor must use a semitone [below the tonic] instead of a diatonic whole tone as ascending leading tone; for example in A minor:

Example 135

The alteration, however, can only be interpreted as a borrowing from the parallel major key, in this case A major (see *Harmony*, §§23, 45).

But this [alone] does not suffice. The requirements of melodic fluency as well as of a most natural conclusion extend further, to the *third* tone from the end—that is, the tone before the ascending or descending leading tone. For in order to get to the leading tone itself in the smoothest way and to support it in its cadential function more effectively, it is again most appropriate to employ the step of a second. But if, as is evident, the desired second can approach the leading tone from above just as well as from below, then there result the following cadential formulas for the *descending leading tone* (seen at a in Example 134):

Example 136

1. (from above)   2. (from below)

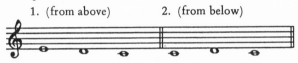

These formulas, therefore, are preferred from the outset to the following ones, where the leading tone is reached through the interval of a third:

Example 137

3.   4.

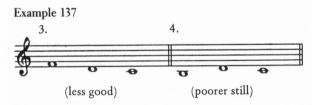

(less good)   (poorer still)

In minor, the formulas shown above appear in the following versions:

Example 138

1.   2.   3.   4.

(from above)   (from below)   (less good)   (poorer still)

If one were to place the four formulas in major and minor on a scale of merit, one would have to consider the first and second equally good, both of them better than the third, and the fourth poorest. The reason for this judgment is that B in C major (or G♯ in A minor) already implies in a way the path of the ascending leading tone, from which it is possible to move directly to C in C major (or to A in A minor). Thus the effect can only be confusing if the original direction is abandoned midstream and the track of the descending leading tone is approached by leap: in this case both avenues, namely that of the ascending as well as descending leading tone, appear to be pursued in a somewhat impure and indistinct fashion.

By analogy, the cadential formulas that result for the *ascending leading tone*—that is, the one at b in Example 134—are the following:

Example 139

in major:

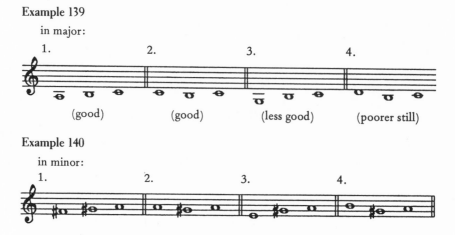

(good)   (good)   (less good)   (poorer still)

Example 140

in minor:

Observe that the minor mode (Example 140) requires in the first case also an alteration of the sixth tone of the key, since the augmented second ($F - G\sharp$) must be avoided (see §7 in this chapter and also *Harmony*, §42). Appraisal of the individual formulas for purposes of the cantus-firmus [exercise] must again be based on the principles laid down for the formulas given for the descending leading tone (Example 138).

From this it can be seen that, regardless of which leading tone and melodic direction is involved, the third must be considered the largest interval of approach to the penultimate tone in the cantus firmus. Larger leaps, such as that of a fourth or fifth, for example:

Example 141

necessarily impair the effect of closure; by nature, they imply the expression of a particular mood and, therefore, also require a reason for such a mood. This requirement, however, can be satisfied only in free composition (where, incidentally, it is also welcome).

In order to gain insight into cadences in free composition it is important to recognize that there the closure is no longer based on the horizontal line alone but rather (and to a larger degree) on the harmony of the vertical [dimension], or, more precisely, on the succession from scale degree V to I; this alone is already a source of innumerable licenses, which the cantus firmus dare not employ if it is to avoid damaging its own purpose—that is, its didatic function.

The following examples of free composition show the unrestricted use of intervals larger than the third in approaching the leading tone, even though the melody may otherwise still retain the order valid for the cantus firmus (first leading tone, then tonic) in its cadence formula.

Example 142

Brahms, Begräbnisgesang Op. 13

4th-leap

Example 143

J. S. Bach, English Suite No. 6, Gavotte

4th-leap

Example 144

Beethoven, Trio Op. 1 No. 3 III

4th-leap

Compare also the leap of a sixth in the Chopin illustration (Example 113) together with the explanation given there.

When we see how Beethoven simplified and improved the conclusion of the Adagio from the *Leonore* Overture No. 2 (see Example 145a) in the *Leonore* Overture No. 3 (Example 145b), we may learn to appreciate his

Example 145

Beethoven, *Leonore* Overture No. 2

Leonore Overture No. 3

forthright and profound insight; in his second attempt, he finally realized that, despite the nature of free composition, it would necessarily remain futile to compose as at a. Why generate tension through augmentation and rests; why overshoot the real closure by moving to D♭ (cf. above, Example 139 under 4!); and, finally, why that mysterious < > ? He obviously saw that at this point there could not, indeed should not, be such a mystery, least of all one with such an exaggerated end in itself; he thus realized that all [such] efforts would necessarily lead to completely lifeless ineffectuality and that, therefore, only the simplest and briefest form, as at b, would be appropriate.

Avoidance of the leading tone can be seen also in the following example, with a downward leap of a fifth to the tonic:[34]

Example 146

Beethoven, Piano Sonata Op. 2 No. 1, IV

Or in the combination of a falling fifth with the leading tone:

Example 147

Haydn, Variations in F Minor, Var. I

Finally, the melody may be permitted in free composition (compare also three- and four-voice counterpoint, incidentally) to close not only always on the tonic itself (as it must in the cantus firmus) but also with the third or fifth of the tonic harmony, as in Example 148. This results from the fact that the downward leap of a fifth from scale degree V to I relieves the melody in

Example 148

J. S. Bach, Sinfonia No. 5

free composition to a certain extent of the necessity of contributing to closure in the manner required in the cantus firmus.

The cadences of chorale melodies mistakenly considered Dorian, Phrygian, or Mixolydian also belong, in a different sense, to this category. If we assign these melodies (to the extent that they are well constructed at all from an artistic standpoint) to one [or the other] of the only two valid systems (that is, major or minor), then we view the closures of these melodies from the perspective of exactly these two systems—for example, as fifth of the tonic harmonies in Example 12 of this volume and Example 107 of *Harmony*.

That *Albrechtsberger* is not afraid to approach the leading tone by a leap of even a diminished fourth (see similar fourth-leaps to the leading tone on p. 75, fifth-leaps and even sixth-leaps on p. 36 of his work), we have seen above in Example 80, where the explanation of this phenomenon from his perspective was also given; it thus becomes evident that he has even less scruple concerning third-leaps. Albrechtsberger's indifference about the problem of the tone preceding the leading tone, however, has to be viewed as a misconception on his part with respect to the true purpose of contrapuntal theory. He himself certainly knew the difference in effect among all possible formulas, but he did not perceive with sufficient clarity that it was his sole task to teach exactly this difference instead of immediately and indiscriminately allowing all kinds of leaps, to say nothing of using them also in the sense of real composition, without having first shed light on the difference.

Only *Bellermann* takes pains to discuss in detail in a separate chapter (IX, p. 120f.) "how to establish closure." It would, of course, take too much space to quote here all of that most instructive chapter; it should be pointed out only that, despite much of value, the author's incompletely developed viewpoint (which we have encountered repeatedly in the foregoing)—specifically his practice of illustrating perceptions and evaluations of effects [in counterpoint] with examples from actual compositional practice—unfortunately comes to the fore once again here, for all that it is never permissible to establish *such an immediate connection* between both areas (see Introduction). What can it mean when he writes, for example: "The downward leap of a third to the seventh degree, however, is allowed and occurs in several chorale melodies," and marks the following example as "good"?

Example 149

Aeolian (good)

What can be gained by referring to the practice of chorale melodies (which, inciden-tally, is so varied) before the effect of such a third-leap in relation to stepwise progression or to other larger leaps is investigated and established? And this alone is what matters in contrapuntal doctrine, even if the intention is to present, on this occasion as well, insights into the free world of tones based on many different principles.

That *Dehn* did not even reach the point of being able to make general remarks about cadences results from his dangerous practice of providing his students with real chorale melodies as cantus firmi. Chorales, after all, have internal occurrences of fermatas and several different kinds of cadences! And what gratuitous complexity and detrimental confusion for the student, who at this stage would and should learn something simple about cadential effects!

In the following I add a few melodies to those already quoted (see the cantus firmus by Fux in §11 and a variant of my own in §27):

Example 150

1. Fux Table II, fig. 11 (allegedly Lydian)

2. Fux II, 13 (transposed to an alleged Mixolydian)

3. Fux IV, 4

4. Fux 11, 17 (transposed to Aeolian)

5. Albrechtsberger p. 24

6. Albrechtsberger p. 29

7. Albrechtsberger p. 32

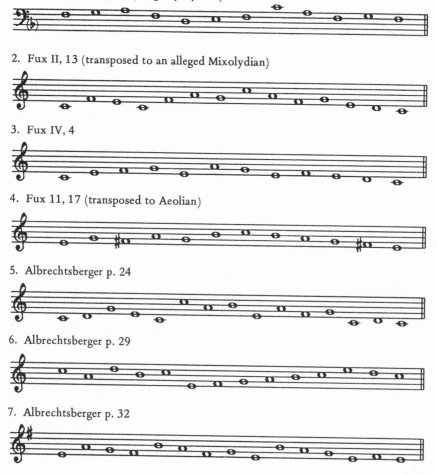

Example 150 *continued*

8. Cherubini Ex. 40

9. Cherubini Ex. 80

10. H. Schenker

11.

12.

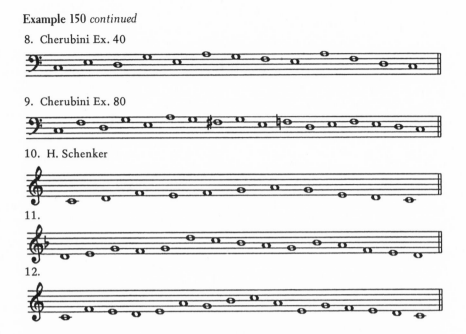

I deliberately cite here melodies by Fux, Albrechtsberger, and Cherubini (Bellermann uses mostly melodies by Fux, while Cherubini introduces melodies by the latter only now and then) in order to show the position of these teachers outside the text proper as well—in other words, in their practice. Many reasons will be found to consider the melodies by Fux better than those by Albrechtsberger and Cherubini, but I leave it up to the reader to make this evaluation in the light of what has been presented so far.

PART TWO

Two-Voice
Counterpoint

Chapter 1

The First Species:
Note Against Note

General Aspects

§1. *The concept of counterpoint*

A second voice placed above or below the cantus firmus is called the *counterpoint.*

Such a [resulting] two-voice structure naturally presents situations whose treatment offers a desirable testing-ground for refinement of the student's musical sense.

§2. *The permitted intervals*

In this species only consonances may be used.

This restriction has to do exclusively with the nature of the situation presented by the first species. Because of the absence of scale degrees (*Harmony,* §84f.) and of any richer contrapuntal movement, the first species lacks the power to clarify the true sense of dissonances.

The use of dissonances, on the contrary, would necessarily lead to the establishment of larger harmonic units, as the following examples illustrate:

Example 151

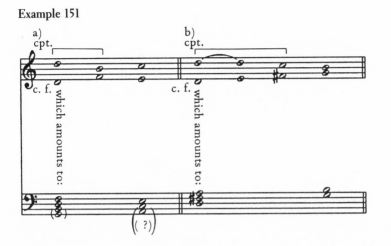

At a the ear would have to collect the interval succession 8 — 4 into a sum comprising $B-D-F$, and at b, the succession 8 — 7 — 5 into a sum comprising $D-F\sharp-(A)-C$ with a passing tone E in the cantus firmus; obviously the equilibrium of all vertical combinations would thereby suffer considerably. Specifically, in the first case two, and in the second case as many as three, harmonic events would be dominated entirely by a single tone: B at a and D at b; only with reference to these tones could the motion of the voices be consistently generated and securely understood.

It comes down to this: the consonant interval speaks for itself; it rests in its euphony, signifying by itself both origin and end. This is not true of the dissonance, whose presence always requires further justification; far from resting at peace in itself, the dissonance instead points urgently beyond itself; it can be understood only in relation to—that is, by means of and in terms of—a consonant entity, from which it follows that the consonant entity alone signifies origin and end for the dissonance.

In this sense, consonance manifests an absolute character, dissonance, on the contrary, a merely relative and derivative one: *in the beginning is consonance!* The consonance is primary, the dissonance secondary!

This implies, however, that the *dissonance* must first be justified (specifically, through a consonance), while the consonance, sustained by its euphonious character and therefore less dependent, needs no justification beyond itself. But how—and this is the question for the moment—could we adduce proof of the necessity of a dissonance in a contrapuntal exercise, which lacks the control and motivation of scale degrees? [Lacking any such proof,] we must, in exercises of the first type to be considered, avoid the dissonance as insupportable, and base all vertical sonorities only on consonance, which, to the extent that grounds for the justification of dissonance are absent, always represents in itself the first principle, the first logical foundation of simultaneity.

We shall see later how, above an explicitly sustained tone of the cantus firmus (and that is the essential difference between the present situation and the ones to be encountered further on), under certain circumstances dissonant sounds as well may occur in passing; but regardless of the outward appearance of such situations, the principle "in the beginning is consonance!" will always hold true without qualification.

Free composition alone can dispense with an actual distinct extension in time of the organizing tone (such as is provided by the cantus firmus in the exercises of the later species) and posit only ideal tones that can be expected to bear the burden of dissonances. Yet these ideal tones certainly are so completely present in our consciousness that they can, in this sense, again be described as actual. First and foremost in free composition it is the scale degrees that have their own secret law of progression (*Harmony*, §76f.), and precisely our intuitive familiarity with that law of progression makes plausible the assumption of those ideal tones that lie outside the realm of actual voice leading.

Regardless of all the freedom of free composition, even there the first principle of the theory of counterpoint—"In the beginning is consonance!"—has practical significance: even in free composition, that which, as dissonance, cannot and may not be substantiated, must be placed upon the foundation of consonance [*FrC.*, §170]. If only the composers of today could at last understand how utopian it is to believe that the nature of our senses could ever grant the dissonance an equal birthright alongside consonance! The two of them, consonance and dissonance, cannot have the same role; that is assured by the basic law of nature in general: never to form a thing twice in the same way!

§3. Why the fourth is prohibited in the vertical direction

Although we have counted as consonances, as they are used by melody in the horizontal plane, the intervals 8, 5, and 4 as perfect, and 3 and 6 as imperfect (*Harmony*, §73 and above, Part 1, Chapter 2, §10), in the vertical direction a single exception must be made. Specifically it is the fourth which here, in the vertical direction, must count as a *dissonance,* and which is therefore prohibited altogether.

The reason for this prohibition is the following. As we learned in Part 1, Chapter 2, §13, the fourth, as a boundary-interval of the harmonic triad, is inferior to the fifth as original boundary-interval in that it is gained only through the artifice of inversion, therefore by a secondary method. As an inverted boundary-interval, it calls attention immediately to the fact that it lacks the perfection of the fifth; moreover, it is the situation of the vertical direction, so essentially different from that of the horizontal line, that causes the lack of perfection suddenly to effect a real distortion, while the same lack in the horizontal direction could not necessitate a prohibition. In the horizontal direction specifically, as mentioned in the passage cited above, the successive occurrence of the melodic tones gives our musical perception time, so to speak, and at least permits us to make the necessary detour by way of the fifth; but in the vertical direction, the simultaneity of attack of the two voices unfortunately simply makes it impossible to sense the corresponding original fifth ahead of time. The simultaneity that characterizes the vertical direction is a *fait accompli* in the face of which we cannot but arrive too late at a perception of the fifth. From this it follows that at the instant in which two tones sound together in the interval of a fourth, just this fact of simultaneity forms an obstacle, and indeed an abrupt one, to any approach to the perfection of the boundary-interval as it is manifested by the fifth, even by way of a detour. Since the effect of perfection (as shown by the fifth) is not to be attained, even after the fact, we can only content ourselves with investigating—at least after the fact—whether the vertical fourth actually strove to represent the inversion of an original fifth and in this sense also to form the boundary-interval, or perhaps something different; for a vertical fourth, just because it is barred from expressing the triadic boundary with absolute clarity—a deficiency which, as we know, must immediately transform the perfect consonance into a dissonance!—, can also represent a suspension or an accented passing tone of dissonant character.

A two-voice model may serve at first to illustrate vividly the uncertainty that attends the vertical fourth: is the fourth [in a given case] the boundary-interval of a triad, as at a in the following example, or a suspension as at b, or an accented passing tone as at c?

Example 152

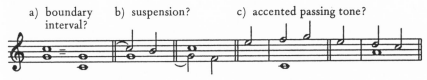

a) boundary interval?   b) suspension?   c) accented passing tone?

To put it differently, the doubt attendant on the vertical fourth about whether it pretends to be an inversion of the fifth and, as such, a perfect consonance, or whether it is merely a suspension or something similar, arises from the following: the simultaneity of the two tones that form the fourth prevents an expression of the character of the boundary-interval (which can also be intrinsic to the fourth) with the same absoluteness and perfection as it is characteristically expressed by the fifth. But here in this new [vertical] situation, where uncertainties about whether the fourth is not perhaps a suspension or the like—uncertainties that were unknown, indeed impossible, in the horizontal direction—, this lesser degree of perfection must at once become the cause that demotes the fourth in this case (but note well: only as an exception!) to the rank of a dissonance.

Conversely, to pursue the problem of the fourth, it follows that the fourth immediately realizes its original potential as a consonance once it is relieved of the pressure of (boundary-interval) competition with the fifth—that is, once its character as a boundary interval at least stands no longer so strongly and exclusively in the foreground. This is the case, for example, when in a setting for three or more voices the fourth does not appear as the lowest interval (in which case the old uncertainty would flare up once again), but rather in the upper voices. For example:

Example 153

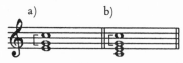

For in this situation, heard upward from the bass, the first effect at a is that of a third, $E - G$, and after it a sixth $E - C$; and at b a third, $C - E$, a fifth, $C - G$, and finally an octave, $C - C$. In no case do the fourths stand any longer in the foreground, least of all as excessively obtrusive boundary intervals.

To put it still another way: the quality of being a dubious boundary-interval of second rank, which attends the fourth even in the cases cited above, is completely redeemed by the more penetrating and more unambigous effects of the intervals formed against the lowest voice.

The deficiency of the fourth as a boundary-interval in comparison with the fifth in this situation, incidentally, is so unobtrusive that even the augmented fourth must be allowed here; for example:

Example 154

—especially in consideration of the fact that the disagreeable juxtaposition of the tones B and F in the same diatony (see *Harmony*, §§17, 18, 58, and 65) makes occasional encounters of the two tones in counterpoint (especially of more than two voices) simply unavoidable.

In free composition, of course, the scale degrees provide a point of reference for quicker and easier orientation regarding the character of the fourth as lowest interval. For example:

Example 155

Haydn, Variations in F Minor

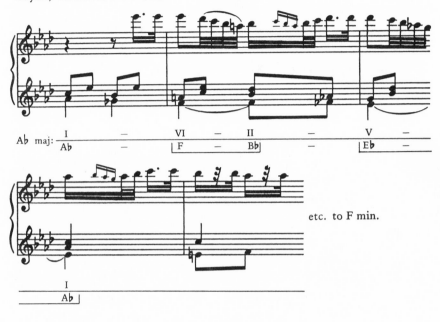

etc. to F min.

Here, specifically, our harmonic sense expects at the second quarter of bar 2 after the F^7 (representing VI) a falling fifth to B♭ (representing II); and even if the latter harmony is expressed only through the inversion with the fourth [i.e., the $\frac{6}{4}$-position]—in other words, less perfectly—, our feeling for scale degrees is nevertheless, by virtue of its logic and strength, fully able to deal quickly with the imperfection of the boundary-interval and with the moment of uncertainty (about whether it actually is a boundary-interval or not), and to decide that here the fourth is intended exclusively as the inversion of the fifth. The same holds true in the following bar with respect to the falling fifth E♭ — A♭ (V — I) at the second quarter, which, in the light of what has preceded, we hear as nothing other than a fifth A♭ — E♭ within the tonic triad [*FrC.*, §§244-245]. Compare *Harmony*, Example 55, bars 3-4, and Example 88, bars 17, 18, and 19!

Obviously the motion of the lowest voice gains fluency precisely by avoiding the fifth-leap at the change of harmony and by taking advantage instead of the $\frac{6}{4}$-position of the new scale degree. Thus the bass is spared the necessity of a strong leap, and it is provided with a more restful movement; and free composition favors the $\frac{6}{4}$-position for reasons of economy also in situations like the following:

Example 156

a) Wagner, *Tristan und Isolde,* Act III

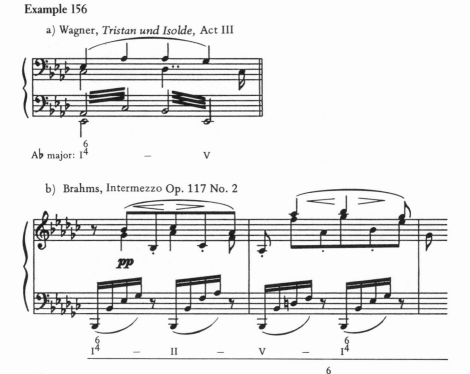

A♭ major: I$^6_4$ —   V

b) Brahms, Intermezzo Op. 117 No. 2

E♭ minor:

Pedal point: I$^6_4$ (followed by VI—II etc.)

Such a procedure must be clearly distinguished, however, from the effect of a $^6_4$-position which is merely an internal component of an organ point: compare *Harmony,* Examples 73, 76, and 81. Finally, it is appropriate here to caution against the misuse of the $^6_4$-chord that is encountered all too often today, in which the intention is merely to keep the bass tone unchanged as long as possible!

Free composition has yet another resource that provides all sorts of benefits to fourths that function as the lowest interval: it adds abstract scale degrees below them, and thereby turns them once again into upper voices [*Counterpoint II (Cpt. II)*, p. 2], as here:

Example 157

Schumann, Piano Quintet Op. 44, I

(l. h.)

*   * *molto cresc.*   *rit.*

Here, scale degree V of E♭—which, incidentally, is made explicit by the two flanking octaves B♭¹ and B♭—consigns the fourths that are apparently the lowest intervals to a higher position, where they move through as permissible passing events above the root B♭.

Although lacking such a clear fundamental tone, similar fourths which appear in the following example are also supported by scale degrees, which our consciousness posits as a foundation for the changes of harmony:

Example 158

J. S. Bach, English Suite No. 6, Gigue

Yet free composition in no way relinquishes the right to make use, under certain circumstances, of the tension that the fourth arouses (exactly as in cantus-firmus exercises) because of its ambiguous nature when it occupies the lowest position; for example:

Example 159

Beethoven, Symphony No. 7, Allegretto

Precisely the doubts caused by the fourth, about whether we are faced here with an inversion of a minor triad on A as scale-degree I or with a freely approached suspension above the root E, as though the continuation would have to be as follows:

Example 160

—just these uncertainties are especially well suited to provide tension in an introduction.

In bar 3 of the following example:

Example 161

Beethoven, Symphony No. 9, I

the logic of scale-degree progression impels us to assume at the second quarter—especially after the raised IV (G♯)—only the V; thus we first want to hear the fourth as a suspension to the third:

But surprisingly, the expected resolution is withheld, in spite of the fact that the double basses in bar 4 have the opportunity to sound the dominant tone once again; instead there follows, at a single stroke, the tonic. Was the fourth not a suspension, then, and was the scale degree to be understood as I rather than V? In any event, it is only the fourth that can pose such riddles when it appears as the lowest interval. As we look at the events in retrospect from the vantage point of the final goal, we cannot deny having heard scale degree V before the tonic, and therefore we must assume an elision of the expected resolution ($^5_{♯3}$); nevertheless it remains true—that is, at least up to the decisive moment—that the tension of the fourth alone was the precondition for our expectation and our deception. (Observe at the same time how Beethoven, at the beginning of the last bar in the above example, tries at least belatedly to satisfy our frustrated expectation of the dominant by means of the two modest thirty-second notes $c\sharp^2$ and d^2; in particular, the $c\sharp^2$, in its tiny slot, sounds like a final parting glance which does not completely succeed in attaining the object of its longing, the harmony of the dominant.

A similarly ingenious construction with a $\frac{6}{4}$-chord in Schumann's *Waldszenen* no. 1, eighth bar from the end, may be compared with this.

In *Fux,* Chapter XVII, p. 38ff., we read:

> Who can fail to see that [Example 162] by no means contains the fourth, but [rather] the fifth and octave? For intervals are to be measured with reference to the bass note [*Grundton*], not the middle components. . . . But if one understands the fourth, which derives from the arithmetic division [see example 163], then I fail to comprehend how such a thing could be included among the consonances.

Example 162

Fux I, 2

Example 163

Fux I, 4

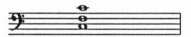

> Anyone [who did so] would have to believe that it was regarded as a consonance by the ancients not only in concept (because the interval originates in the direct division of the octave), but also in practice. I will not dispute it if someone chooses to make this claim; but the practice of so many centuries appears indeed to speak against such a conclusion, and we must proceed in accordance with that practice; because experience now teaches that the employment of the fourth in no way deviates from that of the other dissonances[1] in that it likewise is introduced only as a syncopation or by means of a ligature. The fourth certainly sounds less strident than the other dissonances, and is more tolerable to the ear; yet the sense of hearing is not completely gratified in perceiving the interval, for example:

Example 164

Fux I, 5

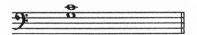

but obviously awaits the arrival of the fifth below:

Example 165

Fux I, 6

With what delicate language Fux pries at the deeply buried mystery of the fourth-turned-dissonance: he refers to the doubt about whether the fourth in the situation under consideration is not merely the inversion of the fifth, a doubt that is held to be the reason the ear still is "not completely gratified." But how insecure and timid the conclusions he draws therefrom!

Let us hear *Bellermann* on the subject (p. 128ff.):

III. In this third class, which stands as though between the consonances and dissonances, we include the perfect fourth and the tritone along with the diminished fifth. As we saw earlier, the first of these, the perfect fourth, as inversion of the perfect fifth, is to be counted among the original intervals, and stands in the simple vibration ratio of 3:4, while the other two intervals originated only indirectly and exhibit the most complex vibration ratios in the diatonic scale (namely 32:45 and 45:64); nevertheless all three will be treated in certain cases to be discussed later as imperfect consonances, and in other cases, in contrast, as authentic dissonances. For the sake of clarity, I shall here discuss the intervals in question individually:

(a) The perfect fourth is always a dissonance in two-voice counterpoint:

Example 166

4   3   4   5

and also in settings of three, four, and more voices when the lower of its two tones is also the lowest of a chord consisting of three, four, or more voices—thus always in the $\frac{6}{4}$-chord, as here:

Example 167

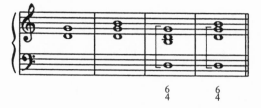

$\begin{smallmatrix}6\\4\end{smallmatrix}$ $\begin{smallmatrix}6\\4\end{smallmatrix}$

It appears as an imperfect consonance, however, when it is produced by two inner or upper voices. If we add to those tonal combinations above [in Example 167] a lower consonant tone, then, the fourth between the inner or upper parts loses its dissonant quality and becomes an imperfect consonance:

Example 168

This phenomenon can be explained as follows: we view the lowest voice of a chord as the basis (*Grund*) upon which the higher voices are constructed, and we measure the [remaining] tones from this basis. Now if we add to a fourth a third, lower tone that is consonant with the two tones of the fourth (thus either the lower octave or the lower sixth of the upper tone of the fourth), then the ear hears in the first case, measuring from the bass, a fifth and an octave, and in the second case a third and a sixth; and the fourth that lies between the upper voices appears to vanish completely.

Such a disappearance of a dissonance through an added bass tone occurs, of course, only in the case of the fourth, which by its very nature is actually a consonance.[2]

Here I interrupt Bellermann and ask, in reference to all of this, just the following: why, then, was the fourth described as a dissonance in two-voice counterpoint? Bellermann appears not to notice that he has in the meantime simply assumed and proclaimed the transformation of the fourth to a dissonant state as a *fait accompli*, without having demonstrated it; and when, in conclusion, he arrives at the statement quoted above that the fourth is "by nature actually a consonance," then his initial principle, "the perfect fourth is always a dissonance in two-voice counterpoint," makes no sense at all. What, then, has Bellermann demonstrated? Nothing except that the fourth ceases to be a dissonance if it is not the lowest interval; but this presupposes that he would have been obliged earlier to demonstrate that the fourth begins to be a dissonance exactly when it occupies the lowest position. Just this, however—the most important thing of all—is missing in Bellermann's discussion of the problem.

Bellermann continues: "It is a different matter, on the other hand, when two upper voices stand in a truly dissonant relationship, for example that of a second or seventh. These intervals, because of their very complex vibration ratios and because they are actually dissonances, can never go unnoticed by the ear." Unfortunately I must interrupt Bellermann again: it is completely unwarranted to make so essential a distinction between a fourth and any other dissonance between the upper voices, since even in cases like these:

Example 169

we hear primarily, in relation to the bass, at a the fourth and fifth rather than the fourth and second, and at b the fourth and third rather than the fourth and seventh.

The truth is, rather, that when a dissonance crops up between two upper voices, such as the second or seventh in the above examples, the dissonant quality of these intervals in the upper voices is due less to their own nature than to the fact that they cannot both be accommodated by the same triad. It is only because a fifth and a fourth cannot both at the same time be components of the same triad that they dissonate against each other in the upper voices as well, and, depending on register, form sometimes a second and sometimes a seventh. But it is clear that this is completely insignificant in comparison to the more important fact that a tone is dissonant precisely in relation to the bass, and in comparison to the question of exactly how it is dissonant with the bass; and thus, in regard to Bellermann's argument, the question remains open of why the fourth is a dissonance only when it is the lowest interval, since it is no longer dissonant when it appears among the upper voices; and there is no point in considering the precise identity of the interval in question, whether consonant or dissonant, whether a fourth, second, or seventh.

Concerning the augmented fourth, finally Bellermann states (p. 129): "the augmented fourth (the tritone), however, together with its inversion, the diminished fifth, both of which will be discussed later, form a characteristic exception to the foregoing observations." And on p. 130:

> (b) The tritone and its inversion, the diminished fifth, were used by the early composers only in rare cases as actual dissonances on the arsis.[3] . . . Between two inner voices, however, or between an inner voice and the upper voice, both intervals occur relatively frequently, and then, like the perfect fourth, they have the rights of an imperfect consonance. The bass tone that accompanies them, however, must stand in a consonant relation to each of their tones. Accordingly, there is but one type of combination in which they are usable, namely:

Example 170

The authors R. *Louis* and L. *Thuille* approach the problem of the fourth as a transient dissonance with incomparably more acute sensitivity in their *Harmonielehre*. We read in §14 (p. 34ff.):

> *Sixth and fourth, in and for themselves, are nothing but undoubtedly consonant intervals; they are such, however, only to the extent and under the condition that they appear in the guise of inversions of the third or fifth respectively.* The reason is that for the ear, which perceives harmonically, it is not the consonant interval that is primary, but the consonant *chord* (the triad). Perfect octave, perfect fifth, and major and minor third are consonant intervals to musicians only because they are constituents of the major or minor triad; the contrary proposition—that the consonance of the major and minor triad might derive from an assemblage of "consonant intervals"—is incorrect.
>
> If harmonic context must always decide whether the intervals of fourth and sixth in a given case are to be regarded as inversions, and therefore as consonant, or as embellishments (suspensions or passing tones), and therefore dissonant, an important distinction between the two intervals is immediately revealed when we compare them with respect to this dual nature that they possess. *In the case*

of the sixth, its interpretation as an interval by inversion is the more plausible, while the fourth, on the contrary, is more easily heard as dissonant than as inversion of a consonant interval. This becomes evident if we consider the two intervals in *isolation.*

If we play a major or minor *sixth,* we immediately hear it as the *inversion* of a minor or major third, thus as an undoubtedly consonant interval. Any different interpretation (perhaps as a suspension preceding a fifth) would have to be forced upon our perception by the context in which the sixth occurred; it would arise only if, for one reason or another, we were to find the first interpretation inadequate. The ear has for the consonant interpretation of the sixth what legal scholars call *praesumtio juris:* the sixth counts as consonant until it is convincingly proven otherwise.

The opposite applies to the perfect fourth. If we hear that interval in and for itself, we do not at first think of the inversion of the fifth; instead, we immediately hear a suspension preceding a (major or minor) third. The harmonic sense *presumes it to be dissonant,* and we admit the consonant interpretation only when the context compels us to do so.

Thus the old controversy of *whether the fourth is to be regarded as a consonance or a dissonance* is definitively settled. On the purely *acoustical* side, the fourth is a *consonance,* and indeed *exclusively* a consonance. But this acoustical concept of consonance is of no concern at all to the *musician* as such. With respect to *harmony,* the fourth can be *either consonance or dissonance,* depending on whether the ear interprets it as inversion of the perfect fifth or as (upper) embellishment to the major or minor third (or possibly also as lower embellishment to the perfect fifth). The characteristic of the musical effect of the fourth, however, resides in the fact that its *interpretation* as embellishment—especially, indeed, in the case of the isolated fourth—is the more *obvious.* This, then, is the reason for the old contrapuntal rule that in *two-voice strict* counterpoint the fourth is always to be treated as a dissonance.[4]

In regard to an interpretation so far superior to, for example, Bellermann's, I am really sorry not to be able to affirm that, as the authors claim, the old controversy has been definitively settled. For just the most profound level at which their interpretation arrives is itself in need of further independent clarification. It is not enough to say that our "harmonic sense presumes the fourth to be dissonant" because "its interpretation as embellishment—especially, indeed, in the case of the isolated fourth—is the more obvious," regardless of the fact that, as the Haydn example [155] above has shown, this presumption is only a conceit which sometimes even vanishes under the strength and overriding power of the scale degrees (which can indeed substitute a different presumption). Just for this reason, the first task would be to explain why one interpretation is more obvious to our perception than the other. That the two authors themselves sensed this basic flaw in their argument is proven best of all by the fact that they sought an answer to the fundamental question. They make this known in a footnote (pp. 36–37):

Treatment of the question of why the fourth and sixth differ so thoroughly in respect to their consonant or dissonant interpretation actually does not belong to the domain of our considerations. Yet it should be indicated at least briefly that here an element enters the picture which indeed does not count as a primary feature (as was believed earlier) but perhaps as an important *secondary* one under certain circumstances for the judgment of consonance and dissonance: specifically, the degree of *agreeability* (that is, of *"euphony"*) of intervals. It can be verified that, all else being equal, an interval will *more readily be heard by the ear as a consonance* the more *euphonious* it is. Now of all the usual consonant intervals, the *perfect fourth* sounds decidedly the *least agreeable*, and in any case far more disagreeable than the major and minor sixth, and this may well be the cause of the difficulty of its interpretation as a consonance.

To this, however, I believe that only the following answer was to be given: only the imperfection of the fourth as a boundary interval should be taken into consideration and cited as the reason the ear must experience doubt about the meaning of a fourth that occurs as the lowest interval—doubt which alone, for an otherwise perfect consonance, would have to suffice in this situation to judge the fourth as dissonant. A discussion of the sixth cited by the authors in this connection, however, is the subject of the following paragraphs.

§4. *More detailed differentiation among the permissible consonances*

The *unison* materializes with full clarity only in counterpoint of two voices—specifically, as the coincidence of two different voices in respect to the absolute as well as relative pitch placement (*Höhe*) of a tone.[5] While it can be accepted in the horizontal direction, if at all, most propitiously in the form of a tone-repetition—and this not in the cantus firmus itself, but, as we shall later see, only in the added voice—, here, in the vertical direction, it is for the first time a real and independent interval, in spite of the fact that it clearly remains foreign to the overtone series.

By contrast it is the overtone series itself that provides valuable implications for practice in regard to the other consonances. (Compare also the pertinent remarks in Part 1, Chapter 2, §§11–15.)

It is the overtone series that affirms that the *octave* is the most perfect interval, since it manifests identity of pitch-class (*Ton*) coupled with differentiation only in pitch (*Höhe*).

After the octave comes the *fifth,* somewhat less perfect at the outset in that it no longer represents merely a repetition of the fundamental but rather sets a new tone against it. Yet this new tone expresses most perfectly a new property—specifically, by forming the ultimate boundary of the triadic jurisdiction (*Dreiklangswirkung*) of its fundamental tone. That is: since the fifth belongs to its fundamental as a boundary in such a way that there is nothing "beyond" it without violating [the properties of] unity and consonance,[6] perfection is achieved in the fifth—albeit in a sense different [from that of the octave]—precisely by virtue of this unsurpassability.

The hierarchy, or valuation, of the perfect consonances, then, is as follows:

(a) 1,
(b) 8,
(c) 5.

Thus from the most perfect identity of pitch-class and specific pitch, as represented by the unison, the path leads to the offspring of the overtone series: to the octave, which, alongside differentiation of pitch, still repeats the pitch-class; and further, to the fifth, which shows differentiation of both pitch and pitch-class, but which on the other hand establishes the final and unsurpassable boundary of consonance in relation to the fundamental.

By virtue of its differentiation of both pitch-class and pitch, the fifth also provides the bridge to the *imperfect consonances:*

(d) 3,
(e) 6.

The imperfect consonances likewise show differentiation of both pitch-class and pitch in relation to their bass notes; but they are distinguished from the fifth in that they are not boundary intervals and therefore are unable to demarcate the harmonic content of a bass note. Rather, they form the content of a triad demarcated by means of a fifth, and therefore it is not possible to determine from these intervals alone the specific triad of which they form the content. For example, does the third at a in Example 171 belong to the triad at b or that at c?

Example 171

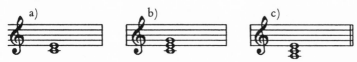

The overtone series, to be sure, presents us with the major *third,* and in this sense it also evokes the assumption that the third $C-E$ of Example 171 might best be counted as part of the fundamental C. Yet it is impossible to do better than such an assumption—especially in the case of the minor third!—and to gain so secure a foundation as for the perfect consonances. The same applies to the *sixth,* except that the latter, unlike the third, is not even ratified by the overtone series itself, but is to be regarded only as the inversion of the third.

We may now be inclined to ask, however, why the sixth, like the fourth, should not be prohibited in two-voice counterpoint because of its simultaneity and the consequences resulting from it; after all, it too is an inversion—namely, of the third.

The answer is this: first, in the case of the sixth the boundary-interval problem does not come into consideration at all, so that the other issue of the detour (specifically, in this case, through the third) is not complicated, as was the case with the fourth, by the more important boundary-interval question. Clearly, the latter issue must be of greater import, because it has the final say regarding the possible consonant content and thereby provides the very *raison d'être* for the third as an interior consonance.

Secondly, the sixth, like the third, is only an imperfect consonance, and, as such, is by origin less sensitive in every respect than the perfect fourth. That is, while the fourth (see §3 above) possesses such purity and perfection that any mutation causes it to slip immediately into a state of dissonance (diminished or augmented fourth), the imperfection of the third makes it more tolerant. Both major and minor thirds retain their character as consonances; precisely for this reason, the process of inversion must cause less damage in the case of these intervals. Indeed, one might say that the imperfection of the third does not suffer when, by inversion into a sixth, it becomes even a degree more imperfect.

For two-voice counterpoint, then, the practical use of both imperfect consonances, all intrinsic differences between them notwithstanding, is permitted without restriction, even if for the purposes of doubling in three- or four-voice counterpoint, as we shall see later, the third, for the reason just presented, is in principle accorded that priority over the sixth [Part 4, Chapter 1, §1] which is its due as a better interval.

Finally it should be stressed here that the inversions under consideration, the fourth and the sixth, are to be understood only in the sense of the voice leading of contrapuntal practice—thus in contrast to the inversions taught by the theory of harmony in an abstract way relative to the meanings of scale degrees. Thus it is entirely inappropriate for the theory of harmony, in presenting the chord of the $\frac{6}{4}$, to abjure the fourth as a dissonance. Rather, it is the task of harmonic theory merely to elucidate the phenomenon in question purely conceptually first of all as a possible derivative of another, fundamental and original, phenomenon, with which the $\frac{6}{4}$-chord in that case must share the position and significance of a scale degree.

Thus the theory of harmony, to return to the Haydn passage in §3 above, Example 155, has only to teach that the $\frac{6}{4}$-chords in bars 2 and 3, to the extent that they represent inversions (in accord with the demands of the scale degrees) rather than suspensions, do indeed form inversions of the triads on B♭ and A♭ respectively, and therefore share with those triads the significance of scale degrees.

After the foregoing observations on the sixth (cf. §3), I must, therefore, respond here to Messrs. *Louis* and *Thuille* that, whatever presumption one may have about the sixth, it is not permissible to view that interval as turning into a dissonance, not even when it occurs in the form of a suspension. There exist, indeed, consonant syncopations and suspensions (see Chapter 4), and this may be the best point of departure for judging the different natures of fourth and sixth: only because the fourth is otherwise perfect, it must become really dissonant once it no longer has that perfection, as is the case in two-voice counterpoint when it appears as the lowest interval. The sixth, however, even when it is no longer an inversion but rather a suspension, still retains its character as a consonance—an imperfect consonance to be sure, which, incidentally, is what it has been from the very beginning. Therefore it is at least insufficiently cautious when the cited authors write: "The sixth counts as consonant until it is convincingly proven otherwise."

§5. *The three types of relative motion of voices*

Two voices can move in any of three different ways in relation to one another; specifically:

1. *Similar motion (motus rectus)*, where both move in the same direction—that is, both upward or both downward; for example:

Example 172

2. *Contrary motion (motus contrarius)*, where the voices proceed in different directions; for example:

Example 173

And finally,

3. *Oblique motion (motus obliquus)*, where one voice sustains, while the other moves in either direction; for example:

Example 174

§6. *The prohibition of similar motion to perfect consonances in two-voice counterpoint*

The consonances unison, octave, and fifth *must not be approached by similar motion in the exercises of two-voice counterpoint.*

The restriction applies in two-voice writing—and *only* there—to *all cases*, regardless of whether the preceding interval is (1) another perfect consonance or (2) an imperfect consonance.

In the first case, incidentally, it makes no difference whether the two perfect consonances have the same name, as here:

Example 175

etc.

or different names, as here:

Example 176

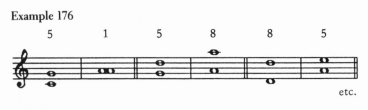

In the second group, obviously, no such distinction exists:

Example 177

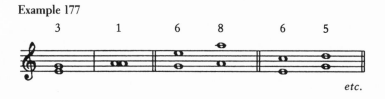

Moreover, within the exercises of two-voice counterpoint, even in examples of *contrary* motion such as:

Example 178

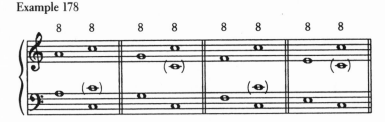

or:

Example 179

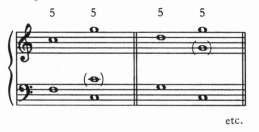

the inversional character of the fourth- and sixth-leaps (cf. Part 1, Chapter 2, §§13 and 15) is set in sharper relief in accordance with the ear's heightened sensitivity, just here in the realm of two-voice writing, to ways of approaching perfect consonances. (The reasons for this sensitivity will be discussed in the following paragraphs.) Add to this the fact that, as a result, our instinctual sense of the original intervals (fifth and third rather and fourth and sixth) compels us to translate the contrary motion back into simple parallel motion as shown, and it follows that at least in the exercises of two-voice counterpoint we should avoid even such contrary motions (which are known as *antiparallels*) to perfect consonances. Such avoidance is facilitated by the fact that a moderate distance between the voices, so long as it is actually observed (see §24 below), will exclude any opportunity for such antiparallels, which, as Examples 178 and 179 show, require such a large separation.

§7. On the nomenclature of the prohibited similar motions

Because, as I shall presently show, the old theory unfortunately misunderstood the true reason for the prohibition, it characterized the cases in Example 175 as *"open"* octave- or fifth-successions, in contrast to all others (those in Example 176 as well as in Example 177), which it designated *"hidden"* successions. At the outset let us agree at least that instead of a variable nomenclature—one speaks, for example, of "parallels" in general, of "similar" and "unequal-similar" motion, and finally, most frequently, of "open" and "hidden" successions—it is perhaps most correct (if, unfortunately, not also shortest) for the sake of consistency to speak only of *parallel* unisons, octaves, or fifths, and (in preference to "hidden" successions) of *nonparallel similar motion* (which is understood as referring to progression to the unison, octave, or fifth).

I say "for the sake of consistency" because in the case of so-called hidden successions it is very misleading to speak of actually "parallel" motion, a designation which, in the strictest sense, correctly applies only to the "open" successions.

But one could, while completely avoiding the older nomenclature, speak of "similarly-named unison-, octave-, or fifth-successions" and (instead of nonparallel similar motion) of "similar nonparallels."

§8. The reasons for the prohibition of similar motion to the perfect consonances in general

The prohibition of similar motion to the perfect consonances in exercises of two-voice counterpoint is based in general on several discernibly different but simultaneously operative reasons:

First, the nature of the perfect consonances (as emphasized in §4 of this chapter), which is to provide either identity of tone or boundary of the harmonic content;

Second, the character of similar motion in general and how it differs from oblique and contrary motion; and finally

Third, the original meaning of polyphony in general,

to which it should be added that in individual cases sometimes one and sometimes another of these factors will predominate.

The first factor, which concerns the *harmonic boundary,* has already been discussed.

The second factor, *similar motion,* is to be interpreted in its psychological effect as a kind of agreement between the two voices to strive toward a common goal; in this respect it contrasts with oblique and contrary motion, whose differentiation of direction acts, conversely, to rule out such agreement.

The third and last of the points mentioned implies that if *two-voice* counterpoint is to have any meaning at all, the second voice, like the first, must be individual—that is, must have an independent course.

To make clear the application of the above rules to specific cases, I now proceed to investigate them in order, beginning with the parallel successions.

§9. *Unison- and octave-parallels (1 — 1 and 8 — 8)*

The exclusion of unison- and octave-parallels as successions of the two unisons or octaves rests mainly on the third reason cited above—that is, on the simple understanding that the added counterpoint must never be a mere repetition of the first voice, whether in unisons or in octaves.

It is self-evident, however, that the other reasons also support this restriction.

§10. *Fifth-parallels (5 — 5)*

With fifth-parallels, however, I believe that the first two reasons stand in the foreground.

To find ample cause for this restriction, one need only consider the effect of a direct transition from one harmonic entity so explicitly bounded as a fifth to another equally bounded entity, especially in two-voice counterpoint, where, in the interest of stronger motivation [to move forward] (about which more detail will be provided in §22), any such boundedness is to be avoided wherever possible. So far the first reason.

If the fifth is approached through oblique or contrary motion, as for example:

Example 180

then, at least, it sounds as though the two voices have arrived at the undesirably bounded entity of the fifth merely by accident, so to speak. Such a coincidence is less propitious, however—and this is the second aspect—in the case of similar motion, which (see §8 above) here can only signify completely conscious pursuit of that faulty succession of undesirably bounded entities.

But why would the voices be allowed, above all as matter of general principle, to seek out consciously a fault of this kind?

§11. *Nonparallel similar motion to perfect consonances*

Similar motion, which we have just interpreted as the common agreement of two voices to strive toward a common goal, and have therefore recognized as the compromising element that contributes to the prohibition of parallel perfect consonances, operates in an equally compromising manner for non-parallel similar progressions to perfect consonances—thus, for similar motion from non-unisons, non-octaves, and non-fifths to unisons, octaves, and fifths.

To invoke here the older terminology of so-called "open" and "hidden" successions—interpreting it differently, to be sure, from the way it was originally conceived—we could say that through similar motion even the so-called hidden succession is really turned once again into an open one: "open," however, only in the sense of the agreement, made manifest through similar motion, of both voices to reach the same goal.

Nonparallel similar progressions, then, like the true parallels, remain categorically forbidden in two-voice counterpoint.

But if similar motion contributes to the bad sound and resulting inadmissibility of non-parallel similar progressions in two-voice counterpoint, it is nevertheless completely unnecessary to give credence to that older theory which tried, in a manner most complicated and at the same time naive, to reduce the "hidden" successions to "open" ones in order to exclude them. The older theory[7] labored under the delusion of the need to fill in the leap of the one voice with a so-called diminution, so that a tone appeared which then actually formed an open succession with the other voice:

Example 181

The designation "hidden" succession has to do with the fact that therein a true "open" succession was allegedly concealed. Such a glaring hiatus between the artistically correct perception of a necessary prohibition, and a grotesque and forced justification of correct instinct!

The interpretation was so contrived that it has long been easy to make fun of its unnaturalness.[8] But what was the point of ridicule without the proposal of a more satisfactory explanation, which would have been accompanied by a more satisfactory nomenclature? Certainly, it appeared easiest of all simply to rescind altogether the prohibition of hidden progressions (as has been done in many quarters)—a solution that would necessarily have eliminated the question of nomenclature. But artistic instinct, which always felt the need for the prohibition, has proven correct to this day, and all that can be done about it—which certainly is so very difficult—is to formulate the artistically correct reason for it in convincing language.

§12. *Refutation of the claim that octave- and fifth-parallels manifest the same doubling-principle*

The attribution of such special reasons for the injunction in two-voice counterpoint against octave- and unison-parallels on the one hand, and fifth-parallels on the other, must here, however, be more precisely grounded from the *historical* standpoint as the definitive solution of the problem of parallel motion.

As is well known, the first experiments of polyphonic music began with the addition to a given melody of parallel motion precisely in fourths and fifths (so-called *organum*). From this one might be tempted to conclude that the poor effect of extended fifth-successions had been perhaps only a conceit of later epochs, since in earlier ones, as is historically documented, a contrary practice was doubtless the norm.

The actual fact, however, is different. In that early period there existed as yet no artistic experience of polyphony whose correct interpretation would have been the only possible basis for a true theory of art—theory, indeed, can only follow art, interpreting and abstracting—; therefore theory, or what was at that time considered theory, had on the contrary to establish the first guidelines for practice. And since theory was certain that the fifth is a perfect consonance, it was naive enough to set as a guideline the simple doubling of the melody in fifths or fourths: can perfection upon perfection (so theory reflected) produce anything other than a perfect effect? Thus the practice of organum was based on fifth-successions, which could be called actual fifth-doublings—"doublings" specifically in the same sense in which we speak today of octave "doublings." But the teachings of theory in this respect were soon revealed to be completely inartistic and flawed, for the specific reason that theory, trapped as it was in its purely speculative view of the perfection of the fifth, had no artistic notion that value and beauty of effect in the combination of voices issued from sources other than merely those of perfect intervals. And when the practice of the ensuing period in fact—partly perhaps in the mere quest for variety, but also partly from correct artistic instinct—began to mix thirds and sixths into the setting along with fifths and fourths, it was the contrast of the intervals, emerging for the first time, which exposed their true nature in the service of voice leading. Exactly the contrast to thirds and sixths made composers notice how bounded in effect was the sound of the fifth—even a single fifth, but especially in a succession of fifths! And also, contrariwise, how the fifth revealed the nature of the third and sixth—specifically the fact that they, far from lending a bounded quality to the sound, rather, through their equivocality (*Mehrdeutigkeit*), provided the stimulus for forward motion. And just here, in the hustle-and-bustle of thirds, sixths, and fifths, it was gradually recognized how detrimental it would be merely on the basis of the fifth's perfection to forget about its boundary effect in counterpoint itself, and how little the fifth is therefore suited to fill out the counterpoint by successive usage—that is, fifth by fifth—and to "double" in fifths. Finally a freshened sensitivity led to the insight that if the fifth provides the boundary of the sound, this effect, which is certainly unwelcome in the contrapuntal setting, at least should *not* be produced by *similar* motion—that is, through mutual agreement of both voices. And thus there arose the restriction—a kind of "rule of battle" for the warring thirds, sixths, and fifths—that in two-voice counterpoint the fifth should not be approached in similar motion. Through this well-grounded fifth-restriction—its first written formulation can perhaps be ascribed to Johannes de Muris in the fourteenth century—expression was given once and for all to the artistic awareness that a succession of fifths could never again be understood and heard from the standpoint of mere "doublings"; that rather, whether for purposes of explanation and justification or only with the aim of cultivating better hearing, only the standpoint of voice leading—and, to be sure, a thoroughly concrete voice leading *(reelle Stimmführung)*—is to be given consideration.

There are, then, no true fifth-"doublings" (however much the external appearance of the music may suggest their presence); but there are, on the other hand, doublings in unisons and octaves. One must therefore altogether avoid such terminology in relation to fifths, if only to protect the ear from incorrect ways of hearing. Thus even in a case like the following often-cited one by Beethoven:

Example 183

Beethoven, Piano Sonata Op. 53, I

or, to mention a still more pungent example, in the following case:

Example 184

Chopin, Mazurka Op. 30 No. 4

Example 184 *continued*

one must not speak of mere fifth-"doublings"; and we will see later in which manner such voice leadings were arrived at by the composer and are to be understood by the listener.

It is highly regrettable that the lesson which so clearly teaches to artists and theorists the development of our art has not (unfortunately!) been better understood in its essence. In particular, the milieu of the first prohibition has been overlooked—that is, the fact that the experiences which had to lead to the prohibition first occurred in the domain of a counterpoint of actually only two voices, and in a terrain where the setting, though free composition, resembled very closely a primitive exercise in our two-voice [strict] counterpoint. Only in two-voice vocal counterpoint could the effects of the parallels be perceived at all in their absolute purity, and thus, on the contrary—and this precisely is the important point of the historical experience!—the prohibition, with its absolute stringency and its true justification, applied only to two-voice counterpoint. By no means is one allowed, however, to evaluate also the later polyphony in exercise and in free composition with reference to the prohibition that rightly applies first of all only to the bicinium of free composition of that [early] epoch, and thereby discover contradictions where none existed.

It redounds to the credit of M. *Hauptmann* that he provides at least an inkling of the truth in his *Harmonik und Metrik:* "The reason for the poor effect . . . is not the same in the two cases [of octaves and fifths]: the *fifth*-succession lacks unity of harmony, and the *octave*-succession variety of melody."[9] The best feature of this formulation without doubt is the recognition that the reasons for the prohibition of fifth- and octave-parallelisms are indeed different. It should be noted, however, that the "unity of harmony" mentioned in connection with fifth-successions is an empty phrase. Although apparently pointing in the right direction, the expression goes too far, since a voice leading such as the following:

Example 185

could also be criticized for its lack of unity of harmony. Hauptmann undoubtedly sensed the harmonic boundary provided by the fifth, but was himself unable to give more felicitous expression to that perception. In addition, like all theorists, he commits the fundamental error of testing the reasons for the prohibition applicable to two-voice counterpoint just in the domain of free composition, where they have long since ceased to be operative in a pure and unmodified form.

So much more regrettable, then, is the regression by *H. Riemann*, who has recently propagandized in favor of regarding the reasons for the prohibition of parallel successions as exactly the same for both octaves and fifths.[10] He states expressly: "Octave-parallels, as a denial of the independence of the voices, are unstylistic and false; fifth-parallels too are faulty *for the same reason*." Further on, he elucidates more precisely:

> A voice that repeatedly presents the octave-tones of the other voice is only a reinforcement of the sound of that second voice; it is not a different voice. And a voice that moves in *parallel fifths* or twelfths with a second voice *also* still blends much too completely with the latter to be regarded as an independent voice.

Thus, in order to account for the fifth-prohibition by the same reason as for the octave, he formulates the hypothesis—attractive in itself—of several different degrees of blending, according to which he attributes to the octave the strongest, to the fifth what might be called an intermediate (note the expression "still blends much too completely"), and to the third—the major third of course—the weakest degree of blending. Concerning the third, he says: "The fifth overtone, the tone that produces the third, is too weak in sound for us to overlook its independent production [in polyphonic contexts] and perceive parallel thirds too as mere doubling."

As is evident, he bases the hypothesis on the phenomenon of the overtone series, which, incidentally, he clearly acknowledges: "The auxiliary voices on the organ give obvious proof that sonic reinforcement throughout entire compositions by means of parallel octaves, twelfths, and in general all pipes that correspond to the overtones is possible and of good effect." And thus he arrives at the following statement:

> But certainly neither parallel octaves nor parallel fifths sound bad in themselves; therefore intentional octave-doublings (sonic reinforcement by added octaves) are always good and completely permissible in orchestral writing, but they lie completely outside the domain of counterpoint in four real voices; reinforcement by parallel fifths (or twelfths), too, is not infrequent in full-textured keyboard [playing] or in full orchestral writing, but it is never to be regarded as real voice leading.

There we have it, then. Even parallel fifths, according to Riemann, are scarcely anything other than tonic reinforcement (like the octave), a doubling voice, so to speak, as in mixture stops on the organ.

This would take us back to the beginning [of art], and all evolution in artistic practice and, following it, artistic theory since the establishment of the prohibition of parallels would prove to be completely misunderstood! And all of this stems only from the fact that the origin of the prohibition, as history teaches it, was not grasped in its relationship to musical phenomena. Riemann too is naive enough to try to understand this prohibition as completely absolute; he too claims that it must either be enforced or be rescinded in an absolute fashion. Since this position, however, will obviously have to founder on the contradictions inherent in the differences of situation (i.e. the distinction between two-voice counterpoint as opposed to that of three or more voices, as well as between an exercise and free composition), it is understandable that Riemann speaks vaguely and timidly in part of orchestral and full-textured keyboard writing, and in part of school exercises, and thus—by constantly shifting the foundation of the prohibition—is all the more unable to arrive at a definitive solution, but instead offers only a formulation that is itself so much more in need of clarification:

> Even in cases of parallel fifths, today we are more permissive and allow them to pass by without admonition if they are covered up by means of contrary motion or dissonances—that is, if the ear is compensated for the decrease in textural richness (for the parallel voice disappears, so to speak, for the duration of the parallel motion) by alternative sources of interest. Parallel fifths between real voices, however, remain a stylistic error under all circumstances; they are to be banned without exception from all school exercises. If the teacher neglects to develop and intensify the natural sensitivity in his young charges for such offenses against purity of counterpoint, he must not be surprised if they completely run amok.

Such a miserably confused and at the same time naive muddle! In school exercises the student is to avoid successions of perfect fifths—because (so Riemann claims) they are, like octave-successions, merely reinforcements. Elsewhere than in school exercises, however—specifically in free composition—, according to Riemann, "parallel fifths between real voices" indeed remain under all circumstances a "stylistic error," yet the composer may use them as a "reinforcement" and only as such. Doesn't the truly most important issue still need clarification by Riemann? He would have to explain the following: first, how exactly it could be determined whether a given case represented a well motivated "reinforcement" or only a true and unintentional contrapuntal and "stylistic" error (this is the point most often addressed in assessments by critics!); second, how it happens that reinforcements with fifths occur so relatively infrequently in comparison to those with octaves; and finally, third, how to reconcile with the license of fifth-reinforcements the far greater number of [parallel] fifth-successions that Riemann himself would never describe as mere reinforcements, but which he would nevertheless tend to judge in a more "permissive" way and "allow to pass without admonition" (compare the above quotation).

Are there, then, perfect fifth-successions of a different nature, successions that are permitted and do not fall within the purview of the principal criterion of the intermediate degree of blending? Are those exceptions, one must ask? Or do they lie within the purview of a different criterion? If so, then why has Riemann applied the criterion of mere doubling [valid for octave-successions] also to fifth-successions? If there are open fifth-parallelisms that are permitted and are not to be considered doublings, what is the point of the prohibition at all? Or, if all parallel fifth-successions are permitted in free composition anyway, isn't the prohibition in the last analysis really only a form of intimidation, whose sole purpose to make students quake (such naive method!) before the supremacy of the "prohibiting" teacher?

To what should Riemann's student adhere when he turns his efforts to free composition? To the prohibition or to the license—where both fundamental situations are so indefinitively defined?

But Riemann's error lies not only in having represented fifth-successions as "doublings," in spite of the fact that he himself incautiously quotes different types of fifth-successions that are said not to be doublings, and that accordingly he ignores the history of the beginnings of polyphony, which has long been able to forestall the reappearance of such a false and discredited interpretation. Of far greater detriment in his case, rather, is the ignorance of purely artistic and psychological perceptions, and the forcible imposition upon art of natural phenomena—here, in particular, once again the results of the overtone series. In *Harmony* (§§10, 19, etc.) I have already called attention to the unfortunate consequences that necessarily accompany the effort to abstract art in its total content only from the overtone series. I called instead for an understanding that nature's suggestion, as it is found in the overtone series, was taken over by artists only up to a certain limit, while from that limit forward they have, with complete originality, worked out artistic elements to which they [alone] hold title—elements which then, certainly, once again flow back into nature, but only at the very end and only in the most exalted sense.[11] Riemann's error lies completely exposed precisely here, where, in his treatment of the parallel-fifths prohibition, he again takes refuge in the overtone series in order to derive the concept of blending-gradation mentioned above. For if the overtones really are only components of an indivisible sonority, and if, therefore, the [tones comprised by the] sounds known as organ mixtures are in this sense once again only elements of a single tone and can claim no independent existence whatever—their dependency is expressed already in the terms "over-," "partial-," or "aliquot-tones"—, then it is clear that that palpable tone which the contrapuntal voice places against the cantus firmus as fifth (or as octave or third) is never truly identical to such an overtone. Rather, the tone of the contrapuntal voice in itself represents another independent tone-phenomenon that carries its own overtones on its back, so to speak, exactly like the cantus-firmus tone against which it sounds ("an unhappy Atlas, who must carry a world, a whole world" of overtones).[12] Each of the two tones is, accordingly, an independent tone—the cantus-firmus tone as well as that of the counterpoint, which forms the fifth; both have their own overtones, absolutely necessary to their tone-production—two infinite columns of tones, so to speak, which are completely different and fundamentally have nothing in common. Consider too the fact that even octave doublings, which according to Riemann manifest the strongest degree of blending quality, nevertheless always signify once again only an encounter of two completely independent voices, and that the independence of the octave-tone is sensed clearly not only in orchestral writing but also—we need only think of couplings—on the organ itself. There is, therefore, a quite essential difference between the organ mixture, which is completely integrated into the sound of a single tone, and an incarnate, independent tone which, activating its own mixture, sets itself against the cantus-firmus tone as a fifth. For if the fifth in the added voice were little more than an organ mixture—the third overtone of the cantus-firmus tone—, then it would be possible to heap upon a given tone a whole world of the most indefinable tones under the label of mere reinforcement, and still expect the sound of the counterpoint to follow a satisfactory course. In short, one should be able to copy literally what the overtone series prescribes (thus [for example] the ninth and fifteenth partials as well), and the voices would nevertheless have to produce only the effect of doubling! And yet, as I see it, such a reinforcement-mannerism and -mania would even offend much more acutely than the modern mannerism of alleged polyphony, which already produces a ghastly state of chaos. Taking its unfair advantage only from a frenetic and obfuscating tempo and, to no lesser degree, also from a misconception of the passing [dissonance], that polyphony already burdens almost every tone with a seventh—but, note well, the seventh that belongs to the [tonal] system, thus a phenomenon completely different from the seventh partial. (See *Harmony*, §10). Yet this procedure does not, as one would have to expect on the basis of the theory [of Riemann] discussed above, represent itself as mere "reinforcement," but rather, haughtily and pretentiously, as true voice leading, in short: "polyphony." While the error of the modern artist, who unfortunately has only a decayed instinct left for his creative work, can often be demonstrated to be bad, I mean objectively bad—for example, in its overestimation of the capacity of a scale degree or failure to understand the technique of the passing tone, etc. (cf. *Harmony*, §89)—, it would be impossible, in spite of one's complete distaste for it, to fend off a way of composing which, invoking nature or the overtone series, moved in the most bizarre doublings.

Although the tone of the added voice which relates to the cantus-firmus tone as its octave or fifth is therefore not *identical* to the second or third partial, the consonant relationship of the two independent tones, and accordingly the specific quality of the resulting consonance (i.e., that of the octave or the fifth), nevertheless rests on the foundation of the overtone series, albeit in a sense different from that assumed by Riemann. With all of the independence of the two tones forming the octave or fifth—each tone carrying the bequest of its own world of overtones—, it is none other than Nature who confirms, according to the standard established by the meaning of octave and fifth within the overtone series, their consonant relationship and its character. In other words: since the second partial represents identity of pitch-class together with differentiation of pitch, while the third partial yields the last tonal boundary (*Grenzton*) of the comprehensible consonant space[13] in the form of a tone that differs in both pitch and pitch-class, this characteristic is preserved even when one completely independent tone sounds against another in such a way that either (1) identity of pitch-class together with differentiation of pitch, or (2) a final consonance-boundary together with differentiation of pitch-class is produced. Or, to quote the presentation in *Harmony*, p. 29, §14:

> To the question: Which two tones are most naturally related? Nature has already given her answer. If G, for example, has revealed itself as the most potent overtone emanating from the root tone C, the potency and privilege of this close relationship is preserved also in those cases where, in the life of a composition, C meets G as an independent root tone: the ancestor, so to speak, recognizes the descendant. We shall call this primary and most natural relationship between two tones the *fifth-relationship*.

It remains to be mentioned that Riemann uses the hypothesis of blending-gradations also to support the prohibition of antiparallels, as follows:

> The prohibition of octave- and fifth-successions must, however, be generalized and sharpened by comparison to the formulation in which it has been handed down to us; for since unison, octave, and double-octave are not significantly distinguished from one another with respect to degree of blending quality, and since the same holds true of fifth and twelfth, all motions from the unison or octave to the double-octave and vice versa:

Example 186

are to be prohibited as contradicting the independence of the voices; and the same applies to all motions from the fifth to the twelfth and vice versa (including also the octave-expansion of the twelfth, i.e., the 19th):

Example 187

Unfortunately Riemann succeeded in intimidating later theorists as well, and thus the *Harmonielehre* by R. Louis and L. *Thuille* already contains the suggestion of at least a compromise between the points of view of Hauptmann and Riemann. There, on p. 376, we read:

> If it were therefore decided to accept the Riemann explanation of the poor effect of parallel fifths as such, we nevertheless consider it necessary to invoke the Hauptmann viewpoint at least as an auxiliary theory if we want to be able to evaluate the actual occurrence of parallel fifths in a harmonic context. Accordingly, the prohibition might be formulated thus: because of the high degree of blending quality of their intervallic relationship, parallel perfect fifths (as also, to a lesser extent, parallel major thirds) *can under certain circumstances* produce a very poor effect. This will happen, specifically, if this type of progression occurs in the direct succession of two chords that bear no mediating relationship to one another [etc.].[14]

To summarize all of the foregoing, we find that as errors in the theoretical justification of the prohibition of parallel fifths, the following should be cited: (1) misunderstanding of the initial artistic experiments in contrapuntal writing that led to the prohibition—that is, the thoroughly inadequate appreciation of the fact that the prohibition originally arose in the domain of counterpoint for only two voices, where it indeed still remains in full force up to the present time; and, finally, (2) evaluation of free composition in terms of prohibitions that originally apply only to exercise-situations.

With our discovery of the fact that the prohibition of parallel octaves and that of parallel fifths stem from two entirely different causes, which can be evident in their full purity only in two-voice counterpoint, we have indeed accomplished all that is necessary for the time being for the first species of two-voice counterpoint. We shall, however, following our established custom, [now] provide a deeper glimpse into counterpoint of more than two voices as well as into free composition, and illuminate how the situations that occur in both affect the application of the prohibition. Nevertheless, we shall of course initially proceed in this only so far as is necessary to understand the problem in a general way, and therefore reserve a more detailed treatment for the proper occasions.

§13. First introduction concerning the influence of strict counterpoint in more than two voices on the prohibition of similar motion

The birthplace of the problem is, as we have seen, two-voice counterpoint. The latter calls attention for the first time to the inevitable consequence that (1) the succession of two unisons or octaves destroys the character of the added counterpoint as an independent voice, and (2) the succession of two fifths means an unpleasant clash of two entities that are harmonically bounded with the same degree of severity. Two-voice counterpoint reveals, moreover, that these effects are caused not by the nature of perfect consonances alone, but also by [the quality of] similar motion as such. Now it would certainly not make sense, just as we are striving to learn how one voice is to be led *independently* against another, to seek out at the same time effects that eliminate this independence or even impair the good simultaneous sound of the two voices. Therefore it is fully in order for the theory of *two-voice* counterpoint, striving to reconcile intent and result first of all in the proper domain of its *two-voice* exercises, to establish the prohibition discussed above just in this area—and this, to be sure, without discriminating between whether the progression to the perfect consonance takes place in parallel motion or only in nonparallel similar motion.

If one knows, however, that this prohibition is to be understood only as a product of the intent and the situations of two-voice counterpoint, then one will naturally avoid from the outset the error (already censured in the foregoing paragraphs) of regarding the prohibition also as an absolute one—that is, as a prohibition which, outside the domain of two-voice counterpoint, would also invariably have to regulate multiple-voice counterpoint as well as free composition. It will be found, on the contrary, that more complex situations, to the extent that they demand their own solutions, cannot satisfy the stringency of that prohibition; especially when the new factors that enter in such situations also introduce exigencies that far more urgently need satisfaction.

Thus even three-voice [strict] counterpoint—here I bypass for the moment the situations encountered in the second, third, and fourth species of two-voice counterpoint with their new differentiations—must at least in principle admit the nonparallel similar motions (the so-called hidden progressions) if it is to accomplish its central purpose of setting *two* voices against the cantus firmus in a state of true melodic independence. For, often enough, melodic fluency of the line itself (as precisely the chief characteristic of such independence of voices) will doubtless require that the voice include in its path exactly a tone with which such a nonparallel similar motion is associated. Thus, from the standpoint of the higher law of independence, it will be altogether appropriate to include nonparallels into the bargain, especially as their poor effect surely recedes into the background in the face of the increased prominence of the effect achieved precisely by means of the good line. We shall see later (Part 3, Chapter 1, §22)—just to give at this point a preliminary glimpse—how in three-voice counterpoint various factors produce altogether new, stronger effects, which under certain circumstances are able to suppress the effect—always poor in itself—of nonparallel similar motion. Such factors include: (1) satisfaction of the requirements of melodic fluency in the form of smaller intervals (best of all the smallest, the second); (2) emphasis on contrary motion [of the voice not involved in the similar motion]; and finally (3) the advantage provided by a rich-sounding, complete triad.

Four-voice counterpoint, in turn—and, to be sure, again by reason of the really numerous and new difficulties attendant on the increased number of voices—, necessarily must admit nonparallel similar motions even under circumstances in which three-voice counterpoint still adheres strictly to their prohibition. Four-voice writing brings with it as an inevitable consequence the necessity that nonparallel similar motion be subject to still less stringent limitations than those required by three-voice counterpoint.

But contrapuntal doctrine does not admit at the same time into its environs also parallel motion of unisons, octaves, and fifths. These instead remain prohibited, always and everywhere, in both three- and more-voiced strict counterpoint, and, indeed, by reason of the effects cited earlier, which other factors of the setting remain too weak to cancel completely under the given limited circumstances of the cantus firmus.

Finally, it may not be uninteresting to mention here that the prohibition of all similar motions to perfect consonances remains from the outset so completely tailored to the first species of two-voice counterpoint that one could (assuming that one wished to) dispense, for this first species, with any further conceptual differentiation among the prohibited similar motions.[15] For, as is evident, it is at bottom only the situations of the other species of two-voice counterpoint—for complete clarity, however, those of three- and four-voice counterpoint (still leaving free composition out of consideration)—which, to the extent that they already tolerate and even require a certain type of similar motion to perfect consonances, now compel the theorizing artist for the first time to put a notch, in the form of a first conceptual differentiation, into this prohibition that originates in two-voice counterpoint and continues to apply there without exception. Thus, what was not at all necessary in the first species of two-voice counterpoint automatically becomes, in subsequent species, a necessity created by the new situations, so that fundamentally one would have to draw the boundary between actual parallels and merely nonparallel similar motion in the second species of two-voice counterpoint at the earliest, so as to carry the two types forward from that point on as permanent categories of similar motion.

But also apart from any particular method of systematic presentation of this problem, it nonetheless remains of essential significance for the understanding and evaluation of the prohibition to grasp the facts of the matter as outlined above: specifically, that the first species of two-voice counterpoint has established the prohibition in its domain as absolute, and that the differentiation of the prohibition enters the scene organically only with the differentiation of situations.

§14.   First glimpse of the status of the prohibition in free composition

Dispensation for the use of even parallel successions finally enters only in the realm of free composition [*FrC.*, §161].

Specifically, in free composition the changing character of the voice, whose contrast with the continuously bound real voice of the contrapuntal exercise will be demonstrated in detail in the last section,[16] has as an attendant consequence the fact that in order (for example) to be able to regulate the number of voices freely and at will, sometimes even parallel octaves become fully a necessity.

Concerning parallel fifths, among the forces that can successfully counteract the poor effect of nonparallel similar motion even in strict counterpoint are the principles of contrary motion, melodic fluency, and completeness of triads. In free composition, these factors are joined by others: the progression of scale-degrees and variation of [foreground] key areas are the strongest forces which, either alone or, better still, in conjunction with the forces mentioned above, can completely remove the harmful effect of even parallel fifths.

To put it differently: precisely by reason of the tonal identity present in the unison and octave, free composition uses octave- and unison-parallelism, for example as so-called "reinforcing voices" (which at the same time reduces the number of voices), and so forth. Moreover, free composition can also—but note well: always only under the rubric of concrete voice-leading![17]—use fifth-parallelisms in abundance, by virtue of the fact that it successfully counters them with new and stronger forces still unavailable in the exercises of strict counterpoint.

Obviously, under such circumstances in free composition the nonparallel similar successions, as well as antiparallels, gain still greater freedom than they already had in three- and four-voice counterpoint.

Considering the end result, however, that free composition is, under certain circumstances, in a position to dispense entirely with the prohibition not only of nonparallel similar motion but even of parallels and antiparallels, it seems all the more curious that the prohibition should be taught at all any more, even if only in counterpoint and in the domain of exercises. For if in free composition, as one might claim, there are no longer any limitations on these progressions,[18] then why should any restriction be imposed in the exercises, whose results are never of practical quality anyway?

This question, however, is only apparently justified, and the answer is simple. For I have already said that only the strong motivations and counter-forces that penetrate clearly and convincingly into the foreground can eliminate the effect, by nature always poor, of similar motion to perfect consonances. This observation also explains, in different words, the fact that with every octave- or fifth-parallelism, with every nonparallel similar motion in all situations (even those of free composition), the knavery of the associated effect returns and lurks in wait for us—just as though free composition were only an exercise of two-voice counterpoint!—specifically in that the bad effect immediately impresses itself on our ear whenever the counterforces (contrary motion, melodic fluency, complete harmony, scale degree, modulation, altera- tion of the character of the voice, and the like) fail to work sufficiently strongly against it. Thus it remains true in free composition, for example, that the interval of the fifth produces a boundary-effect; this can even be obvious, depending on whether it was really intended or was merely the fault of lack of skill. Therefore the school [of counterpoint] must always direct the student's attention to that effect beginning in two-voice settings, even if it later pro- vides him with means to protect himself from it as the need arises. In short, the effect of similar motion—indeed in all possible categories as taught by contrapuntal theory—remains ever a psychological reality, even where, smitten by forces of the foreground, it lurks only in the background![19]

§15. *Mode of departure from the perfect consonances in general*

Since in the exercises of the present species any departure from a perfect consonance naturally also represents at the same time the approach to the next consonance, all that needs to be said about mode of departure has been covered here under the rubric of mode of approach. Therefore no further, special restrictions and prohibitions apply to mode of departure. The only exception to this is mode of departure from the unison.

§16. *Mode of departure from the unison in particular*

The fact of complete agreement and blending of both voices as manifested by the unison obligates the voice leading subsequent to the unison to proceed with caution (which, incidentally, also best fulfills the postulate of melodic fluency); at least the voices should refrain from seeking out in an all too drastic manner a contradictory situation immediately after the unison.

If, for the problem of mode of departure from the unison, we take into consideration the three types of motion, we find the following effects:

(a) The employment of similar motion harbors the danger that ear and sense will find it difficult to decide, especially in the case of larger leaps, which path has been taken by the one voice, and which by the other. Thus here, for example:

Example 188

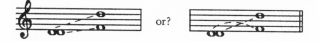

at least the danger of a confusion of voices is present, since it must appear not always completely clear which of the two d^1s has moved to d^2 and which to f^1.

(b) Oblique motion, on the other hand, by means of sustaining in one voice, provides such a strong counterforce of repose that even the largest [melodic] interval can be allowed to follow the unison, for example:

Example 189

(c) With contrary motion, finally, the danger is far more imminent of an explosive effect by the larger interval that follows the unison, just by the nature of the situation itself, for example:

Example 190

This danger is countered best of all, however, by placing an interval of more modest size after the unison, and, moreover, by moving to that interval by small steps; thus the best solution of mode of departure by contrary motion is doubtless the case in which both voices depart from each other in seconds alone, so that they meet in a third:

Example 191

The effects just described, then, yield the following advice for treatment of mode of departure from a unison:

Oblique motion takes first preference, since it is best able to avoid an explosive effect in the succession of intervals. The second best solution is contrary motion, but only under certain favorable circumstances, as described above. The least suitable possibility, finally, is similar motion, which should accordingly be avoided wherever possible in these exercises.

Since the unison, as we shall later see, is prohibited in the main body of the exercise and thus may be used only at the beginning or end in two-voice first-species counterpoint, the question here under consideration has but one practical application—specifically, when the exercise has begun with a unison. Therefore one may test the situation by examining its consequences at the very outset—that is, by determining whether or not the exercise is at all suitable for a unison beginning. For if we have to set an upper counterpoint against a cantus firmus that begins, for example, as follows (cf. p. 54):

Example 192

then it is clear that use of a unison at the beginning would immediately yield that strict necessity of precisely a case of similar motion, for example:

Example 193

unless the device of crossing the two voices (cf. below, §27) were to be used instead; this, however, would appear somewhat out of place, at least at the beginning of an exercise. It is more advisable with such a cantus firmus to use the octave or fifth as opening interval instead of the unison itself.

How free composition proceeds according to its own expressive reasons in handling the effects described above, however, may be shown by the following examples:

Example 194

Schumann, Symphony No. 2 Op. 61, I

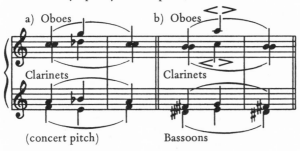

Here we see in the oboes the departure from a unison in similar motion to a fourth at a and even to a seventh at b; just observe, however, how much effect the composer has thereby achieved at a single stroke: measured against the unobtrusive second of the second oboe, the first oboe's detours by leap (the fifth-leaps at a and the seventh-leaps at b) only appear all the more expressive (cf. Part 1, Chapter 2, §18!). Moreover, the fact that the second oboe enters the space of the first oboe's leap exactly with the interval of a second generates a good, genuine portamento effect (cf. Part 1, Chapter 2, §17, especially Example 111!).

In *Fux* we read on p. 73:

[*Aloys:*] It [i.e., the rubric "N.B." in the first bar of an exercise] means that progression by leap from the unison to another consonance is not permitted, nor is progression by leap to a unison, as was explained before. But since this leap appears in a part of the cantus firmus, which is not to be changed, it may be tolerated here. It is different when one is not confined to the cantus firmus and can do as one pleases.[20]

This opinion, clearly, is based on a regrettable misunderstanding, not only of free composition on the one hand, but also of contrapuntal exercises on the other. The misunderstanding has misled Fux in the present instance to grant less freedom to the former than to the latter, since he deduces from the strictness of the exercises, [on the one hand,] the necessity of tolerating possible leaps from a unison, and from the freedom of free composition, on the other, the necessity of greater strictness. In fact it is just the opposite—as may be seen in example 194 above—, for free composition, more often than strict counterpoint, is compelled, by reason of expressive content, to use leaps in such cases.

Treating the question in more detail than Fux, *Bellermann* teaches on p. 136:

The leap from a unison to another consonant interval in similar motion is not good in two-voice counterpoint, and thus should be avoided as much as possible. [Examples follow.] Such a leap is quite permissible, however, if one of the two voices remains stationary on its tone—thus in a case of oblique motion. [Examples follow.] In contrary motion it is likewise desirable to avoid leaps, regardless of whether one or both voices make such a leap. Nevertheless, one very frequently finds exceptions to this rule, and therefore we may be less strict in observing it.

Here Bellermann cites the treatise of Fux, in order to ally himself with the latter in regard to free composition. He confirms this agreement with the following words: "There is, of course, no reason [in free composition] to introduce less beautiful progressions of that kind." What is admittedly correct in these observations is that contrary motion often cannot be avoided; in such cases, however, the reader should adhere to the relevant suggestions in the text.

§17. *The free approach to imperfect consonances*

The approach to imperfect consonances is free, regardless of whether they are preceded by a perfect or an imperfect interval.

Similarly, all three types of motion are unconditionally permitted when they lead to an imperfect consonance, with the possible exception of the following cases.

§18. *The possible prohibition of a succession of two major thirds*

(a) The first exception is the case of a succession of two major thirds, as they are found specifically in the pure, undiluted diatony from the fourth to the fifth degree in major and from the sixth to the seventh in minor—only a single instance [in each mode], as we know:

Example 195

But such thirds will constitute the exception described only if this succession forces on the ear as a *resultant* an *augmented fourth*—a *tritone*—in such an unpleasant way that the ear's attention cannot be distracted from it by any possible later course of the voice leading. Thus in the following voice leading, on the contrary:

Example 196

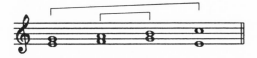

the continuation of the voices certainly cancels the resultant of the augmented fourth quite adequately.[21]

The reason for the prohibition of such third-successions, then, clearly lies less in the juxtaposition of *F* and *B* or in the resultant of the augmented fourth in itself than in a special instance of the latter: specifically, that in which the harshness of the [augmented] fourth-resultant strikes the ear in a particularly drastic manner because it fails to gain sufficient justification through a good subsequent resolution.

But on the other hand a voice leading like the following:

Example 197

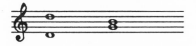

is, therefore, unconditionally permitted; and from this it can be inferred that not just any encounter between *F* and *B* gives reason to apply the prohibition, but only, under especially unfavorable circumstances, an unresolved resultant of an augmented fourth. This, then, is all that can be salvaged of the so besmirched myth of what is unjustifiably known as the tritone "cross-relation" (cf. below, §28)!

(b) Within the pure diatonic system, a seventh-resultant, for example, is no more permissible than the augmented fourth-resultant arising from the succession of two major thirds, especially as it would have to remain unwarranted for other reasons as well:[22]

Example 198

On the other hand, successions of two major thirds like the following:

Example 199

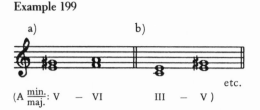

etc.

(A $\frac{\text{min.}}{\text{maj.}}$: V — VI   III — V)

presuppose from the outset a mixed[23] minor key (*Harmony,* §38), in which
the first example represents the progression V — VI and the second the progression III — V. Assuming, then, that the student were to use a mixed minor key
for the exercises, he would have to avoid completely the resultant of an
augmented fifth as well, as it appears in the second example, while use of the
succession in the first example would doubtless be justified without restriction.

It is well known that successions of major thirds (where possible also in
series of sixth-chords) are much favored in our own time in free composition.
How the latter justifies such successions may be shown first of all by an
example:

Example 200

Mozart, Symphony No. 36, I

Admittedly, the scale degree alone (here, the V), with its omnipotence, adequately justifies the series of major thirds (bars 4-5), in that it demotes them to the status of merely transient chromatic advancements through the space from g to c^1. And yet the ear grasps very well too the operation of the whole process that necessarily produced this effect of transience, and we gain finally the insight that we are here dealing with only apparent major thirds, which in fact originate simply from minor thirds instead. It is astonishing how rapidly our perception functions—how it rushes with lightning speed through so many intervening stages and grasps the abbreviation:

Example 201

The illustration at a shows the normal diatonic passing tones that lie between g and c^1 of the lower voice and between b and e^1 of the upper. That is the real background of all later occurrences—the first stage, so to speak.

The illustration at b presents the chromatic filling-in of the normal diatony—at 1. in the lower voice, at 2. in the upper. This is the second stage.

The illustration at c represents the first and initially normal attempt to introduce all of the chromatic passing tones indicated under b into the two voices, while at the same time retaining the given total duration of four quarter-notes.

Yet here the two voices, for the sake of clarity and in order to preserve the passing character of the chromatic tones in a purer form, still interrelate in such an active way that at any given time only one voice executes its passing tone, and only when the first voice has completed its advancement does the second proffer its own passing tone. Thus when the lower voice has completed its passing motion $ab - a$ in the first quarter, the upper voice enters at the second quarter—note well that the lower voice now sustains!—with its own passing motion $c^1 - c\sharp^1$; at the third quarter, the second voice again waits until the first, the lower, has finished with its new passing motion $bb - b$, and then itself advances in the fourth quarter from d^1 to $d\sharp^1$, while the lower voice in contrast remains waiting and passive. This is the third stage.

It is easily recognized, however, that this procedure finally provides the opportunity for a more abbreviating and more complicated one (see Example 200 itself), which is precisely the fourth and final stage of the process. For if it is always only a diatonic tone which, remaining stationary itself, in the meantime provides an opportunity for the chromatic passing tone:

Diatonic Tone	Chromatic Passing Tone
Beneath c^1 of the upper voice	ab—a of the lower voice
Above a of the lower voice	c—$c\sharp^1$ of the upper voice
Beneath d^1 of the upper voice	bb—b of the lower voice
Above b of the lower voice	d^1—$d\sharp^1$ of the upper voice

then it follows that, since the chromatic passing tone $c\sharp^1$ (and later $d\sharp^1$) must in any case chart its course above the diatonic passing tone a (and later b), it certainly amounts to exactly the same thing if the two tones—the diatonic and the chromatic one in each case—instead of waiting and following upon one another, throw caution to the winds and run together.

The ear has come to understand that at the second quarter the third was indeed originally minor: $^c_a{}^1$, until it was enlarged to major: $^c_a\sharp^1$ (and later $^d_b{}^1$, enlarged to $^d_b\sharp^1$) only by means of preempting the chromatic passing tone; therefore it accepts unconditionally the abbreviation as well (that is, the final telescoping of the two-stage process just described into a one-stage one), relinquishes the intermediate stage of minor thirds $^c_a{}^1$ and $^d_b{}^1$ at the second and fourth quarters, and thus arrives immediately at the perception of major thirds in these places.

In the following example, by Brahms:

Example 202

Brahms, Symphony No. 4, I

B minor: VI ———————————————————— I   —

the succession of major thirds in the 'cellos and violas has as its basis the fact that here scale degree VI in *B* minor is composed out altogether in the sense of a genuine minor. However, the harshness of the effect—an intentional harshness—in this case certainly stems far less from the succession of major thirds itself than from the severe dissonance of the passing third *a–c♯* (at *) beneath the harmonic tone b^1 of the violins, and also from the rhythmic peculiarity of this modulation-motive, which begins at the second quarter.

The pair of major thirds in the following example by Wagner:

Example 203

Wagner, *Das Rheingold,* Scene III

C♯ minor: ♮II (Phrygian)

originates in the fact that (1) scale degrees I and VI progressed to II by means of a falling fifth; (2) this scale degree II was lowered (♭II, Phrygian); and (3) within its domain the tone $g\sharp^2$, the upper voice of the succession of thirds, was now called upon to show that we have indeed remained exclusively in the C♯-minor diatony. To be sure, g^2 could have appeared here, if Wagner had preferred to follow the drive of the II toward tonicality—as though it had suddenly turned into a true *D* major (*Harmony,* §137)—; but simple comparison of the effect produced by g^2 shows how much more elegantly the tone $g\sharp^2$ functions in this passage in the service of the diatony to be preserved. Such lovely fruit of the composing-out of scale degrees!

On the other hand, it is instructive to see how in the following example Smetana evades a succession of two major thirds and also is able thereby to achieve a certain mood:

Example 204

Smetana, String Quartet in E Minor ("Aus meinem Leben") I

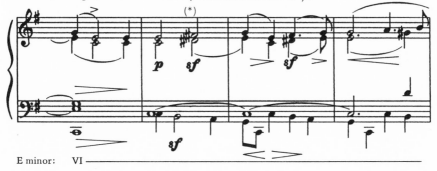

E minor: VI

Fux is not concerned in any particularly strict way with the succession of two major thirds, as can be seen in the following example:

Example 205

Fux IV, 15

Fux V, 16

Albrechtsberger confronts the problem all the more energetically. He too, to state it at the outset, represents the problem only as a matter of disallowed third-successions, but completely avoids speaking *ex offo*[24] of a "cross-relation of the tritone" as such. Thus he writes, on pp. 21–22 under VII:

> Two major thirds are prohibited in the progression of a whole step upward or downward, but not in that of a half step; [they are prohibited] also in the case of a third-leap by both voices; for in these progressions a discordant cross-relation, a *mi contra fa* arises; this is not true, however, of the leap of a perfect fourth. Two major thirds are likewise prohibited when the voices leap a perfect fifth—not because of *mi contra fa,* but because the diagonal product is a major seventh, which is always a difficult thing to seek out, whether it rises or falls in the continuation.

When we place his pertinent examples into order, we arrive at the following picture:

Example 206

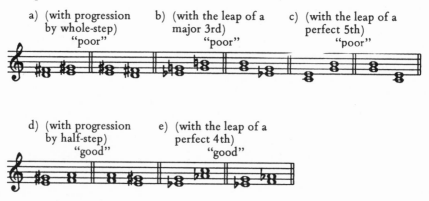

a) (with progression by whole-step) "poor"   b) (with the leap of a major 3rd) "poor"   c) (with the leap of a perfect 5th) "poor"

d) (with progression by half-step) "good"   e) (with the leap of a perfect 4th) "good"

That he permits d at all is connected to his basic way of understanding the mixed minor system, with which we are already familiar (cf. above, Part 1, Chapter 2, §9).

It also follows from the above rule that he by no means prohibits all cross-relations of *F* against *B,* but only the one that occurs along with two major thirds and thus leads to a prohibited fourth-resultant (see Example 206a), so that my Example 197 is equally exempt from his prohibition.

What his rule nevertheless lacks in ultimate precision is that he unfortunately neglects to say that even a progression like that at a can still be permitted under more favorable circumstances, specifically when the effect of the fourth-resultant is effaced by means of a beneficial voice leading. To be sure, an element of this idea, admittedly only unconscious and almost only in the sense of an exception, appears also in Albrechtsberger's own discussion, in the following remarks: "In a cadence with three or more voices, two major thirds ascending a whole-step are permitted, as we can see in the two last examples:

Example 207

c. f.

Yet this idea, in which the author appears literally to have been compelled by the spirit of harmonic theory (here the scale-degree progression II — V — I) to make an exception, unfortunately is unjustly limited to the cadence alone, and thus, as I have said, not expressed accurately enough. In the practical realm of exercises, however, he rightly attended only to the situation at hand in a given case; this can be demonstrated by the corrections, transmitted by Nottebohm, pp. 48–49, that he made to an exercise by Beethoven:

Example 208

etc.

In his Rule 7, (p. 8), *Cherubini* states: "The false relation of the octave, and of the tritone between the parts, should be avoided; these two relations are harsh to the ear, especially that of the octave." (There follows a remark the relevant part of which I have already quoted in *Harmony,* §19.) By his incorrect and wrongheaded assumption that only the relation of the tritone itself (instead of just its situation in any given instance) alone must be the reason for the prohibition, Cherubini unfortunately finds himself compelled for the sake of consistency to prohibit any such relation at all, such as the following:

Example 209

This idea is, admittedly, thorough and consistent, but unfortunately the presupposition lacks inner truth. Cherubini overlooks the fact that for the same reason a succession of this kind, for example:

Example 210

would likewise have to be prohibited because of *B* against *F* (in the form of a diminished fifth); but this prohibition—fortunately, if contradictorily enough—is on the other hand not to be found in Cherubini.

Bellermann returns in this issue to the indifference of the early master Fux. But it almost raises the suspicion that he would tend to judge the matter exclusively from the standpoint of the Mixolydian mode when he writes on p. 149 in an exercise that he represents as Mixolydian:

Example 211

c. f.

cpt.

and then explains:

> In the second example of the Mixolydian mode[25] we see *F* raised to *F♯* in the fourth bar from the end, while according to the stricter rule the sharp should be used only in the cadence itself. This exception can occasionally be permitted in the Mixolydian mode, however, when *F* arrives from above and then moves up again, and when *B* is heard directly after it in another voice. In such a case *F* is not only allowed but sometimes demanded even at the beginning of the setting as well [here follows the exercise whose beginning and end are cited above]; if we keep *F* in the second bar, the *tritone* (*F – B*) between the two voices from the second bar to the third would make a very unpleasant effect, which is called a *cross-relation,* a discordant relationship. In the course of the melody, however, only *F* must be used, in keeping with the mode (bar 5).

This passage clearly relates to the allegedly Mixolydian character of the exercise.

§19. *Mode of departure from the imperfect consonances*

Departure from imperfect consonances is free of any prohibition; since with the departure, however, the approach to the next consonance is also determined, all of the principles set forth in §§6, 11, and 17 concerning mode of approach now take effect.

§20. *Consideration of the traditional formulation of the rules of voice-movement*

To enrich the special instruction given here (in §§9–19) concerning types of voice-movement, a synopsis of the pertinent rules as they are found in other textbooks may now be presented.

Thus we read in *Fux* (p. 61):

First Rule: From one perfect consonance to another perfect consonance one must proceed in contrary or oblique motion.

Second Rule: From a perfect consonance to an imperfect consonance one may proceed in any of the three motions.

Third Rule: From an imperfect consonance to a perfect consonance one must proceed in contrary or oblique motion.

Fourth Rule: From one imperfect consonance to another imperfect consonance one may proceed in any of the three motions.

Here it should be noted that oblique motion is permitted in all four progressions. On the knowledge of these three types of motion and their correct use hangs, as the saying goes, the law and the prophets.

He does not discuss here, as we see, the issue of antiparallels.

According to *Albrechtsberger,* the rules of voice-motion run as follows (pp. 19, 21):

I. If in two chords the second pair of notes forms a perfect consonance, similar motion must be avoided in moving from the first to the second, and contrary or oblique motion must be used; the first chord may then be either perfect or imperfect. [Examples follow.]

One must also avoid two fifths or two octaves even in contrary motion, especially if the accompaniment is provided by an organ equipped with a pedal; for organists play most bass notes with the left foot, and very often turn an ascending fourth-leap into a descending fifth-leap and vice versa. As a result, parallel fifths or octaves are heard.

Since in reference to antiparallels, the prohibition of which he [in fact] creates, Albrechtsberger suddenly invokes a justification derived from free composition, we take this opportunity to respond immediately (regardless of his later amplifications) that, aside from the inadmissibility in principle of such a procedure, the issue under discussion also has a very different appearance in free composition. Consider, for example:

Example 212

a) Beethoven, Piano Sonata Op. 2 No. 1, IV

b) J. S. Bach, Aria variata (BWV 989)

In the first example a, it is by no means necessary to assume an *unisono* in order to validate the parallel octaves (even if this secondary effect has to arise there of its own accord), since the tones G — C of the bass are more nearly incarnations of the scale degrees V — I than voices in the pure contrapuntal sense.[26] That is, we hear the same tone progression in the low register with a different purpose than in the high: in the former, scale-degree progression prevails, in the latter, nothing but melody.[27] If the autographs do not deceive, more complex relationships are present in the Bach example. There are either true parallel fifths from the second to the third quarter: $\frac{b}{E}$—$\frac{e^1}{A}$, or mere antiparallels from the first to the third quarter: $\frac{b}{e}$—$\frac{e^1}{A}$; in the latter case, for the sake of clarity, the *e* of the bass would have to be thought of as a half-note (i.e., without division into quarters). However one wants to view it, as parallels or antiparallels, it is in any case the scale degrees, their expectation and fulfillment, that justify the fifths here.

[Albrechtsberger continues:]

> II. If in two chords the second pair of notes forms an imperfect consonance, one may use any of the three types of motion in proceeding from the first to the second; the first chord may be perfect or imperfect [examples follow]. Since in the following four species dissonances are used as well, they are treated in this respect as imperfect consonances, and the following rule is added to the two preceding: the first chord may be perfect, imperfect, or dissonant.

Cherubini bravely ventures deeper into the justification of the prohibition. We read on page 5, fourth rule:

Several perfect consonances of the same kind should never be permitted to succeed each other, regardless of their particular size; consequently, two fifths and two octaves in succession are prohibited. This prohibition is applicable to every kind of strict composition, in two parts, as well as in more.

There follows the explanatory "Observation":

[*Observation:*] A succession of octaves renders harmony well nigh void; a succession of fifths forms a discordance, because the upper part progresses in one key at the same time that the lower moves in another. For example, if to the scale of C an upper part be added which gives a perfect fifth at each bar, thus:

Example 213

Scale of C

it follows that one part will be in C, the other in G. It is from this concurrence of two keys that the discordance arises, and consequently, the prohibition to introduce several fifths in succession, even when the movement of the parts, instead of being conjunct, is disjunct. The effect always remains the same. [Cherubini's Example 12 follows, which presents several fifth-successions by leap.]

It is easily discernible that Cherubini, in formulating the reasoning contained in the latter comment, was governed by an all too vague notion of what a key might be, and that in its ramifications, the reasoning therefore suffers at least from gross exaggeration. For if one might perhaps be permitted to direct it against a phenomenon like primitive organum (see above, §12) with justification, how, on the other hand, can one use it as an argument against a succession of, for example, only two fifths, whether in strict counterpoint or in free composition? Is it possible at all, then, to express by a succession of (for example) only two fifths even one key, to say nothing of two different keys operating in parallel?

Continuing the rule, Cherubini comments:

Consecutive fifths have been, and still are tolerated in contrary motion. . . . [Cherubini's example 13 follows.]

In this example it will be seen that one is a twelfth, and the other is a fifth, which alters the matter. Nevertheless, it is forbidden to use this liberty in two-voice counterpoint, particularly that of note against note. The method is tolerated only in four-voice counterpoint, where there is difficulty in making the parts flow well.

No justification whatever of the prohibition of antiparallels is given by Cherubini.

The pupil may meet with consecutive fifths in works of the galant style, as in operas, symphonies, etc.; but these are always only licenses, which are tolerated in those kinds of composition.

But how little faith Cherubini himself must have had in his own reasoning becomes clear when he, the ever strict and merciless teacher, nevertheless condescends, after all, to "tolerate" actual fifth- and octave-parallelisms under the rubric of "licenses" in free composition! Instead of the banner of "need to tolerate"—alas! how much insecurity and bewilderment in the treatment of the subject matter are hidden in this word "tolerate"!—it would have been far more useful at this point if Cherubini had stated the reasons, whatever they might be, that would cause him to tolerate licenses in free composition.

But the fifth rule (p. 6) is still more surprising: "Approaching a perfect consonance by similar motion is prohibited, except when one of the two voices moves by a semitone." (His Example 14 follows, under the rubric "forbidden motion.") "This case," he continues, "is allowed:"

Example 214

Ex. 15

And after giving the reason for the prohibition first established in the same rule—we are already familiar with it from Part 2, Chapter 1, §11—he adds the following concerning example 214: "The case of the tolerated movement shown in the example is different, inasmuch as, on filling up the interval-spaces with quarter-notes, there result, it is true, two fifths, but one is diminished and the other perfect." (Cherubini's Example 17 follows, which clarifies the text.) And finally:

These two fifths are tolerated because they are not of the same nature, and because the discordancy of which we have spoken as arising from perfect fifths in succession is not present. The old composers, however, always avoided this progression in two-voice counterpoint. It was only when writing for several voices that they availed themselves of it in the inner parts, to void committing some other offense.

It is perhaps unnecessary for me to state specifically that my argument in §11 (n.7, pp. 352–53) applies also to the exception set up—incidentally, quite inconsistently—by Cherubini (Example 214), and that this example, too, falls under the prohibition. Obviously Cherubini—like Albrechtsberger, incidentally, regarding the issue of two major thirds—has in this case allowed himself to be misled into positing those exceptions only by the association of Example 214 to scale-degree progression in free composition (VII — I); this is the reason for his vacillation.

Like Fux, except with a logically sound transposition of the second and third rules, *Bellermann* formulates the principles on p. 134f. as follows:

Rule 1. From a perfect consonance to another perfect consonance, only contrary or oblique motion may be used. [Example follows.]

Rule 2. From an imperfect to a perfect consonance, likewise, only contrary or oblique motion may be used. [Example follows.]

Rule 3. From a perfect to an imperfect consonance, all three types of motion may be used. [Example follows.]

Rule 4. From an imperfect consonance to another imperfect consonance, likewise, all three types of motion may be used. [Example follows.]

Like Fux, incidentally, he also fails to remark on the matter of antiparallels.

These rules, to touch upon this point as well, are the rules of *voice leading*, which unfortunately are taught already in harmonic theory, and, indeed, immediately in the first lessons. But I have explained in *Harmony* why they belong only in contrapuntal theory as the *ex offo*[28] theory of voice leading, and what harm they inflict on instruction once they are taught in an ill-conceived manner in harmony lessons.

Beginning

§21. *Construction of the beginning*

At the beginning, thus in the first bar, 1, 8, or 5 must be used in all cases; never other intervals, such as 3 (10) or 6.

The ranking of perfect consonances is already familiar from §4 of the present chapter; and whether preference should be given to 1 or 8 or 5 can most aptly be decided on the basis of the situation in the second bar—that is, by considering whether the unison, for example (cf. §16 above), could find a suitable continuation or not, and related matters.

Nevertheless—and this should be scrupulously observed here—when the added counterpoint is in the lower voice, the lower fifth must not be used as an alleged instance of the fifth required [by the preceding paragraph]; because with it, the key would be negated. Thus in C major, an opening-formation such as the following, for example:

Example 215

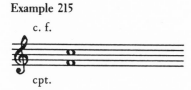

c. f.

cpt.

would point not at all to C major, but rather to F major, in which case we would certainly assume just the opposite situation of the voices, with the lower as cantus firmus and the upper as counterpoint.

The prohibition of imperfect consonances in the first bar of the exercise is, naturally, to be understood as only relative; that is, it derives automatically from the axiom, always to be observed in contrapuntal study, that the solution of all problems that arise is to move always in the direction from the simple and natural to the more complex and less natural (see Introduction, p. 000). But there is no doubt that the perfect consonances here have the significance of the more natural, especially since the purpose of the beginning can be none other than to express the tonic and its harmony (insofar as the latter is attainable at all in two-voice counterpoint) with the maximum of repose and security.

In this sense of purely contrapuntal understanding of the task of simply giving the exercise a beginning, therefore, the scale of values established above cannot be subject to any further vicissitudes of fashion in teaching: it remains immutable under all circumstances, however free composition (be it that of the past, the present, or some future time) may proceed concerning the beginnings of compositions. Exercise and free composition are completely different things, and it is least appropriate of all to derive principles from the latter and consider them binding on the former.

The best statement of the question at hand is by *Albrechtsberger,* p. 21 under III: "The beginning and the end must have a perfect consonance, with the exception that the upper counterpoint cannot end with the fifth, and the lower counterpoint cannot begin with it." (Compare also p. 66.)

Dehn, by contrast, writes as follows (p. 5f.):

For these two [beginning- and ending-notes], the ancients strictly demanded a perfect consonance in the key; we shall be satisfied if beginning and end of the setting clearly define its key, and we may confidently end, for example, with the third in the upper voice, provided only that the bass note gives the root.

He then proceeds, on p. 7, actually to begin an exercise with the interval of a third. All of this is nothing but infantile mania to "modernize" counterpoint—truculence against a rule whose meaning he has completely failed to understand in the first place. Alas, this lamentable confusion of contrapuntal theory and composition-theory!

Main Body

§22. *The preference for imperfect over perfect consonances*

In the main body, more imperfect consonances should be used than perfect ones, for by dint of the harmonic characteristics of imperfect consonances described in §4 of this chapter, they appear more suitable in every case to foster mobility in the setting than the perfect consonances, which either limit the harmonic content too severely or merely repeat the tone of the cantus firmus.

Here, where the concern is to learn the ways and means by which such a modest organism [as the exercise] is to be created, the student's attention must be directed to the incentive for propulsion of content that operates precisely in the imperfect consonances.

On the other hand, good taste precludes that more than three thirds or sixths be placed in succession unless there is a particular reason for doing so. For even if it is certainly most convenient to write counterpoint against a voice using only thirds or sixths, in such as case the poor effect of a *monotony of intervals* cannot be avoided, and the lack of variety and contrasts in the intervals then cannot but diminish the artistic merit of the counterpoint. (Yet it is not, just for this reason, by any means necessary here to invoke the assistance of the artificial hypothesis of Riemann about the degree of blending of thirds. See above, §12 of this chapter.)

On the question of whether sixths, when several of them occur in succession, are better used descending than ascending, see Part 3, Chapter 1, §23.

Fux criticizes ascending motion of several sixths in succession on p. 92; see the citation in Part 3, Chapter 1, §14 concerning Fux's Table VII, Figure 11.

Albrechtsberger, p. 24 under X: "One should not, without necessity, set more than three thirds or sixths consecutively in similar motion, because this produces the effect of a street song or popular melody." Compare also pp. 30, 32.

§23.   Use of the perfect consonances, and a few exceptions encountered therein

It goes without saying, however, that even perfect consonances may and should be used in the main body of the exercise in keeping with the principles of voice leading, so long as the otherwise applicable laws of approach and departure (§§6–20) as well as the law of more moderate usage (at least in principle) are observed.

The only exceptions are:

1.   The *unison,* which is prohibited here in the first species of two-voice counterpoint simply for the reason that it would inhibit far too abruptly and drastically the flow of a setting that is so tonally impoverished in the first place by the limitations of two-voice counterpoint; and

2.   The *octave,* whenever its use in the main body would suddenly produce a cadence, which—if the brevity and tonal poverty of two-voice exercises are always kept in view—would serve as a premature and misleading goal for the voice leading, and thus would have to weaken irreparably the final cadence's sense of close. But the extent to which the mere succession 6 — 8 is to be understood as a cadence in the purely contrapuntal sense will be shown later in §29. (Concerning the same question in three-voice counterpoint, see the discussion in Part 3, Chapter 1, §26.)

Cadences in secondary keys (see §28 of this chapter), however, are certainly permitted.

Fux combines the question at hand of the unison with that of the *"ottava battuta"* (10 — 8) on pp. 72–73, where he expressly forbids the unison in the main body (see the quotation in Part 2, Chapter 2, §12). He does not treat the cadence explicitly. [He deals with] avoidance of cadences only in his theory of fugue (p. 131).

Albrechtsberger treats the prohibition of the unison on p. 21 under V; on cadences he writes, on p. 22 under VIII: "Cadences, including both partial and full cadences,[29] are prohibited in the middle of a piece (*Stück*); a partial cadence is permitted in the last two bars at the end, for example:"

Example 216

"poor"

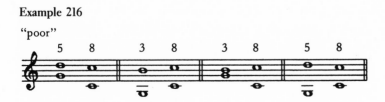

Example 217

"good"

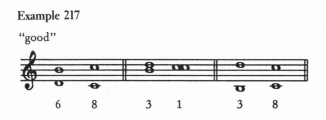

From this it can be inferred that he applies the term "full cadence" to a cadence in which the dominant tone itself participates, while "partial cadence," on the other hand, signifies a cadence that uses only the two leading tones. Concerning the permissibility of partial cadences in three-voice counterpoint, however, see p. 81.

On p. 27 Albrechtsberger teaches—in a purely casuistic manner, to be sure, since there was no other possibility in this case—the other methods to be used when the danger of a cadence arises: ". . . not that the expected chord would always have to follow, since deceptive cadences (*Inganni*) are more beautiful and necessary before the arrival of the final cadence; for example:"

Example 218

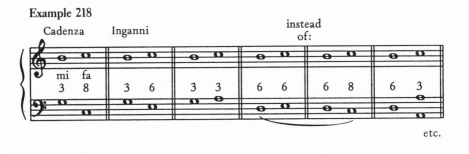

etc.

§24. *Spacing of the two voices*

The need for good sonority itself dictates moderation in the spacing of voices; thus for two-voice counterpoint, registrally adjacent voice types are preferable, such as soprano and alto, alto and tenor, or tenor and bass.

The same postulate of good sonority also stipulates that the distance between the two voices should if possible not exceed a tenth. If the voices should, on the other hand, occasionally move too close to one another, a particularly appropriate countermeasure, among others, is the leap of a sixth; such a leap can regain the contrast provided by separation and, at the same time, yield other benefits for the voice leading.

Fux writes (p. 76):

Second, if the two voices move so close together that one does not know where to take them, and if contrary motion cannot be used, such motion can be brought about by the leap of a minor sixth (which is permissible) or an octave, as in the following examples:

Example 219

Fux III, 11

With regard to the spacing of voices, however, Fux adheres to the principle of close spacing only in the exercises of the first species; later, he violates that principle—unfortunately, to the severe detriment of his own teaching.

Bellermann's comments (p. 143) are excellent:

> If a two-voice setting is to have a really good sound, the two voices must stand in a correct relationship to each other and must not be too widely separated. Therefore the student must, in exercises, always combine two adjacent voices—tenor with bass, alto with tenor, or alto with soprano; but not bass with alto, or (still worse) with soprano, etc. For pure intonation is difficult without instrumental accompaniment in spacings larger than the octave; besides, such spacings sound empty and poor unless they are filled out by inner voices. In two-voice counterpoint, therefore, the tenth is the widest spacing permitted.

One should, however, avoid thinking of the sonic quality of exercises in terms of a free composition, as Bellermann, in the light of the foregoing, obviously does, as a consequence of his profound misconception of [the purpose of] contrapuntal doctrine. For even in regard to sonic quality, the student must here experience for the first time only the most essential things (cf. Part 1, Chapter 2, §20); the sonic quality of the setting should stand purely in the service of the exercise [and its purpose]: to provide a foundation first of all for [understanding] the nature of the singing voice and of voice leading in general.

§25. *The added voice abides by the rules of the cantus firmus*

All rules and prohibitions that apply to the cantus firmus itself are to be used also in constructing the added voice. These include the rules pertaining to intervals (Part 1, Chapter 2, §§5–19) and cadences (§23), those pertaining to melodic fluency in general (§20), and the prohibitions against chromatic progression, monotony, the arpeggiation of harmonic units (cf. Part 1, Chapter 2, §§2, 41), and so forth. In short: the added voice, even in the exercises of strict counterpoint, should be no less melody than the cantus firmus itself!

Clearly, the requirement that the added voice constantly maintain in all respects the bearing of a melody applies to an even greater extent in free composition as well. For the infinitely greater freedom that the principal melody is entitled to require in that domain naturally extends also to the added voice, which accordingly may demand and expect the freest approach to its formation.

§26. Consequences of the dependency of the added voice: (a) The license of tone-repetition

The very fact that the cantus firmus is the a priori given element, in contrast to which the added voice is merely a complement entering the scene a posteriori implies that the latter is, in turn, dependent upon the former in many respects. Consequently, as the "curse" of this dependency, the added voice is quite often forced to deviate from those very rules and norms upon which the essence of the independent cantus-firmus melody was founded.

Accordingly, the postulate of melodic fluency itself (which, as noted, is the primary requirement in the added voice just as in the cantus firmus) can, under certain circumstances, cause the added voice to violate the prohibition of tone-repetition—that is, simply to repeat a tone—in order to maintain the same pitch level purely for the sake of the melodic line.

The unison of the opening bar, incidentally, can itself necessitate a tone-repetition in the second bar, since the unison thereby is assured the eminent advantage of a departure by oblique motion (§16); for example:

Example 220

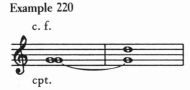

c. f.

cpt.

How many such tone-repetitions may be allowed to occur in succession, however, can be decided only by the conditions present in the given cantus firmus and the line of the added voice. Perhaps not even a threefold repetition could be called the absolutely ultimate permissible limit.

Albrechtsberger teaches (p. 24): "The added voice in two-voice setting may remain stationary for at most three bars (even if the meter is only two-quarters alla breve, or three-quarters or three-halves alla breve), because of the static melody." But when he moreover adds to this, "The *tasto solo* in settings of three and more voices is exempt from this rule," he unfortunately expresses in far too naive a manner an idea that is in itself indisputably correct. The reason for this naiveté, however, is that he neglected to present the necessary intermediate stages in reasoning, as they have been treated more fully in the text preceding, in §§25 and 26. I am afraid that he was unaware of them.

§27. (b) The license of voice-crossing

As a rule, the added voice keeps to its place through the whole course of an exercise—that is, either always above or always below the cantus firmus. Yet under certain circumstances the demands of melodic fluency (and, occasionally, also the need to avoid a forbidden progression) can make it appear altogether desirable to cross the voices. It is obvious, however, that such an exceptional condition should by no means be continued too long and, in particular, should not ultimately lead to a complete reversal of the registers in which we perceive the two voices. Least of all should it prevail in the cadential formula itself.

Albrechtsberger makes the following appropriate observation (p. 32): ". . . that even more than three thirds may follow upon one another in succession if one or several of them are produced by voice-crossing."

Example 221

cpt.

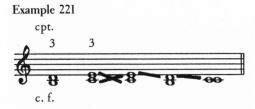

c. f.

Yet at the same time we see from this example that Albrechtsberger unfortunately has no compunction at all about allowing voice-crossing even toward the end of the exercise.

Bellermann, on the other hand, rightly criticizes a similar voice-crossing at the cadence itself (p. 145):

This must always be avoided at the cadence, however, unless the cantus firmus itself has to make a larger ascending leap immediately before the cadence. Such cases are rare, however; for example:

Example 222

cpt.

c. f.

and even here the added voice can easily be led in such a way that the voices need not close in inverted position:

Example 223

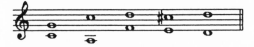

§28. *On modulation and cross-relation*

Through the incorporation of the added voice in two-voice counterpoint, for the first time a harmony can be brought to life in the vertical direction (which, if we disregard harmony expressed in the horizontal direction, naturally could not yet happen in the melody of the cantus firmus alone). And this in turn automatically enables us to incorporate modulations with relatively greater clarity than was possible in the cantus firmus (Part 1, Chapter 2, §22).

It remains nonetheless true even in two-voice settings that a modulation must never be produced by means of a chromatic inflection;[30] this would give rise to either a chromatic progression on the one hand, or the effect of a mixture of modes or of a chromatic modulation on the other, depending on whether the chromatic tone were used in one and the same voice [as its diatonic counterpart], or only in the other voice. But all of these effects must, as established in Part 1, Chapter 2, §4, appear inadequate and overly vague in these exercises; they are therefore prohibited.

If, accordingly, a modulation is indeed correct when it moves as shown by the Albrechtsberger excerpt cited in Example 133, it is on the contrary incorrect if it includes voice leadings such as the following:

Example 224

In such cases, at least a mixture must be assumed, if not an actual chromatic modulation.

The chromatic inflections that regularly characterize these latter situations are called (inharmonic) *cross-relations*, and therefore the limits on any freedom of modulation can perhaps be expressed most trenchantly simply by the prohibition of all cross-relation of this kind.

Thus the concept of cross-relation, to formulate the results definitively, includes only the case of chromatic progression distributed between *two* different voices; completely excluded from the concept is not only chromatic progression used in a single voice, but also the juxtaposition of *F* and *B* (the tritone; cf. §18 above).

Just as free composition has urgent need of mixture and of chromatic modulation, however, the cross-relation that derives from them becomes in like measure not merely a "tolerated license" but a fully justified necessity.

Many examples that incidentally happen to illustrate cross-relation appeared already in *Harmony*; these include the following (all from *Harmony*): Example 72, fourth bar, third and fourth quarters; same example, sixth bar, second and third quarters; Example 79, first and second (!) bars, and later fifth and sixth (!) bars; Example 84, third and fourth (!) bars; and so on.

Accordingly, I can limit myself here to a single example:

Example 225
Brahms, Intermezzo Op. 117 No. 1

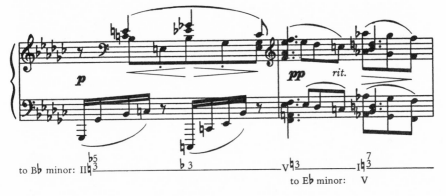

to B♭ minor: II♮⁵₃ ————— ♭3 ——— V♮3 — I♮3

to E♭ minor: V

The first bar of this example exhibits a cross relation by reason of a chromatic tonicization-process which is made to turn back on itself: the e^1 of the melodic line itself ($e^1 - g b^1 - c^1$), as an initially chormatically raised third of II in B♭ minor, juxtaposed with the diatonic third E♭ (incidentally appearing in three octaves) of the same scale degree. (Concerning the resulting interval of a diminished third $e^1 - g b^1$ in the melody, compare Part 1, Chapter 2, §8!)

As a product of the chromatic modulation that occurs in the second bar of the example, the tones A (as third of V in B♭ minor) and A♭ (as seventh of V in E♭ minor) are juxtaposed in the manner of a cross-relation.

Chapter IV (p. 7) in *Albrechtsberger,* entitled "Von den musikalischen Geschlech-tern und Tonarten," treats modulation among other things; as a result of misun-derstanding, however, it deals only with modulation in free composition (symphony, concerto, quartet, quintet, psalm, choral work), so the opinions set forth there can claim no real significance for direct application to contrapuntal study. (It should not be overlooked that Albrechtsberger regards counterpoint as part of an actual "introduction to composition"!) Compare on the other hand the statement by Albrechtsberger quoted in §22 of Part 1, which pertains directly to modulation in the exercises of counterpoint.

Cherubini also exceeds the limits set by the most fundamental tasks of contrapuntal theory; he writes (p. 11):

In no piece should one modulate to keys other than those contained in the scale [of the main key]. In C major, one can modulate to no keys other than G major, A minor, F major, and D minor, and in the latter modulation[s], one must take particular care to touch upon the [key of] F only in passing, because the B♭ which it contains completely obliterates the idea of the principal key (whose leading tone is B), just as the C♯ (the leading tone of D minor) directly contradicts the principal key. One can also modulate to E minor, but this key, because of the F♯ and D♯, must be of even shorter duration than the modulations mentioned above. The key of B is completely forbidden, since its fifth must be raised. In A minor, one can modulate to C major and, in passing, touch upon the keys of F major and D minor; the key of E minor can also appear, but B major is completely prohibited, just as in C major.

All of these modulations are natural and analogous to the principal key. Practice and reflection provide the means to use them appropriately and with good effect, and to shape them so as to form a beautiful whole.

So far Cherubini. In a *Kompositionslehre* all of this would perhaps be appropriate; in contrapuntal theory, on the other hand, it is appropriate only to the extent that it is not put forward as instruction directly applicable to the teaching of counterpoint, but is intended merely as an excursion into the realm of free composition.

Another severe flaw in Cherubini's treatment is that he fails to recognize all cross-relations as what they really are—specifically, modulation by means of mixture or chromatic inflection. Instead, he regards cross-relation as simply a *relation* to be conceived in an absolute sense and at the same time to be condemned in an absolute sense. We read on p. 8, under "Remarks on the Seventh Rule":

> Relation signifies the immediate affinity that exists between two sounds, successive or simultaneous. This affinity is considered according to the nature of the interval formed by the two sounds, so that the relation shall be true when the interval is true; it is false if the interval is diminished or augmented. False relations in harmony are considered to be those in which the two sounds do not belong to one and the same key. The diminished or augmented octave is a false relation in melody as in harmony, however it may be used. The disagreeable effect it produces may be mitigated, but not entirely eliminated. The use of this interval is, therefore, absolutely prohibited [in melody]:

Example 226

Ex. 19

false relation of the diminished and the augmented octave

In harmony, such octaves are completely unusable, especially in proliferation.

Example 227

Ex. 20

There are, however, more recent composers who allow themselves the following usages:

Example 228

Ex. 21

They regard the C♭ and C♯ as merely transient alterations, and as notes which, since the fall on the weak beat, have only little value. That, however, is again a gross license, which, scarcely tolerable in a completely free style, must be absolutely excluded in the strict style.

Such an agglomeration of serious mistakes by Cherubini! Simply because the exercises of strict counterpoint must altogether reject mixture, chromatic modulation, and diminished and augmented octaves—it would have been up to Cherubini to state the very reason for these prohibitions!—must free composition, in turn, also forgo them for that reason? Why? Just for the sake of consistency? Is it not still more consistent if free composition, which is just as entitled to use dissonant passing tones as strict counterpoint, motivates, under the same rubric [of passing tone], also chromatic progressions—to which free composition has indeed inherited a new, independent right (cf. Part 1, Chapter 2, §4)? (Compare Examples 30, 31, etc.)

And why, then—to respond to Cherubini's Example 20 [Example 227 of the present text]—, when so many new motivations enter the picture, should Wagner, for example, hesitate to write the following:

Example 229

Wagner, *Tristan und Isolde,* Act II

Would it not on the contrary have to be criticized as inconsistency if Wagner, with all of the reasons he had to write as he did in this passage, nevertheless had forgone this way of writing—that is, if he had avoided it even in free composition just for the sake of strict counterpoint, which can by no means marshal such reasons in its exercises? (Compare also *Harmony,* §53ff.)

Finally, it should be remembered that Cherubini unfortunately includes among cross-relations the tritone, which is addressed more fully in the comments to §18 of the present chapter.

But let us read further:

There is yet another situation in which one can arrive at a false relation in the harmony between two different chords; for example:

Example 230

Ex. 22

Example 231

Ex. 23

The tone C in the upper voice of the first chord of the first example sounds bad in relation to the C♯ of the lower voice in the second chord; that is indisputable for every trained ear, and it is easily proven for the intellect by the fact that these two tones belong to completely different chords, which stand in no close relationship to each other, and that they cannot be placed in such direct succession without striking the ear as unpleasant.

There is, however, a simple method of eliminating this difficulty—namely, by inserting another note, so that the voice which (in the above illustration, for example) has sung C itself introduces C♯ in advance, or causes the impression of C to disappear by means of such an inserted note, for example:

Example 232

Ex. 24

Through this and other palliatives, the unpleasant impression of false relations can be weakened and the ear made accustomed to them, because the impression then is not so immediate; in the strict style, however, such cases should always be avoided.

How little the utilitarian value of all this in free composition, and how superfluous and misleading in strict counterpoint! It is certainly correct, as Cherubini stresses, that C and C♯, for example, "belong to completely different chords, which stand in no close relationship to each other," but it surely is no less correct that along with modulation through re-valuation or enharmonic change, free composition is for many reasons often forced to use modulation through chromaticism; the content of the latter, however, is provided only by the cross-relating octaves and similar phenomena under discussion here! [*Fr.C.*, §§248–250.]

Cadence

§29. *Construction of the cadence*

Like the cantus firmus, the melody of the added voice (cf. §25 above) must in turn use for the purpose of its own cadence nothing but one of the two leading tones. This automatically implies that only one of the following formulas must be used:

Example 233

These formulas are necessary if parallel octaves or unisons are not to arise from the possible use of the same leading tone in both the cantus firmus and the added voice.

For the above cadential formulas, which have heretofore been called "partial cadence," I prefer the term *contrapuntal cadences*, in view of the fact that they have taken on this form only under the influence of *contrapuntal* voice leading itself, and, indeed, that of the interval of the second, which might be called the primary ingredient of melodic fluency.

Another form of cadence, however, such as the following:

Example 234

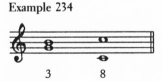

dispenses with the leading tone in the lower voice, substituting the interval of a fifth instead. If on the one hand it thus offends against the contrapuntal postulate of the leading tone as the inevitable penultimate tone of the melody, on the other hand it betrays all too clearly the traces of a purely harmonic origin, the scale-degree progression V — I. Precisely for this reason, however, in contrast to the contrapuntal cadences introduced here for the first time, the cadence of Example 234 may be called the *harmonic cadence*, a designation that gives far better orientation concerning its essence than ·the formerly common nomenclature "full cadence." The harmonic cadence is therefore to be strictly banned from two-voice counterpoint, and should not be admitted before the study of three-voice counterpoint is taken up. Even there, it should be used only when the two leading tones are otherwise present in the cadence and thus pay proper tribute to the spirit of voice leading: such is the immutable adherence of counterpoint—indeed, without exception in the realm of its exercises—to the purely contrapuntal law of the leading tones, a law that counterpoint never sacrifices!

From the above arguments, finally, it can be inferred that a succession such as the following:

Example 235

can be called neither a contrapuntal nor a harmonic cadence: even the involvement of the one leading tone in the upper voice is insufficient, as can be seen, to allow this interval succession to be subsumed under the concept of cadence at all.

From the tendency to maintain constantly in exercises above all the vocal foundation, it follows that the cadential form 3 — 1 is incontrovertibly preferable to the form 10 — 8:

Example 236

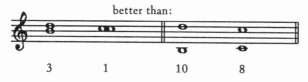

And it must not be overlooked that a closer relationship between the voices is always more suitable to the character of a cadence as such than the more distant relationship of tenth and octave.

However, those who attend less closely to the spacing of voices may, in any case, also employ the form 10 — 8.

Regarding *Albrechtsberger,* compare the quotation in §23 of the present chapter. In his exercises, he freely uses the formulation 10 — 8 along with the others.
Bellermann states (p. 145):

The cadence involving a tenth and an octave is not good and should be avoided in the exercises, since one should take care especially at the cadence that the voices stand in a pleasing relationship to each other, and that the tenth, as the maximum distance between two voices, be used only in passing in the main body of an exercise.

Exercises

Example 237
Fux II, 3 and II, 4 (allegedly Dorian)

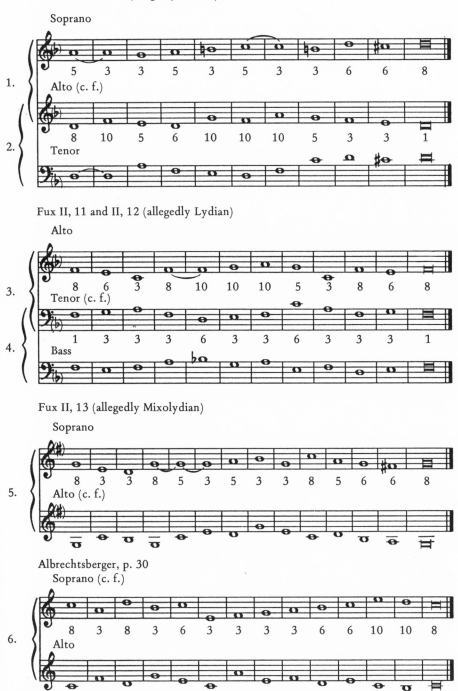

Fux II, 11 and II, 12 (allegedly Lydian)

Fux II, 13 (allegedly Mixolydian)

Albrechtsberger, p. 30

Example 237 *continued*

Albrechtsberger, p. 32

H. Schenker

H. Schenker (c. f. by Fux)

Comments on the Preceding Exercises

No. 1. Fux uses fifths in bars 4 and 7, since they came about so naturally through contrary motion in the fluent line of the melody; under such favorable linear circumstances as he achieved here, he preferred not to avoid the fifths perhaps by substituting sixths or the like in a forced manner. Bars 5 and 6, and likewise bars 8 and 9, pay no heed to "B contra F" (cf. §18 of the present chapter).

No. 2. Beautiful, especially successful mixture of perfect (bars 3, 8) and imperfect consonances.

No. 3. In bars 3–4 and 9–10, the parallelism of [interval] succession protrudes almost with the impression of monotony in the broader sense (cf. Part 1, Chapter 2, §21); by use of the interval 6 in bar 3, this fault as well could perhaps have been avoided without causing still greater damage.

The progression 3 — 8 in the same bars, however, is not a cadence (cf. Part 2, §§23 and 29).

No. 4. The descent below the tonic by the cantus firmus in bars 5–7 (allegedly: Hypolydian mode!) causes Fux to use voice-crossing for the duration of no fewer than four bars. The exercise includes only imperfect consonances, but these nevertheless occur in appropriate alternation and in beautiful mixture.

No. 5. Observe here the tone-repetitions over the span of three bars (bars 4–6).

No. 6. The tenths in the final bars here make an unpleasant effect.

No. 7. The construction of the counterpoint suffers under the unfavorable structure of the cantus firmus itself. In the last four bars, Albrechtsberger oversteps the basic precepts of strict counterpoint by causing the leap of a sixth to be followed by that of a diminished fourth (cf. Part 1, Chapter 2, §9), when he could have simply allowed the tone B in the third bar from the end to be repeated, and thus have moved to the leading tone by the leap of a third (cf. Part 1, Chapter 2, §23).

Chapter 2

The Second Species:
Two Notes Against One

General Aspects

§1. Downbeat and upbeat

This species teaches how two notes in the counterpoint (specifically two half-notes) may be set against one note of the cantus firmus.

This automatically necessitates for the first time a discrimination of two distinct beats.

The first is called the *downbeat,* the second the *upbeat.* This nomenclature is derived from the act of beating time, in which the first beat, called strong, is indicated by a downward motion of the hand or baton, and the second beat, called weak, by a rising motion. From this point of view, it is certainly better to translate the old term "thesis" as "downbeat" and "arsis" as "upbeat" rather than vice versa.

> *Fux* writes (p. 74):
>
> Before I begin to explain this species of counterpoint, it must be known that now we are dealing with a twofold temporal organization, in which the measure or bar consists of two equal parts; the first of these corresponds to downward motion of the hand, and the other to upward motion. The downward motion is called *thesis* in Greek, the upward motion *arsis;* we will use these two words in this study.

Bellermann (p. 150) uses the terminology arsis and thesis in the opposite sense; for his reasons, see Bellermann, p. 2 (footnote).

§2. The dissonance on the upbeat

From what was said in Chapter 1 about the requirement of consonance in strict counterpoint, it is obvious that the downbeat must be consonant. This postulate continues to be satisfied, it is true, if the upbeat too is consonant. But the latter can also, under certain circumstances, present a dissonance against the cantus firmus.

176

§3. (a) The requirement of stepwise motion to the dissonance

If the dissonance is placed on the upbeat arbitrarily and without any constraint, as at a and b:

Example 238

it can easily happen that a relationship of a harmonic nature will be heard between the dissonance and the two tones set at the following downbeat (those of the cantus firmus and the counterpoint)—a relationship (known in free composition as anticipation) which injects into strict counterpoint a thoroughly unwelcome entity of a melodic-harmonic nature.

Or, as at c, it is enigmatically made clear to the ear that, given the tone C in the cantus firmus, the path to G in the counterpoint would have moved far more naturally through E than through F:

Example 239

In this latter case, it is also the two-voice texture that fails—and within the scope of an exercise must fail—to explain why instead of the natural path just the more individual (that is, the less natural) was taken.

If strict counterpoint, as has repeatedly been emphasized, must avoid dubious unified configurations and always prefer the natural to the artificial, then obviously it goes against the grain of counterpoint, at least within the sphere of its own interests, to permit a dissonance-tactic that leads to effects like a, b, and c. In seeking a solution to the problem—that is, in seeking devices that could counteract the danger of an anticipation or of a too differentiated, thus too individual turn of the melodic line—, strict counterpoint found the most suitable device to be the *horizontal interval of the second,* which at the same time can represent, in the vertical-harmonic direction, dissonances other than the second as well:

Example 240

The second used in this way (cf. Part 1, Chapter 2, §16) establishes truly complete neutrality from tone to tone, in that it contributes just as little of harmony to the tone that follows as to the one that precedes. For since it relates to both just as a dissonance, it cannot possibly maintain a harmonic relationship to even one of the surrounding tones. And finally, along with this, the second provides an especially happy fulfillment of the postulate of melodic fluency. What better solution could be found?

Thus it came to pass that long ago, in consideration of the attendant benefits for both harmonic neutrality and melodic fluency, the basic principle was established: *the dissonance on the upbeat may be introduced only by step.*

To leap either into or away from the dissonance on the upbeat is therefore—to formulate this law also in widely used schoolbook terminology—not permitted under any circumstances.

§4.   (b) About the direction of the stepwise motion

To judge only on the basis of the foregoing considerations, however, it would certainly be only consistent to approve also the following solution to our problem:

Example 241

since here, just as in Example 240, the dissonance on the upbeat still appears only in passing. But the two consonant tones surrounding the dissonances are identical; this unfortunately has the obvious disadvantage that all three tones enter into a higher-level melodic unit, in that here the one tone C of the counterpoint appears as though melodically unfolded. If this effect is to be suppressed in the interest of the balance requisite for counterpoint, then one must, as follows *e contrario* from the preceding, simply avoid returning to the same tone, while otherwise adhering strictly to the principle of the passing tone. Or in other words: *The dissonance introduced by step on the upbeat must also continue in the direction by which it entered.*

§5.   (c) The phenomena of the passing second and the neighboring note

The problem of the dissonance on the upbeat thus leads finally to the following graduated set of solutions:

1.   The first and most natural solution, which at the same time precludes all error, is that which demands of the passing tone a continuation in the same direction.

In this case the dissonance is called a *passing second*.

2.   Less natural, because bound to a consequence undesirable in strict counterpoint and thus of second rank, is the solution that permits a return to the same consonant tone at the downbeat of the next bar.

The dissonant second appearing in this case between the two identical consonant tones is called *neighboring note*.

3.   By contrast, all other solutions, which approach or leave the dissonance by leap (and there are infinitely many of these), must be considered completely unsuited for strict counterpoint—that is, for exercises. They are instead reserved only for free composition, which alone (in contrast to strict counterpoint), in direct proportion to the compositional disposition, can elicit and validate the psychological reasons for any more individual kind of solution.

It must not be forgotten, however, that the neighboring note offers an important advantage to the setting, specifically that of the interval of a second. For precisely because of this, it is often possible to use a second, so beneficial to melodic fluency, even in situations in which otherwise (because dissonance cannot be used in the form of a true passing tone) it would perhaps be necessary to leap. If the neighboring note shares with the passing second the advantage of the second, the two nevertheless differ significantly in that with the former, one note of the melody turns as though upon its own axis, as we can see more clearly from the following example of free composition than from an exercise of strict counterpoint:

Example 242

F. Couperin, Pièces de Clavecin: Troisième Ordre *(La favorite, chaconne à deux tems)*, ed. by J. Brahms and F. Chrysander

In the light of the preceding, it is easy to differentiate the passing second and the neighboring note from the so-called *Wechselnote* or accented passing tone (see *Harmony,* §167),[1] which has its place only in free composition. It, too, like the first two types, represents a dissonance enclosed between two consonances, except that it occurs on the downbeat instead of the upbeat:

Example 243

The scale of values of weak-beat dissonances established above is completely independent of time and fashion; it is therefore idle and childish to cite—just on the pretext of trying to write a "modern" theory of counterpoint—inclusion of the neighboring note as alleged evidence of an advanced point of view. The effects depicted in the above scale remain the same through all eternity, and are ranked only among themselves! And exactly at the cost of sacrificing the distinction, one can adopt sometimes a stricter standpoint (which excludes the neighboring note), sometimes a less strict (which includes it); but the possibility of such a choice merely emphasizes the differentiation inherent in the problem, never any kind of "modernization" of it.

Unfortunately all previous treatises have neglected to provide a foundation for the principle of the passing second. Thus [often] a perfectly correct solution of the dissonance-problem that arises just here for the first time (admittedly, it is only one of several solutions) is worked out in a completely preemptive tone, as a panacea. It is obvious that the student is ill served by such instruction; but the teacher is also at a disadvantage in that he himself does not have a thorough understanding of the rule he adopts and teaches. For when the time comes to decide whether the neighboring note or, finally, a still more remote solution like the accented passing tone should be permitted in exercises, he simply lacks the security of any guiding principle. According to the above account, each solution with its own particular effect is clearly circumscribed; and as I have said before, all that remains for the teacher is to decide at the outset, in full consciousness and free of any individual whim, to favor either the strictest or a less strict position. Let each teacher and each student decide the matter as he wishes—so long as he understands just which side he is taking.

Fux disposes of the problem, without providing further justification, as follows (p. 74):

In this species no dissonance may occur, except by filling the space between two notes a third apart, e.g.:

Example 244

Fux II, 21   *diminutio*

diminutio

It makes no difference whether the filling note is consonant or dissonant; it is satisfactory if the space between the two notes a third apart is filled out.

It is clear that this definition of the dissonance permitted here applies only to a passing dissonance moving in a single direction, and consequently excludes any form of neighboring note. In fact, Fux avoids the neighboring note in his exercises as well, and uses dissonances only in the strictest form of the stepwise passing tone. Thus the following voice leading, in Table IV, Figure 1 (admittedly an isolated case), is all the more striking:

Example 245

As can be seen, a seventh is taken *by leap* at the upbeat.[2] If one respects the principle of consonance, and understands that such voice leading [as in the above example] belongs only in the realm of free composition, which from the outset is co-determined by purely harmonic concepts, then one can in no way excuse Fux just because of the truly severe difficulty in which he found himself. There is no question that the tenor in the second bar had to reach *D* by contrary motion if similar motion to a fifth were to be avoided; on the other hand, the tenor voice as such (cf. Part 1, Chapter 2, §2) could not drop below *C*. So what could be done? Obviously the voice leading would have had to take a different course much earlier if such an irregularity were to be avoided at the end.

Albrechtsberger, probably only obsessed with pursuit of a falsely understood modernity, permits not only the passing dissonance at the upbeat but also the neighboring note, and, significantly, without discriminating between upper and lower. After setting forth the rule of the passing dissonance—unfortunately without providing justification!—he adds (p. 35): "It is also permitted to enclose dissonances (including augmented and diminished ones) between two occurrences of the same tone, [both of] which must, however, be consonances . . ." (examples follow); but he makes no references here to the differences of effect. In fact, Albrechtsberger freely uses neighboring notes as well as passing tones in his exercises, as if use of the former in contrapuntal settings had exactly the same effect as that of the strict passing dissonance. Such a practice, however, which ignores actually present distinctions as though they simply did not exist, makes ear and judgment ever duller; for the ear neglects to discriminate properly among effects that are in themselves differentiated, whereby a blurring sameness in goal and execution necessarily arises in the exercises.

Still more freely than Albrechtsberger—and for that very reason farther removed from the true goal of contrapuntal instruction—, *Cherubini* teaches on p. 12 in his rule X:

The strong beat must have a consonance. There are particularly difficult cases in which a dissonance can also be placed on the strong beat, but they occur seldom, and then only when it is not otherwise possible to avoid faults of a different kind, such as those that cause an excessively disjunct melody and the like. The weak beat can bear either a consonance or a dissonance, provided that the latter stands between two consonances and the melody that it forms is fluent. Such a dissonance is called *passing.*

In this rule, then, passing dissonance, neighboring note, and even accented passing tone lie side by side, and no further discrimination or justification indicates how different these concepts are! But this much is clear in any case: Cherubini's textual presentation includes the neighboring note, and he thus proceeds to use it freely in the exercises. But the most astonishing thing in his discussion is the inclusion of even the accented passing tone in the exercises of strict counterpoint. Compare his example 48:

Example 246

Whoever cannot believe that this is nothing but a lamentable, serious misunderstanding on Cherubini's part concerning the purpose of contrapuntal doctrine need only read the following remark of his, which concerns the example cited above:

> I could have proceeded differently, but by placing the dissonance on the strong beat I achieve a more graceful and pleasant melody, and that is sufficient reason to justify nonobservance of the rule. During the course of his studies, the student will find many other cases in which he will want to take advantage of this procedure. Incidentally, one can learn from this example how the counterpoint must be constructed in conformity with the strictest rules of art if it is to conjoin both pleasant melody and the style uniquely appropriate to this genre of composition.

The contrapuntal exercise, with its modest resources, is supposed to inform the ear for the first time about the manifold phenomena of the tonal world—for example, in this case, about passing dissonance, neighboring note, and accented passing tone. Now if we insist on immediately infusing it with what is called "style"; in other words, if we represent the exercises as actual examples of a particular compositional genre and, citing necessities inherent in that genre, attempt to justify the violation of "rules" in them; in short, if we write actual *compositions* where we should instead learn to differentiate effects within the realm of an exercise constructed expressly for that purpose, then the hodgepodge of concepts and principles undoubtedly reaches its apex! And yet, I almost suspect that Cherubini's aberration, like that of Albrechtsberger, is again only the result of an unfortunate delusion of modernism, which, as we have already seen and will see often again, prevents the theorist from grasping what alone should be taught as the true task of counterpoint.

Bellermann (see pp. 150–151) was the first to return to the strictness of Fux in its entirety, in keeping with his preference for transmitting the latter's teaching. He requires the dissonance to progress by step in the same direction, and explicitly excludes the neighboring note with the following words:

Note well that this can be done only as indicated here, and that the *passing* dissonance is not to be confused with the *neighboring note*. The latter term likewise signifies a dissonance on the weak beat; however, this dissonance does not move ahead in the same direction, but returns to the first tone or sometimes progresses by a foreign interval,[3] such as:

Example 247

The composers of the sixteenth century knew this type of dissonance as well, to be sure, but they used it only in quicker note-values—quarters and eighths—and even then only rarely.

Leaving aside the fact that Bellermann, like his predecessors, fails to provide any foundation for the most basic rule of the passing second, he commits, besides, the error of introducing disorder into the concept of the neighboring note in that he confuses it, in the second and third examples, with the anticipation. Bellermann's reference to the compositional practice of the sixteenth century would have to be considered admirable if, along with it, he could have seen his way clear to remark that the effects of neighboring note and anticipation certainly have been sought out in composition for a very long time (for this is true, and must be mentioned even in contrapuntal theory); unfortunately we must conclude from his closing phrase that he sees in these dissonances, even if they could really be sufficiently motivated on a given occasion by affect or other technical grounds, fundamentally only a license, an infraction of the rule; and apparently all that can comfort and reassure him about this infraction is the observation that it occurred "only in quicker note-values . . . and even then only rarely." Bellermann simply overlooks that even in the free composition of the sixteenth century in general, only little opportunity and equally little necessity for those dissonances existed; and therefore it is completely improper in principle to approve Bellermann's thought process and doctrine, even though in other respects one must concur with his position on the neighboring note.

§6. *The psychological significance of the passing dissonance*

If consonance between two voices expresses most exactly their will to belong together, so to speak—the commitment to unity—in the dissonance, conversely, we can find the mark of an independence, albeit only transient, of the one voice in relation to the other.

If, however, as in this case, the dissonance remains bound for the time being to the rather strict specification that it must flow back into a consonance, and therefore can count only as a path, or a bridge from the one consonance to the other, there is still no danger whatever that such a dissonance might destroy the unity of the two voices. Rather, the transient independence increases the value and power of the unity of the two, a unity that was intended from the beginning and is indeed once again asserted. Exactly in this situation we are provided a beautiful, deep insight into free composition, which strives similarly to abstract the unity of its "scale degrees" (see *Harmony,* §§82ff.) from the independence of *many* voices. The aesthetic effect of this unity will be the more complete the more richly the independence of the individual voices is constructed.

Here in two-voice counterpoint, however, where the *dissonance* is introduced *for the first time,* one should first learn to grasp its initial function, and the prerequisites of that function. And one should not forget that, however modestly the problem of dissonance here presents itself, in this beginning, nevertheless, we greet the wellspring of countless beauties in free composition.

The basic moral of this problem, however, like that of the permissible intervals in the first species (cf. Part 2, Chapter 1, §2), accordingly runs as follows:

In the beginning is consonance, that is, agreement!
Only after a consonance follows the antithesis, the dissonance, and ultimately agreement has the last word!
Thus dissonance, here as well, absolutely presupposes consonance.
Consonance precedes, and only through its contrast with consonance does the dissonance set itself off clearly!

As far as free composition is concerned, it emancipates the passing dissonance from the postulate of the second, so that it is possible, as an extension of the concept, to regard as passing dissonance even a dissonant note that leaps between two points of a given definite harmony.

The construction, permitted and sought in free composition, of varied harmonic entities leaves no doubt about the character of such passing tones, no matter what kind of leap they execute.

Compare, for example:

Example 248
J. S. Bach, English Suite   J. S. Bach, Organ Prelude and Fugue in C Minor
No. 6   (BMV 546)

Free composition solves in particular the problem of the passing dissonance within the space of a *fourth* (in other words: not just within the space of a third, as strict composition does)—indeed, in such a way that each of the two intermediate tones is equally entitled to function as passing tone. For example:

Example 249

How special the effect, in particular, when, within the space of a fourth that contains the leading tone of the key, that very leading tone is omitted and replaced by another passing tone.[4]

Example 250

Brahms, *Ein deutsches Requiem*, IV

Wie   lieb - lich   sind dei - ne   Woh - nun - gen,   Herr

Or:

Example 251

Brahms, "Nachtwache," Op. 104 No. 2

ru - fet das Horn des Wäch-ters   drü - ben aus We - sten

Or:

Example 252

Mendelssohn, Symphony No. 3, IV

See for comparison, on the other hand, an especially interesting example showing the use of the leading tone within the space of a fourth in *Harmony*, example 241, bar 5, left hand, first quarter-note; observe there the circumstances in which the leading tone d^1 itself appears in passing between the tones bb and eb^1.[5]

In free composition, the passing tone can even move in a *direction different* from that of the two harmonic tones, for example:

Example 253

J. S. Bach, Twelve Little Preludes, No. 12

On this occasion we may recall that in early music—see J.S. Bach's Suites, Handel's keyboard works—the passing tones (even accented ones) were sometimes not written out at all but only notated with a sign like this: ∽ (compare *Harmony*, Example 271[6]).

The innocent but charming passage shown in Example 254 illustrates the highly delicate and fascinating effects that can be achieved by providing

Example 254

Schubert, Deutsche Tänze, Op. 33 No. 11

h = harmonic tone
p = passing

just the passing tone with a *longer duration* than the harmonic tone to which it resolves. In spite of many other secondary effects that catch our ear, the above example really has to be understood this way:

Example 255

Free composition, furthermore, makes it possible also to *interrupt* the passing motion. In the following example:

Example 256
Handel, Suite in E Major

we find that the passing motion $d\sharp^2 - e^2$ in the soprano is even interrupted by another tone, so that the tone $d\sharp^2$ almost assumes the effect of a neighboring note temporarily, at least until the appearance of e^1.

Several other examples of interrupted passing motion may be cited here:

Example 257
R. Strauss, *Till Eulenspiegels lustige Streiche*

The possibility of replacing smaller intervals also with *larger leaps* (cf. part 1, Chapter 2, §17) leads in free composition to a passing motion such as that in the next example, where a ninth is used instead of a second.

Example 258
Brahms, Piano Trio Op. 8, I

The abbreviation common in free composition of two or more tonal processes—usually called ellipsis—leads, when applied to the passing motion, to the following phenomena:

Example 259

R. Strauss, *Till Eulenspiegels lustige Streiche*

We perceive the $g\sharp^1$ as coming from an implied g^1 that was omitted by ellipsis: $(g^1-)g\sharp^1-a^1$.[7] Such occurrences may very well be called *elliptical* or directly superimposed passing tones (cf. *Harmony,* example 264).

I mentioned already in *Harmony,* §164, that free composition, furthermore, has the power of suddenly changing, if necessary, the character of dissonant passing tones that first appear as simple passing tones. Therefore, the portamento based on *anticipation* (cf. Part 1, Chapter 2, §17) in many cases is nothing but a second which originally has the effect of a passing note. Compare with Examples 116 and 117 in the cited paragraph also the following illustration:

Example 260

Schubert, "Der Kreuzzug"

The first eighth-note of the uppermost voice is an appoggiatura to $f\sharp^1$.

The second eighth-note is the harmonic tone, the fundamental of the chord itself, which appears here in inversion as a $\tfrac{6}{3}$-chord.

The third eighth-note brings once again the same tone $f\sharp^1$; our perception subsequently interprets the tones in retrospect in an entirely different way, as here:

Example 261

suspension-resolution

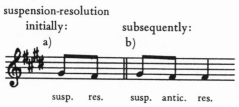

and understands the second eighth-note only as portamento anticipation of the third eighth-note, as shown at b.

The fourth eighth-note is another second-step; thus, the question arises whether this step is only a passing motion or something else.

The fifth eighth-note provides an answer; since it is itself an appoggiatura, the preceding eighth-note appears to us in reality again only as an anticipation—that is, a portamento.

The sixth and seventh eighth-notes show again the same situation as the second and third.

Observe at the eighth eighth-note the tie, the sign of the keyboard-portamento (cf. §17 of Chapter 2, just cited).

The following exhibit, finally, shows the assemblage of effects so delicately intermixed by the succession of eighth-notes:

Example 262

In this context one should also study the fluctuation of such passing tones especially in the aria[8] from Beethoven's Piano Sonata op. 110.

This category encompasses also anticipations—most of them even involving steps of a second, and thus having the initial appearance of a passing tone—as Liszt writes them:

Example 263
Liszt, *Rhapsodie hongroise No. 12*

(observe especially the legato applied to the whole melody!) and, in Liszt's tradition, also Richard Strauss, for example:

Example 264
R. Strauss, *Till Eulenspiegels lustige Streiche*

(observe in the first violin the original sign of a genuine violin portamento between d^3 and c^2).

By presenting also *complete chords* only in passing, incidentally, free composition gives the concept of the passing dissonance its maximum expansion. [See Part 6, first section, especially §§7, 10.]

As far as the neighboring note is concerned, even strict counterpoint, as we shall see in Chapter 5, uses both neighboring notes, the upper and the lower, in direct succession; this occurs at first, however, only as a means of resolving suspensions, whereby the first neighboring note is [actually] not so much a neighboring note as, rather, the dissonant suspension itself. Aside from suspension-resolutions, free composition creates, from the intent and possibility of forming larger melodic units, a great number of reasons to provide the principal tone with both of its neighboring notes (that is, the upper and lower seconds). The order within these groupings can take various forms, as illustrated in the following discussion.

We saw already in Example 77 how both neighboring notes occurred between the principal tones in the following order:

1   2   3   4
Main Tone—Upper Neighbor—Lower Neighbor—Main Tone

In the following example we see an even larger melodic unit:

Example 265

Handel, Suites de pièces, 2nd collection, No. 1, Air with Variations, Var. IV

which contains, in addition to the two neighboring notes of the principal tone c^2, also the harmonic tone a^1:

1   2   3   4   5
Main Tone—Upper Neighbor—Lower Third—Lower Neighbor—Main Tone

And how ingenious Mozart is in constructing the neighboring notes in the following figures:

Example 266

Mozart, Symphony No. 39, Andante, b. 10ff.

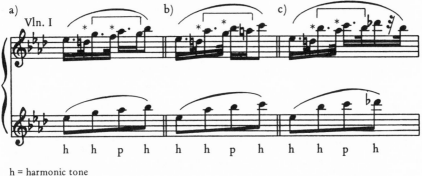

h = harmonic tone
p = passing

The first neighbor d^2 (at the asterisk at a) at first implies the return of the principal tone eb^2, but instead another harmonic tone, g^2, occurs (compare the previous example). In addition, the ear hears the bracketed passages as independent melodic units, as though, for example, the tone g^2 at a were the principal tone followed by its neighbors f^2 and ab^2, while the latter tone ab^2, independently of its neighboring-note character, expresses by virtue of the continuation a passing-tone quality even more strongly. (The effect of the figures cited here is especially interesting, because they appear in a later passage, bars 40ff. in the bass.)

That the neighboring note in free composition can occur simultaneously in two or more voices is due to the free number of voices in free composition in general.

Here is an example for neighboring notes in thirds:

Example 267

Handel, Suite No. 7, Passacaille

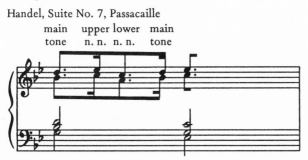

Compare Examples 113 and 167 in *Harmony* for neighboring notes in three voices; J.S. Bach especially was a master of this type.

Most recently it has been Richard Strauss who could compose neighboring notes conceived even in four voices in a most masterful way:

Example 268
R. Strauss, *Till Eulenspiegels lustige Streiche*

One should avoid interpreting here the fluctuation between C^{b7} and $B^{\sharp\frac{7}{5}}_{\sharp 3}$ (shown in Example 269) as a real modulation; this is an assumption contradicted by the basses alone, which, as can be gleaned from what precedes,

Example 269

present only the V of F major throughout. Instead, one may give the concept of the neighboring note its due even in such an application as this, without finding it an obstacle that the four-voice neighboring note is composed out by means of a motive. (Incidentally, Strauss attempted in the same composition—miniature score, p. 18, bars 1–4—a similar, even more daring experiment, which in my opinion, however, is a complete failure, since the harmony $B–D–F\sharp–A\flat$ (or $G\sharp$) placed between the F^{b7} harmonies is much too remote for voice-leading reasons alone (the B of the bass moves to F) to be perceived either as a modulation or as a neighboring-note harmony.)

By the same token, one should avoid hearing in the following passages anything but neighboring-note harmonies:

Example 270
Schubert, *Winterreise*, "Frühlingstraum"

Example 271

Wagner, *Das Rheingold*, Scene 3

(Rhine-maidens)

In the Schubert excerpt the sustained e^1 in the inner voice (bar 1, fourth eighth-note) shows in itself that the tones F♯ and A undoubtedly should be heard only as neighbors of G and B; therefore, in the next measure, where in the high register an E is again sustained, the event at the third eighth-note has to be perceived similarly—indeed, as a configuration of three neighbors:

Example 272

In the Wagner excerpt, one need only imagine an $e\flat^2$—that is, the fifth of the harmony—at the first quarter-note:

Example 273

From this, one grasps immediately the true character of mere neighboring-note harmonies in the original example as well.

Georg Capellen comments on the latter example in his *Musikalische Akustik* as follows:

> In Wagner's music one occasionally encounters these formations; for example: [see Example 271], in which G – B – F♭ is not an enharmonic E minor triad but an elliptical $E\flat^9_5$ sound with the fifth raised and the ninth lowered *(Hochquinttiefnonklang)* so that the succession of sounds belongs to the cadence MRM; anyone who has developed acoustical sensitivity will hear this immediately.[9]

Here I can only advise Mr. Capellen that he would do better to become an acoustician and leave hands and ears off our art. For whoever perceives a somewhat more individual manifestation of the neighboring note—how much higher J.S. Bach's daring neighboring-note in example 148[10] ranks, for example!—as nothing more nor less than an "elliptical *Hochquinttiefnonklang*" (sic!) is a barbarian and deserves his "exotic music"! I must repeat my remark in *Harmony*, §63: "How easy it is to fabricate theory and history of music when one hears badly!"

Highly stimulating is the study of neighboring notes in Beethoven's Piano Sonata op. 111, Arietta, Variation No. 4 ($\frac{9}{16}$), particularly in the triplet figures of the right hand.

The following example shows how, finally the *accented passing tone* (*Harmony*, §167) is used in free composition.

Example 274
Chopin, Prelude Op. 28 No. 24

D minor: I

Here the passing tone c^2 (within the space of the fourth $d^2 - a^1$) is frozen as an accented passing tone on the strong beat.

Or another, even more daring example:

Example 275
Mozart, Symphony No. 40, Andante

Here the accented passing tones (see the asterisked notes) do not enter freely, as one might believe, but represent passing tones of the most regular kind: One need only extend the fifth eighth-note of each bar beyond the eighth-note rest to the first eighth-note of the subsequent bar to perceive clearly and immediately the underlying passing character of the accented notes even here. (Compare the same figures later, bars 88, 89, 92, and 93!)

Albrechtsberger mentions on p. 17 "cast-out" notes (*notae abjectae*) and defines them thus: "A cast-out note is a tone that occurs as a leap in passing, but which does not belong to the chord; for example:"

Example 276

etc.

Beginning

§7. *Construction of the beginning*

The prescriptions for the beginning, demanded by the first species and certainly retained here as well, are expanded by the option of using, as a license, a half-note *rest* in the first bar, which, as is self-evident, must then be followed on the upbeat only by one of the perfect consonances: 1, 8, or 5.

While we will learn the usage of still other rests in the remaining species of counterpoint, here only the half-rest is under consideration—indeed, because it indicates the character of the intended species (two half-notes) with the same power and logic as a half-note would do.

For exercises in triple meter [notated in $\frac{3}{4}$], however, it goes without saying that only a quarter-rest should be used instead of the half-rest.

Albrechtsberger mentions this point explicitly on p. 71, where, at the conclusion of two-voice counterpoint, he writes exercises in triple meter as well for each of the species.

Main Body

§8. *Variety in treatment of the upbeat*

We may well elevate to the rank of an important issue the question of whether the upbeat should have only consonances or perhaps only dissonances throughout. If the latter is, of course, not always possible because of the structure of the given cantus firmus, the former—even though certainly always possible—is nevertheless prohibited. As a reason for this prohibition may be cited not only the goal of learning the application of passing dissonances but, far more, also the aesthetically pleasing effect that results from a felicitous *mixture* of consonant and dissonant passing tones on the upbeat.

The artistic principle of *variety* already manifests its beneficial effect in contrapuntal exercises, and it is for this reason that the student is here alerted to it at the proper time.

§9. *Spacing of the two voices*

It is imperative here as well (cf. Part 2, Chapter 1, §24) to attend to [the maintenance of] a suitable distance between the voices, to the extent that one takes at all seriously the pure realization of the vocal principle and strictness of setting. Especially the vocal element requires a correct distance between voices throughout, and only when it is desired to relax the strictness or perhaps to experiment temporarily with effects of an instrumental nature may teacher and student allow the two voices to arrive at a distance from each other greater than that permitted by the vocal principle. It should be kept in mind that the first stage of study should be devoted exclusively to pure vocal writing, while only the second belongs to the instrumental idiom.

It has been discussed already in Part 2, Chapter 1, §24 that larger leaps, especially the sixth (the minor sixth in particular, cf. Part 1, Chapter 2, §15) and the octave, under observance of the principle of melodic fluency, are best suited to regulate the spacing of the voices and to separate them in those instances where they have moved too close together.

In his exercises for the species under consideration, *Fux* unfortunately does not pay too close attention to the spacing of the voices, so that all too often they go astray into an instrumental idiom. I repeat that such inaccuracies, by necessity, only confuse the study and the purposes that accompany it. See above (p. 162) for the quotation concerning the sixth.

Albrechtsberger, too, unfortunately, pays little more attention [than Fux] to the strictures of the vocal principle, and solves his exercises mostly in an instrumental manner, wherein the spacing between voices is of but little relevance for him.

Cherubini treats the leap of a sixth in a bit more mannered fashion than Fux, but without any real reason. On p. 16, rule 7, he states: "In the first species of counterpoint the leapwise progression by the minor sixth is permitted; in this second species it should not be used unless the voices, because of the nature and pitch level of the given melody, have moved too close together and there is no other means to separate them," etc. And in an "Observation" concerning this rule, he says: "In the first species of counterpoint the leap of the minor sixth is in some measure prohibited, because this interval, especially ascending, is more difficult of intonation than any other permissible interval. This difficulty is amplified here because the notes of shorter duration allow less time to prepare the intonation." Cherubini's advice, formulated somewhat less strictly, may hold good: it is exactly the quality of the cantus firmus and the contrapuntal line that may make it advisable to use the leap of a sixth or octave even in instances where one or the other would have to be completely avoided according to the rules of Fux or Cherubini. For it is not only the purely material distance between voices that is a decisive factor, but also the aesthetic quality of the line, and this applies even in the strictest writing technique!

§10. Use of the unison permitted on the upbeat

The unison, still entirely prohibited in the main body of the exercise in the species discussed up to now (cf. Part 2, Chapter 1, §23), is on the contrary permitted here—if not on the downbeat, at least on the upbeat—provided that it can be continued in the most propitious way (that is, by stepwise motion in the direction opposite to that of the leap), as here:

Example 277

Only *Bellermann* writes about this at length (pp. 152–53):

It is permitted to use the unison, completely disallowed in the previous species, on the unaccented part of the bar; progression that otherwise would be faulty can thus be rectified [examples follow]. One must always take care in using the unison and see that the counterpoint is set in a melodically pleasing way: that is, if the counterpoint moves by leap into a unison, it should not continue in the same direction, which would lack elegance [examples follow]. A good use of the unison, on the contrary, occurs when the counterpoint moves by step back into [the space of] the leap (be it ascending or descending) [examples follow].

§11. A possible extension, resulting from new situations that now arise, of the prohibition of both parallel and nonparallel similar motion

In this species, the prohibition of parallel and nonparallel similar motion [to perfect consonances] receives new nuances of application because of the addition of a note on the upbeat.

To study these nuances, we can identify within the content of two bars (twice two half-notes) three cases, as marked by brackets 1, 2, and 3:

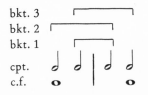

1. In the first case, that is *from the upbeat to the downbeat* (see bracket 1), the prohibition under consideration is still always in full and unmitigated force. Only this immediate succession is fully identical to the original situation familiar to us from Part 2, Chapter 1, §6, and, for that reason, it is the only case in which every exception [to the exclusion of parallel or similar motion] continues to be prohibited under all circumstances.

An interesting problem, however, is suggested by the *neighboring note*—assuming that one decides to use it here occasionally. The question arises whether the neighboring note used on the upbeat exudes so much individuality that it has the power to undo the bad effect of nonparallel similar motion. I would be disinclined to ascribe such compensating effect to the neighboring note, since nonparallel similar motions caused by it do not seem to sound at all better; and I can understand it when Albrechtsberger (who in principle allows the neighboring note [in this species]—see above, §5) regards Beethoven's voice leading in the following exercises as containing faults in need of correction (cf. Nottebohm, *Beethovens Studien,* pp. 51 and 52):

Example 278

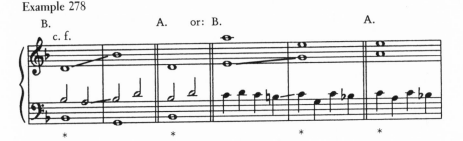

Finally, I should point out that especially in this case particular caution needs to be taken with respect to the so-called *ottava battuta,* of which we will learn in §12.

2. The relation of *downbeat to downbeat* (see bracket 2) should, strictly speaking, be completely exempted from the prohibition even of parallel progressions, since it no longer represents an immediate succession of tones. Nevertheless, the ear demands that the prohibition—exactly this constitutes a new extension of its range of application!—has to be respected to a certain extent in this case as well. For it becomes evident that under certain unfavorable circumstances [the progression from] downbeat to downbeat, despite the intervening note on the upbeat, nevertheless sounds almost exactly like a direct succession of parallel octaves or fifths—so strong is the connection made by the ear between both downbeats. In other words: the poor effect of parallel motion manifests itself so strongly here that it cannot be made tolerable to the ear even by the intervention of a third note. In particular, [the leap of] a third at the upbeat turns out to be an interval much too small and unassuming to be able to banish completely the bad impression of parallel motion from downbeat to downbeat:

Example 279

poor:

Only a larger leap, for example that of a fourth, is capable of removing the impression of parallel motion by attracting the attention of the ear to its own greater significance. For that reason it is possible to admit parallel motion from downbeat to downbeat, provided a leap larger than a third is used [after the first downbeat].

Two things, however, are not to be overlooked: first, that the tone on the upbeat, which has the function of remedying parallel octaves between downbeats, must occur only in contrary motion to the cantus firmus, since, for reasons stated under 1, one may not write as in the following example:

Example 280

poor:

and, second, that because of the leap, no note may be used on the upbeat that is not consonant with the cantus firmus; thus, it is not permitted to write as in the next example:

Example 281
   poor:

4

The question to what extent, on the other hand, parallel fifths as well can and may occur on the upbeats in connection with procedures for avoiding parallel octaves on downbeats—for example:

Example 282

—will be discussed later on under 3.

Finally, since the prohibition of parallel motion extends only under special circumstances to the relationship between the downbeats, and such successions are in principle allowed—that is, since the prohibition must cease to apply to more remote relationships—it is self-evident that *nonparallel similar* motion from downbeat to downbeat is generally permitted.

3. In the case of *upbeat to upbeat* (see bracket 3), which again does not constitute a direct succession of tones, parallel octaves, fifths, and unisons strike the ear as unpleasant only if several of them occur in succession. Without such a provocation of the ear, however, the *parallel* motions in this category—they are called *afterbeat* parallel octaves, fifths, and unisons—are quite tolerable; this in turn frees *nonparallel similar* motion of any restriction whatever.

It is worth noting, however, that it is more advantageous by far in the case of afterbeat relationships if at least the downbeats are free of parallel motions that might on their own again have to invoke the prohibition (see above, Example 282).

If I shed some light with a few examples already here, in continuation of the ideas expressed in Part 2, Chapter 1, §14, on how free composition treats parallel and nonparallel similar motion, I do so notwithstanding that a more detailed discussion in a special section will follow later. [*FrC.*, §§162–164.]

First, a prefatory remark:

It goes without saying that ideas in free composition are expressed mostly in a texture of more than two voices; nevertheless, it may be noted that any such texture ultimately contains aspects of two-voice counterpoint as well. The two-voice counterpoint between highest and lowest voice alone already justifies the citation of examples of free composition within a section on two-voice counterpoint. (One should not overlook, however, that composition for more than two voices permits licenses to a considerably greater extent than does two-voice counterpoint!) For example, the following content:

Example 283
Brahms, Variations on a Theme by Handel Op. 24, Var. XXIII

can be reduced to a clear two-voice counterpoint:

Example 284

The real connection between strict counterpoint and free composition can in general be discovered only in reductions similar to the one just quoted.

Finally, it should yet be emphasized that the special cases as indicated by brackets on p. 197 do not manifest themselves quite so exactly in examples of free composition, but this should be expected in view of the nature of the latter.

And now the examples.

Schubert writes:

Example 285
Schubert, Piano Sonata Op. 42, Andante poco moto

If one is so inclined, the octaves here, since they occur in direct succession, could be considered octaves of the *first* category (bracket 1). Free composition justifies the parallel octaves in this case, however, in that the bass progression strictly coincides with the scale-degree progression; that is, the lowest tones D—G themselves represent scale degrees to such an extent that their character as obbligato bass movement (*obligater Bassgang*) recedes into the background by comparison. Thus, it follows that a voice expressing the scale degree progression itself can under certain circumstances also permit parallels exactly for this reason.

The same reason is also decisive for the parallel fifths of the following example:

Example 286

Mozart, Piano Trio K. 496, I

Here, too, it is permissible to speak of a direct succession of fifths (bracket 1, as it were), because one may disregard the composing out of the harmonies as represented by the eighth-note motive of the violin; it is the power of the scale degrees, however, that suggests the necessity of the parallel fifths. For better understanding, the sequence of scale degrees may be clarified by assuming ellipses (cf. *Harmony,* Example 165) as follows:

$$G \text{ major: } I^{\sharp 7} - (II-) V - (I-) \sharp IV - V^{6-5}_{4-3} \text{ etc.}$$

But if one wanted to avoid parallels such as proved necessary in the Schubert example, one would have to resort to anti-parallels; compare Example 212 as well as the following examples:

Example 287

a) Chopin, Prelude Op. 28   b) Beethoven, Piano Sonata Op. 27 No. 2, I
    No. 3

If we consider the following examples, which again seem to present parallel octaves in direct succession:

Example 288
Mendelssohn, Piano Concerto Op. 25, I

Example 289
Mozart, Piano Concerto K. 482, I

these and similar octave-parallels are justified not only by the fact that the bass also produces the scale degree itself (as in Example 288 in particular), but also by the aspect of composing out, which carries even more weight here. The last eighth-notes in both examples are basically elements of the composing-out process and, therefore, represent only melodic detours (cf. Part 1, Chapter 2, §18), so to speak, that can easily be omitted; after the detours are eliminated, however, only nonparallel similar motions remain—specifically, from the first eighth-note of the fourth quarter to the first eighth-note of the next bar:

$$\begin{cases} a^1 - g^1 \\ d - G \end{cases} \text{ and } \begin{cases} ab^2 - bb^2 \\ f - bb. \end{cases}$$

These are progressions that are clearly justified in free composition, especially in composition for more than two voices. (Compare the Wagner excerpt, Example 182, and also Example 285.)

In the Mozart example, moreover, the principle takes effect that a voice of free composition can always abandon its character as an obbligato voice and strike out along the path of mere doubling; in this latter function it likes to join with another voice—indeed, precisely in parallel octaves!

A situation similar to that of the *second* bracket (concerning the relation of downbeat to downbeat) is found in the Chopin example in *Harmonielehre,* Fig. 370 bars 8–9.[11] The fact that the bass progression embodies the scale degrees is again the reason that justifies the parallel octaves. That, furthermore, the melody leaps by a fourth—a device that had a remedying effect already in strict counterpoint (see p. 198)—carries, therefore, certainly much less weight in comparison to the principal reason.

In the following two examples of antiparallels:

Example 290
Brahms, Symphony No. 4, I

Beethoven, Piano Sonata Op. 27 No. 2, I

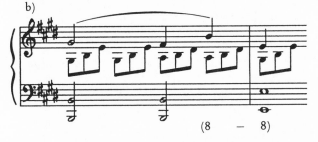

one may justify the passages not only by reason of scale-degrees and of bracket 2[12] but also by the considerations mentioned in connection with Example 288. However, it is clear that antiparallels, as can be seen, can occur even in the middle of a passage, and are not always limited, as is often believed, to cadences alone.

The masters avoid octave-parallels involving *neighboring notes* even in free composition. They write, for example:

Example 291
a) J. S. Bach, Two-Part Invention   b) Handel, Suites de pièces, 2nd collection,
    No. 1   No. 1, Prélude

At a, there occurs on the second eighth-note in the bass the tone *a* instead of *d¹*, and at b, *B♭* instead of *e♭*. (Compare also *Harmony*, Example 200, where, at points marked with an asterisk, the neighboring note is avoided for the same reason as in Example 291, and the path to the tonic had to be taken instead.)

On the other hand—if I may discuss this point here—the masters write nonparallel similar motion to fifths without hesitation in the same situations involving neighboring notes, for example:

Example 292
Handel, Suites de pièces, 2nd collection, No. 1, Prélude

Concerning *nonparallel similar* motions, however, their justification in free composition is the more natural in that the composing out of harmonic concepts and the elaboration of latent polyphony (compare pp. 59 and 63) already lead to them of necessity. Here are two additional examples:

Example 293
J. S. Bach, English Suite No. 6,   Handel, Suites de pièces, 2nd collection,
Prélude   No. 1, Air with Variations, Var. III

Afterbeat octaves (see above, bracket 3) enjoy complete freedom in free composition. For if in examples such as the following:

Example 294
J. S. Bach, English Suite No. 2, Prélude

the unifying spirit of the scale degree is added (in this case, the harmony A – C – E), then there is even less reason to criticize such octaves, when the downbeats[13] have thirds and sixths, respectively.

Another example:

Example 295
Brahms, Piano Sonata Op. 5, II

Fux teaches (pp. 75–76):

It should be noted, then, that the leap of a third can avoid neither two successive fifths nor two successive octaves, because the note [which] occurs on the upbeat in such a way is regarded as if it were not present; thus, because such a note, as a consequence of shortness of duration and limited space, cannot communicate the interval in such a way that the ear fails to recognize the relationship of two successive fifths and octaves. . . .

It is different in the case of a leap that contains a larger space—for example, the fourth, fifth, and sixth—since there the distance from the first note to the second has the effect that the ear has, in a manner of speaking, already forgotten the first note on the downbeat by the arrival of the second note, likewise on the downbeat. . . .

Fux even mentions that nonparallel similar motions, for example 6 – 5, are remedied by the leap of a fourth (cf. Table III, Figure 8). To state this explicitly, however, was basically superfluous, since it was self-evident.

Albrechtsberger discusses the problem at hand (pp. 36–38) in the same way as Fux. He concludes the discussion of so-called *afterbeat* octaves, fifths, or unisons with the following comment: "However, I advise beginners not to write many afterbeat fifths or octaves, since they affront many an ear in two-voice counterpoint."

Cherubini (pp. 13 and 14, rule 3) couches his thoughts in stricter terms. Despite a different formulation, even he arrives only at the same result as the teachers mentioned previously, but he is very much inclined to prohibit in general all parallel octaves and fifths from downbeat to downbeat, as can be seen from the following:

I note, however, that these ways of avoiding fifths and octaves were considered very reproachable licenses in two-voice counterpoint by the strict masters of old. I share the same opinion, and believe that two octaves or fifths on the strong beat can by no means be eliminated by intervening notes, whatever they may be, on the weak beat, unless the tempo is so extremely slow that all beats can be interpreted as strong. This restriction, however, does not suffice in all cases and, therefore, should not be viewed as a rule.

I conclude from this that the above method [of avoiding octaves and fifths] should be used only in case one writes for more than two voices or in rare instances where one cannot find a different solution.

I have made all these remarks and examples concerning the avoidance of octaves and fifths for the purpose of demonstrating the insufficiency of the rule rather than proving that they really can be avoided [by such means]. The rule, which I prefer to regard as falsely attributed to the old theorists, is nevertheless not entirely without value and can occasionally serve a useful purpose.

The basic error, however, that leads Cherubini to such strictness is again the fateful confusion of counterpoint and free composition. What role does tempo play in the exercises of strict counterpoint? Isn't the principal goal here to explore tonal effects in relation to their causes, without concern for tempo and rhythm? And isn't this purpose served if the ear is made aware of the fact that, in the case of two octaves on successive downbeats, it makes a difference whether a leap of a third or a fourth is used on the intervening upbeat? Even Cherubini couldn't ask more of the theory of counterpoint. Another error of Cherubini's is that he obviously considers it implicit in the rule itself that the prohibition of parallel octaves and fifths extend also to downbeats under all circumstances. But this is not the case. The extension of the prohibition to tones that do not occur in direct succession is, on the contrary, an exceptional situation caused only by the special circumstance of the third-leap; in case the latter does not occur, the prohibition, too, is canceled and again the *norm* prevails that the prohibition cannot apply to tones that do not occur in direct succession. This result, however, is just the opposite of that given by Cherubini in the above remarks.

§12.   *The so-called* ottava battuta

While motion to an octave is usually not only permitted but also required to occur by contrary motion, there is an exception to this rule, in which the octave, though arrived at through contrary motion, nevertheless makes a bad impression; this has led to the prohibition of such an octave. Specifically, when the lower voice progresses simply by step from upbeat to downbeat and the upper voice at the same time moves by a larger leap such that the two voices suddenly meet in an octave on the downbeat, then the bad effect of a so-called *ottava battuta* is produced.

Consider, for example, the following octaves, all of which are arrived at through contrary motion:

Example 296

A difference in the effect of these examples will easily be discovered.

While perhaps only an "empty" impression on the downbeat can be observed at a and b (a result, especially in two-voice counterpoint, simply of the octave itself), we feel the emptiness of the octave at c and d, on the other hand, to a much stronger degree, for reasons that have to do less with the octave itself than with voice leading. The poor effect is essentially softened at c in that here the upper voices as well at least progresses by step from the upbeat to the downbeat, but at d it protrudes more strongly because the *upper* voice moves by a larger *leap*.

This poor effect at d can be defined in the following way: our ear perceives the melody as too peculiar and individual, because the leap A to D occurs in the soprano.

First, every modestly musical ear senses that, instead of the actually chosen path, a simpler and more natural way would have led here to the same goal, such as:

Example 297

Two-voice counterpoint, however—and this must be stressed—is unable to make us understand why, instead of the simpler and more natural course given in Example 297, the singular path, as at d in Example 296, was chosen.

Second, the decidedly melodic nature of the leap attracts our attention especially because it is at the same time highlighted as a sharp contrast by the more tranquil step of a second in the lower voice. Our instinct, however, seems to require—not without justification, to be sure—that the more extensive leap, on the contrary, should instead occur in the lower voice, while the upper voice, which attracts our ear first of all, ought to maintain the natural quality of the melody and, therefore, move only in smaller, more fluent and singable intervals.

Third, the brevity of the upbeat emphasizes the unpleasant effect of the situation even more drastically; in particular, it appears as though the exaggerated tension in the melody were almost entirely disproportionate to the brevity of time during which it occurred.

Fourth, finally, one cannot disregard the effect of anticipation (A to D), which doubtless adds to the poor effect.

In view of so many disturbances of the natural effect, it becomes clear that a voice-leading such as that at d has to be prohibited entirely.

I mentioned already that at c all bad effects, in so far as they can be attributed to the leap alone, are absent; besides the empty effect of the octave, there is only the disturbance that the lower voice lacks the larger interval, which, by its nature, would have established a counterweight to the emptiness of the next octave. The question, therefore, is whether this deficiency alone is enough to prohibit such a voice-leading. I myself would prefer to let only the given situation decide this question: in two-voice counterpoint, at least, an octave of the kind at c will sound too empty under certain circumstances; on other occasions, especially in composition for many voices and in a more favorable milieu, however, the effect can be good. Thus, within the prohibition of the *ottava battuta,* one would have to differentiate more closely between cases c and d, and limit the prohibition to the latter in particular—that is, to cases in which the upper voice progresses by a larger leap.

Furthermore, since the *ottava battuta* involves *motion from upbeat to downbeat*—a progression that by its very nature highlights the bad effect—, it is clear that the prohibition could not be taught already in the context of the first species, where the distinction between downbeat and upbeat is still lacking, but had to await the second species (as here), which manifests those categories (analogous to the accented and unaccented parts of a bar in free composition) for the first time. The only alternative is to remove the problem of the *ottava battuta* from strict counterpoint altogether and treat it instead only in the context of free composition.

For the same reasons as in the *ottava battuta,* I consider it a fault when, instead of an octave, a *unison* or a *fifth* is approached in such a way that the lower voice moves only by step while the upper voice progresses by a larger leap. In the following example:

Example 298
a) Albrechtsberger, p. 90   b) Fux IX, 1

the effect of such voice leading may be experienced; note especially how in the example at b the size of the leap in the soprano contrasts with the unassuming second of the lowest voice in an all too individual manner.

As examples of *ottava battuta* in free composition may be cited:

Example 299
a) Mendelssohn, Piano Concerto   b) J. S. Bach, St. Matthew Passion, Aria "Blute
    Op. 25, I   nur"

Example 299 *continued*

c) Mozart, Piano Trio K. 496, I

The following example shows a *quinta battuta:*

Example 300

Brahms, Piano Quartet Op. 25, I

And when Brahms writes in the song *Auf dem Kirchhofe* op. 105 no. 4, bars 9 – 10, as follows:

Example 301

Brahms, "Auf dem Kirchhofe"

in view of the fact that the bass also could have been written this way:

Example 302

we may recognize a *quinta battuta* avoided in a most interesting way.[14]

Fux's discussion of the *ottava battuta* (pp. 72–73) has certainly become the definitive one. I therefore quote it in full:

[*Aloys:*] Then, from the tenth bar to the eleventh [of the exercise under discussion], you have progressed from a tenth to an octave in such a way that the lower part moves up a step while the upper part descends a step; such an octave is called *thesis* by the Greeks and *battuta* by the Italians, because it appears at the beginning of the bar. This octave is prohibited. I have often pondered this matter, but I can find neither the reason for the prohibition nor the difference that makes this octave permissible:[15]

Example 303

Fux II, 18

while the next is disallowed:

Example 304

Fux II, 19

where both octaves are produced by contrary motion. It is different with the unison that arises by progressing from the third to the prime—for example:

Example 305

Fux II, 20

in which case the unison, wherein the proportion is that of one to one, is heard only very slightly, and appears as though engulfed and lost; for that reason, the unison is never to be used in this species of counterpoint, except at the beginning and end. But to return to the octave called *battuta* mentioned above, I leave it up to your free choice whether you use it or avoid it; for it is not a matter of great importance. But when the octave is so constituted that the lower voice rises a step while the upper leaps downward several steps, in my opinion that is not to be tolerated even in composition for more than two voices:

Example 306

Fux II, 14

This also holds true especially of the unison:

Example 307
Fux II, 15

In composition for eight voices, such leaps in the bass and in voices that represent the bass can scarcely be avoided, as will be mentioned at the proper time.

Fux presents these thoughts in the context of the first species. This in itself already signifies a misunderstanding of the *ottava battuta*, because here the element is still lacking which so clearly exposes the emptiness of the octave in the first place—namely, the differentiation of downbeat and upbeat. The *ottava battuta* in general cannot really produce its full effect until free composition, where the accented and unaccented parts of the bar play such a prominent role; see Examples 299 and 300 above.

However, we do not learn from Fux what effect it has when the upper voice progresses by leap instead of the lower one, and why in this case the *ottava battuta* is to be prohibited; it is simply his "opinion" that such a voice leading should not be tolerated, even in counterpoint for more than two voices.

Albrechtsberger deals with the *ottava battuta* as follows (pp. 28–29):

It remains to be noted that the old teachers prohibited the *ottava battuta* in composition for two as well as more than two voices. I prefer to use it neither in strict nor in free writing for two voices; it may be acceptable in three-voice writing, even more so in four-voice, especially if double counterpoint at the octave is involved. The *ottava battuta* (in German: *Streichoktave*) is that octave which occurs on the stroke or beat, that is, the accented part of the bar. [Here follows an explanation of what constitutes an accented part of the bar through all meters.] When a perfect octave is approached in the upper voice by leaping through a fourth, fifth, or sixth from an unaccented to an accented part of the bar and the lower voice ascends only by a half- or whole-step in contrary motion, the *ottava battuta* results; it can occur in the following ways:

Example 308
In strict setting of the first species   In free settings

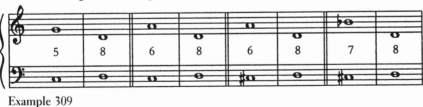

Example 309
In strict setting of the second species   In free settings

[Examples follow of both third-species counterpoint and free composition.] The reason it is prohibited may be that it becomes too faint and almost resembles the unison; for example:

Example 310

likewise in
all modes

As is evident, Albrechtsberger is no more able than Fux to specify the true reasons for the prohibition; in attributing the poor effect solely to the emptiness of the octave, Albrechtsberger, too, disregards the extent to which it is caused by the larger leap itself as well as the downbeat. True, he formulates the prohibition somewhat more precisely, in that he stipulates the leap of at least a fourth in the upper voice as a condition for its application; for that reason, c in our Example 296 would not be an *ottava battuta* for him. This alone already marks an essential step forward, as compared to Fux, in understanding the problem of *ottava battuta*.

Cherubini seems in general to ignore the prohibition of *ottava battuta;* he does not mention the term anywhere, nor does he concern himself in practice with the traditional prohibition. On the contrary, he writes in Example 40 on p. 14:

Example 311

and since he considers the octave-parallels of the downbeats to be avoided more convincingly by the leap of a sixth than, for example, a fifth or a fourth, he is not even deterred by the unpleasant effect of the *ottava battuta* that is undoubtedly produced in this case!

Bellermann follows entirely on the track of the venerable master Fux, whom he cites, incidentally, on pp. 136–137. Nevertheless, we find in his work (p. 205) the following voice leading:

Example 312

which, according to Fux's views and, thus, also those of Bellermann, would better have been avoided. On his own, Bellermann adds the following thoughts in a footnote (p. 137):

I find this rule too somewhat strict; nevertheless, one must admit that it originated in a very correct observation. In connecting the following two triads, for example, in four-voice writing:

Example 313

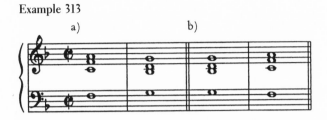

it will be noticed that the second triad at a sounds far less voluminous—one could almost say empty—in comparison with the first one. In free composition, where one is not limited by a cantus firmus, this usage at the accented part of the bar is not recommended; the same triads, however, sounded in reverse order as at b, have an exceptionally beautiful effect.

Unfortunately, everything in this remark is misguided. Whether the approach to the octave from the tenth, as at a in Example 313, is not, on the contrary, strong and convincing and, thus, the opposite of an empty effect, can obviously be decided only by the special circumstances of a given piece. I note also that neither Fux nor Albrechtsberger viewed a motion to an octave like that shown at a as a prohibited *ottava battuta.* Bellermann, therefore, should have demonstrated with different and more convincing examples as well as with more persuasive arguments that the problem of the *battuta,* nevertheless, exists also in free composition. That the example at b has nothing whatever to do with the problem is obvious.

The more recent theorists have little concern for the effect of the *ottava battuta;* nevertheless, it cannot be disavowed and, therefore, also cannot be ignored in theory.

§13. *The possibility of a change of chord at the upbeat*

The second beat, that is, the upbeat, can occasionally even present a *change of chord.*[16]

This type of occasion is, to be sure, limited to a single situation—specifically, when a sixth follows a fifth, or vice versa:

Example 314

This is a direct consequence of the following consideration: on the one hand, passing dissonances must be excluded from the present issue because, precisely as a result of their dissonant nature, they can establish no new harmony (consonance) at all [Part 3, Chapter 2, §2]; on the other hand, however, any other consonance [than a fifth or sixth] would quite simply only complete or continue the harmony of the downbeat:

Example 315

etc.

In free composition, unlimited freedom of harmonic change awaits the composer: it may be executed within a bar, within a single beat, and, moreover, also with devices other than merely the successions 5 — 6 and 6 — 5. By contrast, the change of harmony mentioned above is the *only* one admitted by strict counterpoint. Just in its preliminary uniqueness, however, it forms the entrance, the portal, of the problem of change of harmony altogether.

But from the necessity of clearly expressing the key at the very beginning of an exercise there follows the obligation at least not to use such a change of harmony immediately—that is, not in the first or second bar—because otherwise it would lead too quickly away from the key.

To make this point clearer still, I quote here the following (analogous) correction by *Albrechtsberger,* which applies to an exercise by Beethoven in triple meter (see Nottebohm, p. 49, No. 4):

Example 316

etc.

The unfolding of the intended key, according to Albrechtsberger, has to be rigorously observed even this far into the exercise. Decisions about this matter, however, can be made only on the basis of the given cantus firmus.

Cherubini writes in rule 4 on p. 15:

> Counterpoint of this type [second species] provides the license of having either one or two chords per bar; thus, if one decides to use only one chord, each half note must be a different consonance, but both must also belong to the same chord.

Example 317

Ex. 41

If two chords are desired, the chord on the accented part of the bar must be consonant; the chord on the unaccented part must also be consonant, but should differ from the first.

Example 318

Ex. 42

However adroit these observations may be, they contain an erroneous and regrettable contradiction that cannot be reconciled with the spirit of counterpoint. Why introduce here the concept of harmony (see Example 41) in the sense of *harmonic theory*? How is it possible in counterpoint to conceive of a sixth-chord and cause the voice leading to be influenced by this preconceived notion? Isn't it necessary, on the contrary, to generate voice leading in contrapuntal exercises only in accord with its own laws—that is, the requirements of the line, of melodic fluency, and the like? Furthermore, despite the second part of the rule, and despite Example 42, Cherubini seems not to have been aware that in strict counterpoint only the intervals 5 and 6 can signify a change of harmony.

§14. *The prohibition of tone-repetition is now reinstated*

Repetition of tones is *prohibited* in the second species. Thus we return here to the original prohibition, as it applies to the cantus firmus, and we justify this return (a contrast to the first species, which permitted the repetition of tones—compare Part 2, Chapter 1, §26) by observing that the enriched possibilities provided in the second species by the two half-notes make it possible now to achieve a beautiful melodic line even without any licenses; thus it is necessary to permit an exception to the otherwise universal prohibition of tone-repetition.

Obviously viewing the renewed prohibition of tone-repetition as self-evident, *Fux* and *Albrechtsberger* remain silent on this point. In *Cherubini's* text, on the other hand, the prohibition is already implied in his formulation of rule 4 cited in §13 above, especially by his words "a different consonance." *Bellermann* explicitly discusses the prohibition on p. 150.

§15. *Certain faults that can result from the proliferation of tones*

The proliferation of tones in this species could, more easily than in the cantus firmus and in the first species, lead to certain violations of contrapuntal voice leading and the postulate of melodic fluency. For this reason, one must beware of outlining a triad, a major or minor seventh-chord, or (still worse) a ninth-chord with three or four tones. It is equally important to remember to change direction after a larger leap.

Compare the comment by *Albrechtsberger* quoted in Part 1, Chapter 2, §§19 and 20. Here I want to emphasize again the results of that discussion; in strict counterpoint, only the construction of the cantus firmus and the course of the contrapuntal voice can decide whether or not several tones necessarily group into a unit. If they do, it is unimportant whether the unit itself is a triad [or not], since any unit-formation is strictly forbidden in the exercise. Therefore, Albrechtsberger is correct in writing on p. 42:

Example 319

and in commenting on the voice leading as follows: "Secondly, it is of significance that especially this *C* [that is, the concluding *C*] permits and justifies the major-seventh chord produced by leaping through four notes: *C, E, G,* and *B,* because as octave of the preceding *C* it makes the sensitive note *B* move upward, whereby the last three bars of the counterpoint establish a good melody." And similarly, he allows the following voice leading of a Beethoven exercise (compare Nottebohm, *Beethovens Studien,* p. 49):

Example 320

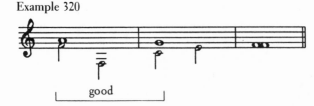

and remarks: "It is an error if the two notes that form a seventh fall on downbeats," for example:

Example 321

It may, however, be risky to prejudice such cases of actual writing procedure, which under more favorable circumstances could scoff even at this rule. Really, enough has been said if the student is instructed to avoid unit-formations, no matter how they originate.

From our strict viewpoint it is obvious, however, that Albrechtsberger oversteps the limits of strict counterpoint by writing, on p. 99 in a three-voice exercise of the third species, as follows:

Example 322

c. f.

In counterpoint of quarter notes, he outlines the diminished triad and, furthermore, even uses the interval of a diminished fifth!

§16. The prohibition of "monotony"

The proliferation of tones, however, could evoke, even more than in the first species, the danger of a unified motivic, melodic-thematic formation; for that reason, I again emphatically caution against such shapes.

Compare above, p. 101, the quotation from *Albrechtsberger. Fux,* however, writes without scruple as follows (Table IX, Figure 2):

Example 323

Fux IX, 2

Cadence

§17. Cadential formulas

The stipulation requiring both leading tones in the cadences of strict counterpoint can be satisfied in exercises of the present species only by using 5 — 6 | 8 in the upper counterpoint and 5 — 3 | 1 in the lower (compare also Part 1, Chapter 2, §23).

Example 324

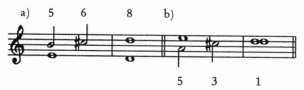

In this context it is to be expressly emphasized that the leading tone must actually be the *penultimate* tone of the counterpoint, never the antepenultimate; thus it is never permitted to reverse the order of tones as follows (compare Part 2, Chapter 1, §29, Examples 234 and 235):

Example 325

3   5   1

Only in exceptional cases, when the above formulas would be entirely impossible for one reason or another (for example, because of the peculiar construction of the cantus firmus), is it permitted to fall back on the closing formulas of first species—that is, to use a whole note in the penultimate bar.

Fux remarks already in the context of first species (p. 66, but compare also pp. 67, 69, 74, 76, etc.) that "if the cantus firmus is in the lower voice, a major sixth must be used with the penultimate note; if it is in the upper voice, the minor third is required." Thus Fux at the same time opts for the requirement of raising the leading tone in the Dorian, Mixolydian, and Aeolian modes: *c* to *c♯*, *f* to *f♯*, and *g* to *g♯*!

It deserves to be mentioned in this connection that *Beethoven,* too, has dealt in his own way with the problem of the raised leading-tone in the Dorian mode (compare *Harmony,* p. 77ff.) In one of Beethoven's sketchbooks kept in the archive of the *Gesellschaft der Musikfreunde* in Vienna there is a curious and ingenious idea, hastily written in the margin in Beethoven's hand and, so far as I am aware, unnoticed until now; it is an attempt to avoid the *C♯* in the cadence of the Dorian mode, as follows:

Example 326

6   5   8

Instead of 5 — 6 — 8 (compare Example 324 above) he uses 6 — 5 — 8—in other words, a kind of plagal effect, as though III — I. Beethoven failed to see, however, that the cadence in the Dorian mode too requires both leading tones always in direct succession [to the tonic]: $\frac{C-D}{E-D}$, and that there was only one remedy for the defect that bothered him: to give up the Dorian mode altogether!

Albrechtsberger indulges on p. 36 in various cadential formulas which, however, in many cases really belong to the domain of free composition. That he at least retained the requirement of always having the leading tone directly precede the final tone, however, can be proven by pointing not only to the cadential formulas to be cited later (p. 93f.) but also to the following correction of an error by Beethoven (Nottebohm, p. 52):

Example 327

Bellermann, too, speaks on p. 153 of the whole-note in the penultimate bar as an exception.

Regarding *Cherubini*'s absurd lapse in this matter (p. 31, rule 7), see the citation in Part 3, Chapter 2, §7.

Exercises

Example 328

Fux III, 3 and III, 12

Example 328 *continued*
Fux III, 15 and III, 16

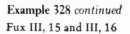

Fux IV, 4 and 5
Soprano

Example 328 *continued*

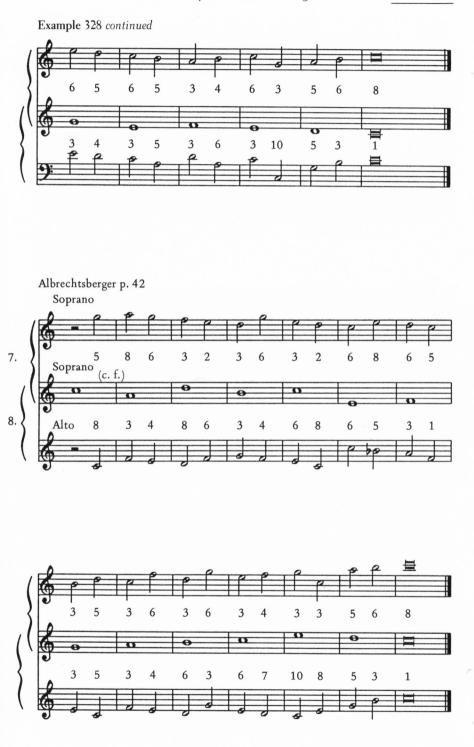

Albrechtsberger p. 42

Example 328 *continued*

Albrechtsberger p. 43

Albrechtsberger p. 70

Example 328 *continued*
Cherubini Ex. 48

Cherubini Ex. 48

Bellermann p. 154 (c. f. by Fux)

Example 328 *continued*

H. Schenker

H. Schenker (c. f. by Fux)

Example 328 *continued*

H. Schenker

20.

Comments on the Preceding Exercises

No. 1. The melodic line of the counterpoint lingers in an almost too monotonous way at the pitch-level of d^2; furthermore, it meanders awkwardly and aimlessly in the region of the fourth between a^1 and d^2.

No. 2. In bars 2 and 3, the two *a*s of the tenor are somewhat disturbing, because they appear twice in succession. Observe that in the last three bars the effect is already reminiscent of free composition.

No. 3. The line is beautiful; the only disturbing element is that it touches twice on the apex-tone a^1 (bars 7 and 10). Bellermann is unjustified when he "corrects" this exercise—incidentally, with little success—in the cantus firmus as well as in the counterpoint (bars 7 and 8) as follows:

Example 329

No. 4. A more instrumental approach. (Compare above, §9.) Bellermann uses this exercise as well, but streamlines the leaps in bars 7 and 8 by changing the counterpoint as follows:

Example 330

No. 5. A counterpoint with a most beautiful line. Observe the fortunate location of the apex-tone e^2.

No. 6. In bars 8 and 9, an effect similarly unpleasant to that in the second exercise at bars 2 and 3.

No. 7. Bars 5 and 6 as well as 7 and 8 show an inappropriate repetition. (Compare above, §16.)

No. 8. In bars 6 and 7, a modulation to F major. Concerning the last three bars, see the quotation above in §15.

No. 9. In the penultimate bar the sixth as well as the seventh tone of E minor is raised (compare Part 1, Chapter 2, §23, Example 140).

No. 10. Written entirely in an instrumental fashion. The intervals are no longer notated in actual size, but are mostly measured from the upper octave of the counterpoint. Unity of space (compare §9) has been completely abandoned here.

No. 12. Instrumental, so far as the distance between voices is concerned. Neighboring note in bar 3! See the quotation above in §5 concerning bars 9 and 10.

No. 14. A flowing, beautiful melody. But observe that Bellermann, even though he believes in the Dorian mode, uses the tone Bb in bars 4 and 5.

Chapter 3
The Third Species: Four Notes Against One

General Aspects

§1. *The principle of the passing dissonance in its application to the rhythm of four quarter-notes*

The use of four quarter-notes in the added counterpoint against each whole note of the cantus firmus makes it possible for passing dissonances to occur at any of three points in the bar: on the second, third, or fourth quarter.

As before, however, dissonances, wherever they may be introduced, must always occur as stepwise passing tones between two consonances, except in the following instance, which is perhaps the only other conceivable possibility:

Example 331

Here, for inevitable reasons that reside both in the fourth $D-G$ of the added voice and also in the tone B of the cantus firmus itself, the diminished fifth actually takes on the role of a consonance, so that the dissonant fourth appears in passing between it and the third.

Particular attention, however, should be paid to the effect of a dissonance that is to be used on the third quarter. To be specific: initially, the third quarter is heard simply as a weak beat; but the ear, by virtue of the further subdivision present of half-notes into quarters, is made conscious that the third quarter contrasts with both the preceding second quarter and the ensuing fourth quarter as a relatively stronger event, as a kind of strong beat. As a result, a typical secondary effect intrudes into the principal effect: it is as

227

though the dissonance were actually placed again on a strong beat, as though a "first" beat:

Example 332

In this secondary effect, then, is in fact to be sought the origin of the *accented passing tone (Wechselnote)* of free composition, which, accordingly (cf. *Harmony*, §167, and here Part 2, Chapter 2, §5), should be understood as a dissonance that is indeed conceived once again as a passing event, but at the same time gains a position on a strong beat.

Further, it is the artistic principle of *variety*, already articulated in Part 2, Chapter 2, §8, that demands constant pursuit of diversity—just for the sake of aesthetic contrast!—in the use of dissonant passing tones. The student should therefore strive, to the extent that the voice leading permits it at all, to introduce passing tones in colorful succession, so to speak—that is, alongside those on the second and fourth quarters, to use them without hesitation on the third quarter as well.

At the same time, however, it may further be inferred from the continuing validity of the law of the passing second that even here, as before, it remains incorrect to leap away from a *fourth*, for example:

Example 333

This holds true regardless of the extent to which the clarity of the harmonic conception (here the chord $F-A-C$) expressed by the counterpoint is intensified by the multiplicity of four tones, and regardless of how closely that harmonic clarity approaches our perception with something approximating the expression of a harmony composed out in the manner of free composition (see below, §8).

The exception described above of a fourth which, although it follows a diminished fifth, nevertheless retains the effect of a dissonance passing between two consonances, is taken from an exercise by *Albrechtsberger* (p. 52). I should like to point out only that Albrechtsberger himself obviously remained unaware of any peculiarity of this case. He considers it completely self-explanatory, even though on p. 43 he requires that every dissonance in this species "occur between two consonances." On p. 53 he intentionally constructs the following error:

Example 334

This provides an occasion for the following remark:

The . . . error is the B in the bar under consideration, because it does not proceed upward to the adjacent C; for if in two-voice counterpoint a perfect fourth on the third quarter is not led upward or downward by step, and is instead enclosed between two occurrences of the same tone, the impression made on the listener is that of a dissonant chord; this is just as faulty as if the fourth were to be approached by leap with two half-notes in the second species, for example:

Example 335

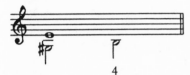

But from this it is perfectly clear that Albrechtsberger understood very well the peril of the present species—that of attempting, with the given means of four quarter-notes and even in violation of rules, to project a harmony, as though the environment were that of free composition, where such a thing could indeed occur without restriction. Albrechtsberger therefore marks as incorrect the following voice leading by Beethoven in the exercise cited by Nottebohm on p. 53 under No. 15:

Example 336

B.

He corrects, with good reason, as follows:

Example 337

A.

But the following precept in *Bellermann* (p. 158) may be considered an exaggeration:

> . . . thus here one must take care first of all that the first and third quarters in the bar are consonant with the cantus firmus, while on the second and fourth quarters a passing dissonance may be used [examples follow]. After preliminary exercises in which this stricter rule is diligently and repeatedly observed, one may later, in consideration of melodic fluency in the counterpoint, now and then take the liberty of placing a passing dissonance on the third quarter as well; but in that case the second and fourth quarters must always be consonant [examples follow].

But Bellermann appears not to be at all aware that even in contrapuntal exercises the principle of variety exerts influence in this matter.

§2. *Use of the neighboring note*

The remarks made in the preceding species concerning the *neighboring note* (cf. Part 2, Chapter 2, §5) should also be taken into account in connection with the third species. At the same time, however, one should remember a possibility easily overlooked, namely that the neighboring note (like any other dissonance, and also like the cambiata) can be used to very good advantage across the bar line—that is, from the fourth quarter of one bar to the first quarter of the next.

In a certain sense, because of the increased number of notes in the counterpoint, the need for the neighboring note is even more urgent here than in the preceding species. Nevertheless, for the sake of practice, it is desirable at first to adhere in the exercises to only the strictest formulation, in order to learn to solve the problem of melodic fluency and beauty also, insofar as possible, without using the neighboring note—and thus under more difficult conditions.

Accordingly, *Fux*, too, in keeping with his view cited in Part 2, Chapter 2, §5, appears to prefer complete avoidance of the neighboring note. He deigns to use it now and again only in the most pressing circumstances, such as in an exercise of the fifth species:

Example 338
Fux VI, 11

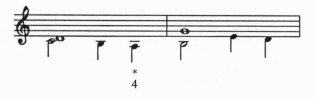

*
4

or the following:

Example 339
Fux X, 3   **Fux XVIII, 1**

A voice leading such as the following, however:

Example 340
Fux XVIII, 2

which uses even the anticipation (Bellermann's alleged neighboring note), occurs in Fux's work only this one time.

Like Fux, *Bellermann* too makes a commitment to the stricter formulation (p. 158): "Although the neighboring note is occasionally found in counterpoint of this species by sixteenth-century composers, its use in exercises is not permitted, because if it is used, quarter-note motion can be achieved without effort." The only misleading part of this is his reference to sixteenth-century compositions, which certainly have at least no direct relevance to the topic.

Beginning

§3.   *The quarter-rest as a license*

If a rest is to be used at the beginning, as in the preceding species, it must always be a *quarter-rest,* for that alone is able to give prior notice to the coming quarter notes.

In exercises in triple meter ($\frac{6}{8}$), for similar reasons, only an *eighth-rest* is to be used.

Main Body

§4.   *Increased use of the unison*

In the third species, the unison finds a more favorable environment than in the second. For in addition to the possibility of *contrary motion—*which remains available here in the third species when the unison occurs on the fourth quarter—, if the unison is placed on the second or third quarter, it enjoys also the advantages of oblique motion, which were unknown in the second species:

Example 341

1   1

§5. The prohibition of parallel and nonparallel similar motion may have still wider application

Concerning ranges of application of the prohibition of parallel and nonparallel similar motion, the four quarter-notes of the present species allow for the discrimination of four relationships, illustrated here as in the preceding species by means of brackets:

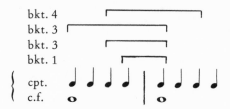

1. In bracket 1, concerning the actually *direct* succession of two tones, the prohibition applies in its strictest form and entirely without exception (cf. Part 2, Chapter 1, §6 and Part 2, Chapter 2, §11—bracket 1—and the pertinent remarks).

2. The relation of *upbeat to downbeat* (bracket 2) takes a form analogous to that of the second bracket in the second species (see Part 2, Chapter 2, §11), though certainly with the distinction that the second bracket there (in the second species) depicts the relationship of downbeat to downbeat. Accordingly, here as in the earlier case, the rule can be applied directly—that is, *parallel* motion is in principle better forbidden than allowed (although here again, as in the second species, the possibility exists of redemption by means of a leap larger than a third); *nonparallel similar* motion, however, is completely exempt from the prohibition.

3. But in the relationship of *downbeat to downbeat* in this species—which provides at least the further advantage that three tones of the counterpoint intervene and lay claim to our attention—*parallel* motion can be at least in principle all the more easily tolerated. Yet it should be scrupulously observed that if the counterpoint is not skillfully constructed, even in the relationship depicted by this bracket—thus in the most remote relationship—the ear nevertheless recognizes parallel motion and actually perceives it as a fault. So

the prohibition, since it is able to assert itself even in this relationship, can boast of another advance over what had already been achieved in the second species: just see how it has managed to extend itself from its initial area of application—the direct succession of two tones (see Part 2, Chapter 1, §6)—to the extent that it is here able to regulate the succession of tones so far removed from one another!

That parallel motions can still be painfully obvious to the ear in spite of the three intervening quarters of the counterpoint, however, is doubtless connected to the fact that it is precisely the downbeats that are strongly impressed on our hearing by the very rhythm of the cantus firmus itself. Or in other words: if the cantus firmus had a still further subdivision, perhaps into half-notes or the like, the impression of the downbeats at such a distance from one another would undoubtedly be very much weakened.

In view of this perception [of the prominence of downbeats], however, the best recommendation is rather to avoid parallel motions in the main body of the exercise, so that they can be used with so much better conscience only in cadential formulas or with the nota cambiata (to be discussed shortly), because of one or another attendant difficulty.

Finally, it goes without saying that *nonparallel similar* motions may be used without restriction, as was the case already in bracket 2.

4.　In bracket 4, from *upbeat to upbeat,* the formation known as *"after-beat"* octaves or fifths may be completely exempted from the prohibition.

It may be reported here that in regard to "afterbeat" octaves or fifths, neither *Fux* nor *Albrechtsberger* displays any kind of reticence; they use them freely in their exercises as well. Compare Fux, Table VI, Figure 6; Table VI, Figure 9; Table XII, Figure 5; also Albrechtsberger, p. 112 (bars 11 – 12).

Cherubini has the following to say on this matter (p. 20, rule 3): "In two-voice counterpoint, neither one, two, nor even three quarter-notes can avoid a prohibited octave- or fifth-succession, or cancel its effect, even if in certain cases contrary motion is used, or leaps greater than a third:"

Example 342

one quarter-note:

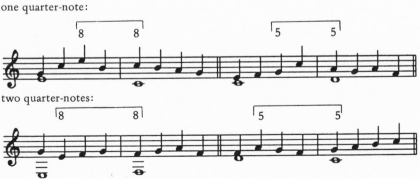

two quarter-notes:

Example 342 *continued*

three quarter-notes:

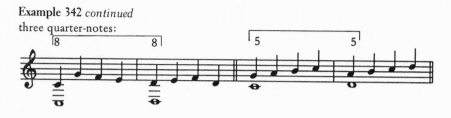

Obviously, this is the same exaggerated, in a way already fossilized and unprincipled strictness that we observed in connection with his treatment of the same problem earlier, in the second species. (Compare the remarks in Part 2, Chapter 2, §11.) And when he goes so far as to create a new field of application for the prohibition—indeed, in the relationship of second quarter to subsequent downbeat—, we can endorse such aural sensitivity only to a very limited extent: under certain circumstances a parallel motion even in this relationship could strike the ear in an all too unpleasant way; it remains, nevertheless, an exaggeration to formulate the prohibition so strictly, even if only for the exercises of strict counterpoint![1]

§6. A *faulty third-leap*

Among the contrapuntal theorists, Albrechtsberger is the only one who calls attention (on p. 44f.) to the following "offense against good melody," which occurs "when after four, or even only three, stepwise ascending notes an upward third-leap is made into the next bar; and also conversely, when a downward third-leap is made into a bar after three or four notes descending by step"—for example:

Example 343

He continues: "Larger leaps after the same type of motion also are seldom good"—for example:

Example 344

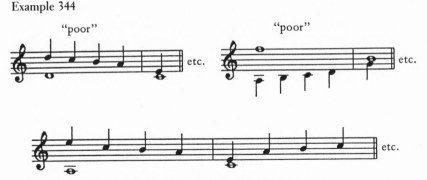

"good, because the chords are almost the same"

Albrechtsberger is certainly correct with this stricture. As the reason for this poor effect—unfortunately Albrechtsberger neglected to give one himself—the following should be cited: after the strong and extended succession of seconds, even the smallest leap will have to be noticed as melodically altogether too particular and individual. And sometimes, when the interval of the leap is added harmonically to the preceding tones, an unwelcome diminished chord or a seventh- or ninth-chord suddenly results. If one observes further that the leap is forbidden not in the middle of the bar but only when it leads "into a new bar," then it is in the last analysis also the measure-boundary that exposes the poor effect of the leap, reproachable already from the melodic standpoint, also in the rhythmic domain—hence all the more glaringly.

But certainly, it depends completely on the particular situation in such a case whether contrary motion is to be recommended as the best solution; if neutrality and complete equilibrium of all tones of the counterpoint are kept in view as the unalterable final goal, then other methods will also be found to avoid such "offenses against good melody."

Consider the following example from free composition:

Example 345
J. S. Bach, Prelude and Fugue BWV 894 (Arpeggio-passage)

This example shows the danger of the error discussed in this paragraph. One need only insert at the bracketed place the tone *b* (as in the first figure)

after $c\sharp^1$, thereby creating a third-leap $b—g\sharp$, to be convinced of the poor effect of the latter! (This is above and beyond the additional necessity in this case of expressing the $\frac{6}{4}$-chord $[a-d-f]$.

§7. The nota cambiata (changing-tone figure)

Traditionally and generally, the formation called *nota cambiata* is taught in the third species.

The phenomenon represents an organic *unit consisting of five tones* whose course is immutably fixed; for example:

Example 346

The infraction in this example of the rule of passing dissonance can be noticed immediately: the dissonance of the seventh at the second quarter, which is first introduced in compliance with the rule (that is, by step), is unfortunately left in a manner contrary to the rule (by leap) as the counterpoint moves ahead to the third quarter.

In essence, however, the offense is only apparent; for the second quarter (d^2 in our example) is very well connected—connected indeed, above and beyond the interpolated third quarter, to the fourth quarter (c^2). By virtue of this connection, the mandate of the passing second nevertheless finds its complete and just fulfillment, if only through the path of a detour.

The detour, to be sure, has its own further consequences; for the offending third quarter, as though under penalty for having delayed the immediate consummation of the seventh that entered as a passing tone, must seek its own support in the form of an absolutely consonant relationship to the cantus firmus; that is, it must at least be underwritten and supported by the latter through the quality of consonance if it is successfully to play the role of a delaying interloper. Moreover, the alien third quarter establishes a new base for a second, normal passing tone; for the situation it has brought about is such that the fourth quarter (c^2)—although, according to the foregoing, psychologically representing the destination, so to speak, of the first passing motion (the first, second, and fourth quarters)—itself functions simultaneously as a passing tone between the third quarter of the first bar and the downbeat of the next (i.e., between the third and fifth notes of the complete figure in our example).

Or, to put it differently: the nota cambiata represents *two passing-tone motions,* which, although interlocking, are nevertheless genuine and complete; see the bracketed tone-successions a and b in the following illustration:

Example 347

Each individual passing tone otherwise exhibits completely normal construction in that the dissonance is actually presented in stepwise motion. It is just that the middle tone of the second passing motion must at the same time be understood as the final tone of the first; and it is exactly this feature that produces the interlocking character and the apparent irregularity of the phenomenon.

The following, then, can be viewed as prerequisites for the nota cambiata:

(a) the first quarter of the group must be consonant;
(b) the second quarter introduces the dissonance, which begins according to rule with a stepwise approach;
(c) the third quarter contains the apparently faulty third-leap, but must itself in all cases be consonant with the cantus firmus;
(d) the fourth quarter continues the stepwise descent by which the second quarter arrived, and is therefore to be heard as both endpoint of the first passing-tone motion and middle tone of the second;
(e) the fifth quarter, the last tone of the group, is again consonant with the cantus firmus.

Accordingly, the following possibilities exist:

1. A genuine nota cambiata may also span its five-tone group from upbeat to upbeat, for example:

Example 348

2. A nota cambiata may be constructed equally well in the ascending direction as in the descending, for example:

Example 349

Under no circumstances, however, may phenomena such as the following count as a nota cambiata:

Example 350

a)

where the second quarter is in any case a genuine consonance, which may be left by leap at will; or this:

Example 351

b)

where the third quarter is not consonant with the cantus firmus; or:

Example 352

c)

where most of the characteristic requirements of the nota cambiata are satisfied, but the group begins with the second quarter, thus producing the overall impression of a certain lack of precision and transparency in comparison to the genuine nota cambiata; or:

Example 353

d)

which deviates from the genuine nota cambiata in that the dissonance on the second quarter, instead of being introduced by step, is approached by leap—we shall see below, in the commentary on the literature, what this actually represents—; or:

Example 354

which falls two tones short of being a nota cambiata; the configuration instead represents a harmonic anticipation (see *Harmony*, §167)[2] such as is often used in recitatives, especially at the conclusion.

From the aggregate of prerequisites listed above, however, it can ultimately be inferred that the nota cambiata, as a unit so extensive as to embrace five tones, fundamentally stands in contradiction to strict counterpoint itself, which, as we know, invariably postulates a state of complete balance. In the strictest sense, then, it can hardly be counted as a phenomenon of strict counterpoint.

That the earlier theorists nevertheless carried over this genuine element of free composition into the domain of strict counterpoint proves only with how little care and clarity they conceived the boundary between free and strict settings.

Since the structure of the beginning of the nota cambiata—specifically from the first to the third tone—manifests the space of a fourth, it is not only necessary but instructive to learn to distinguish between the nota cambiata and the passing tone in the space of a fourth, as I have presented it above, p. 184ff.

First, let us consider passing tones. As Example 249 shows, two [different] passing tones in the space of a fourth are possible from the outset; and it is the order of the intervals by which the passing tone is approached and left that distinguishes the two forms from one another. In one case, the smaller interval of the second is executed first, and only after it the larger leap of the third, while the other case uses the reverse succession in that the third precedes the second. It is precisely the latter form, however, that produces the more natural effect. The definitive psychological reason for this is that the more distant, so to speak more strenuous, leap of a third clarifies the direction with greater accuracy, and actually brings us closer to the goal than the step of the second; the latter, indeed, leaves open the possibility that the very next tone a second removed may be the goal of the passing motion rather than the tone of the fourth, which still lies at the distance of a third. For the same reasons, then, of the two possible descending passing tones in the space of a fourth:

Example 355

again the form at a has the advantages of naturalness in comparison to that
at b. Obviously, under certain circumstances, only the less natural form can
bring forth a correspondingly marvelous effect. This is corroborated, in respect
to the fourth in the ascending direction, by the previously cited Examples
250–252; for the descending direction, on the other hand, the following
example may serve, whose profoundly poetic effect is based on nothing other
than form b of Example 355:

Chopin, Prelude Op. 28 No. 6

The simple fact, however, that in the case of passing tones in the space
of a fourth, regardless of direction, the postulate of naturalness is satisfied by
having the leap of a third precede the step of a second, implies the intrinsic
differences between such a passing tone and the nota cambiata, which in all
cases demands the reverse order. Just this observation permits a clearer and
deeper insight into the nature of the nota cambiata: it invariably adheres to
the order of second followed by third, because only in this way can it express
the fact that the step of a second initiates the intended normal passing-tone
motion, which is completed, with the aid of a second passing-tone motion,
only at the fourth quarter. The nota cambiata thus represents, to be sure, a
form of passing motion, but one of such unusual and intricate construction
as is not yet exhibited by the passing tone in the space of a fourth.

The heightened awareness that has here been achieved of the existence of
so many and varied effects of the different forms of passing events—as such
we have thus far encountered the neighboring note, the accented passing tone,
the passing tone in the space of the fourth, and now also the nota cambiata—gives me an opportunity, finally, to explain further the diversified
phenomena of those disjunct passing tones of which several instances (Examples 248, 253, 257, etc.) have already been cited.

Strict counterpoint totally lacks the power to make us sense in advance
the coming harmony at any given point, since the force of its voice leading,
in spite of all the necessity intrinsic to it, is by no means adequate for this
purpose. Free composition, on the other hand, makes available such signposts
to the future in the form of scale degrees and other auxiliary forces of
harmonic logic. By thus sensing in advance—leaving aside possible
surprises—along with the composer the coming harmony (much as we read or
hear ahead when we read written matter or listen to speech), we also
immediately grasp in free composition the function of those tones that bind

themselves in advance to the coming harmony as neighboring notes or accented passing tones. Beyond that, incidentally, free composition is able to bring to life in our imagination not only the immediately present concrete tonal edifice, but, far more, the total complement of constituents of the harmony in all their possible registers and octaves. Thus if we find, for example, in a passage that we recognize in advance as cadential, the following:

Example 357

Handel, Chaconne in G major, Var. II

we understand the second eighth-note *c* of the bass as first of all in the service of the expected V, as the neighboring note of the coming fundamental *D;* but besides this, our imagination independently supplies, before *c,* components (either *B* or *d*) of the major triad on *G* that is being left:

Example 358

Consequently, however—and precisely this is the result inaccessible to superficial perception—even the second eighth note, the passing tone approached by leap, embodies nothing but the original form of the passing tone itself! One sees, then, how one and the same basic phenomenon manifests itself in so many forms, yet without completely losing its identity in any of them! However much a given variant may conceal the basic form, it is still the latter alone that occasions and fructifies the new manifestation. But to reveal the basic form together with its variants, and [thereby] to uncover only prolongations of a fundamental law even where apparent contradictions hold sway—this alone is the task of counterpoint!

After the foregoing, it is obvious in an example like the following:

Example 359

J. S. Bach, WTC I, Prelude in C♯ Minor

that a passing tone in the space of a fourth is undoubtedly present in the bracketed succession; that this passing tone, however, differs completely from a nota cambiata; and further that it deviates from ordinary passing tones in the space of a fourth in that it places in the foreground nothing less than the effect of an anticipation.

The passage from Handel's *Messiah* chorus "And with His stripes we are healed," quoted by Bellermann on p. 162, represents a genuine nota cambiata:

Handel, *Messiah*

Alto

Bass

Fux teaches (p. 78ff.):

Further, a deviation from the common rule occurs when the note is changed, a case called *cambiata* by the Italians. It arises when the second, dissonant note leaps to a consonance, as can be seen in the following examples:

Example 361

Fux IV, 10

This third-leap from the second note to the third should actually take place from the first note to the second, since then the second note would form the sixth, a consonance, in the following way:

Example 362

Fux IV, 11

If it were then desired to fill out this third-leap, the result would be as follows:

Example 363

Fux IV, 12

But since the beamed notes are not available in this species of counterpoint, good authority has approved the first example, where the second note is a seventh, perhaps because the melody is more agreeable.

Such commendable effort toward investigation of the problem, and yet—alas!—in these last words, how timid the attempt at a solution! If I nevertheless reject the solution, it is for reasons of my own that have been presented in the foregoing, and because Fux's utterances appear to me not to be in accord with the intuitive feeling that he himself must have experienced on executing a nota cambiata in composition. Besides, my treatment of the problem provides a still broader overview encompassing several other phenomena similar to the nota cambiata, and offers the means to distinguish and differentiate among them.

Albrechtsberger first cites Fux, with examples expanded as follows (p. 48f.):

Example 364

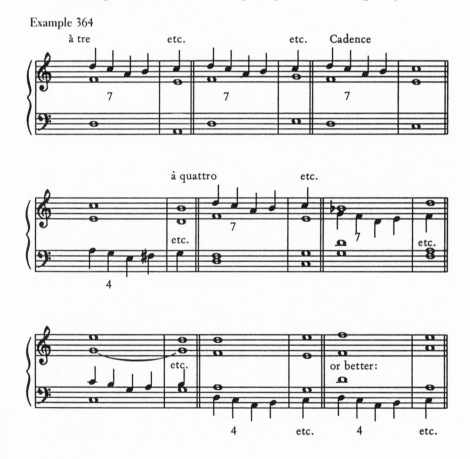

He then adds the following comments of his own:

These two changing tones (*Wechselnoten*), the seventh above and the fourth below [the cantus firmus], are quite often found in inversion among the works of other good masters, even though in settings of three or more voices, hidden fifths are involved; for example:

Example 365

Or in the following way, where they moreover use the $\frac{6}{4}$-chord without preparation:

Example 366

A critique of this changing-tone figure newly added by Albrechtsberger can pose no difficulty. One need only consider that, as he himself admits, it is derived from the works of "good masters." Does this not itself signify that they were found only in free compositions, and that, strictly speaking, they also belong only in that domain? What they have in common with our nota cambiata is in any case only the number of tones (five); for the rest, because the third-leap precedes the step of a second, they are all the more closely related to the passing tone in the space of a fourth. As a genuine trait of free composition, however, they are most appropriately recognizable simply as composed-out seventh-chords (*Vierklänge*), to which only free composition, but not strict counterpoint, has a just claim; and this is the basis of the merely apparent $\frac{6}{4}$-chord in four-voice counterpoint presented by Albrechtsberger in Example 366 as a "license": in fact, it signifies a $\frac{6}{2}$-chord instead! Albrechtsberger nevertheless uses such "changing tones" of free composition in his exercises of strict counterpoint as well. See Albrechtsberger, pp. 68, 69, 95, 96, 97, 119, 133.

Cherubini (p. 19) at first bows respectfully to the usage of the "classical composers"—as though they really had everything in common with strict counterpoint, even in its most primitive formulation!—but ultimately opposes the rule of the nota cambiata and announces:

> In any case, I would not know how to justify such an extreme violation of the rule; and tradition also has offered us no grounds on which this faulty practice of our forebears could have rested. I cannot understand why, instead of writing as follows:

Example 367

Ex. 52

they did not instead prefer this:

Example 368

Ex. 53

Likewise in the following case:

Example 369

Ex. 54

where they could also have written:

Example 370
Ex. 55   4   4

  In the last example there are two dissonances that occur in succession and violate the rule; this is sometimes allowed, if the dissonances move by step: sometimes one is forced by circumstances to write in such a way. But how the classical composers could justify writing dissonances by leap I do not comprehend—unless they did so for the sake of greater variety and in consideration of the short duration of the quarter notes, or finally, because the third is only a very small leap and therefore always rather easy to sing in tune.

With his wondrous thought process, Cherubini placates us really only with the confession that he has not understood the basis of the nota cambiata: that surely disarms any criticism! But it would have been better if Cherubini had rejected the nota cambiata by reason of good understanding rather than failure to understand; for in that case he would undoubtedly also have sensed the obligation of consistency, and would have spared himself the unquestionably more serious error of possibly allowing the voice leading of Example 370. In the latter, there are altogether too many licenses at one time; and if a similar idiom may elicit the most frequent application in free composition, it is nevertheless a self-deception and an obfuscation not to perceive that this idiom must then remain all the more alien to strict counterpoint. In the first place, Cherubini's example presents a combination of species, which can best be accomplished only along the path to free composition (see Part 6); further, the most primary law of the neighboring note according to strict counterpoint is violated, in that the third quarter is not once again a consonance; and finally, the dissonance of the third quarter by no means occurs between two consonances, which also must absolutely be counted as an error. Cherubini's explanation of his own example, incidentally, is inadequate: if the only requirement were that "dissonances move by step," what manner of bad voice leading would then have to be permitted under all circumstances even in exercises! The true reason Example 370 nevertheless has merit—but only for free composition, to be sure—lies rather in the following fact: the figure represents an abbreviation of two normal acts, which have been compressed into a single one; the graphic form of the first act appears as follows:

Example 371

and is to be understood as meaning that against one tone of the cantus firmus, four quarter-notes form a counterpoint with a neighboring note introduced in a perfectly regular way on the second quarter. The second act consists in the circumstance—to be seen later in the combined species—that the lower voice does not await the completion of all four notes, but moves ahead in advance to the next passing tone; in doing so, it counts on the fact that our instinct, in spite of everything, is privy to the true situation. The case is similar, for example, to that of resolution of a suspension:

Example 372

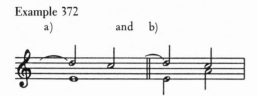

wherein our instinct is so familiar with the suspension's innate necessity of resolution that the ear can even be further burdened by [simultaneous] advancement of the lower voice, without risk that it will become confused and fail to perceive that the origin of the phenomenon at b is to be derived from that at a, as the first act of the process. It is clear, then, that Cherubini's dispute with the "classical composers" is therefore completely insupportable in the present instance; and for the rest, it is nothing but a flight of mad fancy to believe counterpoint and compositional theory to be completely identical concepts!

Bellermann writes at length (p. 159) in explanation of the nota cambiata; only excerpts from his remarks will be quoted here:

> The following practice was favored by the older composers. They considered a leap in smaller note values (quarter-notes) to be easier from a weak beat to a strong beat than vice versa. . . . They much preferred to make this leap from the *second* to the *third* quarter rather than from the first to the second, even when the second quarter thereby entered into a dissonant relationship to the other voices and, strictly by the rule, would have to proceed *by step*.[3]

And similarly again on p. 160.

This explanation is deficient, however, just because it is able at best to explain only the first three tones of the nota cambiata, but not the total phenomenon comprising five tones! Admittedly, Bellermann enlists the further aid of the following naively confused explanation (p. 160): "One finds almost without exception that the three notes following the leap again rise by step, so that use of the changing tone almost always leads to this pattern":

Example 373

But how could he defend himself against the still more damaging objection that he has, with his explanation, proclaimed as allegedly general a principle which finds no application outside the nota cambiata itself? Because if attention is supposed to be paid in counterpoint to "accented and less accented" notes (p. 160), as Bellermann's position requires, then it is impossible to avoid the question of why, as in the nota cambiata, a leap from the strong to the weak beat would not have to be prohibited in all cases. Further, I call attention again to that third-leap across the bar line which was forbidden earlier—see §6! And so, in Bellermann's case, we witness the following curious scene: although he comes rather close to an intuitive grasp of the phenomenon, he is not able to explain and defend it adequately, and thus, for lack of thoroughgoing comprehension, permits himself to be carried way by completely false ideas. He allows, for example, that "the changing tone can occur just as well on the fourth quarter of the bar as on the second" [p. 160], but on the other hand feels obliged to "excuse" the changing tone that moves upward with the following words [p. 161n]: "In the fifteenth and sixteenth centuries the changing tone is found only in the descending direction; in modern compositions however, it can be well used even in ascending":

Example 374

He has still more to say about the changing tone: "The changing tone was treated exactly as a consonance, and even in polyphonic compositions in which one or several voices had to sing passing tones, no heed was paid to its dissonant relationship" (a quotation from a motet by Palestrina follows); then on p. 450, in paragraph 4: "The changing tone should be used only in melismas; the latter must never be broken up by [changing] syllables"—a thought which reveals clearly that Bellermann perceived the nota cambiata as a self-contained entity only in the form of a unit of five tones. Nevertheless, he rebuts Cherubini, in an (indeed extremely) ill-conceived polemic, with the following words (p. 161): "And doesn't more modern music exhibit very similar idioms, which, if adjusted to fit the rule as Cherubini would have it, would sound very awkward? I think for example of the idiom not uncommon in our recitatives":

Example 375

In this remark he himself again takes into account only the first three tones of the figure, as though these alone formed a complete nota cambiata, or, rather, as though the recitative-idiom quoted represented use of a genuine nota cambiata (see the explanation given above of a similar phenomenon as anticipation).

§8. Recollection of several earlier principles

So far as the arpeggiation of harmonies is concerned, the prohibition with which we are already acquainted (cf. Part 1, Chapter 1, §3; Part 1, Chapter 2, §19; Part 2, Chapter 2, §15) remains in effect; it is all the more necessary because the presence here of several tones within the bar makes such an arpeggiation more tempting and at the same time easier.

    Special care must be taken here to ensure that dissonances are never left by leap. (Precisely in this connection, the fourth, as I have said already in §1, plays a dangerous role!) In case of necessity, then, when there is no other solution, one can therefore write as follows:

Example 376

But never this:

Example 377

Here—on the pretext of composing out, which is always insupportable in strict counterpoint—on the third quarter a fourth occurs, which, instead of functioning as a passing tone, is both approached and left by leap.

As for *monotony,* its avoidance is now all the more imperative, since the danger of consolidation into units is still more present by virtue of the four quarters than in the preceding species.

The effect of a *change of chord* (cf. Part 2, Chapter 2, §13) can be manifested still more acutely by the third species, with its medium of four quarter-notes, than by the second. Since the harmonies in the third species can be given a more distinct shape, their succession is also more clearly perceptible; and it makes a significant difference whether a change of chord takes place from bar to bar or only within a single bar. Instruction in counterpoint therefore has the task first of calling attention to the difference of effect in the two cases; if it nevertheless goes still further and proclaims that the delineation of only one chord in each bar is initially better and more natural, that advice is founded on the fact that before the tone of the cantus firmus is harmonically divided, so to speak—that is, before it is assigned two different harmonies—it would have to be more appropriate to present the single tone first of all in a single harmonic environment. (Often enough, it is precisely the neighboring note that most easily aids in this task, and facilitates, better than some other note, the retention of the same harmony throughout the entire bar.) Yet one is, certainly, allowed to carry out a change of chord by means of the succession of 5 and 6; only the first bar, whose unified harmonic profile (as said already in the second species) is simply a prerequisite for comprehension of the key, must be kept free of such a procedure.

The tendency and necessity of free composition to compose out harmonies, however, and thereby to generate content, at the same time provides a reason for the fact that within its domain, all manner of triads and seventh-chords may be arpeggiated. But in the same measure, then, in connection with composing out and the support of harmonic fundamentals, even the leap away from such a (merely apparent!) fourth[4] is desirable and permitted without restriction; for example:

Example 378

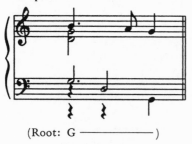

(Root: G ———————)

Albrechtsberger is explicit on p. 53:

> The best counterpoints of two, three, or more voices in this species are those in which each bar has only a single chord type, because those counterpoints are more straightforward and more solemn (as befits the liturgical style), and can be used also in quicker tempos when necessary. Yet it is not prohibited to cause a change of chord at each beat, with the following provision: the first chord, like the last, must be perfect.[5] And the perfect chord is by preference retained throughout the first bar, because listeners want to be instructed, so to speak, concerning the main key, and want to be made ready for it. . . .

Here too, it would have sufficed if Albrechtsberger, instead of creating a misunderstanding by citing the "liturgical style" as a real argument, had simply endeavored to describe the effect, which is indeed different depending on whether a harmony lasts the whole bar or changes within the bar. And finally, it is unfortunate that Albrechtsberger himself deviates in one case from the principle, otherwise so strictly observed, of presenting the keys securely at the beginning: in an exercise on p. 106, he modulates to G major already in the second and third bars, where the cantus firmus is instead in C major.

It should be noted already in the present context that Albrechtsberger, in concluding his treatment of three-voice counterpoint (cf. pp. 113 and 114), abruptly announces:

> The "NB" here [see Example 379] at the D in the bass signifies that it is not at

Example 379

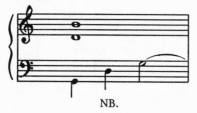

NB.

all faulty as a weak beat, even though a $\frac{6}{4}$-chord is implied with it. If this bar had to be set in four voices, or to be accompanied by the organ, the octave of the first note G would be added; the second note, D, would then have the passing—or better, arpeggiating—$\frac{6}{4}$-chord, as at No. 1 below [see example 380].

Example 380

No. 1   No. 2

"All good"

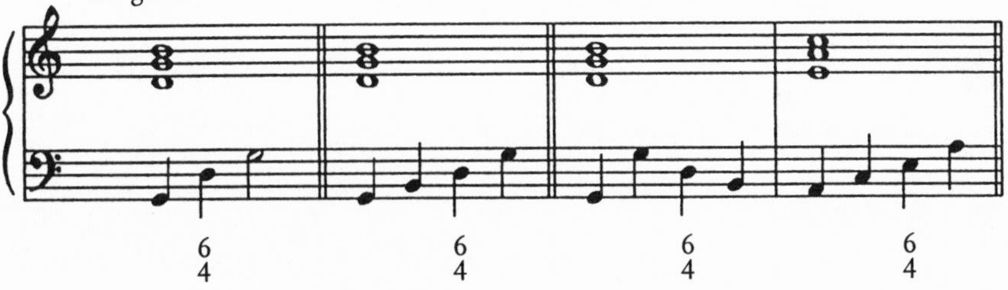

No. 3

Here, when the bar has four quarters, as in the third species,[6] the $\frac{6}{4}$-chord may be used on the third or fourth of them, when the bass arpeggiates an entire perfect chord or sixth-chord. It remains forbidden (without the use of a ligature) only on the first [quarter] note.

The author's confusion, which led him to such an inordinate admixture of strict counterpoint and free composition, is obvious for all to see. Yet I do not want to neglect, given such a fitting opportunity, to mention that the above invoked octave that the accompanying organist would be entitled and perhaps even obliged to add in the low register is nothing other than the scale degree or fundamental, as it is known only to free composition, and which there, with its own necessity, account for and justifies the content generated from within it!

Cadence

§9. Construction of the cadence

Since the other leading tone[7] must under all circumstances occur only on the fourth quarter [of the penultimate bar], the following, among others, are available as possible cadential formulas:

Example 381

Albrechtsberger marks as "poor" (p. 51f.) the following formulas:

Example 382

As can be seen, this is because of the parallel unisons or octaves from upbeat to downbeat.

Exercises

Example 383

Fux IV, 15 and IV, 16

Example 383 *continued*

Fux V, 2 and 3

Example 383 *continued*

Albrechtsberger, p. 52

Cherubini Ex. 61

Example 383 *continued*

H. Schenker

Comments on the Preceding Exercises

No. 1. Observe in bars 4 and 5 the added original flat sign, in spite of the Dorian mode. In bars 7 and 8, on the contrary, evidently because of the approach of the cadence, Fux avoids a similar use of a flat sign; as a result, however, he commits the error of two [successive] major thirds in bars 8 – 9—about which more detail has been given in Part 2, Chapter 1, §18. It is not without irony that Bellermann, who cites this Fux exercise on p. 165, uses the B♭ instead of the Dorian B♮ in bars 7 and 8 as well—what becomes then of the Dorian system, in which Bellermann certainly believes (cf. Bellermann, p. 49)?

No. 3. The B♭ in bar 3 is original, in spite of the Lydian mode; Bellermann, however, who also reproduces this exercise, removes the flat sign; thus he here does the opposite to what he did in the first exercise. In bar 9, Fux's counterpoint can hardly be called fluent and good; Bellermann is justified in changing it as follows:

Example 384

No. 5. In bar 6 the arpeggiation of the C triad makes a thoroughly poor effect. Bar 8 exhibits the figure discussed in more detail in §7. The parallel fifths on the strong beats in bars 8 – 9 are, under the circumstances, not to be condemned.

No. 6. Bars 1 – 2 yield a deadly, inexcusable monotony in their relationship to bars 3 – 4. In bar 5, the tone F is no neighboring note, although the D in bar 6 is, and likewise the G of bar 9. Bar 12 shows an arpeggiation of a triad (cf. Exercise 5).

No. 7. This exercise shows modulations in bars 6 and 9, and a neighboring note in bar 3.

Chapter 4

The Fourth Species: Syncopation

General Aspects

§1. The concept of syncopation

If in strict counterpoint based on a binary division of the bar (compare the second species) a *consonant* note on an upbeat is extended into the following downbeat, which is indicated specifically through *connection* by means of a tie, the resulting phenomenon is called *syncopation;* for example:

Example 385

Strict counterpoint emphasizes, however, that the note on the upbeat must always consonate with the cantus firmus. Thus, for reasons that will be revealed later, it excludes from its domain at the outset any case in which the note of the upbeat forms a dissonance that, although obviously first conceived as a passing tone, is nevertheless turned into a syncope by means of tying; for example:

Example 386

The following example from free composition shows the same thing:

Example 387
Beethoven, Piano Sonata Op. 110, Fuga

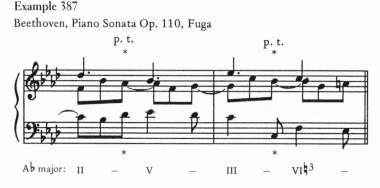

Ab major: II — V — III — VI♮3 —

We shall see later, to be sure, the circumstances under which even strict counterpoint itself, daring a first step toward free composition, nevertheless permits a dissonance at the upbeat: $^6_4$ | $^5_3$.[1]

Fux (p. 80) defines syncope as "two half-beats (*halbe Schläge*) against a whole beat such that the two half-beats remain in place and have a tie over them; the first must be on the arsis, the second on the thesis."

Albrechtsberger's correction of an error by Beethoven (Nottebohm, p. 50):

Example 388

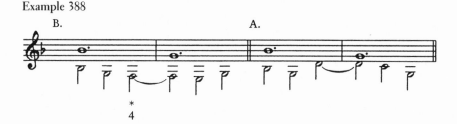

confirms strict counterpoint's immutable requirement of consonance at the upbeat.

Cherubini writes (p. 22): "Syncope is the name given a whole-note whose first half lies on the weak beat, and whose second half lies on the strong beat of the following bar"; thus:

Example 389
Ex. 62

Bellermann erroneously takes up the further development of the syncopation concept somewhat prematurely in that, even as he introduces the discussion, he speaks of the dissonant syncope in particular, and then forms the general concept. Only later, on p. 174, does he correct the error—only by accident, as it were: "The note that is tied to this on the arsis [= downbeat!] is either a consonance or a dissonance. . . ."

§2. *Classification of syncopes*

If the principle of syncopation—that is, the continuation of the consonant note of the upbeat into the following downbeat—remains always the same, the material content of the syncope, on the contrary, can be further differentiated. Specifically, in spite of [the immutable requirement of] tying and consonance on the upbeat, the interval that arrives at the downbeat may be consonant or even dissonant, and for this reason we speak of *consonant* and *dissonant* syncopes (*ligatura consonans, dissonans*):

Example 390

Strict counterpoint unquestionably allows both types.

Still, if the consonant syncope, in spite of its different external appearance, obviously belongs to the same family as the other consonant phenomena observed in strict counterpoint up to now, the *dissonant syncope* on the contrary offers a completely new technical and psychological principle: in it, by contrast with the single dissonance passing through on the upbeat and, indeed, between two consonances (the only one permitted so far), we at last encounter—for the very first time in strict counterpoint!—a *dissonance on the strong beat*. The new prerequisites and effects presented by the latter will be treated in detail shortly.

§3. *The consonant syncope*

Once the mechanism of a consonant syncope (consonance on both upbeat and downbeat) appears immutably fixed, all that remains is to form a clear notion of its continuation. And this is very easy to describe in strict counterpoint. For if, according to the principle of the present species, a consonance must always be placed on the upbeat, then motion away from the consonant syncope must always lead to another consonance, whether by step or by leap.

Apart from the fact that the new consonance on the upbeat becomes itself the basis for the next syncope, it now enters either (a) as a third party along with the cantus firmus and the note of the preceding strong beat to express the same harmony, or (b) as a second party with the cantus firmus alone to produce, necessarily, a change of harmony (cf. Part 2, Chapter 2, §13 and Part 2, Chapter 3, §8). The latter, as we know, is possible only with the successions ⌒5 — 6 or ⌒6 — 5:

Example 391

Moreover, especially in extended use of consonant syncopations, wherever possible the old rule should be applied, according to which an imperfect consonance is more desirable on the strong beat than a perfect (cf. Part 2, Chapter 1, §22).

Finally it should be noted that the unison, too, can appear in a series of consonant syncopations. More about this later.

Although *Fux* does not speak explicitly about them, *Albrechtsberger* (pp. 57–58) says: "The consonance-ligatures may move at their resolution [sic!] either by leap or by step to another consonance; but the latter mode of progression can apply only to the perfect fifth and the two permitted sixths":

Example 392

(Examples follow also of continuation by leap.)

It should not be overlooked, however, that in the example just cited he initially pays no further attention to fifth-successions, since he has set on the downbeat at a and on the upbeat at b as many as three fifths in succession.

§4. *The nature of the dissonant syncope*

If we compare the dissonant syncope with the phenomenon, familiar from the second species, of the passing dissonance, we are surprised to find that they have a common characteristic, namely, that in both, the dissonant element is situated only between two consonances!

The phenomena of strict counterpoint under comparison here are in fact made more similar to each other by this characteristic than they are differentiated from each other by the circumstance that in the syncope the two consonances enclosing the dissonance in the middle position are placed on upbeats, while in the passing dissonance they are placed on downbeats:

Example 393

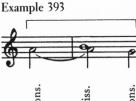

And their similarity is in no way canceled by the fact that in the syncope, the dissonant note of the downbeat is identical to the so-called consonant *preparation* on the upbeat, while in the passing dissonance, upbeat and downbeat must exhibit different tones.

In both phenomena the essential course of events—cf. Part 2, Chapter 1, §2, and Part 2, Chapter 2, §6!—is the same:

Consonance—Dissonance—Consonance!

In this light even the dissonant syncope is fundamentally nothing but a type of passing dissonance, a part of the general problem of dissonance altogether, which in the realm of strict counterpoint therefore includes, along with the passing dissonance on the weak beats (second and third species), also the passing dissonance on the strong beat, specifically the dissonant syncope (fourth species).

Fux is the only theorist who, although chiefly concerned with another problem, at least made an effort at the same time to explain the inner nature of the dissonant syncope (p. 80):

> Since dissonances come about here not accidentally or as a result of filling out [a larger interval] (*per diminutionem*) as in earlier species but, rather, essentially and on the downbeat, and since they have no attraction in and of themselves (as they strike the ear rather in an annoying way) but derive their beauty [*Wohlklang*] from the immediately following consonance to which they are resolved, the subject of resolution of dissonances must now be treated.

(Compare the citation in §15 below.) Thus we find here already an inkling that even the dissonance of the syncope, just like that of the simple passing tone on the weak beat, is to be grasped only from the standpoint of consonance!

§5. The law of downward resolution of the dissonant syncope in strict counterpoint and the limitations it imposes on the types of syncopes

The dissonant syncope in strict counterpoint must always be led *downward by step* to the nearest consonance.

The following table presents first of all every possible dissonant syncope:

Example 394

A) in the upper counterpoint

a) with descending stepwise resolution

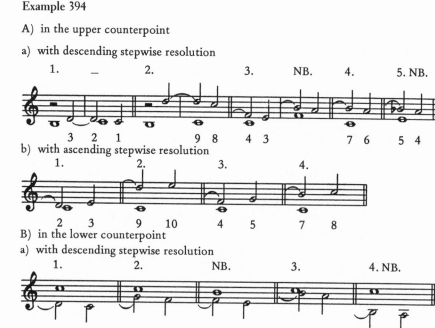

b) with ascending stepwise resolution

B) in the lower counterpoint

a) with descending stepwise resolution

b) with ascending stepwise resolution

All syncopes under A, b and B, b, however, are excluded at the outset from use in strict counterpoint.

"NB" above A, a 3 and B, a 2 is to indicate that the *augmented fourth* in both upper and lower counterpoints, so long as the paths of the syncopes in a strictly maintained diatony are not blocked off, must be allowed to appear without restriction even in strict counterpoint. In this matter—as remarked already in Part 2, Chapter 1, §3—one must consciously, if also reluctantly, take into account the artificial organization of diatony.

"NB" above A, a 5 refers to the fact that in itself, even the *diminished fifth* could be regarded as a dissonant syncope, if the requirement of downward resolution did not call attention to the insurmountable obstacle of the dissonant fourth, as an insupportable resolution.

Now to the most difficult aspect of the subject, namely the *reason* for the rule according to which only a downward resolution is admitted in strict counterpoint.

If we consider an example of free composition, like the following:

Example 395

Beethoven, Piano Sonata Op. 13, I

we find that a number of factors cause us fully to expect in advance—just according to the logic of the harmonies—the C triad (in $\frac{6}{4}$ position) that arrives at the third quarter of bar 2. Contributing to this expectation is the presence of scale degrees (see *Harmony, §84*) together with the composed-out entities that result from them, as well as the development of richer devices of polyphony. Consequently, given the clarity of the total situation, we then must sense perfectly correctly the function of all of the tones conceived as suspension formations, such as $b—c^1$, $d^1—e\flat^1$ and $a\flat^1—g$; these tones represent either (from the standpoint of the scale degree C itself) the suspensions $\frown 7—8$, $\frown 2—3$, and $\frown 6—5$ respectively, or (from the standpoint of the tone E♭, as bass note of the sixth-chord) the suspensions $\frown 5—6$, $\frown 7—8$, and $\frown 4—3$ respectively.

Because of its lack of scale degrees and its very considerable reduction of other resources, two-voice texture in strict counterpoint is unable to offer any possibility of attaining an equally desirable clarity concerning the function of the syncopes that arise in its milieu. But precisely the fact that downward resolution of dissonant syncopes was used in practice and justified in theory at a very early time—in fact, long before composers had learned to fructify the horizontal dimension through harmonies, to elevate the harmonies to the rank of scale degrees, and finally to bind the latter together as diatony and as system—makes it our obligation today to seek the reason for this rule (cf. Part 2, Chapter 1, §12!) only in the causes and effects of strict counterpoint itself!

Compare with Example 395 the following:

Example 396

a)
J. S. Bach, French Suite No. 1, Sarabande

b)
J. S. Bach, English Suite No. 3,
Sarabande

Here too, in both cases, it is the tonic that we fully expect in bar 2 under both a and b—indeed, after the preceding V in the first bar of both examples; and therefore the contributions of the harmonic components of the I are welcome and comprehensible, regardless of how they are brought in, even if it be by means of ascending or descending suspensions.

And similarly:[2]

Example 397

Mozart, Piano Sonata K. 333, I

On the other hand, if we consider any arbitrarily selected tone within the course of a two-voice exercise, for example the tone c^1, strict counterpoint cannot explain what this tone c^1 might be—whether a scale degree itself, or a harmonic component of one, or perhaps just a passing tone within some scale degree, or something else. Therefore, dissonant phenomena such as the following:

Example 398

whose ancestry and significance in a given place could be explained to the last detail by free composition, must remain unsolvable riddles in strict counterpoint, and no device (cf. Part 2, Chapter 1, §2) would be able here to help us crack these riddles. Strict counterpoint, then, in order to lend at least *some* kind of interpretation to the tone, invokes the only means available to it, namely consonance. Since it can by no means certify the dissonance as independent, under such duress it provides the tone in each case with the consonance that is only fitting.

I call attention once again in this context to the idea expressed on p. 153, and I repeat here: consonance signifies the a priori principle in the tonal universe. After all, strictly speaking, consonance adds to a tone only that which the tone carries within its own bosom by nature in the form of the overtone series, regardless of whether the particular interval is an octave, fifth, third, or only the artificial inversions of those (unison, fourth, sixth)!

Thus the tone c^1, to return to our example, must first, under all circumstances, acquire its consonance, before dissonances such as 7, 9, 4, 2, etc. (see Example 398) can pass above or below it. In the most fundamental sense of strict counterpoint, then, there can be only the following passing tones:

Example 399

A) in the upper counterpoint
1. the 7th:

2. the 4th:

3. the 9th:

4. the 2nd:

B) in the lower counterpoint
5. the 2nd:

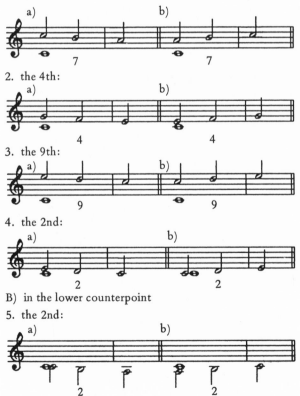

Example 399 *continued*

6. the 4th:

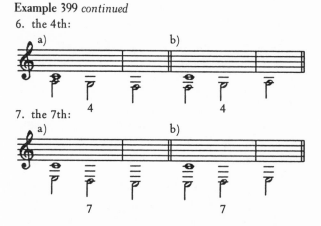

7. the 7th:

With this let it be once again most emphatically established that in strict counterpoint there logically can be no *fundamental* and endemic way to introduce a dissonance on the downbeat—that is, just on the head of the cantus-firmus [tone].

Yet strict counterpoint does undertake, given a preceding definite consonance, to place a dissonance on the strong beat, as an act of force, so to speak. This act of force consists in a *conflating* of two situations which were originally separate.

Specifically, in the *first* stage of this process (consider the following example):

Example 400

the consonant beginning (c^1) of the passing motion is deleted (see the parentheses), whereby an appeal is justifiably made to our instinct, which here is able to supply on its own the necessary consonance on the downbeat.[3] Therefore the passing dissonance can be moved forward, onto the unoccupied downbeat, so that the passing tone as such apparently ceases to exist.

In the *second* stage, the sacrificed consonance of the downbeat finds a substitute at least in the consonance of the upbeat of the preceding measure. The mark of this substitution is the tie, which, to be sure, presupposes *identity* of the preceding consonances with the dissonant tone. By this means, finally, the so-called syncope of a seventh is produced:

Example 401

among others. This phenomenon shows a stricter form than the accented passing tone and the free suspension, which will be discussed later.

If the phenomenon of the syncope is thus to be understood only as a product of abbreviation—the first *elliptical* process in strict counterpoint itself!—then it is also possible to answer the question of why the dissonant syncope in strict counterpoint must always be resolved downward. For if the tied dissonance is from the outset only a passing dissonance, then the basic rule of the dissonant passing tone remains fully as applicable here as before, specifically, that the direction of motion by which it arrived (cf. Part 2, Chapter 2, §4) be maintained. In the light of this, then, the answer to the question just posed depends upon which *direction* of passing motion (see Example 399) should be assumed in the case of a seventh, fourth, ninth, and so forth. This means that if we argue, in the case of the seventh, for example, for the passing motion as seen in Example 399 at 1a, then the seventh, as a passing tone coming from above, must continue downward; but if we gave preference to the other passing tone, as seen at 1b, the seventh would then have to continue its upward path; and so on, *mutatis mutandis,* for all the remaining dissonant syncopes.

Nothing is simpler, however, than to answer this latter basic and preliminary question, if we begin with the only logical point of view. It is, specifically, that in the absence of any more exact orientation concerning the meaning of the cantus-firmus tone, the latter must be supplied with the fullest possible, or most *definitive,* measure of consonance, so as to shape at least the brief moment of consonance-effect for the tone in the most satisfactory way.

So far as suspensions in the *upper counterpoint* are concerned, in deciding our preliminary question about the point of departure for the passing seventh—see Example 399, 1a and b—our instinct prefers the octave to the sixth, simply for the reason that the former interval (cf. Part 1, Chapter 2, §11) is more natural than the latter, which is only a product of inversion, and, ultimately, even points to a different fundamental:

Example 402

For the passing *fourth*—see Example 399, 2a and b—the fifth is more suitable than the third as point of departure of the passing tone, because the former draws the boundary of consonance of the fundamental better than the latter.

Since in the case of the *ninth*—see 3a and b—we must choose between third and octave, we decide in favor of the third, which provides more harmony to the lower tone than the octave. For the same reason, in the case of the *second*—see 4a and b—we prefer the third to the unison.

In the *lower counterpoint* the question of the beginning of the passing tone for the *second*—see 5a and b—is decided in favor of the unison, for the reason that it at least fits into the characteristic harmony of the tone *c* itself, while the lower third *a* deprives the *c* of its roothood-tendency by reducing it to the status of a third.

The lower fifth expresses still more drastically than the lower third the complete loss of roothood-tendency of the given tone c^1, and therefore in the case of the passing *fourth* in the lower counterpoint—see 6a and b—we decide for the third in preference to the fifth.

The passing *seventh*—see 7a and b—, from the standpoint of quantity of harmony, is better imagined as beginning with the lower sixth than with the octave: the latter interval, at least, is the inversion of the upper third! (For the seventh in the upper counterpoint, however, the upper sixth was rejected, precisely because it is the inversion of the lower third.)

As the point of departure of the passing tones has finally been decided for the absolute reasons cited—specifically, 8 before 7, 5 before 4, 10 before 9, and 3 before 2 in the upper counterpoint; 1 before 2, 3 before 4, and 6 before 7 in the lower—, at the same time the direction of the passing tone is established; as we see, it is a *descending* passing tone.

Selection of the other departure-points would, on the contrary, necessarily have suggested an ascending direction for the passing tone; although the other departure-points are certainly possible per se, just here, in strict counterpoint, they had to be rejected. In any case, this much is clear: dissonant syncopes with ascending resolutions are peripheral to the problem under consideration; therefore strict counterpoint can refer to them only as, in a sense, more distant relatives, which have their place only in free composition. There, under the aegis of scale degrees (which clarify all relationships from the start), they can manifest their characteristic passing effect and expressive value all the more effectively and securely.

Let us finally solve this problem definitively on the basis of strict counterpoint: if the postulate of descending resolution of dissonant syncopes establishes at once the path of three tones, from precisely that fact we can see the reason that, as mentioned in §1 above, [in the fourth species] only a consonant character must always be demanded of the note on the upbeat. For suppose it were permitted in strict counterpoint to place a dissonance in passing also on the upbeat. In such a case one would have to arrive at a unified formation comprising two full bars (see Example 386a), because, regardless of the dissonant passing tone, the dissonance of the syncope now demands for its own part a fixed continuation. But wouldn't such an extensive and, by its lack of motivation, moreover incomprehensible formation stand in contradiction to the uppermost postulate of strict counterpoint—that of maximum neutrality of the tones? If one tried to avoid such a danger perhaps by suddenly turning the syncope into a consonance (as in Example 386b), wouldn't one be guilty in that case of a transgression against another crucial prescription by abruptly and arbitrarily depriving the dissonance, conceived as passing tone, of its natural and proper downward motion?

Among all of the teachers, *Fux* is the only one who at least acknowledges for the student the problem of the prohibition of upward resolution as such. On p. 80 we read:

Before I begin to explain how dissonances are to be resolved, it must be said that a tied note is nothing but a delaying of the following note, which then, as though liberated from its servitude, again finds itself in a free condition. For this reason, dissonances are always to be resolved downward by step to the nearest consonance, as is seen clearly in the following example:

Example 403

Fux V, 6

When the delaying process is removed, this figure appears as follows:

Example 404

Fux V, 7

This reveals that it can easily be understood which consonance any dissonance is to be resolved to: namely, that which is found at the downbeat of the following bar once the delaying process is eliminated. Thus it happens that when the cantus firmus lies below, the second will have to be resolved to the unison, the fourth to the third, the seventh to the sixth, and the ninth to the octave.

And moreover, on p. 81:

Joseph: . . . With your permission, I should like to ask whether the delaying or tying of dissonances occurs also with the ascending motion? For the following examples appear to be essentially the same:

Example 405

Fux V, 15

Aloys: You raise a question that is harder to untangle than the Gordian knot—one which you, as a beginner in this discipline, cannot understand, and which, therefore, will be taken up in another context. Regarding whether the thirds indeed remain the same both rising and falling after the delaying is eliminated, as said, it will be explained at the proper time that some difference is present. In the meantime, you must believe me, as your teacher, that all dissonances must be resolved by descending to the nearest consonance.

Albrechtsberger does not attempt to justify the prescription of downward (or prohibition of upward) resolution under discussion; he rather simply decrees the rule as self-explanatory (p. 57) and adds only this: "It is certainly well known that the diminished fifth in all settings tends to resolve downward to the third; but here this cannot occur immediately, at least not in the upper voice. When it [the diminished fifth] is tied there, the minor third or minor sixth must be struck at the upbeat, before [it resolves]"; for example:

Example 406

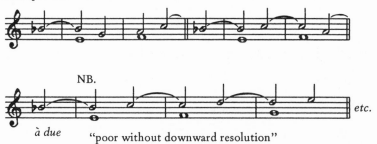

à due   "poor without downward resolution"

Compare the voice leading in Albrechtsberger, p. 103, in an exercise of three-voice counterpoint:

Example 407

And finally an excerpt from a Beethoven exercise (see Nottebohm, p. 52), approved by Albrechtsberger expressly as a "license":

Example 408

Here the diminished fifth even appears to be resolved in a different voice.

As can be inferred from this, Albrechtsberger admits as a dissonant syncope the diminished fifth as well, even though its resolution necessarily comprises two full bars. Just this fact, however, provides us with sufficient reason to exclude this syncope, which leads to such a broad unified formation, from the domain of strict counterpoint and consign it instead to free composition.

On pp. 75–78 and 100f. he shows—in a disorganized manner, to be sure, because only among other things—also the upward resolution of dissonant syncopes ⌢2 — 3, ⌢7 — 8 [in the upper counterpoint], ⌢7 — 6, ⌢9 — 8 [in the lower] for use in free composition.

Concerning the augmented fourth, see the citations below in §9.

Bellermann's citation concerning the augmented fourth is in §§9 and 10.

§6. *Certain syncopes which, even though they resolve downward, are either entirely prohibited or only tolerated*

Even syncopes that are given downward resolutions—see above, A, a and B, a—are subjected to a further reduction for the purpose of strict counterpoint: despite their downward resolution, one among them is altogether prohibited, and several others are only tolerated. To be specific, ⌒7 — 8 in the lower counterpoint is prohibited, while others are more or less tolerated: ⌒2 — 1 and ⌒9 — 8 in the upper counterpoint and   4 — 5 in the lower counterpoint. The reasons for this restriction are now to be discussed in detail.

§7. *The total prohibition of the* ⌒7 — 8 *syncope in the lower counterpoint*

The prohibition of the ⌒7 — 8 syncope in the lower counterpoint is based on the fact that the passing motion whose middle tone (see above, §5) is the seventh begins with the *sixth below* [the cantus firmus].

Among all the consonances which can initiate a passing motion—octave, fifth and third (or tenth) before the seventh, fourth and second (or ninth) in the upper counterpoint, and unison, lower third and lower sixth before the second, lower fourth and lower seventh in the lower counterpoint—the lower sixth, as is evident, represents without doubt the least appropriate initial interval. Consider that we arrive at the lower sixth only by way of the inversion of the upper third (which by itself shows the questionable derivative quality of the former interval with sufficient clarity); and consider, further, that in strict counterpoint the syncope of the lower seventh is in danger of being mistaken for the syncope of the upper seventh (especially as in the latter case we can easily posit the very propitious interval of an octave as point of departure for the passing motion): these two reasons explain our instinctual resistance to following the path of inversion or to giving preference to the lower sixth over the octave. In other words: it is difficult, even impossible, for us to posit directly the lower sixth; this, however, is absolutely necessary in the case of syncopation (according to §5) if we want to determine the direction of the passing motion. Strict counterpoint, therefore, lacks all means to compel us to accept the lower sixth, and this eliminates the ⌒7 — 8 syncope in the lower counterpoint.

The conditions for this syncope are completely different, however, and far more favorable, in free composition. There, we intuitively follow the logic of the scale-degree progression; just for that reason, since we are entitled to expect one or another harmony, we are also able under certain circumstances to interpret at once the downward-resolving suspended seventh of the lower voice as a suspension of the octave of the expected harmony. Moreover, in free composition such a syncope can, without being misinterpreted, even occur between an inner voice and an upper voice:

Example 409

Schubert, Piano Sonata Op. 42, II

regardless of the fact that, measured from the fundamental, the intervals would be different. Thus in the above Schubert example, the syncopes would represent either $\overset{\frown}{}{}^9_4{}^8_3$, if the tone C itself (scale degree I) were to be considered the fundamental, or $\overset{\frown}{}{}^7_3{}^6_4$, if the $^6_4$-position of the harmony were to be taken into account.

Fux devotes the following passage to this difficult question (p. 81f.):

Aloys: I must confess that I deliberately omitted the seventh. Hardly any reason can be cited here except the authority of great masters, to which we must always pay attention in practical matters. Almost none can be found who used the seventh resolving to the octave in this way:

Example 410

Fux V, 13

One might say that the seventh so resolved cannot be tolerated because the octave to which it moves is a perfect consonance, from which it can derive little harmony, if it were not for the fact that these same masters often resolve the second (which is the seventh in inversion) to the unison, from which a dissonance can derive even less harmony, since it is the most perfect consonance. I maintain that one must follow the usage of renowned masters in this matter. Here is an example of the inverted seventh, or second:

Example 411

Fux V, 14

It is always a serious mistake, as I have stated repeatedly, to call upon the practice of the masters in free composition to decide problems in strict counterpoint. Even more surprising, however, is that Fux nevertheless uses this very ⌒7 — 8 syncope in the lower counterpoint in an exercise (Table VI, Figure 1; see below, Exercise 4), apparently only to avoid doing violence to the melodic line.

Albrechtsberger, if only subconsciously, comes closer to the truth than Fux when he writes, "[Fux] forbids the resolution of the lower seventh to the octave, which in two-voice counterpoint is a very appropriate prohibition; but it is well-known that other famous composers have often used it as a suspension to a complete chord in multi-voiced compositions; for example":

Example 412

No. 1   No. 2

Albrechtsberger expresses here his intuitive notion that it is only two-voice counterpoint itself that causes the restriction; admittedly, he is not able to express this idea with greater precision.

While Fux and Albrechtsberger approve of the syncope ⌒7 — 8 in the lower counterpoint at least in free composition (even though they are not yet able to gain clarity about why it is permitted there but prohibited in strict counterpoint), *Bellermann* commits the gravest error that can be committed by a theorist, in that he extends the prohibition also to free composition (p. 216):

> The inversion of the ninth—that is, a seventh prepared in the lower voice which would resolve to the octave—is, because of its rough sound, prohibited not only in a capella composition but generally in any kind of polyphonic music that conforms to rules.

Example 413

By the same token, the situation just described also must not occur between two inner voices, even though similar things can occasionally be found in smaller note values in the works of the best masters. Compare the four-part motet "Dies sanctificatus" (No. 1 of the first book of four-part motets) by Palestrina, bar 16. Such occasional exceptions, however, are not to be imitated, and have no influence whatever on the stricter rule.

Such a wretched abuse of theory! It is all the more reprehensible as the author's perception did not even suffice to recognize the effect of the prohibited syncope as beautiful and good in free compositions; it thus remains in arrears vis à vis indisputable facts of the tonal world, which find their justification in the beautiful effect so attained! I almost fear that Bellermann invented the "rough sound" in order to find some way to motivate the restriction.

§8.   The necessity of restricting the use of: (a) The ⌒2 — 1 and ⌒9 — 8 syncopes in the upper counterpoint

Use of the syncopes ⌒2 — 1 and ⌒9 — 8 is best restricted in counterpoint, for the following reasons:

First, the resolution leads to perfect consonances, in particular the unison and the octave, that are less appropriate in counterpoint.

Second, because of those consonances, greater caution must be used with regard to voice leading (cf. later, §15); this leads necessarily to a certain inconvenience in the practical execution of the exercises.

It should be stated now, however, that an important law originates from these syncopes that are to be used only in moderation; it is the law of the *identity of the tone of resolution.* Since unison and octave are identical with the tone of the cantus firmus, the above-mentioned syncopes really lead back, even though by way of a dissonance, to the tone of the cantus firmus. What damage this fact must cause in other difficult circumstances will be demonstrated later in parts 3 and 4.

Leaving aside the restriction [of these syncopes] in counterpoint, we are obliged nevertheless to distinguish clearly the two syncopes mentioned here as two completely different phenomena. Thus it is not permissible in strict counterpoint to consider ⌒2 — 1 merely a ⌒9 — 8 syncope transposed down an octave. Decisive for the distinction is only the voice-leading in the exercises themselves; here the intervals ⌒2 — 1 or ⌒9 — 8 simply have to be taken literally, precisely in the way they occur in the voice leading!

We will see later that most theorists tend to understand ⌒2 — 1 as contained in ⌒9 — 8—that is, to deny the independent quality of a ⌒2 — 1 syncope. The reason for the difference of opinion appears to me to lie in the following. Theorists promise in their introductions to base the exercises of counterpoint on a purely vocal foundation, and accordingly teach [the necessity of] a proper distance between the voices; later on, however, they unconsciously abandon their original (and correctly conceived) intention in order to be able to equate (that is, confuse) counterpoint with free composition: under the influence of the latter, they already use in exercises voice-spacings that can no longer be understood as vocal but only as instrumental. But if theorists decided to explain intervals beyond the tenth, for example, such as 11, 12, 13, 14, by suggesting to themselves as well as to their students that these intervals are not what they appear to be but rather 4, 5, 6, 7 merely transposed up an octave; or, put differently, if the distance between two voices is taken only figuratively and not in its literal reality, then, of course, a theoretical vacillation must arise concerning the syncopes ⌒2 — 1 and ⌐9 — 8. Then one must ask: Is ⌐9 — 8 really ⌐9 — 8 or perhaps only ⌒2 — 1; and, vice versa, is ⌒ 2 — 1 also something different from ⌒ 2 — 1? That teachers in this predicament decided in favor of assuming one single syncope ⌐9 — 8 and abandoning the ⌒ 2 — 1 can be explained on two grounds. First, they viewed the interval of the octave in counterpoint as a more suitable consonance than the unison (especially in three- and four-voice counterpoint where the octave can have a better harmonic effect than the unison). This point of view, which belongs to the realm of strict counterpoint itself, certainly cannot be disputed; the second point, however, which is invalidly derived from free composition, must be rejected all the more emphatically. The aural image of triads, which, in the name of scale degrees of free composition, always lives within us, leads quite naturally to the acceptance of the octave rather than the unison as an interval of further reinforcement; in other words, in free composition we expect the harmony C–E–G, for example, to appear in the form at a rather than at b in Example 414.

Example 414

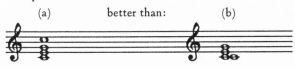

In this case, too, we are inclined to view as more compelling the octave, whose better quality has already been certified by the overtone series. Nevertheless, it is unjustified to transfer this inclination to counterpoint, where the decisive factor is voice leading alone, not scale degrees and other elements of reinforcement. Therefore, in the given situation—that is, when it is required by voice-leading—⌒2 — 1 had to be used without hesitation; and if, according to principles of counterpoint alone, it is justified to consider the unison inferior to the octave, and thus to regard the syncope that resolves to the unison as likewise inferior, then we may draw as a consequence [of this] only the distinction between "superior" and "inferior" in a purely contrapuntal sense; we may not for this reason alone deny the contrapuntally independent quality of the "inferior" syncope. In other words: anyone who insists most strictly on the vocal foundation in the execution of exercises, and, thus, is accustomed to regard the distance between voices as an irrefutable reality, must also view ⌐9 — 8 as something materially completely different from ⌒2 — 1, regardless of the fact that, for the reasons presented here, he will prefer the former syncope to the latter, and, for the rest, will find it best to limit the use of both syncopes only to cases of greatest necessity.

Despite scale degrees, free composition does not abandon the principles of voice-leading altogether; therefore it remains true even here that ⌒2 — 1 and ⌒9—8 certainly represent different phenomena, depending on whether they function—again only in terms of voice leading—as suspensions to the fundamental or to the octave, as for example here:

Example 415

J. S. Bach, French Suite No. 2, Sarabande

to E♭ major: II ———————————————————— V ——————— I

The phenomenon of ⌒2—1 at the asterisk is not canceled by the fact that the lower voice moves away during the resolution of the syncope (cf. Part 6).

From the passage (already quoted in §7) that *Fux* devotes to the ⌒7—8 syncope [in the lower counterpoint], one can at least infer that he appears to recognize the independent quality of the ⌒2—1 syncope and does not want it confused with ⌒9—8.

Albrechtsberger, on the other hand, expressly denies the independence in the upper counterpoint of the ⌒2—1 syncope, which he regards as assimilated by the ⌒9—8 syncope. Thus he writes on p. 57: "Seconds always resolve in the contrapuntal *lower voice* down a half- or whole-step to thirds." This means that he does not recognize the syncope of a second in the upper voice. Moreover, on p. 58 we find the following figured-bass notation:

Example 416

that is, the same figure for ⌒9—8 and ⌒2—1 together with an NB remark which becomes completely clear only when we read Albrechtsberger's explanation on p. 161:

The second is resolved in the lower voice to the third, and in the upper voice to the unison. It is always erroneous to figure the latter in compositions for three or more parts—for example:

Example 417

Example 417 *continued*

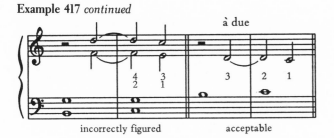

incorrectly figured   acceptable

I have touched upon this point already in my discussion of fourth-species two-voice counterpoint in the context of dissonant ligatures in the upper voice; I repeat it here once more so that aspiring composers are not misled by many an erroneous figure. They should keep in mind that the second-ligature can never be figured [as such] in settings of three or more voices if the ligature or delay is contained in the upper voice, but only if it is in the lower voice, which, being a half- or whole-step below [the upper voice], is delayed by means of a ligature and resolves downward to the minor or major third. The ninth is indeed literally identical to the second above, but not in accompaniment and resolution. [Compare also p. 104ff.]

We read something similar in *Bellermann* (p. 173), who in this case abandons the Fuxian trail: "The ninth is therefore a second which, depending on the distance between its elements, resolves to the octave or the unison . . . etc." (Compare also later on p. 215). Soon thereafter he remarks: "The ninth has not been used so frequently as the other dissonant intervals. In two-voice counterpoint it really should be avoided *completely*." Such a statement about [musical] practice can hardly be considered a satisfactory rationale for his assumption that ⌐2 — 1 and ⌐9 — 8 are identical.

§9. (b) The ⌐4 — 5 syncope in the lower counterpoint

The ⌐4 — 5 syncope in the lower counterpoint has a value similarly inferior to the syncopes just discussed; when we consider that this syncope is based on the passing motion 3 — 4 — 5 (whereby, unfortunately, the third is only the lower third), we immediately understand that our instinct prefers under all circumstances the syncope of a fourth in the upper counterpoint, which originates from a much more favorable passing motion, namely 5 — 4 — 3. Moreover, since in the ⌐4 — 5 syncope the interval of resolution is a fifth, it is clear that this syncope, because of the inconveniences of voice leading connected with that interval, is of inferior value in that it poses a greater technical danger; therefore it is advisable at least to limit the use of this syncope.

Concerning the *augmented fourth,* see above, §5.

Fux uses ⌐4 — 5 quite frequently, from which it may be inferred that he has no scruple concerning this kind of syncope.

Albrechtsberger, on the other hand, articulates the following thoughts on p. 59 without further elaboration: "These tied fourths in the lower counterpoint are not authentic fourth-ligatures, but only an accompaniment to the second-ligature, which must go along with [the fourth-ligature] in settings for three or more voices." Through this remark alone he indicates that he certainly does not have a very high opinion of this syncope.

Apropos of an augmented fourth he uses in an exercise (see Exercise 6, bar 10, p. 000) he remarks as follows on p. 63: "The second NB at the interval *f — b* excuses the otherwise faulty *mi contra fa,* because the next measure does not lead to C major but to A minor. Besides, the strictness and constraint of this species excuse much." (Compare also the illustration on p. 105, with the text on p. 106, quoted in Part 3, Chapter 1, §10.)

Bellermann (p. 172f.) also opines that ⁀4 — 3 [in the upper counterpoint] is more frequently used than ⁀4 — 5 in the lower counterpoint; and if the fourth should be augmented, it is said to be prohibited in two-voice counterpoint in the form of a syncope in the lower voice. See §10 for a quotation [from Bellermann] concerning the augmented fourth in the upper counterpoint.

§10.   *Final codification*

In the light of the foregoing, we can state definitively that in the upper counterpoint ⁀7 — 6 and ⁀4 — 3 would be preferable, but in the lower counterpoint only ⁀2 — 3.

The completely unquestionable character of these latter syncopes, incidentally, can be explained most simply just through the fact that their intervals of resolution are precisely 3 and 6, which are so desirable for counterpoint and which raise no further problems of voice leading.

Regarding the syncope ⁀2 — 3 we may add that it is the inversion of ⁀7 — 6, which (because it stems from the passing motion 8 — 7 — 6) is to be regarded as original. Thus ⁀2 — 3 shares the particular high value of ⁀7 — 6. And this, finally, is also the reason ⁀2 — 3 in the lower counterpoint appears so much more plausible to our sense than ⁀2 — 1 in the upper.

I have already said that it contradicts the essence as well as the history of the rule under consideration if its justifications are sought only in the realm of free composition. (This unfortunately is what is done by, for example, Riemann, whose theories, so fatally divergent from art, will be refuted at every suitable opportunity.)

Free composition, incidentally, shows mostly *prolongations* of the basic form; how can they even be understood in their true significance, not to mention be systematized, before the basic form has been grasped in and for itself—which can happen only in strict counterpoint? With the following discussion I offer an attempt, within the bounds of a modest outline, to familiarize the apprentice of art with the panoply of syncopation-forms, whose common point of emanation is just that basic form I have set forth in the preceding series of paragraphs. It is obvious, however, that with respect to most categories, a more detailed explanation and treatment can be offered only in the later sections.

1. First let us cite the *upward resolution* of dissonant syncopes, which incidentally has already been mentioned frequently in §5 (cf. Examples 395–397 and p. 268). Specifically it is the scale degree in free composition which permits—indeed compels—us to assume ascending passing motions as well as descending ones. In this sense, free composition (in contrast to strict counterpoint) includes the syncopes 7, 4, 2, and 9 in the upper counterpoint, and 2, 4, and 7 in the lower; these syncopes resolve upward. But the relation of all of these to the basic form of the dissonant syncope of strict counterpoint is not at all that of "exceptions," as is unfortunately taught in textbooks and schools both in print and orally: they represent on the contrary new solutions to new *problems*—problems completely foreign to strict counterpoint. On the other hand, it would be equally incorrect to place them alongside the descending resolution as though they were of equal rank from the outset, as, for example, Riemann does. [Voice-leading] situations differ among themselves in rank, and nobody can deny that the situations constructed intentionally for teaching purposes in a syncopation-exercise of strict counterpoint are more primitive than those of free composition. Thus the downward resolution of strict counterpoint must be accorded psychological priority in comparison to the upward resolution of free composition! May teachers finally stop speaking of "rule" and "exception," then, or at least get accustomed to recognizing these phenomena as two branches—one of them younger than the other—that sprout from the same trunk (the passing tone!).

2. Since in free composition the harmony of the triad or seventh-chord is conceived also in its respective inversions, as $\frac{6}{3}$, $\frac{6}{4}$ or $\frac{6}{5}$, $\frac{4}{3}$, and $\frac{4}{2}$ (see *Harmony,* §§98, 106), it is clear that there the *material content* of a dissonant syncope is accordingly better understood—specifically, as a suspension resolving precisely to a $\frac{6}{3}$-, $\frac{6}{4}$-, $\frac{6}{5}$-, $\frac{4}{3}$-, or $\frac{4}{2}$-chord.[4] Add to this the possibility of upward resolution and of chromatic motion, and new intervals become available to serve as preparation—intervals that strict counterpoint could not yet allow, such as 4 before 5, 6 before 7, etc.[5] More on this in the later sections.

But to gain a better overview of the varieties of dissonant syncopes, it is advisable to review once again how the basic form consists of three elements: the tone on the upbeat forms the first, which serves as preparation of the suspension; the same tone immediately introduces the second, in that it is continued (tied over) to the downbeat; the third element finally is the resolution to the upbeat. The spirit of variety penetrates into these elements here, so as to transform them individually or collectively in one respect or another.

3. I begin with *time* as a basis of variety. Since free composition eschews the rhythmic rigidity of the cantus firmus, it proceeds on its own to use a variety of *different note-values* instead of the half-notes of the original form: ♩♩ ♩. (More detail will be provided in the next chapter.) But however these values may be organized, they can be perceived in an artistically correct way, and—which is still more important in free composition—at the same time

performed correctly, if their deviation from the basic norm (that of equal halves) in each case is assimilated into artistic consciousness.

4.   Another basis of variety, which, like time, can reshape the syncope, is *harmonic character* within the individual elements. In applying this new basis of variety to those elements, we achieve the following results:

(a) The *preparation* itself may take on a *dissonant* character in free composition, in contrast to strict counterpoint, where it may have only consonant character. Such a dissonance stems usually from a *passing tone,* which derives its necessity and justification from the scale degree,[6] if it is not otherwise based on an *elision* (see below under 5). To this category belong those cases of which C.P.E. Bach (*Versuch,* Part 2, Kap. XXVI) speaks as *"displaced notes" (rückende Noten),* and about which he states the following: "Through *displacements (Rückungen)* the usual *harmony* is either *anticipated* or *delayed."*[7] From his examples, the following may be cited:

Example 418

(b) The tone at the *downbeat* can, in free composition, be consonant in a sense completely different from that which applies to a consonant syncope of strict counterpoint. Since free composition, in contrast to strict counterpoint, includes clearly defined suspensions to seventh-chords (see above under 2), it accordingly presents under certain circumstances even, for example, an octave as suspension to a seventh—or, under the assumption of upward resolution, a sixth suspended to a seventh and the like. Another example from C.P.E. Bach's *Versuch,* cited earlier under a, may be quoted here as an illustration (see Kap. XXV, §8):

Example 419

To the same category belongs also the *suspension of a sixth* before the fifth of a triad, for example in the double suspension $\frac{6}{4}-\frac{5}{3}$ of free composition. But in such a case, it is not permissible to speak of a sixth that has turned into a dissonance (see above p. 126) or of a "make-believe consonance" (*Scheinkonsonanz*) as Riemann does. Because in actuality it is only our consciousness and prescience of the scale degree itself (or of the harmony to come, whatever its rank) that sets off so much more emphatically the suspension-character under consideration. But even though we sense the consonant sixth-suspension in $\frac{6}{4}-\frac{5}{3}$ —under the guidance of the predicted harmony!—just as clearly as the dissonant fourth-suspension, and sense both suspensions again more clearly than would be possible in strict counterpoint, we must never draw the monstrous theoretical conclusion that culminates in the proposition that just on account of increased clarity (intrinsic to free composition) a sixth should be counted as a dissonance! Wouldn't it then be necessary to treat all other consonances similarly, and to regard them as dissonances the moment they occur with the function of suspensions? For example, in a case like the following:

Example 420

Haydn, Piano Sonata Hob. 46, I

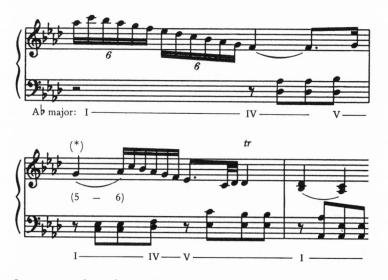

I maintain, then, that in the case of the sixth-suspension we must always be content with just the feeling of suspension, at the same time allowing the sixth to retain fully its consonant character. Otherwise we get onto the precipitous track of Riemann's theory—see his *Handbuch der Harmonielehre*, Part 2, §25. Through misunderstanding and exaggeration of an otherwise correct idea,[8] he arrives at complete misconstrual and falsification of chordal values that are forever regarded by the artist himself as consonant, and simply proclaims them to be dissonant. For example, p. 139: "A chord represents consonance or dissonance only when understood in its relationships to others—that is, in its logical context. We will discover, therefore, that it can be possible, or rather, necessary, to understand a major or minor triad as a dissonance." Or the following, p. 140:

> If a harmony acquires its full aesthetic value only through its relation to a tonic—that is, if the discrimination of simple- and contra-fourth sonorities is to yield not just empty names but concise formulas for definite functions of harmonies in the musical fabric—, then any chord that is not itself a tonic will actually be heard not as itself, but rather in relation to that chord which is tonic. In other words, only the tonic chord itself is truly an absolute consonance.

But where does it lead, I ask, to call every "relationship"—just because it is a relationship—an adequate ground for conversion to dissonance? Wouldn't one then necessarily have to consider even the fifth of a fundamental—just by virtue of its undeniable "relationship" to the latter, certified as "adequate" by the overtone series—a dissonance? And finally, isn't the thing we call a "relationship" in truth merely a mode of our way of conceptualizing (like "time" and "space"), and in no way an objective reality? But why should a "mode of thought" have such power over the natural phenomenon of consonance as to alter its innermost nature?! Therefore I caution most emphatically against yielding to the obsession with "relationship," as Riemann does, and hearing dissonant chords where only consonant ones rule—admittedly maintaining their "relationship" all the while, like everything in the world!

(c) Finally, at the *upbeat,* which is supposed to present the consonant resolution of the dissonant syncope, a *dissonance* can also appear. It will be shown below under 5 how this is usually combined with an elision.

If we add to the varieties just shown under a, b, and c the liberty of upward resolution, of chromatic progressions, of modulations and so forth, the number of hybrids among all of these varieties soars to infinity. An example may illustrate. Instead of the following:

Example 421

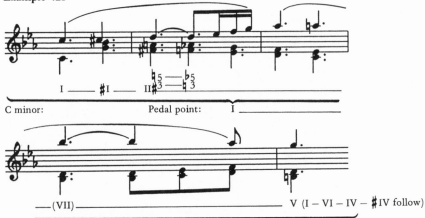

Brahms writes in a syncopated form:

Example 422
Brahms, Symphony No. 1, Introduction

f espress. e legato

From this we discover the following: The fundamental of scale degree I itself, c^2, functions as a suspension to $c\sharp^2$ (at the last eighth-note of the first bar) as fundamental of scale degree $\sharp$I, so that the step is a chromatic one; the $c\sharp^2$ then serves as a suspension to the following fundamental of scale degree II, d^2—to be exact, as a consonant suspension $\frown 5 - 6$. The next suspension is found at the first quarter of bar 3, and has the form $3\uparrow 4-5$; next follows $5\uparrow 6\flat - 6\natural$, $6\uparrow 7 - 8$ etc., thus syncopes with ascending resolutions and chromatic progression (see above under 2).

5. Moreover, the syncope is subject to modification brought about by *elision:*

(a) Thus the *preparation* itself can be elided and the dissonance placed on the strong beat in its absence. *Dissonant* chords thereby arise, for which in certain circumstances a purely *implicit preparation* (see *Harmony,* Example 281) through the preceding harmony can be assumed; otherwise the apparently free dissonance must be understood as the clearly established internal element of a *latent passing motion* (see above, Example 399). In the latter case, the elided consonance that would initiate the passing motion is to be inferred from and supplied by the harmony belonging to the dissonance itself. In this way we arrive at the so-called *free suspensions,* and it may be that the ultimate origin of seventh-chords (see *Harmony,* §99) is best explained with reference to the elision of a preparation or of the consonant beginning of a passing-tone motion.

When, for example, Brahms, in the last movement of his Fourth Symphony, writes:

Example 423
Brahms, Symphony No. 4, IV

Winds

Strings

we find here that a seventh-chord is applied to each bass note (*E, F♯, G, A*);
in each case we can assume an implicit preparation, or, in the last analysis,
also a passing motion whose consonant initial interval has been elided. (The
resolutions, granted, are perfectly regular.)

(b) Further, in free composition a second act of independent character can
be *mixed* with the *resolution* in such a way that the latter is prevented from
taking place, at least in such a pure form as in strict counterpoint.

And yet even when another voice moves simultaneously, the *consonant*
character of the resolution can still be preserved (cf. Example 415), about
which, incidentally, more detail will be given in the section on the combined
species.

Or, the resolution can be apparently fully divested of its consonant
character if it moves directly to a second dissonance. In the latter case one
often speaks of a so-called *preparation of dissonance by dissonance,* while in
fact the act of consonant resolution of the first dissonance implicitly accompanies the second one—even granting that the rhythm of the basic form is
obscured and, simultaneously (for purposes of explanation), a texture of several
voices is reduced to an underlying three-voice model. Thus, for example,
behind the chain of seventh-chords in Example 230 (bars 2 and 3) in
Harmony there stands the following basic voice leading, in which I have
placed the elided resolutions in parentheses:

Example 424

And still further: scale-degree progression, to which free composition has
access, makes the consonant resolution clear even in cases where such
preparation [as that in Example 424] is completely lacking. For example, when
Beethoven writes in his String Quartet op. 59 no. 1 (first movement):

Example 425

scale degree II is to be implicitly supplied after VI^7 (cf. *Harmony*, §127); the II—observe the chromaticization of the third! (*Harmony*, §139)—is to be viewed as bearer of both the consonant resolution (*g* after *f*) and at the same time as preparation of the next seventh (V^7). (Compare examples 35–38 above and the explanation, particularly on p. 51!)

6.   The possibility of eliding the preparation of dissonant syncopes or resolving them on the strong beat, as well as the possibility of modifying the harmonic character of all elements of the syncope, leads quite logically to ultimate reduction of the basic form to a mere *concatenation of weak and strong beats,* thus to a purely *rhythmic form,* which then fully resembles the form of the consonant syncope of strict counterpoint (see above, Example 391). This reduction to a purely rhythmic nucleus may now—insofar as any system at all can be introduced into such a plethora—be considered the final transformation of the basic form.

I would include here the following, for example:

Example 426
Beethoven, Piano Sonata Op. 27 No. 2, Allegretto

Without doubt the purely rhythmic effect of the syncopation-form stands in the foreground here, and, if you like, along with it the effect of anticipation (see the third quarter of the first bar: G♭), which, however, in the last analysis (see p. 188) certainly stems from a passing motion (F — G♭)—the "displacement" of C.P.E. Bach (see p. 280).[9] So far as the scale degrees are concerned, their progression can be identified as I — V — I, unless one prefers first to ignore the tone A♭ (the fifth of scale degree I, in the left hand of bar 1) and thus to arrive at the following:

$$I - II - V - I$$
bar: 1,   2,   3,   4

The A♭ could then be considered simply an organ point.

Still more instructive is example 427 on page 286. Genuine syncopes, prepared and resolved downwards, are found here in bar 6 (⌢7 — 6 in relation to the bass A♭, or ⌢4 — 3 in relation to the scale degree D♭ itself) and in bar 8 (⌢4 — 3 in relation to the bass G♭). The remaining syncopes, on the contrary, show a deviation from the basic form, which can be understood only if the scale-degree progression is taken into consideration. Because if at bottom it is the third quarter in each case (here, admittedly, along with the downbeat) that is to be related to the

Example 427

Beethoven, Piano Sonata Op. 27 No. 2, Allegretto

harmony (see the dotted lines), then at least in this sense the basic form is apparently still preserved, in which, likewise, it is not until the tone of resolution at the upbeat that the true harmony (belonging to the cantus firmus) is completed. It is still more justifiable, however, to compare the syncopes under discussion with those that rest purely on rhythmic bases when one considers that here it is only the roots of the seventh-chords (that is, the tones Bb, Eb, Ab, Db, and Gb) which receive the syncopated form, not the actual dissonances (in the left hand the sevenths: ab, db, gb, cb), which alone, instead of the fundamentals, should according to the rule have been treated in syncopated form. (Regarding the mode of progression of the dissonances, see above, Example 424.)

Incidentally, in those places where the syncope emphasizes its purely rhythmic nucleus it is not always absolutely necessary that the connection from a weak to strong beat be literally expressed graphically by means of a tie. The latter can rather be tacitly supplied according to the meaning of the passage. Haydn writes, for example:

Example 428

Haydn, Variations in F Minor

Example 428 *continued*

in order to express the following melody:

Example 429

Now observe how, once the notation is completed by the use of longer values,[10] the true rhythmic placement of the tones reveals itself completely differently!

The following example, incidentally:

Example 430

Beethoven, Piano Sonata Op. 110, Arioso dolente

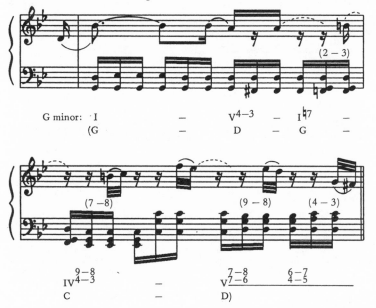

shows that even rests, far from intending to be actual rests, can carry with them and express the effect of ties! Measured in relation to the scale degrees, the first sixteenth-note chord of each 3/16 group in the bass introduces a syncope, resolving sometimes upward, sometimes downward; moreover, in each case the preceding tone of the melody is to be considered as though still sounding, or—which comes to the same thing—tied in syncopation, into the rest. This effect is completely clear especially in those cases in which the melody even repeats the preceding tone after the rest—for example, b^1 and eb^2. The performer must therefore take special care to give expression to the concealed syncopes in spite of the notation with rests!

Insofar as rhythm alone is under consideration, it must be noted that in duple or quadruple meter, forms like ♪♪↑♪♪ or ♪♪♪↑♪♪♪ are to be regarded as syncopes; but that on the contrary, in triple meter the connection of the second and third quarters: ♪♪|♪♪ does not yet count as a syncope, since in comparison to the first quarter, the last two together represent the weak part of the bar.

Thus the following example:

Example 431
Haydn, String Quartet Op. 64 No. 5, I

offers genuine syncopes, but in the next example:

Example 432
Haydn, String Quartet Op. 20 No. 4, Menuetto (alla Zingarese)

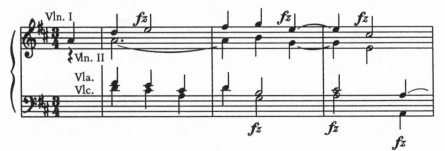

Example 432 *continued*

which likewise has conjunctions of second and third quarters (♩), the longer values do not yet represent syncopes. Compare in particular the rhythm, maintained with inimitable virtuosity, in Schubert's "Des Fischers Liebesglück": 𝄴: ♪♩ ♪♪♩♪ ♪♩, which by no means represents syncopes. Concerning "hemiola" (for example, in 𝄴: 𝅝 ♩♩ 𝅝) see the lexicon of Koch-Dommer, or Riemann.

To draw the final conclusion from all these considerations, the dissonant syncope of strict counterpoint represents the basic form of all possible forms of dissonance in free composition which occur on the strong beat, as well as many other derivative phenomena. And if the basic form, in keeping with the environment of the cantus firmus, appears at first to be bound only to the strictest specifications, free composition in no way contradicts this if, for its own stronger reasons, it relaxes the specification, and perhaps retains only the core of the phenomenon under discussion.[11]

How the *accented passing tone* differs from the dissonant syncope can be learned easily from Example 243 or 332: in that the dissonance of the accented passing tone is placed on the strong beat, its similarity to the dissonant syncope is undoubtedly well grounded; but since on the other hand in the accented passing tone both of the consonances that surround it are different tones, and since moreover the tie is lacking, its genus approaches more closely that of the simple passing dissonance.

Cherubini goes too far when he proclaims, without any defense (p. 24, rule 4), that "in two-voice counterpoint of the present species it is necessary to abstain as much as possible from employing the dissonances of the fourth and the ninth. That of the seventh is preferable when the counterpoint lies in the upper voice, and that of the second when it lies in the lower voice." That is admittedly correct, but on purely artistic grounds one could imagine a more thoughtful approach to a problem that certainly remains one of the most difficult and important in our art.

Also a propos here is *Bellermann's* comment regarding ⌢4—3 in the upper counterpoint (p. 130):

The tritone and its inversion, the diminished fifth, were used as actual dissonances on the strong beat only in rare cases by the old composers. According to the rules set forth later (two-voice counterpoint, fourth species), their use would be (a) in two voices, as here:

Example 433

and (b) polyphonically, that is with accompanying voices, as here:

Example 434

In the strict liturgical masterworks of the sixteenth century, however, this type is seldom encountered.

Compare the dissenting view on p. 262.

Beginning

§11.   *Construction of the beginning*

It is permitted in exercises of fourth-species counterpoint, as in those of second-species, to use a half-rest in the first bar.

It is already evident from the use of the syncope, however, that the upbeat must be consonant.

How flexible even this principle is in practice will be shown by two of *Fux's* exercises when the same problem is treated in the context of three-voice counterpoint. [See Part 3, Chapter 4, §7.]

Main Body

§12.   *Preference for dissonant over consonant syncopes*

In general, dissonant syncopes are preferable to consonant ones.

Decisive for this preference is not so much the specific appeal of the dissonant suspension alone, but, rather, its technical value for the voice leading of the counterpoint itself, which can only gain in fluency and smoothness by its frequent and skillful application. (The situation is exactly the same as that regarding the use of the passing dissonance in the second species, cf. Part 2, Chapter 2, §8.)

The student is thus given an opportunity to become acquainted with a new source of effects that are significant for the voice-leading.

There is no doubt that the necessity of tying causes difficulties for the voice leading; but it is all the more important in this context to be mindful of melodic fluency in the counterpoint.

To understand more fully the spirit latent in the historic development of our art, it is prudent to find precisely in the dissonant syncope a means of establishing a purely musical *causality*—a means whose suitability could scarcely be equalled for settings of the vocal epoch. In the instinctive search for technical devices to expand the length of a setting (compare in particular in *Harmony* the note on pp. 163-173) within the context of a voice-leading which—apart from its own laws—had otherwise no compelling necessity, the artistic instinct discovered in the *compulsion* to prepare and resolve a dissonance a most welcome means of feigning a kind of musical causality and necessity at least from harmony to harmony. Considering that a seed of such propulsion was contained even in the simplest *passing motion* (the issue of developing length should be kept always in mind in investigating the nature and history of our art!), it is clear that the compelling force of the dissonant syncope must be viewed as incomparably stronger and more urgent.

The effect of musical causality just described remained an inherent quality of the dissonant syncope even in instrumental music. There, even in the most advanced stage of development, harmonies appear to be linked more intimately and with seemingly greater necessity the more drastically and obtrusively a tone of one harmony hooks into the flesh of the following one. The higher degree of structural necessity as well as length is then further provided by *scale-degrees* (including all that derives from them, such as tonality, chromaticism, modulation, etc.) and *form!* Considering that the artist was able to receive only the major triad from Nature's domain (cf. *Harmony*, §8ff.), we must marvel at the creative power of the human kind to erect, on a foundation so modest, such a proud edifice of musical art and to imbue it with such strong and compelling necessities! Through these very necessities of a completely individual nature, music acquires "logic" no less than language or the other arts! Thus, it is obvious that there is ample reason to place music, which provides such a proud testament to the autonomy of human creativity, highest among all the arts.

Concerning this issue, we may very well quote *Fux's* remarks on p. 83: "However, since music derives no small amount of appeal from the ligatures, I advise you not only to set the remaining three cantus firmi in the same manner, but also to practice very thoroughly with other, similar cantus firmi as well; for one can never be too diligent in such studies." Compare, in addition, also the statement on p. 136: "Moreover, take care to apply ligatures sometimes in one voice, sometimes in another; for it is astonishing how much grace the melody receives, even originates, by making each note with a particular motion clearly perceptible to the ear. This applies not only to this kind of composition but to all others as well."

In the context of three-voice counterpoint in the same species, we read the following in *Albrechtsberger* (p. 103): "The remaining bars may have on the downbeat a consonant or dissonant ligature, the latter of which is preferable if ligatures are used frequently." Moreover, he does not neglect to make the following requirement on p. 62: "Melodic fluency must be observed here as well."

Cherubini brings a different perspective (p. 23, Example 72): "If dissonances are not used, there is a danger of writing parallel octaves and fifths." We will soon see what this rule is all about (cf. §15); in any case, it contributes at least a technical reason for ranking the dissonant syncope in counterpoint higher than the consonant one.

§13. The preference for imperfect consonances

As everywhere else in the exercises of counterpoint, the imperfect consonances have a better effect than the perfect ones here as well.

As I have said before, this is the reason the syncopes ⌒2 — 1, ⌒9 — 8, and ⌒4 — 5 are considered less desirable than ⌒7 — 6, ⌒4 — 3, and ⌒2 — 3 (cf. §10).

§14. Use of the unison also on the downbeat

Because of the good occasion provided by oblique motion (made possible by the ligature for the first time in counterpoint in relation to the downbeat), the unison is permissible here also on the downbeat—a situation that, as we know, was not allowed to occur in the second or third species.

That the unison is, however, permitted on the upbeat is—again for the same reason—self-evident.

Compare *Albrechtsberger*, p. 58.

Bellermann states further (p. 175): "To place [the unison] several times in succession (either on the upbeat or on the downbeat) is, of course, prohibited according to the rules set down above about the use of perfect consonances." As we will see presently, the unison—precisely because it is a perfect consonance—is subject to the same caution as the other perfect consonances.

§15. Parallel and nonparallel similar motion in the present species

Among the three relationships that we had to distinguish in treating this problem in the second species (cf. Part 2, Chapter 2, §11), only two remain in the present species; the first and strongest of the former relationships—the direct succession of upbeat and downbeat—has, of course, been absorbed here by the ligature. Here is a diagram of the two possible relationships:

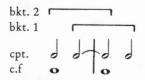

1. Because of the special circumstances of the present situation, the *afterbeat* successions (see bracket 1) here take first consideration.

It makes an essential difference, however, whether the syncopes in these situations are (a) dissonant or (b) consonant, and also whether only the strictest or a less strict standpoint is applied in both cases.

Ad a: The *dissonant* syncopes (the only ones under consideration here), specifically 8 ↑ 9 — 8 and 1 ↑ 2 — 1 in the upper counterpoint and 5 ↑ 4 — 5 in the lower counterpoint, viewed for the time being from the *strictest* standpoint, admit of neither parallel nor nonparallel similar motion in the situation indicated by bracket 1. It is therefore not permitted to write, for example, as follows:

Example 435

This prohibition results, first of all, from the nature of the dissonant syncopes, as well as from the requirement that they resolve downward. Because it is completely bound to the latter requirement, the dissonant syncope appears as nothing but a delay of the tone of resolution; thus, the above-cited examples are scarcely anything but delayed parallel or nonparallel similar motions:

Example 436

This, however, exposes all too clearly to our perception the poor result of similar motion.

Second, in addition to what was said about these progressions already in the first species (to the extent that they were faulty—cf. Part 2, Chapter 1, §§8–11), the problem is compounded by a circumstance that presents severe difficulty from the psychological standpoint: the obligation and necessity of the downward resolution announce in advance the imminent danger of a prohibited similar motion; therefore, those aspects of obligation and necessity must be considered the actual, treacherous source of the mistake. For if one knows that the dissonant syncope will have to move in a downward direction, why seek out at all (consciously, that is) the error that lurks in it? The ear always shows us the truth of this matter, beyond any shadow of doubt. (From this, incidentally, we can now finally understand even better why earlier—cf.

§§8 and 9—we had to recommend limitation of the use of ⌐9—8 and ⌐4—5 syncopes.)

The *necessity* of syncopes, as it is posed precisely by the exercise as such, leads, on other hand, also to a certain *leniency* regarding the absolute strictness of the prohibition of parallel motion involving dissonant syncopes; otherwise, all voice leading in exercises would soon be rendered impossible. In this exigency we are aided by the more discriminating valuation of perfect consonances from Part 2, Chapter 1, §4; and since, for reasons discussed there, the fifth is preferable to the octave for contrapuntal purposes, we permit the syncope 5↑4—5 in the lower counterpoint under certain circumstances, but we never grant an exception to 8↑9—8.

Ad **b:** The *consonant* syncope, even though it may be considered (in a more remote sense, to be sure) a delay of the tone following the upbeat, is, on the other hand, free of any requirement of a downward resolution. Therefore, from the outset, even from the strictest standpoint, this syncope may demand, if not complete access to prohibited progressions, at least a certain *liberty* with regard to parallel motion, to say nothing of nonparallel similar motion—for example:

Example 437

etc.

—especially in view of the fact that no better possibility may be available [in a given case]. This liberty is required even more urgently as the successions involved are by nature only afterbeat successions.

The following, however, should be kept in mind: the more attention is paid in such a situation to placing imperfect consonances at least on the downbeat, the better even parallel progressions can be tolerated. Thus, 6—8↑ 6—8 is better than 5—8↑5—8 (cf. Part 2, Chapter 2, §11, under 3, and the remarks under 2 in the present section).

The same principle would apply, strictly speaking, also to the succession of consonant syncopes in the upper counterpoint, that is, 6—5↑6—5, which signifies a change of harmony (see above, Part 2, Chapter 2, §13 and Chapter 3, §8)—for example:

Example 438

But the descending second-step contained in the falling succession ⌢6 — 5 creates for our ear at least the illusion of a required downward resolution to such an extent that, psychologically, our syncope comes close to the realm of actually dissonant syncopes. Our ear automatically reacts with greater sensitivity toward that succession—obviously, indeed, only because of the falling second-step, as though it were a true parallel succession involving dissonant syncopes—; therefore, it may be advisable to exempt the falling succession 6 — 5 ↑6 — 5 from the liberties granted above to the consonant syncope, and to include it in the prohibition mentioned under a. In other words: the descending consonant syncope 6 — 5 ↑6 — 5 occupies an *intermediate* position, and, therefore, it is best to extend the prohibition of parallels involving dissonant syncopes (see under a) to this syncope as well, even though it lacks by nature the requirement of a downward resolution. On the other hand, this kind of illusion is not present in the succession 6 — 5 ↑6 — 5 in the ascending direction; therefore, its use is again characterized by relative freedom.

Nevertheless, what was said above (under a) should not be forgotten: in case of a *more lenient* treatment, it is again the fifth that requires the strictness of the prohibition to a lesser extent than the octave.

As a final result of the considerations set forth under a and b, it should be kept in mind that there can never be an exception in the case of a dissonant [syncope that yields] similar motion to an octave, but that, because of the lesser perfection of the fifth, dispensation may be granted under certain circumstances for a parallel succession of fifths (whether ascending or descending, dissonant or consonant, or in the upper or lower counterpoint) provided only that such a succession not be misused by excessively crass and unnecessarily repetitious application.

2.   A still greater degree of liberty, however, is called for from the outset in the relationship of *downbeat to downbeat* (see bracket 2) than could be granted in the case of the consonant syncopes discussed earlier. Nevertheless, since the repeated use of perfect consonances on the downbeat would have to result in an overly empty setting, it is clear that the liberty must be applied sparingly in the present situation as well.

Free composition from the outset knows nothing like this. A requirement of uninterrupted syncopes, which is necessary in strict counterpoint for didactic purposes, is from the outset alien to free composition. While this alone reduces the dangers inherent in syncopes with regard to prohibited progressions, an additional factor is the interpretative force of the scale-degree, which can bind together a longer *chain* of syncopes into one single unit—a phenomenon that counterpoint is unable either to originate or to demonstrate. In this context, compare *Harmony,* Example 195, where scale degree VI in *B* major by itself generates a chain of seven syncopes: 6 — 5 ↑6 — 5 ↑6 — 5 ↑6 — 5 ↑6 — 5 ↑6 — 5 (moving in a rhythm of sixteenth-notes over seven eighth-notes). It goes without saying that the repetition of the fifth as a sixth, as seen there, is equivalent to the ligature of counterpoint, even though the articulation with legato slurs appears to indicate something different.

In this context may be cited the remark by J.J. *Quantz* in his *Versuch einer Anweisung die Flöte traversiere zu spielen*,[12] Chapter XV, §24, on the execution of cadenzas in two parts (cf. also §20ff. in the same work):

> In a passage in sixths where you do not wish to touch any dissonances, one of the two parts must anticipate a note, whether ascending or descending, so that the other may adjust accordingly:

Example 439

> Here the lower part has the movement, and indicates that in the first bar the upper part should ascend, and later that it should descend again.[13]

How subtly the effect of the anticipation—indeed, in the form of the syncope 6 — 5 ┼ 6 — 5, etc.—is here placed in the service of improvising two-part cadenzas, and how delightful the words with which Quantz describes all this! How far the overall level of our musical culture has declined since then—in spite of all the spiritual heroes who have come and gone in the meantime! In general, today's musicians are no longer able to improvise preludes or modulations; they are no longer able even to execute cadenzas and fermatas in their leisure time! And which of today's teachers, incidentally, would be in a position to provide such a clear rationale for a technique like the one just discussed for the execution of cadenzas, and thereby convince the student of its necessity!

In the context of two-voice counterpoint, *Fux* discusses all these problems as though only in passing. He merely presents the basic principle by taking his theory (discussed earlier in §4) as a point of departure (p. 81):

> Therefore, it is impossible to progress from a unison to a second or from an octave to a ninth by way of a ligature, as the following examples show [examples of Table V, Figure 8 follow]. If the retardation were to be eliminated, there would be two unisons in succession in the first example and two octaves in the second [examples of Table V, Figure 9 follow]. However, it is good if the motion from the second to the unison or from the ninth to the octave occurs as follows:

Example 440
Fux V, 10

These progressions are permissible, because no mistake is contained in them after the retardations are eliminated (Table V, Figure 11).

That is all he considered it appropriate to say about the subject in two-voice counterpoint.

He makes up for his omissions all the more thoroughly, however, in his discussion of the fourth species in three-voice counterpoint. Observe the surprisingly subtle and discriminating train of thought on p. 101:

> To treat the subject more thoroughly, however, I must repeat what has been said elsewhere about the [various degrees of] perfection of the consonances: the fifth is a perfect consonance, the octave even more perfect, and the unison the most perfect; the more perfect these intervals are, the less harmony they contain. Furthermore, experience has taught that dissonances by themselves have neither grace nor harmonic beauty, but whatever is perceived as euphonious and charming [about them] is generated solely by the consonances to which the dissonances resolve. Thus, we can see that a dissonance that resolves to a fifth is more tolerable than one resolving to an octave. Therefore, it is not surprising that the following example is discarded by good masters as faulty:

Example 441

Fux XI, 5

the next one, however, is considered suitable to counterpoint:

Example 442

Fux XI, 6

> Finally, a resolution is the more easily tolerated and excused the more the perfect consonance to which the dissonance resolves approximates the nature of an imperfect consonance.

Thus, it becomes more clear that from the outset Fux distinguishes between 8↑9 — 8 and 5↑6 — 5 in order to disallow parallel 8↑9 — 8 successions under all circumstances (note well that no mention is made here of the consonant syncope 8 ↑ 10 — 8), but to present 5 ↑ 6 — 5 (see above, p. 294) as tolerable. The question remains open whether, in view of [allowed] fifth-successions in the upper counterpoint, the syncope 5 ↑ 4 — 5 in the lower counterpoint is also tolerated. Fux defends his principle of granting syncopes from the outset a greater degree of freedom in fifth-successions than in octave-successions with the following argument [p. 101]:

> In order to respond to your not inconsiderable reservation, I point out that much that is disallowed in the upper register is tolerated in the lower, because higher tones are perceived with greater accuracy by the ear, while lower tones become

somewhat dark because of their lower pitch, and do not impress the ear so forcefully. For higher elevations clarify, while lower elevations obscure.

Even though, as can be sensed from the context, this remark does not relate to the syncope 5↑4—5, we may nevertheless conclude that, precisely because it occurs in the lower register, this syncope appears to him less reproachable than 8↑9—8 in the upper counterpoint—leaving aside the intrinsically more desirable quality of the fifth, which, of course, remains the essence of Fux's argument (compare the above quotation from Fux, p. 101).

And, as if all these elaborations were not enough, he adds, using the examples in Table XI, Figures 3 and 4:

Example 443

Fux XI, 3

Example 444

Fux XI, 4

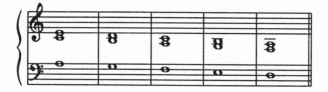

the following consideration (p. 100), so very characteristic for recognizing the essential quality of tying (cf. §12):

> Beyond the fact that one must attend to the authority of great masters, who approve the first example but disapprove the second, you should know that my remark, "ligatures change nothing," applies only to the nature of consonances, which is the same in both examples. For the rest, who can deny that ligatures have a great effect, and have the power to avoid errors and to modify settings?

How beautifully Fux formulates here the double effect of the syncope: on the one hand, it means only a delay of the resolution-tone, so that the suspended tone could simply be disregarded and omitted; on the other hand, however, it manifests a certain transforming power by virtue of which we must attribute to the syncope a purpose and beauty in its own right. (Compare to this the following treasurable definition of the appoggiatura in C.P.E. Bach's *Versuch über die wahre Art, das Clavier zu spielen*, Part I, Section 2, Chapter 2, §1:

> Appoggiaturas are among the most essential embellishments. They enhance harmony as well as melody. They heighten the attractiveness of the latter by joining notes smoothly together and, in the case of notes which might prove disagreeable because of their length, by shortening them while filling the ear

with sound. . . . Appoggiaturas modify chords which would be too simple without them. All syncopations and dissonances can be traced back to them. What would harmony be without these elements?[14]

(Compare also my "Contribution to the Study of Ornamentation" [see Appendix], §1.)

In his own exercises, Fux strictly observes the above theories. He by no means avoids parallel successions with consonant syncopes—for example, 8↑10 — 8 (cf. Table V, Figure 18, or Table V, Figure 20), or the succession 5↑4 — 5 (cf. Table V, Figure 19, or Table VI, Figure 1; etc.), which, on the contrary, is frequently used by him with little scruple; that he then uses a nonparallel succession—for example 6↑4 — 5—with still less scruple can easily be understood. The relationship of downbeat to downbeat is not discussed at all by Fux; without hesitation he writes, for example, as follows (Table XII, Figure 5, Bars 5 - 7):

Example 445
Fux XII, 5, bs. 5-7

Albrechtsberger's theories are different in many respects; to provide a better overview, I have reordered them:

1. In the relationship of upbeat to upbeat, according to him the following rules apply:

(a) 8 ↑ 9 — 8: "Here the tied ninth is prepared by the octave. Even a single occurrence of this is prohibited, because it sounds almost like two parallel octaves" (Example no. 4, p. 61).

(b) Octave-successions with consonant syncopes, however, he describes on pp. 59–60 as "good, especially in three and four-voice settings, even though they seem to sound 'octave-and-fifthish' *(oktaven- und quintenmässig)*." (Examples follow, showing 8↑ 10 — 8 in the upper counterpoint and 8 ↑ 3 — 8, 8 ↑ 6 — 8 in the lower; in this connection, see also Albrechtsberger, p. 103.) From the qualification added to the above explanation, however, we may surmise that *two*-voice counterpoint requires some caution.

(c) Regarding 5 ↑ 4 — 5 in the lower counterpoint, he teaches on p. 60f.: "The following three ligatures [one of these is 5 ↑ 4 — 5, the others are described below under d*β* and 2a], if used more than once in direct succession, are prohibited in settings of two or more voices, in both strict and free styles, because they sound too 'fifthish'." In other words, while he prohibits 8↑9 — 8 without exception, he allows 5↑ 4 — 5, but only under the condition that it be used only once. He gives no reason for this or that opinion, but finally contradicts himself on p. 61 by nevertheless approving successions like the following:

Example 446
Albrechtsberger, p. 61

(d) Parallel successions of fifths in consonant syncopes are differentiated by Albrechtsberger as follows:

(α) He considers them good when they ascend (see above under b), no matter whether the ascent occurs by step or in larger intervals (compare the examples on p. 58: 5↑6—5↑6—5↑6, or on p. 60: 5↑3—5↑3—5 in the upper and lower counterpoint);

(β) He prohibits them in the descending direction only if they descend by step in the upper counterpoints: 5↑6—5↑6—5 (see above under c). The other descending fifths are allowed without hesitation, for example:

Example 447

　　　5　　　　　5　　　　　5

In a certain sense Albrechtsberger's theory is thus more specialized than Fux's; concerning point c and dβ, it even contradicts the latter. Nevertheless, it lacks aspects that would provide depth and orientation, without which contrapuntal doctrine must remain only a collection of casual rules, restrictions and prescriptions of obscure origin.

2. The following rules apply for Albrechtsberger to the relationship of downbeat to downbeat:

(a) Descending successions of fifths in the lower counterpoint, for example:

Example 448

　　　5　　　　　5

are prohibited by the same restriction as [that which applies to] 5↑4—5 (see above under 1c).

(b) All other possible types are allowed—for example, 6↑5—6↑5—6 in the ascending direction (p. 58), 5—3↑5—3 in the descending direction (p. 60); see also p. 100, etc.

Unfortunately Albrechtsberger provides no justification for the rules even here.

Again in this matter, *Cherubini* assumes the strictest possible standpoint, one that is rigid almost to the extent of obtuse lack of principles. He prohibits 5↑4—5↑4—5 (p. 23, Example 70), without any differentiation and under all circumstances, and also prohibits 8↑5—8↑3—8, etc. (Example 72), 5↑6—5↑6—5↑3—5, etc. (same example). In practice, however, we see him contradicting himself by using 5↑6—5↑ 6—5 (see p. 24, Exercise 2). Strangely enough, Cherubini does not discuss parallel successions from downbeat to downbeat at all. From this strict standpoint, one understands more easily his statement (quoted in §12) recommending more frequent use of dissonant syncopes.

Finally, it should be mentioned that he also cites the example of Fux (quoted in this volume as Examples 443 and 444), and appends to it a little polemic that unfortunately is characterized only by naive sincerity. It may be found on pp. 36 and 37.

Bellermann seems at first to follow the doctrine of Albrechtsberger (p. 175): "Since the tied note on the downbeat is considered an extension of the preceding note on the upbeat, it is not good to use the same perfect consonant interval several times in succession on the unaccented part of the bar." Therefore, he considers "bad" also the example 8↑6 — 8↑6 — 8, while the grade "marginally acceptable" is given 5↑6 — 5↑ 6 — 5↑6 — 5 (in the descending direction). Then he prepares to draw from this a bold consequence: "The same reason explains also why fifths, as they appear in the following settings with both voices ascending, are not unpleasant to the ear, even though they occur on the accented part of the bar." Thus, he approves 6↑5 — 6↑5 — 6 (ascending) with the predicate "good," but immediately revokes as much as he has conceded: "The student must not repeat such turns too often, but must always aim for an appealing variety of intervals." Does this mean that he might admit, from the outset, the application of less stringent principles from downbeat to downbeat? And even though he explicitly speaks only of fifth-successions, are octave-successions implicity included here?

How the prohibited octave succession that always threatens in the case of a ⌐9 — 8 syncope can be avoided, he discusses only in the context of three-voice counterpoint, on p. 214:

> It should be noted that the ninth is to be prepared by the tenth, or some other such interval, from which the bass must ascend if it is to form a ninth with the voice in question on the next accented beat, so that if the ninth were to be replaced by its resolution, the voices would move in contrary motion. Preparation by the octave is completely faulty, since very ugly hidden octaves would result.

Example 449
Bellermann, p. 214

Riemann approaches this question in his *Grosse Kompositionslehre*[15] (Vol. II, Chapter 9, §3); however, he immediately obscures its origin: instead of determining the effect of prohibited progressions in the context of the phenomenon of syncope in counterpoint, he immediately speaks of the mannerism of "chain suspensions," which, of course, find application only in free composition. A critique of this improper procedure will follow later.

§16. *The possibility of an interruption of the ligatures*

The law of syncopes is, of course, uniformly valid for the duration of the exercise; nevertheless, it is permitted, as an exception, to interrupt the syncopes and replace them with two ligature-free beats, for which, in some cases, a half-rest and a half-note can also substitute. This is appropriate when a repetition (*monotonia*) is to be avoided, or to give a new stimulus to a line, once its continuation has become impossible for one reason or another.

Fux explicitly cites monotony as a reason [for an interruption of ligatures] on pp. 81–82:

> *Joseph:* I could indeed have used a ligature there, but I deliberately avoided it in order to preclude an unpleasant repetition, since I had used the same ligatures immediately before in the third and fourth bars.
> *Aloys:* Your remark is prudent, for one must pay careful attention to matters of melodic fluency and continuity.

That he views the interruption of ligatures, nevertheless, only as a concession necessary in a difficult situation, can be seen from the following basic idea stated in the context of three-voice counterpoint [p. 104]: "The ligatures here constitute the main purpose, a thorough understanding of which can be gained through such exercises." (Compare the quotation in §12.)

Albrechtsberger (p. 62): "Finally, it is important to know that, in case the invariable use of ligatures is not of good effect, it is permitted if necessary to use once or (at most) twice a freely introduced consonance on the downbeat in the counterpoint." (Compare also p. 103.) We may also recall, however (see above, §5), how, as a result of the use of the dissonant diminished fifth as a syncope in the upper counterpoint, he (precisely Albrechtsberger himself!) arrives at yet another and individual interruption of ligatures.

Cherubini proceeds this time with greater precision (p. 24, rule 5):

> The law of syncopating is to be observed in every bar. However, if this obligation makes it difficult to keep the melody in a middle register—in other words, if the syncope would carry it too high or too low—or if the syncope causes similar phrases to have too much resemblance [cf. Fux, above], or, finally, if phrases become too confusing through syncopes, then it is advisable not to syncopate for one or (at most) two bars. This remedy, however, should be used only if there is no other possibility.

For *Bellermann's* comments on this matter, see p. 175f. of his treatise.

§17. *The prohibition of tone-repetition*

It should be emphasized that here, as well as in the second and third species, the repetition of tones is entirely disallowed.

Cadence

§18. *Cadential formulas*

Without exception, $\frown 7 - 6 \mid 8$ is to be used in the upper counterpoint, and $\frown 2 - 3 \mid 1$ in the lower. This is evident already from the required presence of both leading tones:

Example 450

A different type of cadence, which appears in an exercise by *Beethoven* (*Nottebohm,* p. 50):

Example 451

is expressly criticized by *Albrechtsberger* with the remark: "N.B. not too often"; he adds as a correction ("better") the syncope ⌒2 — 3 | 1. Compare the same situation in *Nottebohm,* p. 52, and in Albrechtsberger's own treatise, pp. 105–106.

Nevertheless, one must consider that, if the cantus firmus were to have, for example, the following cadence:

Example 452

the closing formula ⌒2 — 3 | 1 would not be possible at all from the outset. Since it is impossible to give up the other leading tone, B, would it not be better, instead of writing as follows:

Example 453

or

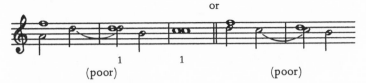

1   1
(poor)   (poor)

to proceed in this way:

Example 454

§19. The misguided treatment of syncopes in the conventional theory of harmony

The theory of syncopes represented here treats, to state it once again and most emphatically, precisely the same subject matter that is taught in conventional textbooks on harmony in chapters about the preparation and resolution of the seventh and the other dissonances. May the type of treatment to which this problem has been subjected here demonstrate that the problem of the syncope can have its real home [only] in counterpoint, not in the theory of harmony.

Exercises

Example 455

Fux V, 16 and 17

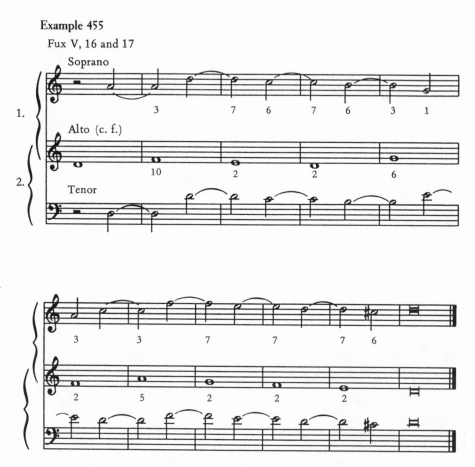

Example 455 *continued*

Fux V, 20 and VI, 1

Albrechtsberger p. 62

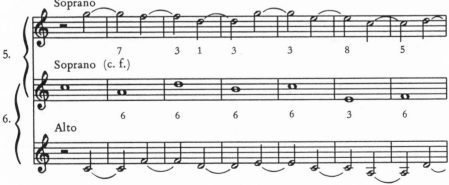

Example 455 *continued*

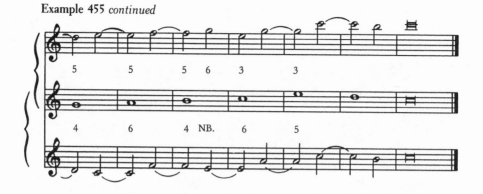

Albrechtsberger p. 63

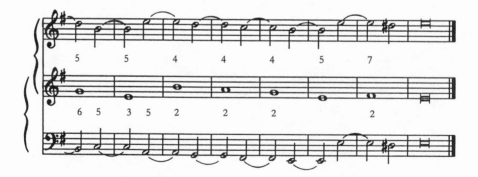

Example 455 *continued*

Albrechtsberger p. 74

Bellermann p. 176 (c.f. by Fux)

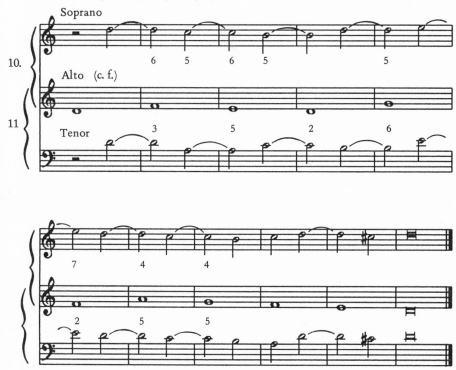

Example 455 *continued*

H. Schenker

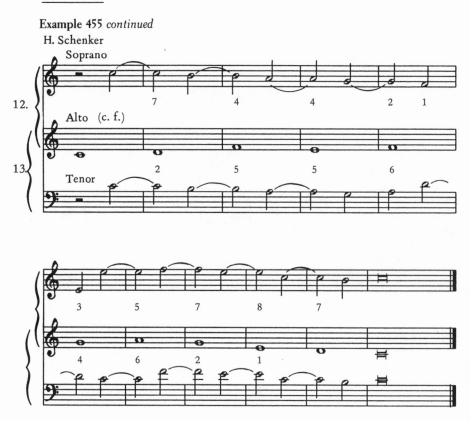

Comments on the Preceding Exercises

No. 1. Concerning the interruption of tying in bar 5, see §16. Bellermann, who uses the same exercise (p. 176), disregards monotony and makes the following change:

Example 456

which certainly does not succeed in improving the effect.

As to the succession of two major thirds in bars 5 - 6: $\frac{B-A}{G-F}$, see above, Part 2, Chapter 1, §18.

No. 2. This exercise (also taken over by Bellermann) basically shows, if the ligatures are removed, only successions of thirds. If this is in a certain sense to be considered a fault of the counterpoint—one that can be excused only in part by the basic requirement of ligatures and the difficulties resulting from it—, one should nevertheless at least not overlook the octave, sixth, and fifth on the downbeats of bars 2, 5, and 7, which do improve the effect here.

No. 3. In bar 5 the counterpoint moves beyond the limit of a tenth; this results in the ambiguity of the intervals of bars 6 and 7: are they really 11 — 10 and 9 — 8 or only 4 — 3 and 2 — 1 (see p. 274)? As to the parallel octaves in the upbeats of bars 9 and 10, see above, p. 294 (note that the downbeats in these bars show the preferable intervals 5 and 10); concerning the fifth-successions in the downbeats of bars 3 and 4, see p. 295. In both cases we encounter non-dissonant successions of syncopes, and therefore Bellermann's cautionary attitude is exaggerated. He changes bars 9 – 10 (p. 177) to the following:

Example 457

obviously in order to avoid parallel octaves—unless perhaps he merely wanted to avoid a second touching of the tone a^1.

No. 4. In bars 3 – 5 there are third-leaps with fifth-successions; they have been discussed above on p. 294. About the unusual occurrence of the ⌒2 — 1 syncope in bar 7, see above, pp. 269 and 274-277. In order to avoid this syncope, Bellermann changes the passage as follows (p. 177):

Example 458

No. 5. Concerning the fifth-succession on the downbeats in the ascending direction (that is, 5 — 6↑5 — 6↑5 — 6 in bars 7 - 10), see p. 295, and [later on, p. 300] in the commentary on the literature, under 2b in the section dealing with Albrechtsberger. As to the syncope of the diminished fifth and its resolution in bars 10 - 11, see the commentary on Albrechtsberger in §5.

No. 6. Concerning the NB at tone 10 regarding the augmented fourth in the lower counterpoint, see the Albrechtsberger quotations in §§5 and 9.

No. 7. The double figuration in bars 5 – 7 is by Albrechtsberger himself. Whoever follows him in disregarding the actual distance between voices (cf. above, §8), can, of course, substitute a higher octave in this case and, accordingly, think of the syncope ⌒7 — 6 instead of ⌒2 — 3.

No. 8. In accordance with his conception of the minor mode, Albrechtsberger uses the raised sixth and seventh tones of the minor scale in the main body of the exercise (bars 2 and 4) without hesitation. Concerning the fifth-succession in ascending direction on the downbeats of bars 7 - 10, see p. 300 under dα. The exercise, because apparently instrumentally conceived, is unfortunately misleading; one need only transpose the added voice an octave higher to be convinced that it is not at all necessary to exceed the limit of a tenth in this case. This is nothing but an all-too-convenient mode of writing.

Chapter 5

The Fifth Species: Mixture of the Preceding Species

General Aspects

§1. The purpose of the fifth species

The fifth species presents a free mixture of all species learned heretofore. Accordingly, the exercises to be carried out in this species approach unawares the realm of free composition itself, with which they already share that foremost principle of *free variety.*

Here for the first time, then, the student is afforded an opportunity to identify the phenomena of diversification in their embryonic form and to differentiate one from another; at the same time, however, also to gain insight into the methods through which the effect of an increased diversity may be attained. And if constraint by the cantus firmus above all, as well as by the limited span of at most fifteen bars, remains as always the prerequisite of these exercises as well, the student will nevertheless find the first steps toward diversity—the results in the small—to be in many respects prototypical also for the results in the large, and will thereby secure a correspondingly better insight into the great world of free composition.

According to *Fux's* definition (Fux, p. 83), "this species is called florid counterpoint *(contrapunctum floridum),* because in it, all manner of embellishments, fluent motions, and divers variations must be present, just as in a flower garden."

Albrechtsberger, p. 64, writes: ". . . for here, one is allowed to introduce all manner of note values in mixture"; and on p. 109: ". . . where one may present the three predominant species at the same time in alternation, and also use a few notes of quicker value than in the third species."

See *Cherubini,* p. 26, and *Bellermann,* p. 179, for their respective comments.

§2. Inclusion of eighth-note values in exercises of the present species

In deference to the tendency toward mixture, for the first time, even *eighth-note values* are integrated into the exercises of mixed counterpoint. They are to be regarded as not unlike a representative of a hypothesized final species—to be precise, a species of ♪-values.

How strict counterpoint nevertheless guards against erosion of its established assumption of the quarter note as the smallest unitary value—that is, how it ensures that in exercises the ultimate rhythmic unit remains not the ♪-value but, as previously (in the sense of the third species, to be exact), only the ♩-value—will be shown clearly later on (§10).

See *Albrechtsberger's* definition above in §1. But for the rest, certainly, the theorists provide no insight at all concerning the real meaning of eighth-note values in mixed-species counterpoint.

Beginning

§3. *Construction of the beginning*

As a rule, the first bar contains a half-rest followed by a ♩, which, however, is usually tied as a syncope into the next bar.

Fux (p. 84): ". . . [you] have also, in beginning, made frequent use of oblique motion, or syncopation. This expedient I should like to recommend to you further, since it imbues the counterpoint with much grace." Fux himself nevertheless writes, in Table VI, Figure 7, as follows:

Example 459

Compare Table VI, Figure 11.

Albrechtsberger begins on principle with a half-rest (see Albrechtsberger, p. 66f.), so as to introduce a syncopation at once; but see also an instance of an unsyncopated half-note, p. 69 (cf. Example 514, Exercise 5).

Main Body

§4. *The postulate of equilibrium among the individual species blended to form mixed counterpoint*

It is clear that if the mixture is to preserve its character as such, no species may be allowed to gain quantitative predominance over the others. From the outset, then, a strict state of *equilibrium* among all species must be postulated.

If we bear in mind the duration of at most fifteen bars within which the exercises must unfold their diversity, we find that the balance postulated above must always be sought only in a way commensurate with this number of bars; and in view of the modest dimensions of the exercise, we can easily see that the individual species will have to curtail their egoistic tendencies and submit to regulation.

The mixture must also promote constancy of rhythmic movement—that is, it must be successfully carried through in such a way that no sudden stasis occurs. Upbeats and downbeats, therefore, must always present "attacked" notes, so that their rhythmic impulse remains aurally present. In this respect, no "dead point" must be allowed to impede unpleasantly the flow of the whole. This principle—admittedly in its broadest extension—again provides a fruitful view of the forms of free composition, in regard to which avoidance of the dead point of the action (in the higher sense of the word) likewise demands the full art of the composer.

Finally, in a certain sense the "caesura," to be studied presently (see §8, p. 316), can also be included among the forbidden devices that disturb the equilibrium of mixture.

In the following paragraphs we will determine, species by species, the extent to which each may be used in mixed counterpoint.

Albrechtsberger articulates the principle of the rhythmic presence of all beats of a mixed-species exercise only in his teaching concerning fugue (Albrechtsberger, p. 199): "To conclude the rules for fugue, I have still to mention that an attacked note, at least in one voice, must occur on each beat in every meter, so that instead of lifeless melody, a delicate contrapuntal setting is always achieved." In *Nottebohm,* too, we find the following corrections from the hand of Albrechtsberger, which pertain to Beethoven's infractions of this very rule (Nottebohm, p. 53):

Example 460

Or, another example (p. 77):

Example 461

A. "license"

§5. *Extent of application: (a) Use of the first species in mixed counterpoint*

The whole-note under consideration here is, however, to be understood only in the sense of the first species—that is, as a note that lasts from downbeat to downbeat; it is not, for example, to be understood as possibly also a syncope, which, if its two half-notes are added together, finally also yields the value of a whole-note.

Given this stipulation, one understands that such a whole-note, if placed at the beginning of the mixed-species exercise—that is, in the first bar—would necessarily disorient the listener about the character to be expected of the intended mixture; therefore, in the first bar only a rest with a half-note following it is employed (see above, §3).

Used in the main body of the exercise, however, a whole-note must necessarily cripple all nimble motion of the counterpoint, and the incongruity of a suddenly so pretentious note will be more sharply and unpleasantly noticeable to the ear the more skillful the construction of the mixture in its immediate environment.

Use of a whole-note, therefore, must be completely avoided both at the beginning and in the main body; it must be restricted to the cadence alone—that is, to the final bar itself.

Albrechtsberger writes (p. 64): "The first [species], however, has no place until the final bar." And on p. 109: "Avoid the first [species] up to the last bar." And as *Nottebohm* shows (see, for Example, p. 76), Albrechtsberger pursues such an error by his student all the way into fugal exercises.

Similarly, *Bellermann,* p. 182:

The whole-note beginning at the bar line (thus consisting of *arsis* and *thesis*) is best avoided in this species, since it makes the movement of the counterpoint appear sluggish; two tied half notes, on the other hand, which together also have the value of a whole-note but consist instead of *thesis* and *arsis,* always have a very pleasant effect.

§6.   (b) Use of the second species in mixed counterpoint

Obviously, the smallest quantity of second species counterpoint that can appear is the single half-note. It will be shown later how just such a single ♩ can nevertheless be used here only if certain preconditions are fulfilled, since in unfavorable circumstances it, like the whole-note, can produce only an inappropriate effect in the main body.

In seeking the quantitative maximum, however, we find that within the framework of the exercise, and measured according to the standards of the other species to be used, an uninterrupted series of four half-notes causes the impression of the second species to be quantitatively excessive, and thus threatens the intended effect of a mixture. We infer from this that the uninterrupted succession of only *three half-notes,* wherein the emphasis falls equally on the condition of being uninterrupted and on the number three, must signify the desired quantitative maximum of the second species in mixed counterpoint. But it should be expressly added that if after three ♩s there follows a fourth, syncopated half-note, this by no means counts as a violation of the limit, because with the syncopation of the last of them, the status is changed to that of the fourth species.

Example 462

good:

poor:

Albrechtsberger, p. 64: ". . . to avoid dull and boring melody, one should not use the second species longer than four beats at a time, the last of which must indeed be tied to the fifth beat":

Example 463

"good":   "poor":

"still poorer":

Compare Albrechtsberger, p. 67.

§7.   (c) Use of the third species in mixed counterpoint

As in the preceding case, a full symmetry of four bars must be avoided if the balance of all species is not to be tipped in favor of the third species alone. Therefore, again a maximum of *three bars* should be observed in the exercises.

How to proceed with only a single quarter note, or with an affiliation of two, will be shown later.

"Here the third species, too, should never last longer than six beats," according to *Albrechtsberger* (p. 64); but unfortunately he himself writes as follows on p. 68:

Example 464

where the specified quantitative maximum has certainly been exceeded, unless one is inclined to view the use of eighth notes—perhaps this is exactly Albrechtsberger's intention (?)—as a sufficient interruption of the third species. In any event, the monotony present in the same example—see the brackets I have added—must be criticized. Compare, incidentally, a similar contradiction in Albrechtsberger on p. 164 (in four-voice counterpoint).

§8. The three possible combinations of a half-note with two quarters in the same bar

If in a single bar a ♩ is to be combined with two quarter-notes, three different possibilities exist, all with completely different effects:

1. First Combination-Type: ♩ ♩♩ This is the first and most natural ordering, because a certain inner psychological congruence prevails between the stronger value of the downbeat with its ♩ on the one hand, and the weaker value of the upbeat with its two quarters on the other: *the note of greater value on the downbeat, the notes of smaller value on the upbeat!*

Here, however, two possibilities can be discriminated: (a) downbeat and upbeat are both treated as consonant:

Example 465

or (b) the upbeat is dissonant, in the form of a passing tone, which was permitted already by the third species—in its own context, to be sure—; for example:

Example 466

That type a has conceptual priority over type b is obvious according to the principles of strict counterpoint—that is, to the extent that naturalness is to be observed.

Fux uses only type a in his exercises. Could it be that the exercises simply gave him no opportunity for type b?

Albrechtsberger, on the other hand, writes type b as well—for example:

Example 467

p. 67   p. 68

And likewise on p. 69, etc.

Type b is found also in *Bellermann,* p. 186 for example.

2. Second Combination-Type: ♩ ♩ ♩ The psychology of this type is to be understood in the following way. First, since it offers in comparison to the first type exactly the opposite situation, for the reasons specified under 1, it makes a less natural effect. Because it is precisely the smaller values that are placed on the downbeat, they invite us to expect only quarter-notes also for the duration of the upbeat; but since a half-note unexpectedly appears instead, we suddenly sense a kind of stasis of rhythmic movement—our ear misses the beat of the fourth quarter!—a contradiction that we designate by the word "caesura."

The error of such a caesura can be eliminated in the above combination-type only by syncopating the half-note that causes the stasis. For the syncope then produces two new effects that remedy the defect: first, through the syncope, the downbeat is reclaimed for the half note of the upbeat, which, as the larger note value, was entitled to that position from the beginning; and second, the cantus firmus has an attacked note at the downbeat against this very [tied] note—psychologically speaking, therefore, a compensation of a rhythmic nature, which would otherwise have to be absent from the ♩ ♩ ♩- type if it remained unsyncopated.

Strict counterpoint accordingly admits the combination-type in question here only when it is allied with the remedial syncopation; thus:

Free composition, on the contrary, has access to countless reasons that justify the second combination-type [even without syncopation], and incorporates this type without hesitation precisely because of its unique and special expressive value; for example:

Example 468

Haydn, Symphony No. 104, Finale

If the appoggiaturas in bars 1 and 2 are removed, we have in each bar only two half notes: $g^1 - e^1$ / $f\sharp^1 - d^1$; since our instinct has knowledge of this, it accepts such a combination-type without resistance in free composition.

Often, too, it is the distribution of note values among voices[1] that indirectly combines two such rhythms into a succession of four quarters that is perfectly normal from the standpoint of strict counterpoint:

In *Fux* we read (p. 84ff.):

But what I would like to give you now is not so much a law as, rather, good advice: when at the beginning of the bar one writes two quarter-notes in direct succession without tying, it appears as though the melody were about to cadence; therefore it will be better, if only two quarters are to be used at the beginning of the bar, to use a tie or to facilitate the continuation by means of two additional quarters, as in the following example:

Example 469

Fux VI, 16

The word "advice," however, shows that Fux has by no means mastered the problem.

Albrechtsberger has the following to say (p. 68):

The . . . error is the overly static half-note C at the upbeat, after the two quarters *e* and *d,* for here caesuras are not permitted on the upbeat. Such an error can be corrected only by means of a subsequent ligature, or by the use of several notes [instead of the half-note] in the following ways [examples follow].

It is not without interest that Albrechtsberger continues:

Caesuras that are concluded by a half-note on the downbeat, however (and also those half-notes that do not define a caesura), are permitted, and should frequently be introduced here and there for singers and players of wind instruments, who are able to breathe on such ligature-free notes without having it noticed.

Nevertheless, we occasionally see Albrechtsberger himself violate this rule—see, for example, pp. 110 and 111—when he writes (albeit only in the cadential formula) as follows:

Example 470

Perhaps *Bellermann* is most comprehensive in this matter. His teaching—which, however, is correct only in small part—runs as follows (p. 180):

1. If half- and quarter-notes are used in combination without ties, it is better and more natural to place a half-note on the accented beat and two quarter-notes on the unaccented [example follows]. The opposite procedure, that is, to put the two quarter-notes first and the half-note after [example follows], sounds harsh and was almost completely avoided by the composers of the sixteenth century. We do, however, find two quarter-notes at the beginning of the bar in their works under the following conditions:

(a) if the first quarter of the bar is tied to a preceding half-note on the upbeat—for example:

Example 471

(b) if, as in the third species of counterpoint, two quarters occur in the second half of the bar as well [example follows];

(c) if the last note of the preceding bar was a quarter-note—for example:

Example 472
Palestrina, II, 14

(d) if the half-note that follows the quarters is tied to the following note [examples follow].

There are, as I said, several matters here to be corrected. Specifically, point a, strictly speaking, belongs to the issue of the syncope in the mixed species (cf. point d), so that it has nothing at all to do with the matter of caesura in the first place, and therefore remains without significance for our problem. Point c rests on an incorrect assumption (since, as we will see later, a ternary note value in mixed species cannot be realized by ♩. but only by ♩♩♩). Thus the only remaining correct element is point d, which, however, in fact involves the solution given first priority by all other theorists—that is, the solution by means of syncopation, under which point a, as said earlier, was to be regarded as included.

Nevertheless, Bellermann himself writes at the cadence of an exercise (p. 234, No. 6):

Example 473

c.f.

This formation, however, was discussed earlier in greater detail. Compare also the citation [of Bellermann] later in §10.

3. *Third Combination-Type:* ♩♩ ♩ For strict counterpoint, a form such as this reveals itself to be completely unsuitable. And, indeed, the irreparable flaw of this form is to be found in the circumstance that the upbeat receives no rhythmic expression at all. The rejection of this third combination-type must appear all the more justified in view of the fact that we have already disavowed the second if it occurs without any syncopation, and if the fourth quarter is thus deprived of its own rhythmic animation.

If we now consider all three combination-types together, it finally becomes clear why a single half-note by itself—that is, as the sole representative of the second species—was presented above in §6 only as bound to specific prerequisites.

All of this, on the other hand, certainly says nothing against the special individual value of the third combination-type in free composition, where, either in cadential formulas or as rhythmic circumscription of a tone by arcing through its neighboring note or the like,[2] it can and may find ample use. In an example like the following:

Example 474

J. S. Bach, St. Matthew Passion, Recitative
"Da Jesu diese Rede vollendet hatte"

we see the combination-type under discussion used at the fourth quarter; specifically, it is a passing tone, *a♯*, which occupies the value of an eighth-note between two sixteenths. The passing-tone character is explained in this case, however, by the fact that free composition brings passing tones with leaps of all possible intervals,[3] since it can also actually establish the harmony as such on the basis of the progression of scale degrees; the emphasis that results for our perception, however, makes it possible for us to bring into relationship with one another the tones that belong to the same harmony, even when they are widely separated: thus in the above example, we automatically add to $c\sharp$, as the true root of II$\sharp$, its seventh, b, and we grasp all the more easily the passing-tone character of the intervening tone $a\sharp$. Add to this the fact that the latter tone ($a\sharp$) at the same time manifests the passing-tone character (see Part 2, Chapter 2, §3ff.) also in the strictest sense of the term, in that the tone $g\sharp$, which can very well replace the root $c\sharp$ before $a\sharp$, can be generated from the harmony $c\sharp - e\sharp - g\sharp - b$. In this manner, we are always able to identify the passing tone in the space of only a third (or a fourth) even where free composition, by reason of the possibility of substitutions for harmonic tones, uses larger leaps!

Later, in the combined species—see part 6—we will be able to use still another, similar combination-type (with a $\frac{6}{4}$-chord prepared by a dissonance),[4] albeit in augmentation, thus in the following form: ♩ ♩♩♩ ♩ ♩.

The following example, from free composition, manifests the latter scheme:

Example 475
Beethoven, Piano Sonata Op. 27 No. 2, I

The rhythm of the inner voice beginning on $b\sharp$ can easily be recognized as the combination-type under consideration here:

$$b\sharp \quad c\sharp^1 \quad b\sharp$$

(3 - 4 - 3)

Albrechtsberger deals with the third combination-type only in four-voice counterpoint, where, a propos of the $\frac{6}{4}$-chord, he writes on p. 149 the examples [shown in Example 476, p. 321]. He comments: "The four NBs [in Example 476] indicate that in strict counterpoint no syncopated note of this kind can be used; because otherwise the second beat would be too stagnant." At the same time he does overlook the fact that the $\frac{6}{4}$-chord is more problematical than the rhythm.

Example 476

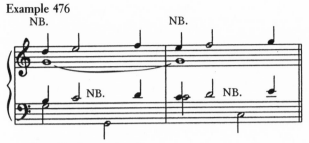

"good in free settings"

Bellermann expresses the following opinion in a footnote on p. 181: "In the works of good composers, cadential figures such as the following do occur now and then:

Example 477

In exercises, however the student must initially avoid completely idioms of this kind, and try to invent the most smoothly flowing melodies." Initially?! I beg to differ: even the teacher himself must avoid completely the error of compromising counterpoint through free composition or vice versa, especially when he is so unable to specify the differences between situations that account for the fact that so many things that must be permissible in free composition are entirely inadmissible in strict counterpoint!

§9. *The new syncopation-types in the mixed species*

The mixed species gives us the possibility, finally, of constructing syncopations in still other note-values than those we have learned so far.

A free combination of note-values leads us for the first time to the following table [of durations] that are possible under the rubric of syncopation:

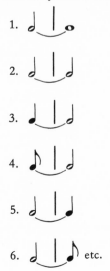

Yet on the other hand, so many of these forms lack from the outset the necessary qualifications for any use at all in strict counterpoint, as will be established in the following discussion.

Form 1 is automatically excluded from strict counterpoint since in the mixed species a whole-note may not be used at all (cf. §5 above).

Forms 3 and 4 represent less natural types in comparison with form 2, whose foundational significance is known to us, to the extent that in them, it is precisely the smaller value—that is, the quarter or the eighth—that is called upon in the upbeat to lead dynamically into the longer value, the half-note, on the downbeat. This is to be understood not only figuratively and poetically, but also actually and literally. True, forms 3 and 4 have their own charm precisely for that reason—as observed, it is the charm of a transformation of weakness into strength—; strict counterpoint, nevertheless, must in the protection of its own interests remain aloof from them: it must, for the promotion of naturalness as foundation of the exercise, reject those forms.

Form 5, however, is free of the error that sullies the preceding forms 3 and 4, and, since here once again it is only a smaller value on the downbeat that follows the half-note of the upbeat (this having to do with naturalness of relationship), it stands next to basic form 2 in order of priority. But the quarter-note on the downbeat, insofar as it may appear within a syncopation after a half-note, is clearly a product only of the mixed species, and therefore, as we know, it must here satisfy certain requirements, in the absence of which form 5 as well would be inadmissible. The continuation must therefore proceed as follows:

Also important to observe in connection with form 5 is that in it, *for the first time, a ternary note-value* appears in strict counterpoint! As far as the ternary nature of the note value is concerned, the following different form would indeed also be possible:

But for reasons similar to those we learned already in §5, where we preferred a whole-note value in the form of a syncopation to an unsyncopated form, here too the syncopated form is to be given priority over the unsyncopated.

Form 6 must be excluded from strict counterpoint for reasons that will have to be presented only later (§10), in our investigation of the problem of eighth-notes.

It follows, then, when we formulate the final result, that in the mixed species only forms 2 and 5 are permitted, thus:

Strict counterpoint has fulfilled its obligation in pointing to the varieties of syncopation-forms; and in the manner in which it has selected among them for its own domain, as well as in the justification of this selection, we find implicit reference to the unrestricted use of all syncopation-forms in free composition. But to discover here, in free composition, which form of syncope is present in a given case, we often find it necessary to take refuge in that ideal aural image of the preparatory harmony which has on several occasions[5] aided us in tracing apparently contradicting phenomena of free composition back to strict counterpoint, and recognizing them simply as prolongations of phenomena observed there.

A few examples may clarify. In *Harmony*, Example 14, bars 6–7, a syncopation with the following note-values is undoubtedly present:

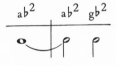

And in bars 10–11 of the same example:

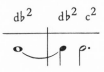

In Example 31 of *Harmony*, in the lowest voice of bars 2–3 we find the following situation:

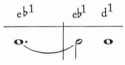

(Concerning the character of the syncope ⌐7—8 in the lower counterpoint, compare p. 271ff.!)

In Fig. 94 of *Harmonielehre*[6] bars 2–4 present the following:

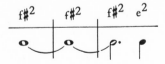

The occurrence of a syncopation-form 𝄽 𝄽 in the passage by J.S. Bach quoted in *Harmony*, Example 72, bar 3, has its origin in the composing-out of the sixth-suspension and the anticipation caused by it.[7] Exactly such an example—bear in mind how much right free composition has to demand composing out, diminution, anticipation, and the like!—can teach the subtle effect expressed by the syncopation whenever the smaller note-value precedes a larger one. (Compare also in the present volume Example 422.)

The sudden appearance of |♩. ♩| in the three-voice exercises of mixed counterpoint by *Fux* is surprising; see Table XIII, Figure 7, and Table XIV, Figure 1.

Albrechtsberger's teaching, although presented without accompanying justification, is nevertheless thorough. On p. 64 we read:

> Thirdly, one should strive to make frequent use of short and long ligatures within beautiful and florid melodies of the liturgical style. From practical musical experience, every musician will certainly have learned that there are four kinds of ligatures in counterpoint. I call them here the short and the shorter; the long and the longer. Others may call them by different names. The shorter ligature is that which consists of one quarter beat, in meter of any type. The short is that which consists of a half beat. The long is that which lasts a whole beat. The longer, finally is that which consists of two full beats. The following example will refresh the memory concerning all four types, or, if they have not previously been known so exactly, will provide an opportunity to learn them.

Example 478

Observe that here only the short and long forms are to be used.

Albrechtsberger says nothing explicitly about the form ♩. ♩ ; it would perhaps not be an error, however, to invoke his opinions on the use of the whole-note, and on the necessity of an attack [on each beat] on p. 199 (see above, §§4 and 5), as proofs that he would prefer it to be prohibited.

He deals with the remaining aspects of the problem only in his discussion of three-voice counterpoint, p. 109, with the following remarks:

> Ligatures in which the tied note itself is longer than the preparation are always faulty and contrary to good melody; if the opposite is true, however, or if both are equally long, they are good. For example:

Example 479

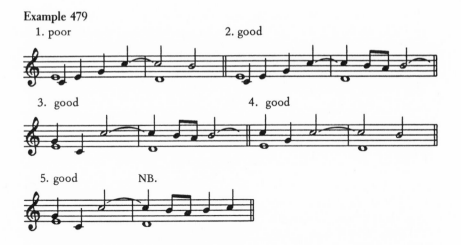

It should be added here that it would not be desirable if the ligatures in 2 and 3 were not [either] followed by quarter-notes, as in 5, or by still another ligature; because without the following ligature, it resembles a caesura, like that caused by two quarter-notes and a half-note in a bar; . . . the fourth form, however, is most often used with the short ligature.

Thus Albrechtsberger, as can be seen in Example 479, 2, admits the form  for use even in strict counterpoint; this is a form I have rejected above. It should not be overlooked, however, that he himself uses such a syncope only seldom (see, for example, Albrechtsberger, p. 110).

From *Cherubini's* Example 76 (p. 26), which contains the following figure:

Example 480

it is clear that he appears to allow the ternary value also in the d. form. About the other problems that have concerned us, however, he has nothing at all to say.

In more detailed instruction, *Bellermann* (p. 181) takes the correct point of view; he too rules out a quarter-note as preparation, and concludes:

> . . . and from this can be inferred the rule that in general to a note on the *thesis*[8] there must never be tied a note on the *arsis* of longer value than this note itself [example follows]; and further, that the note to be tied must be exactly as long or half as long as the note on the *thesis*. Accordingly, it is inadmissible to tie a quarter- or an eighth-note to a whole-note.

True, he lets this instruction stand without any justification; it is all the more reproachable, then, when he regresses in a footnote as follows:

> In modern music, the rule that no long note should be tied to a short one is very often violated. Under No. 2 it was stipulated that in the stricter style all

notes must be divisible by two or three. We find this law strictly observed in
all compositions of the sixteenth century. The mensural notation of that period
did not even allow for the writing of five-unit or seven-unit notes or the like;
the reason, indeed, was that the dot was the only lengthening sign available,
and use of the tie (⌒) was still unknown. More recent music has no reservations
about writing, for example, as follows:

Example 481

I believe that here the limits of beauty (and also of comprehensibility) even for
instrumental music are exceeded, and I consider it important that the student
adhere in his exercises to the *above established* stricter rules.[9]

Except for the last clause, which has full validity, how much absurdity otherwise in
this remark! Why should the composer be bound by an alleged "rule" that at best
can serve only as a key for the understanding of certain syncopation-forms within the
bounds of strict counterpoint? Why shouldn't forms that differ according to their
different causes be introduced to the student successively and simultaneously in exactly
such diversity? To be sure, this should be accompanied by the instruction to use each
at the proper time—thus, in the framework of a strict exercise, at first the simplest and
most natural, and, to the extent that expressive quality and freedom are increased, then
the more complex as well. Why should what Haydn wrote in the passage cited earlier
(Example 428) be called an "error," when this very effect is such an intentionally and
successfully individual one? We see here where we are led by the conceit that
contrapuntal doctrine should be binding on free composition as well!

The remark by Bellermann concerning Example 472 in §8 reveals that in order to
present the ternary note-value, he has adopted already for exercises the form used in
free composition ("the composers of the sixteenth century"), and that therefore he
freely writes ♩ ♩ instead of ♩|♩ (pp. 182, 183, etc.); he does this even though he
opposed with correct reason the appearance of the whole-note, and demanded ♩|♩
instead of o .

§10.   *Eighth-notes in mixed-species counterpoint*

In a small world of tones[10] where, consciously and intentionally, the principle
of a mere ♩ is posited as the basis of all motion—this postulate is most easily
recognizable when we consider the form of syncope required in strict counterpoint—and where the diminution of that value is carried only as far as the
♪, an uninterrupted longer series of eighth-notes must necessarily act as a
perilous and excessive diminution that can no longer be brought into any
equilibrium with the other dimensions.

This is the reason, then, that in mixed-species counterpoint, in spite of the
incentives that favor mixture and in spite of the tendency of the setting to
incorporate eighth-note values as well into its sphere, even a series of four

eighth-notes: ♪♪♪♪ is nevertheless sensed as an insupportable element. Indeed, four eighth-notes in direct succession would have to disorient and upset and our sense of the fundamental unit ♩, and of ♪ as, by initial assumption, the smallest of values.

The succession of two eighth notes: ♫, therefore, is to be designated as the quantitative maximum, with respect to which, however, it makes no difference whether such an eighth-note pair were to appear within the span of the downbeat or that of the upbeat.

Observe, then, that—significantly enough—in the case of eighth notes, too, it is once again necessary to avoid that symmetry which is by nature intrinsic to the number four (see above, §§6 and 7).

Further still, let the apprentice learn from this artistically conscious adjustment of equilibrium between the basic unit of the half-note and the remaining values (whole-, quarter-, and eighth-notes) how an artistic intent is to be given consistency—in other words: how unity of intent and execution is achieved! Translated into free composition, this takes the form of just a similar consistency—the one to be called style!

The use of eighth-notes, already severely limited in mixed counterpoint, is further subject to the following restrictions:

(a) The rule according to which the stronger beat belongs to the larger values and the weaker beat to the smaller values (§8) applies also to the pair of eighth-notes within the downbeat or upbeat, in that in neither case may the eighth-notes occupy the initial position, which rather must be reserved for the quarter. Therefore only ♩ ♫ may be used; and not ♫ ♩.

The prohibition of the latter form must be observed all the more strictly in view of the fact that it lacks access to the remedy by means of syncopation (which could be used in the pattern ♩ ♩ ♩♩♩), since according to §9, syncopation-forms such as |♫ ♩♩ ♩ | or |♫　♩♩ | must remain completely excluded.

At the same time, however, this explains definitively why in §9 the syncopation-form ♩♪ was declared inadmissible: if location in the first quarter of the downbeat or upbeat is denied the eighth-notes from the outset, the syncope that would have to lead directly to such an error must be rejected at the same time.

(b) Moreover, the two eighth-notes that are at least permissible here must not at the same time try to achieve an extensive, independent melodic character, but should simply content themselves with serving as a suspension-resolution (see below, §12) or in some other subordinate role of simplest embellishment. What is meant by this can be clarified more easily [later] in the discussion of syncopation-resolution.

Fux, p. 83: "Moreover, a pair of eighth-notes may sometimes be included in the next species, but only on the second and fourth beats of the bar, never on the first and third":

Example 482

Fux VI, 3

Yet, as this very example shows, Fux uses eighth-notes melodically as well—that is, in contexts other than merely the suspension-resolution. (Compare also Table VI, Figures 9 and 10; and, in three-voice counterpoint, Table XIII, Figures 4 and 7.) Whether his avoidance of twice two eighth-notes in the same bar () is mere coincidence or actual intent, however, cannot be demonstrated with certainty.

In *Albrechtsberger* we read first of all on p. 64 ". . . that four quick notes must not be placed on a beat in the added voices, but only a pair here and there; not, however, at the beginning of a beat":

Example 483

Further, Albrechtsberger, p. 68: "The . . . error is the four eighth-notes, which are out of place here. . . . It is a different matter when, for the sake of convenience, a complete piece that could have two-quarters or four-quarters meter is written in alla breve meter so that many double-flagged notes may be represented by single-flagged ones."

And finally on p. 146: ". . . in which one may also use a pair of quick notes, which form only half a beat."

A first trace of justification makes its appearance with the words "which are out of place here." Granted, this idea would have needed development and enrichment.

Albrechtsberger, incidentally, like Fux, uses the eighth-note pair in a melodic sense; see pp. 68, 69, 110, 146, 148, etc.

And once, on p. 146, we find also the form ♩ ♫ ♩ ♫ in his counterpoint.

From *Cherubini's* rule 1 on p. 25, the following may be quoted:

The eighth-notes that are to be used should occur by step, and only seldom by leap. To follow the old masters, one should never use more than two eighth-notes in a bar. . . . If four eighth-notes are used in a bar, they should be distributed between the last halves of the two beats, and should not occur in direct succession [example follows]. In general, this figure must be used very sparingly; otherwise the counterpoint would become too springy, and alien to its true character.

Just here, then, the otherwise so blindly radical Cherubini failed to find the courage simply to prohibit eighth-notes with melodic significance.

Bellermann's formulation (p. 182), although it makes no attempt at a justification, is nevertheless good: "Of eighth-notes, only two may be used in succession on the second or fourth quarter of the bar, as a small embellishment or decoration; in such a case, the neighboring note is also permitted, as in the cadence for example":

Example 484

§11. New resolution-forms for dissonant suspensions, first made possible by the mixture of species: (a) with the aid of quarter-notes

The discussion in §§9 and 10 has shown that the new possibility of using two quarter-notes, or even a quarter and two eighths, on the downbeat automatically leads to new forms of suspension-resolution as well—forms, indeed, in which quarters or eighths play a role.

Now it is the proper concern of contrapuntal doctrine to indicate the strong difference of effect between the resolution of a dissonant syncope according to the principles of the fourth species on the one hand, or with the aid of quarter-notes on the other. In the first case, the succession of preparation, suspension, and resolution unfolds in the uniform rhythm of half-notes; in the latter case, however, only the preparation retains the value of a half-note, while both suspension and resolution appear in reduced form as only a quarter-note each—that is, as half the value they require in the fourth species.[11] As a result, the pulse of the events appears as though it were accelerated, and the ensuing upbeat, which, according to the principles of the fourth species, would be the first possible location for the resolution of the dissonance, may already devote itself to new tasks—it may either continue in quarters or prepare a completely new syncope. To understand this, refer to bar 2 of the exercise by Fux cited below as Exercise 4, for example, and the text on p. 279ff.

There can be no doubt that the most natural effect is that which results from uniformity of values of preparation, suspension, and resolution. But this effect is still indirectly attainable if, according to the principles of the fifth species, two quarter-notes are used in the resolution of a dissonant suspension. The present discussion will be concerned with that possibility alone.

We shall now go through the possible forms and attempt to explain the specific basis of each.

If we take the following as an example of the syncope:

Example 485

then the following resolutions are possible:

Example 486

where the second quarter is an anticipation of the tone of resolution itself,[12] since it lies at the same pitch level as the latter (this type was formerly called *ligatura rupta*); or

Example 487

where the second quarter is the [upper] third of the tone of resolution, which results in an anticipation of the latter's harmony;[13] or

Example 488

where the second quarter is the [upper] fifth of the tone of resolution, and, again, has the effect of an anticipation.

The forms presented so far, examples 486, 487, and 488, exhibit the common characteristic that the second quarter is also *consonant* with the cantus firmus, and that consequently a *harmonic sum* is made possible, as $\frac{8}{3}$ in Example 487 and (richer still) $\frac{5}{3}$ in Example 488.

If we consider the latter—that is, the harmonic sum in particular—, we advance further to the following important result: since in Example 485, in keeping with Part 1, Chapter 2, §15, the sixth is to be interpreted as inversion of the third ($e^1 - c^2 = c^1 - e^1$), the harmony produced in Examples 486, 487, and 488 is completely identical to the one that has c^1 as its root ($\frac{6}{6}$, $\frac{8}{6}$, and $\frac{6}{3}$

above $e^1 = \frac{5}{3}$ above c^1). From this it follows, however, that if two quarter-notes are used in the resolution of a dissonant suspension, not only is it possible still to present the resolution on the upbeat, as in the fourth species (and, indeed, regardless of the fact that the downbeat manifests the more animated movement of quarters), but further still: it is not even necessary that the second quarter contradict the harmony produced by adding the tone of resolution on the upbeat to the tone of the cantus firmus!

With this discovery, however, we arrive at a most remarkable basis of differentiation, whose nature will become still clearer when we consider the following example:

Example 489

4   6

Here the second quarter, a^1, is to be rejected first of all just because it is dissonant with the cantus firmus. But what is more important is the property that the dissonant second quarter here of itself forces the establishment of a *new* harmony, which certainly was not (and could not be) the case in the previous resolutions. Thus in Example 489, the tone a^1 would yield the root of the new harmony $e^1 - a^1 - c^2 = a - c^1 - e^1$, which is a completely different harmony from that intended by the normal resolution: $c^1 - e^1 - g^1$. Thus through use of the tone a^1, the c^1 would be deprived of its own roothood-tendency; this, however, to judge by the sixth in Example 485, is something to which above all it was entitled in the first place. In other words: the more natural effect in our example is the one that includes the harmony $c^1 - e^1 - g^1$, while the other effect, which includes $a - c^1 - e^1$ is less natural. But it is clear that strict counterpoint, which has to reflect the preference for the more natural effect, must not entrust the definition of a new harmony specifically to a note of smaller value if that note (as here) is bound by a merely attributive character to the following tone of resolution, in comparison to which it can claim only the subordinate status of an embellishment! [Compare *FrC.*, §294.]

Equally inadmissible, therefore, is the following:

Example 490

both because the second quarter is dissonant with the cantus firmus and also because the harmonic sum leads to nothing less than $\frac{6}{2}$, a formation that can in no way provide a consonant resolution for the suspension.

The following figure, on the other hand:

Example 491

provides a more propitious situation, so that there is no obstacle to its use in strict counterpoint. It is true that the figure contains no harmonic anticipation, as did those of Example 486–488; but because the second quarter is heard above all as the lower *neighboring note* of the tone of resolution, the figure escapes the possible danger of establishing a new dissonant harmony $(c^1 - e^1 - b^1)$. All that remains to be done, then, is simply to justify the neighboring note as such in this case; and in my opinion, if there is any place at all in strict counterpoint where it is appropriate and good to introduce the neighboring note, that place is above all here, in the resolution of the dissonant suspension; this, indeed, is consistent with the strictest point of view (see above, p. 178ff.). For in this case, it is a question not so much of the neighboring note as end-in-itself (which would have to be the only danger connected with its use in the second species), but, by common agreement, merely of an embellishment of the intrinsically unalterable tone of resolution! It should certainly be observed, further, that in spite of the obviously dissonant relationship (caused by the interval of the second) in which the neighboring note must stand to the tone of resolution, the neighboring note permitted here is no less obliged to be consonant with the cantus firmus than the respective second quarter notes in Examples 486–488.

The result derived from the totality of forms permitted here can, therefore, finally be stated as follows:

(a) the second quarter note must always be *consonant* with the cantus firmus;

(b) the second quarter must *never effect a change of harmony*—that is, introduce, in collaboration with the cantus firmus and the tone of resolution, a new harmony.

Applied to the syncopes permitted above,[14] then, our principles now lead to the following permissible resolution-forms:

Example 492

Example 492 *(continued)*

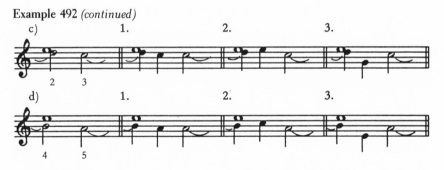

The following forms, however, remain inadmissible in strict counterpoint:

Example 493

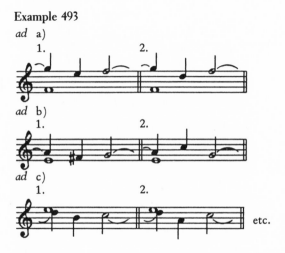

etc.

They are excluded because in some the tone of resolution is preceded by a neighboring note that is dissonant with the cantus firmus, while in others the second quarter projects a harmony different from that which would above all have to appear in consideration of the cantus firmus and the tone of resolution.

If strict counterpoint had also permitted upward resolutions of suspensions, it would have been consistent to make use of quarters in the ascending direction as well; for example:

Example 494

etc.

But these possibilities, as noted, belong to the realm of upward resolution, and, for that very reason, to free composition.

§12.   *(b) With the aid of quarter- and eighth-notes*

The derivation of the following forms, first made possible by the mixture of quarters and eighths, from the original forms presented in §11 will be readily apparent:

Example 495

(cf. Examples 486 and 491 in §11);

Example 496

(cf. Example 487 in §11);

Example 497

(cf. Examples 487 and 491 in §11) and

Example 498

(cf. Examples 488 and 491 in §11).
   It is clear that through combination of Examples 486, 487, 488, and 491, other possibilities exist; for example:

Example 499

and the like, where fifth and third of the tone of resolution (see Examples 487, 488) appear in combination; but these, as more remote solutions, belong entirely to free composition, where they benefit greatly from the advantages of polyphonic texture and, no less, from the increased precision of harmonies in their unobstructedly free unfolding.

A figure such as the following, on the other hand:

Example 500

also can doubtless be admitted in strict counterpoint as decoration of a resolution, in spite of the fact that it involves a consonant syncopation (specifically, of the sixth), which in essence has no need whatever of a resolution, nor, consequently, of a decoration.

Even in those places where free composition adheres to the prescription of strict counterpoint to resolve the dissonance in the *same bar,* it already offers the possibility of expanded liberties in the embellishment of a resolution:

Example 501

Haydn, String Quartet Op. 20 No. 1, IV

If we find in bar 2 of this example the completely regular embellishment according to Example 488, bar 3 on the contrary shows the so-called *ligatura rupta* of Example 486, with the difference that the step of a second has at the same time been transformed into the leap of a seventh, $ab^1 - g^2$; this transformation, however, can readily be allowed for a stringed instrument (see above, pp. 55, 64, 85).

And free composition, as we know (see p. 284), can also combine with the resolution a *change of harmony.*

While in strict counterpoint, therefore, a course of voice leading such as the following would have to be executed in full:

Example 502

free composition, on the other hand, can express it more concisely:[15]

Example 503

If an elaboration is at the same time applied to such an abbreviation, from the following basic form:

Example 504

with free rhythm and with the aid of a change of harmony, we arrive at the following construction:

Example 505
Schumann, Piano Quartet Op. 47, Andante

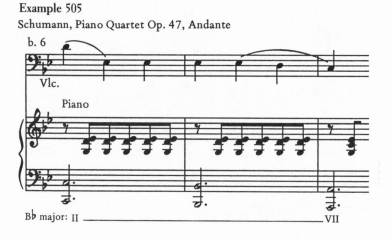

That the suspension of the ninth in this example is resolved only by the *c* of the third bar is established by the accompaniment's retention in bar 2 of the suspension-tone d^1; the bass of bar 2, moreover, shows a passing tone.

A second example:

Example 506
J. S. Bach, WTC I, Prelude in C♯ Minor

C♯ minor:(V-)I   —   VI   —   II   —   V   —   (I)

This approximates the following form of strict counterpoint:

Example 507

provided that allowances are made here for the nature of the cantus firmus, which can never move in such leaps as those shown by Example 507. (Incidentally, what a great difference this example reveals between a bass of an exercise and one of free composition!)

While the use of quarters (or eighths) in strict counterpoint ultimately signifies the first seed of freedom in the resolution of dissonant suspensions (and, no less, at the same time the greatest extent of that freedom), free composition has access to countless other methods which imbue the resolution with still greater intensity. Consider only the possibility, for example, of using the components of a single harmony in such a way that one can be introduced as a *substitution* for the other! How superbly fruitful a principle! The basis of this is simply that in free composition, we are able, with the guidance of the scale degrees (which are indeed abstract and ideal), to imagine all harmonies—as though above the ground of the actual voice leading. This possibility of substitution, which we have already encountered in regard to leaping passing tones (see pp. 241, 242; cf. Example 273) and implicitly prepared dissonance (see p. 283f. and Example 423), can now, just as with leaps and preparations, play a role in the resolution of dissonance as well.

Consider the following example:

Example 508
Chopin, Prelude Op. 28 No. 21

Bb major: I ———————————————— II ———————————————(V)

Bar 3 contains a prepared dissonant suspension; significantly, however, its resolution takes place in a still unchanged harmony.[16] The II occurs first in the sixth-chord inversion, to be sure, and does not take a place above the actual root c until bar 4; nevertheless, we are dealing here with one and the same scale degree, the same harmony, and this makes our example altogether similar to the strict-counterpoint exercises under consideration here, which present the resolution of the suspension along with an unchanged tone of the cantus firmus. And yet, if we nevertheless take into account the change of bass note within a single scale degree, we can say that the suspension here can be understood in a dual sense: measured against the bass note of the II scale degree itself, the c, d^2 is a ninth, while in relation to the bass note of the sixth-chord, it is a seventh. In any case, its resolution would normally have moved to c^2; when g^1 appears instead, it signifies only the substitution of one harmonic tone for the other. But how much greater appeal this offers than mere embellishment!

A second example:

Example 509
Haydn, String Quartet Op. 20 No. 1, IV

Bb major: V^6_4 $^5_4$ — 3

Such a substitution can, however, be used equally well with a change of harmony, as the following examples attest:

Example 510

Haydn, String Quartet Op. 33 No. 2, I

a)

J. S. Bach, St. John Passion, No. 14

b)

öff - ent - lich ge - re - det vor der |Welt

Fux (p. 83):

. . . the ligatures mentioned so far may also be used in another way. This does not alter them essentially, but causes the melody to move quickly:

Example 511

Fux V, 21

. . . The ligature may also be interrupted in this way:

Example 512

Fux VI, 2

This is all Fux has to say of a factual and explanatory nature in the matter; yet the remark "this does not alter them essentially" shows that he understood very well how little the embellishment cancels the basic rhythm of preparation, suspension, and resolution, which remains, as always, the normal rhythm of half-notes!

Albrechtsberger, on the other hand, lists on p. 65f. all possible types of resolution in random order, without adhering to any sort of plan.

Cherubini, too, offers all the forms usable in strict counterpoint, but with a rather peculiar justification. On p. 26, rule 3, we read:

> The dot serves to diminish the value of the whole-note, by first reducing it to a dotted half-note followed by a quarter or two eighths. [Example follows.] These types of variation could also be used with syncopes, and would shorten the duration of the dissonances. These reductions of duration give the melody a very appealing quality.

(Cherubini's Example 79 follows, presenting the various types of suspension resolution.)

Bellermann vacillates somewhat insecurely among Fux, models from early compositions, and ideas of his own. On p. 179, he writes:

> . . . that the dissonance on the first half note of the bar is subdivided into two quarters; the second quarter leaps to another, lower, consonant interval, and the regular resolution is presented only at the third quarter [example follows]. This type of resolution is still very rare in the Palestrina era; I nevertheless thought it necessary to mention it, since Fux permits its use in his *Gradus ad parnassum.* To use it frequently in the following exercises is not advisable, for it would have to be viewed only as an incidental embellishment of the voice.

(Also apposite to this is the earlier citation in §10 concerning eighth-notes.) Finally, Bellermann accepts the *ligatura rupta,* with the following explanation (p. 182):

> It is good, moreover, for the student to become accustomed to writing in such a way that the singer has adequate opportunity to breathe. In the case of dissonances on the downbeat, the earlier composers solved this problem by bringing the resolution already at the second quarter, and then repeating the same tone on the third quarter [example follows]. The singer should never pass over such places, which occur very often in the compositions of the sixteenth century, without taking a breath.

Regardless of the truth of the latter comment, it would have been better if Bellermann had derived the justification of the phenomenon he here allows from the tonal world itself rather than from the technique of the singer.

§13. *Recollection of several earlier principles*

In spite of the tendency of the mixed species toward elements of free composition, *tone-repetition* nevertheless remains excluded here. Express warning must also be given once again about the danger of *monotony.*

Cadence

§14. *Construction of the cadence*

Two formulas are possible:

(a)   in the sense of fourth species, $\frown$7 — 6 | 8 or $\frown$2 — 3 | 1; or

(b)   with the use of eighth-notes and the license of a caesura (see above, §8):

Compare *Albrechtsberger,* p. 67; and the following correction in *Nottebohm,* p. 50:

Example 513

See also *Bellermann,* p. 179f.

Exercises

Example 514

Fux VI, 4 and 5

Example 514 *continued*
Fux VI, 8 and 9

Albrechtsberger p. 69

Example 514 *continued*

Cherubini Ex. 80

Alto (c. f.)

7.

Tenor

Example 514 *continued*

Bellermann p. 187 (c.f. by Fux)

H. Schenker (c.f. by Fux)

Example 514 *continued*

Comments on the Preceding Exercises

No. 5. Concerning the melodic use of eighth-notes, see above, §10.

No. 7. The exercise begins with a syncope. In bars 6 and 8, internal modulations to G major and E minor, but without the clarity and force attainable in free composition. Also notable, finally, is the use of neighboring notes in bars 10 and 12.

Notes

The editor's notes and additions are enclosed in square brackets. All others are from Schenker's original text.

Author's Preface

[1. *Monodie,* in its original meaning of "unaccompanied song."]

[2. See Appendix A, Works of Heinrich Schenker. All citations of *Harmony* and *Harmonielehre* without further specification refer to Schenker's own works.]

[3. ". . . die paralysierende Kraft der Mehrstimmigkeit." The force of polyphony "paralyzes" the opposing force of similar motion in its effort to expose and emphasize the undesirable quality of the perfect interval.]

[4. This observation hints at the subject-matter to be treated more precisely in Part 6, "Bridges to Free Composition," and especially in its third section, "On the Elision of a Voice as Bridge to Free Composition."]

[5. Berlin, 1753 and 1762. Translated, by William J. Mitchell, as *Eassay on the True Art of Playing Keyboard Instruments* (New York: Norton, 1949).]

[6. Friedrich Marpurg, *Versuch über die musikalische Temperatur, nebst einem Anhang über den Rameau- und Kirnbergerschen Grundbass* (Breslau, 1776).]

[7. What Schenker means by "archetypes" and "prolongations" here may be illustrated by a simple example. In thoroughbass, at the resolution of a $\frown 9 - 8$ suspension (an archetype) it is entirely possible for the bass to initiate a descending passing motion. The resulting $9 - 9$ interval succession represents a prolongation that shows the suspension-formation in an "already advanced state."]

[8. See especially Jean-Philippe Rameau, *Nouveau système de musique théorique* (1726), the first clear presentation of the theory of three functions.]

[9. See Example 212 and the accompanying discussion.]

Introduction

[1. J.J. Fux, *Gradus ad parnassum* (Vienna, 1725; rpt. New York, 1966); German translation by Lorenz Mizler (Leipzig, 1742; rpt. Hildesheim, 1974). The section on species counterpoint has been translated into English and edited by Alfred Mann in Fux, *Steps to Parnassus* (New York: Norton, 1943), second edition as *The Study of Counterpoint* (New York: Norton, 1965). The discussion of fugal technique appears in English translation in Mann, *The Study of Fugue* (London: Faber and Faber, 1958). Schenker worked mainly from Mizler's German translation, although in at least one instance he consulted the Latin original (see Vol. II, p. 243); accordingly, our translations of Fux are based on the passages of Mizler quoted by Schenker.]

Throughout *Counterpoint* Schenker quotes repeatedly from the treatises of Fux, Albrechtsberger, Cherubini, and Bellermann, usually in this (chronological) order. The sources for all such quotations are the treatises identified in this note and in notes 2 (Cherubini), 3 (Albrechtsberger), and 7 (Bellermann).]

[2. Luigi Cherubini, *Cours de contrepoint et de fugue* (Paris, 1835).]

[3. Leipzig, 1790. Second, revised edition, ed. I. von Seyfried, in *J.G. Albrechtsberger's sämmtliche Schriften über Generalbass, Harmonielehre, und Tonsetzkunst* (Vienna, 1837; rpt. Leipzig, 1975). All page-number references in Schenker's text are to the 1790 edition.]

[4. *Lehrbuch des einfachen und doppelten Contrapunkts* (Leipzig, 1872).]

[5. *Lehrbuch des einfachen, doppelten, und imitierenden Kontrapunkts* (Leipzig, 1888).]

[6. *Lehre vom Contrapunkt, dem Canon, und der Fuge* (Berlin, 1859).]

[7. *Der Kontrapunkt* (Berlin, 1861).]

[8. *Prolongationen.* This concept is fundamental to Schenker's thought. Highly general, it pertains to the relationship between simple phenomena and their more complex derivatives; thus, just as complex tone-successions are derived from simple ones by *Prolongation,* so also are complex laws of setting tones derived from simple ones by *Prolongation* in the (more figurative) sense of ramification, extension, and adaptation to more elaborate situations.]

Part One, Chapter 1

[1. *Harmonielehre* (Stuttgart, 1907).]

[2. A requirement of a beginning.]

[3. The target of this critique is, of course, the theory of tonal functions, of which Riemann was the chief architect. The application of this theory, which recognizes only three principal functions (tonic, subdominant, and dominant), is especially problematical in passages involving "sequences" by descending fifths. This led Riemann to declare that "as was recognized first of all by Fétis, however, the true harmonic movement—the cadential progression—remains stationary for the duration of the sequence" (*Handbuch der Harmonielehre* [7th ed., Leipzig, n.d.], p. 202).]

[4. See the above quotation from Louis and Thuille.]

[5. Hermann von Helmholtz, *Die Lehre von den Tonempfindungen* (5th ed., Braunschweig: Vieweg, 1896), p. 389. The language in the second (1865), fourth (1877), and fifth editions differs somewhat from Schenker's quotation, which may have been based on the first edition (1862).]

Part One, Chapter 2

[1. The song is dead, long live the mode!]

2. Unfortunately we again encounter such descriptive superfluity and excess in lieu of uniform—but [therefore] all the more simple and profound—conceptions today as well, in the theories of Riemann, Capellen, and others. The lack of artistic perception and knowledge that characterizes both epochs, past and present, finds its expression similarly in the form of a surfeit of concepts, terminologies, and the like!

[3. Obviously, Schenker's example shows only three principal vocal ranges.]

[4. The other error, the leap of a seventh, is also deliberate and is commented upon later by Albrechtsberger.]

5. Compare Nottebohm, *Beethovens Studien* (Leipzig, 1873), p. 70f.

6. This same aspect of tone-repetition, incidentally, is the reason suspensions in free composition can be considered *prepared* even if the tone in question undergoes chromatic modification. See *Harmony*, pp. 309–310 and Example 282.

[7. In English-language terminology, only the raised version of $\hat{7}$ in minor is called the leading tone; the diatonic version is usually called subtonic.]

[8. Some sources for the Bach Sarabande in Example 31 show, at the second quarter in the left hand, instead of *ab* a repetition of the *bb* of the first quarter (thus a 4 — 3 suspension to *a* of the third quarter); this seems more plausible than the version quoted by Schenker, which may have been the only one accessible to him.]

[9. The example was not included in *Harmony*.]

[10. *Spannung*, which normally means "tension," but this cannot be Schenker's meaning here, since he explicitly rejects the notion of varying degrees of dissonance or tension among intervals (see *Cpt. II*, p. 58). Schenker really means *Spanne*.]

11. It is this ability of the ear which is still lacking in exotic peoples (see Part 1, Section 1, Chapter 5).

[12. Schenker again uses *Summen* (sums) as he did in the preceding paragraphs with respect to sums of intervals. Here the reference is to tones, however, and thus the translation must be different.]

[13. "Den 'starrenden' Blick. . . ."]

[14. The same explanation applies equally well to Example 53.]

[15. The seventh in question is that of the flute in bar 143. See Schenker, *Beethoven: Neunte Sinfonie*, p. 67ff.; the bar-number citation on the last line of p. 67 should be 143 instead of 141.]

[16. There is no such appendix to *Counterpoint;* a somewhat detailed refutation is given in *Beethoven: Neunte Sinfonie*, p. 67ff.]

[17. The table was not included in *Harmony*.]

18. When I recently heard Richard Strauss conduct this symphony, I realized to my dismay that he failed completely to empathize with the principal motive's painful experience just described, and obviously regarded the diminished fourths merely as purest sixths or thirds! What can the diminished fourths of a "classicist" signify, asks a "modernist" who credits only himself with blood, pain, dissonance, and temperament, and therefore takes only his own diminished fourths and the like seriously! Didn't the classicist remain always "in equilibrium as man and artist," and doesn't the truly human and passionate element in art begin only with himself? Such are his banal reflections. Need I expressly add that the other conductors likewise fail completely at this point in the development section?

[19. *Durchgang*. The reference is vague here; Schenker might later have expanded it along the following lines. The outer voices move from an octave *F* (bar 21) to an octave *Eb* (bar 27); the bass supplies the chromatic passing tone *Fb* (bars 25–26). At this point the upper voice has reached *D♮* (via the passing *Eb* of bars 23–24), which transforms the bare 8 — 8 interval succession of the outer voices into 8 — 6 — 8 (see *FrC.*, §§162–163). This causes the last of the violin's motivic sixth-arpeggiations to define the augmented sixth $d♮^2 - fb^1$, the second tone of which is chromatically altered for the sake of the chromatic passing tone of the bass.]

[20. The sentence preceding those quoted is "Don't you remember that the leap of a major sixth is prohibited?"]

[21. Here Schenker alters Bellermann's language slightly.]

22. As a horizontal inversion of the second, the seventh (see above, §10) is naturally also a dissonance. Only after we move beyond a given triadic boundary do we find the seventh; it occurs only as the third of another triad, which, being based on a different root and therefore essentially different from the initial triad, necessarily dissonates against it.

23. It is a pity that the principle (which is so important in vocal music) of using larger leaps with moderation and always for good reasons has been so frequently and carelessly abandoned in our time. How erratically the vocal part often leaps about in the music of, for example, Richard Strauss, who treats the voice as if it were simply a keyboard instrument, disregarding the psychological values implied by the leaps! Nevertheless, the double infraction evident here—namely the offense against the nature of large leaps as well as against the nature of the human voice—will, I am convinced, very soon become obvious even to less musical listeners.

[24. Page 159 in the Peters edition reprinted by Dover Publications (New York, 1973). Isolde has the same tone-succession earlier, on p. 137, at the words "Blutschuld schwebt. . . ."]

25. It should in no way be viewed as a contradiction that I speak here of ninths, tenths, and so forth—intervals that I had to renounce in *Harmony*, §§113 and 63. For while those intervals are judged there only in the harmonic sense, and with reference to the issue of harmonic capacity, in counterpoint they are admissible without restriction as intervals of the horizontal direction (regardless of subsidiary harmonic meaning), especially as the horizontal dimension in its artistic implementation has access to more than two, three, and four octaves.

26. An authentic and so painfully overwhelming leap of a ninth in Mozart's Piano Quartet in G minor (first movement, coda):

Example 103
Mozart, Piano Quartet in G Minor K. 478

has been "corrected" (presumably in order to avoid the academic bugaboo of dissonance) by the editor at Litolff into a tenth ($c^2 - eb^3$)!! Alas, these editors—what a deplorable state of affairs! [The tenth, on the contrary, appears in Mozart's autograph.]

[27. The example was not included in *Harmony*. The music quoted is from the Prelude in E♭ of Bach's *Well-Tempered Clavier*, Book II; bar 6 of the example is bar 34 of the prelude.]

[28. Bar 39 of the prelude.]

29. Compare H. Riemann's *Musiklexikon*, articles *"Akzent"* and *"Portament."* [The term *Akzent* (accent) is used here in an older sense that was equivalent to *Vorschlag* (appoggiatura); a portamento effect was always to be associated with the "release" (*Abzug*) of the appoggiatura.] The so-called double accent (*accento*

doppio) is really an anticipation (*Harmony*, §163f.), which in certain circumstances may really be an ingredient of the portamento. In addition to the examples of anticipation given already in *Harmony*, several others showing portamento with anticipation may be cited:

Example 106
Beethoven, Piano Sonata Op. 57

[Compare *Der Tonwille*, Vol. 7 (see Appendix).] Or, across separating rests but with an even more overwhelming longing toward the note of anticipation:

Example 107
Mozart, Piano Quartet K. 478, I

Or in Beethoven:

Example 108
Beethoven, Symphony No. 9, Adagio   Beethoven, Piano Sonata Op. 111, Arietta

[30. Compare Chopin's Mazurka op. 59 no. 3, bars 45 – 46, 47 – 48, etc.]
31. Compare, in my critical edition (Universal Edition No. 548) of several keyboard works by C.P.E. Bach, No. 12, p. 92.
32. The ligatures under consideration here (bar 1, fourth and fifth eighth-notes; bar 2, second and third eighth-notes) are presented in this way in almost all editions of

Handel's Suites, even in the old Nägeli edition, but—strangely enough—are lacking only the *Gesamtausgabe.*

33. See my "A Contribution to the Study of Ornamentation," [trans. by H. Siegel (*Music Forum* 4), p. 24ff.].

[34. Compare Example 212a and Part 2, Chapter 1, note 27.]

Part Two, Chapter 1

[1. *Consonanzen* in Mizler's text, an error that was not corrected in Schenker's quotation; we here follow Fux's original Latin (see *Gradus ad parnassum,* p. 26).]

[2. The bracketed interpolation is by the editor.]

[3. Recall that in Bellermann, "arsis" refers to the downbeat.]

[4. Italics in the quotation are in the original text, but were not retained by Schenker.]

[5. That is, in respect to pitch-class as well as specific pitch.]

[6. The sixth, although consonant, would deprive the lowest tone of its roothood-tendency.]

7. See, for example, Mizler's remark in Fux, p. 89ff., and Albrechtsberger, p. 31. In a comment on page 6 concerning Example 16 Cherubini concludes:

> This rule at first glance appears poorly founded, for since the intervening tones are not written, the fifths and octaves do not really exist either. But since it is possible for the singer to add these intervening notes, octaves and fifths are always produced; and singers have long had this unrestricted freedom. Thus the prohibition. The rule requiring that preference be given to contrary motion is excellent also because it deters us from making even concealed errors. This is also a second example of mistakes caused by the use of similar motion.

> Cherubini is historically correct here in his citation of the older singing-practice. He has in mind specifically the so-called diminution-period, when it was left up to the singer himself to decorate a given tone-succession with all kinds of ornaments and coloraturas. Instead of older examples, which anyone may study by consulting music-historical works and the like, I shall cite here an analogous one from the most recent period:

Example 182

Wagner, *Faust* Overture

We observe here (see violins I and II, bars 3 – 5) the initially conceived interval $g^2 — c^3$ in violin I, which, instead of being written in its original form as half-notes, is filled in by quarter-note values; we find—as our principal matter of concern in this connection—just as a result of this diminution a genuine parallel fifth-succession between the two violins:

$$\frac{b^2 — c^3}{e^1 — f^1}$$

from the fourth quarter of the third bar to the first quarter of the fourth. Nevertheless, it was a mistake for Cherubini to invoke this and other similar diminution-practices as a justification for the prohibition of so-called hidden successions: such practices speak rather against the prohibition. In fact, it is well known from the many textbooks (treatises) of that period that often enough, whenever diminution was involved, theory—yes, even theory!—despite all its cautionary reminders still granted dispensation from the prohibition! And such dispensation was only too well justified. For the vocal part of a solo singer, or a choral setting, already represented free composition; and even in that early period it may have been evident that the prohibition of fifths and octaves would have to yield to the psychic foundations of diminution as a stronger force, and therefore could no longer claim absolute applicability under these circumstances—just as we today, for many reasons (which will be treated later), must approve the voice leading in the above Wagner excerpt (Example 182) in spite of the parallel fifths. [Compare "Brahms, Octaves and Fifths"—see Appendix A, "Works of Heinrich Schenker."]

But how illogical, especially in an exercise of two-voice counterpoint, to invoke the principles of diminution, as Cherubini does! Are such two-voice settings intended to be embellished and ornamented in the first place? Are they really to be performed and perhaps elaborated? If not, what can diminution-practice prove, in a situation in which no such practice is appropriate? Therefore I regard it as more artistic to derive the prohibition and its justification from the given situation of the two-voice exercise alone.

8. See, for example, C.G.P. Graedener, *System der Harmonielehre* (Hamburg, 1877), §38.

[9. Moritz Hauptmann, *Die Natur der Harmonik und Metrik* (Leipzig, 1853), p. 70. The last part is cited by Brahms in "Octaves and Fifths" (see Appendix A, "Works of Heinrich Schenker"), MS p. 5, transcription p. 84. Brahms comments "Geistreich, doch nicht genügend" ("perceptive, but not sufficient").]

10. *Handbuch der Harmonielehre* (3rd ed., Leipzig: Breitkopf und Härtel, 1898), p. 29ff. [Emphasis in this and the following quotations of Riemann is added by Schenker. The language in these passages differs somewhat in the second edition (1887) from the version given here by Schenker. The third edition, from which Schenker quotes, was not available to me.]

[11. Schenker's meaning may be that since man is himself part of Nature, in the end even man's highest achievements are indirectly also products of Nature.]

[12. An adaptation from the first lines of Heine's *Der Atlas*.]

[13. Better, the last tonal boundary of the *triadic region*. Later (*Cpt. II*, p. xxi), Schenker writes: "The intervals 5 and 6 signify the limits of the consonance-concept. . . ."]

[14. Louis and Thuille go on to explain that among the harmonic "elementary relationships" I — V, I — IV, V — I, and IV — V it is only the last that lacks such a mediating relationship, and therefore it is only the fifths between the roots and fifths of IV and V respectively that are "thoroughly faulty."]

[15. E.g., with that between *parallel* and *nonparallel* motion.]

[16. Schenker apparently refers here to the last section of *Counterpoint II*, "Bridges to Free Composition."]

[17. That is, never in the form of simple reinforcement, but only through the leading of obbligato (essential) voices.]

[18. This, of course, is something of an overstatement; see *Free Composition*, §161.]

[19. Or vice versa. See *Free Composition*, §162.]

[20. The bracketed interpolation is by the editor.]

[21. To be fully consistent, Schenker should disallow even the voice leading of Example 196; for although it is true that the tritone's effect is canceled, this is accomplished only by virtue of a larger context—that is, a state of interdependency among several intervals—that vitiates the equilibrium of the exercise. (Schenker frequently inveighs against such procedures elsewhere.) In fact, the A and B must be understood as passing tones in a fourth-space, hence as resembling the third species more closely than the first.]

[22. Specifically, because of the overlap of voices.]

[23. That is, "harmonic."]

[24. Our best conjecture is that this expression is a variant of *ex ovo*, literally, "from the egg."]

[25. An example on p. 148 in Bellermann, not quoted here.]

[26. Compare the Preface, p. xxxi; also Example 287b.]

[27. Later, Schenker would probably have added that the basic melodic progression comprises the stepwise succession $e\flat — d — c$, with the octaves serving as covering tones. This additional degree of precision is fully compatible with the explanation Schenker gives here.]

[28. See note 24.]

[29. ". . . sowohl halbe, als ganze [Cadenzen]. . . ." No established English term corresponds exactly to this German usage of *halbe Cadenz* (least of all the literal "half cadence"); the term has consistently been rendered here as "partial cadence."]

[30. *Chroma*. As will become clear in the discussion, Schenker actually means the direct succession of a diatonic and an altered scale degree, whether in one voice or divided between two voices. His approval, in the following paragraph, of the Albrechtsberger setting quoted in Example 133 shows that he does in principle allow the inclusion of a chromatic tone, so long as it does not directly succeed its diatonic counterpoint.]

Part Two, Chapter 2

[1. *Wechselnote* unfortunately was consistently translated as "changing note" in *Harmony*. In Schenker's writing, it invariably means accented passing tone.]

[2. This is due to a misprint in the Mizler German translation; the bass *c* should be B. Strictly speaking, this, as Schenker observes, takes the tenor part out of range.]

[3. That is, an interval other than a second in either direction.]

[4. Later, Schenker might well have renounced his explanation of the c^2 in Example 250 as a passing tone in the space of a fourth. So far as the upper voice is concerned, this c^2 undoubtedly progresses to the d^2 in the fourth bar of the example; this connection is confirmed in that the basses express the direct connection $C - D$ from the end of the second bar to the beginning of the third, and the resulting tenth $\frac{f^2}{D}$ is then prolonged by an exchange of voices. In Examples 251 and 252, the asterisked notes are neighboring notes from which the upper voice leaps away; in both cases, the normal complete neighboring-note configuration is executed by another voice or instrument—by the first alto in the six-part setting of Brahms's "Nachtwache," and by the second violins in Mendelssohn's Scotch Symphony. Generally speaking, the dissonant tones by leap discussed in this section all represent prolongations of more basic phenomena (e.g., suspensions in Example 248).]

[5. Bach, Fugue in D Minor, *Well-Tempered Clavier* Book I. Schenker's reference to the d^1 as a "leading tone" is singular, for it is by no means a leading tone in this context.]

[6. Fig. 339 of *Harmonielehre*. The signs in question unfortunately were omitted from the example in *Harmony;* the last two bars of the example should appear as follows:

[7. Thus $6 - \sharp 6$ over bass $b\flat$ is abbreviated by omission of the diatonic 6.]

[8. The "arioso dolente (klagender Gesang)."]

[9. Georg Capellen, *Musikalische Akustik* (Leipzig: Kahnt, 1903), p. 93. Capellen writes as follows on pp. 24–25: "The sonorities constituting a key are more simply and briefly indicated according to their positions in relation to each other—that is, by the following general abbreviations: M = middle sonority (middle tone = tonic), R = right-hand sonority (right-hand tone = dominant), L = left-hand sonority (left-hand tone = subdominant)."]

[10. Schenker probably means Fig. 148 of *Harmonielehre* (Example 114 in *Harmony*).]

[11. Chopin, Prelude in A Minor op. 28 no. 2. The example was not included in *Harmony.*]

[12. The appeal to "bracket 2"—nonadjacency—applies only to the first excerpt.]

[13. *Aufstreiche* in the original, by mistake.]

[14. That is, the fifth after the bar line. It might be remarked that to write the bass as in Example 302 would sacrifice the imitation by the bass of the immediately preceding quarter-notes $F\sharp - G$.]

[15. Example 303 is as it appears in both Fux's original and Mizler's German translation. Alfred Mann, in *Steps to Parnassus* (p. 37, Fig. 16), plausibly emends the first soprano note to c^2.]

[16. *Akkordwechsel.* Schenker later uses *Harmoniewechsel* (change of harmony); the two expressions are interchangeable.]

Part Two, Chapter 3

[1. The last of Cherubini's examples (see Example 342), however, surely provides an instance of a counterpoint that is "not skillfully constructed" (cf. Schenker's remarks to bracket 3 above): melodic parallelism and metric strength combine to produce unmistakable parallel fifths.]

[2. *Harmony* §167 concerns the accented passing tone; this reference probably should be to §163, which treats the anticipation.]

[3. The emphases are in Bellermann's text, but were not retained by Schenker.]

[4. That is, a fourth within an arpeggiation, like that of example 377. In an appropriate context of free composition, such a fourth will be "merely apparent" because it will be formed only between upper voices above an (ideal) fundamental.]

[5. That is, a $\frac{5}{3}$.]

[6. The present context deals with the fifth species.]

[7. That is, the one not in the cantus firmus.]

Part Two, Chapter 4

[1. Schenker's meaning is unclear. Evidently he has in mind the so-called "consonant fourth," which, in its full context, appears as follows: $^6\!-\!\!_4 + \frac{5}{4}\!\!-\!_3$ (see Part 6, second section).]

[2. Later, Schenker would probably have added that the upward resolution in Example 397 is motivated also by a stronger force, a descending linear progression from f^2 (in the upbeat to the first bar of the sonata and again as an appoggiatura in bar 2) through eb^2 (bar 2 of the sonata) to the d^2 in Example 397.]

[3. Schenker here takes a fateful step that will lead to some rather unconvincing argumentation in his treatise—the explanation of the downward-resolution requirement given below and in Part 3, Chapter 4, §3. He directly contradicts his present claim, incidentally, with his remark in Part 6, Chapter 3, §8, that "we are unable to adjoin conceptually to the passing tone of the seventh the consonant point of departure presupposed by it (as by any passing tone whatever)."]

[4. That is, in free composition, even when there is no actual dissonant interval in relation to the bass, we can recognize the essential effect of a dissonant suspension.]

[5. There is evidently a mistake here; strict counterpoint does of course allow 6 as a preparation before 7. It is possible that Schenker intended either 8 before 7 or 7 before 6; even these are possible in free composition. (Compare below, p. 280.)]

6. See above, Example 387; and in *Harmony*, Example 185, bars 1–2, and Example 187, bars 9–10.

[7. *Versuch*, Part 2, p. 219 (emphasis in original). See *Essay on the True Art of Playing Keyboard Instruments*, p. 348; the translation there of *rückende Noten* as "syncopated notes" could not be used here, since "syncope" has been used in a more limited sense.]

8. "Dissonance is therefore completely general: disturbance, by foreign elements, of the clarity of chordal meaning" (p. 138).

[9. Schenker rather freely amalgamates several ideas here. The "passing motion" (*Durchgang*) is to be understood in the broadest sense, and is actually not the same as Bach's "displacement" (*Rückung*), as Schenker seems to suggest; nevertheless it is obvious that the "displacement" concept applies to the example. The G♭ can be heard as passing to the A♭ of bar 3 (by means of *reaching-over*—see *FrC.*, §§129–134 and 231–232) and also as returning (in the bass) to *F.*]

[10. *Durch Bindung*—the connection in this case is not accomplished by literal ties.]

11. Incidentally, this is exactly the meaning of the technical hint given by Brahms and transmitted by Henschel: "And then, no sharp dissonances on unaccented beats, please! That is a weakness. I myself am very much in favor of dissonances, but on strong, accented beats, and then I resolve them gently and gradually."

12. Reprint, Leipzig: Kahnt, 1906. [Originally published Berlin, 1752. Translated, by Edward R. Reilly, as *On Playing the Flute* (New York: Schirmer Books, 1985).]

[13. *On Playing the Flute,* p. 187.]

[14. *Essay,* p. 87.]

[15. Berlin and Stuttgart, 1902.]

Part Two, Chapter 5

1. See in Part 1, Chapter 2, §1 the chorale by Bach in Example 13a, bars 1, 2, etc; and the same in Bellermann's arrangement, Example 13c, bar 4.

2. Compare above, in Part 2, Chapter 2, §5, the quotation from Couperin in Example 242.

3. See above, p. 184, and especially pp. 241–242!

[4. See Part 6, second section. More precisely, the voice-leading pattern to which Schenker refers contains a dissonance prepared by a ♮-chord, which latter is in turn *preceded* by (but not *prepared* by, in the technical sense) a dissonant ♮-sonority.]

5. For example, in our explanation of the leaping passing tones (see pp. 184, 241), the implicit preparation (p. 283), the free suspension (p. 283), and the like.

[6. Not included in *Harmony*. The passage is bars 153ff. of Liszt's Sonata in B Minor.]

[7. Schenker measures the suspension $\frown e^2 - d^2$ intervalically against the moving voice (g♯) in the tenor register rather than against the pedal-point bass *e*. Thus the term "sixth-suspension." The syncopation Schenker refers to actually involves an anticipation of the resolution.]

[8. Upbeat, in Bellermann's usage.]

[9. The emphasis is in Bellermann's text.]

[10. That is, the world of species counterpoint.]

[11. This remark and the remainder of the paragraph apply only to the rare situation in which the second quarter of the bar must itself actually be understood as the tone of resolution. (See Schenker's reference at the end of this paragraph to bar 2 of Exercise 4 in Example 514.) In almost all cases in which suspension-resolutions involve quarter-notes, the underlying rhythm of suspension and resolution remains half-notes.]

[12. Compare Bellermann's explanation of this form, according to which "the earlier composers . . . brought the resolution already at the second quarter, and then repeated the same tone on the third quarter" (p. 182).]

13. Because of the seventh-leap, it is prohibited in strict counterpoint (see p. 52) to place this third in a lower register.

[14. That is, in fourth-species counterpoint.]

[15. A fundamental difference between Examples 502 and 503, however, is that the seventh-chord in the latter does not represent a true suspension, but rather the adjoining of a passing seventh. See Part 6, Chapter 3, §8, and also Part 3, Chapter 4, §6(a).]

[16. Bar 3 can plausibly be heard as IV (especially because of strong fifth Bb — Eb across the barline), with the change to II occurring only at bar 4 (anticipated by the left hand's diminution in bar 3).]

Appendix A
Works of Heinrich Schenker

The following is a list of Schenker's major publications, both in the original German as well as in English editions and translations.[1] The German publications marked with an asterisk are in print.

Ein Beitrag zur Ornamentik. Vienna: Universal Edition, 1904.
  *New and enlarged edition, 1908. (See also under English translations.)
Neue musikalische Theorien und Phantasien.
  Vol. I: *Harmonielehre.* Stuttgart: Cotta, 1906. (See also under English translations.)
  Vol. II, Part I: *Kontrapunkt I.* Vienna: Universal Edition, 1910.
      Part II: *Kontrapunkt II.* Vienna: Universal Edition, 1922.
  Vol. III: *Der Freie Satz.* Vienna: Universal Edition, 1935. *Second edition, edited and revised by Oswald Jonas. Vienna: Universal Edition, 1956. (See also under English translations.)
J.S. Bach. *Chromatische Phantasie und Fuge, Erläuterungsausgabe.* Vienna: Universal Edition, 1909. *Newly revised edition by Oswald Jonas. Vienna: Universal Edition, 1970. (See also under English translations.)
Beethovens neunte Sinfonie. Vienna: Universal Edition, 1912.
Erläuterungsausgabe der letzten fünf Sonaten Beethovens. Vienna: Universal Edition.
  Op. 109, published 1913.
  Op. 110, published 1914.
  Op. 111, published 1915.
  Op. 101, published 1920.
  (Op. 106 was never published.)
  *New edition of Op. 101, 109, 110, 111, revised by Oswald Jonas. Vienna: Universal Edition, 1970–71.
Der Tonwille, 10 issues. Vienna: A. Gutmann Verlag, 1921–24.
Beethovens funfte Sinfonie (reprinted from *Der Tonwille*). Vienna: Universal Edition. (See also under English translations.)
Das Meisterwerk in der Musik. Munich: Drei Masken Verlag.
  Jahrbuch I, published 1925.
  Jahrbuch II, published 1926.
  Jahrbuch III, published 1930.
  *Photographic reprint in one volume. Hildesheim: Georg Olms Verlag, 1974. (See also under English translations.)

---

[1] A complete, comprehensive, carefully annotated list of Schenker's writings is to be found in David Beach, "A Schenker Bibliography" (*Journal of Music Theory 3,* no. 1 [1969]: 2–26; a revised edition has been published in *Readings in Schenker Analysis,* ed. Maury Yeston [New Haven: Yale University Press, 1977]). This bibliography also includes the most important books, monographs, and articles by other authors.

Fünf Urlinie-Tafeln. New York: David Mannes School, and Vienna: Universal Edition, 1932. (See also under English editions.)

*Brahms, Oktaven und Quinten. Vienna: Universal Edition, 1934. (See also under English editions.)

Editions of Music

*Ph. Em. Bach, Klavierwerke (selections). Vienna: Universal Edition, 1902.

Beethoven, Klaviersonaten: Nach den Autographen und Erstdrucken rekonstruiert von Heinrich Schenker. Vienna: Universal Edition, 1921–23.

> *New edition, revised by Erwin Ratz. Vienna: Universal Edition, 1947. (See also under English editions.)

Beethoven, Sonata op. 27 no. 2. Facsimile, with an introduction by Schenker. Vienna: Universal Edition, 1921.

English Editions and Translations

"J.S. Bach, The Largo from Sonata No. 3 for Unaccompanied Violin" (from *Das Meisterwerk in der Musik,* vol. 1). Translated by John Rothgeb. In *The Music Forum,* vol. 4. New York: Columbia University Press, 1976.

"J.S. Bach, The Sarabande of Suite No. 3 for Unaccompanied Violoncello" (from *Das Meisterwerk in der Musik,* vol. 2). Translated by Hedi Siegel. In *The Music Forum,* vol. 2. New York: Columbia University Press, 1970.

J.S. Bach's Chromatic Fantasy and Fugue: Critical Edition with Commentary. Translated and edited by Hedi Siegal. New York: Schirmer Books, 1984.

Beethoven, Complete Piano Sonatas. Reprint of the edition of 1921–23, with an introduction by Carl Schachter. New York: Dover, 1975.

"Beethoven, Fifth Symphony, First Movement." Translated by Elliott Forbes. In *Beethoven, Fifth Symphony* (Norton Critical Scores). New York: Norton, 1971.

"Brahms, Octaves and Fifths." Translated and annotated by Paul Mast. In *The Music Forum,* vol. 5. New York: Columbia University Press, 1980.

"A Contribution to the Study of Ornamentation." Translated by Hedi Siegel. In *The Music Forum,* vol. 4. New York: Columbia University Press, 1976.

Five Graphic Music Analyses. Photographic reprint of *Fünf Urlinie-Tafeln,* with an introduction by Felix Salzer. New York: Dover, 1969.

Free Composition. Translated and edited by Ernst Oster. New York: Schirmer Books, 1979.

Harmony. Edited and annotated by Oswald Jonas. Translated by Elisabeth Mann Borgese. Chicago: University of Chicago Press, 1954. Paperback edition, Boston: M.I.T. Press, 1973.

"Organic Structure in Sonata Form" (from *Das Meisterwerk in der Musik,* vol. 2). Translated by Orin Grossman. *Journal of Music Theory* (1968). Reprinted in *Readings in Schenker Analysis,* ed. Maury Yeston, New Haven: Yale University Press, 1977.

Appendix B

Bibliography of Works Cited

Albrechtsberger, Johann Georg. *Gründliche Anweisung zur Composition*. Leipzig, 1790.

Bach, Carl Philipp Emanuel. *Versuch über die wahre Art, das Clavier zu spielen*. Berlin, 1753 and 1762.

Bellermann, Heinrich. *Der Kontrapunkt*. Berlin, 1861.

Capellen, Georg. *Musikalische Akustik*. Leipzig: Kahnt, 1903.

Cherubini, Luigi. *Cours de contrepoint et de fugue*. Paris, 1835.

Dehn, Siegfried Wilhelm. *Lehre vom Contrapunkt, dem Canon, und der Fuge*. Berlin, 1859.

Fux, Johann Joseph. *Gradus ad parnassum*. Vienna, 1725.

————. *Gradus ad parnassum, oder Anführung zur Regelmässigen Musikalischen Composition*, trans. by Lorenz Mizler. Leipzig, 1742.

Graedener, Carl Georg Peter. *System der Harmonielehre*. Hamburg, 1877.

Hauptmann, Moritz. *Die Natur der Harmonik und Metrik*. Leipzig, 1853.

Helmholtz, Hermann von. *Die Lehre von den Tonempfindungen*. 5th ed. Braunschweig: Vieweg, 1896.

Louis, Rudolf, and Ludwig Thuille. *Harmonielehre*. Stuttgart, 1907.

Marpurg, Friedrich. *Versuch über die musikalische Temperatur, nebst einem Anhang über den Rameau- und Kirnbergerschen Grundbass*. Breslau, 1776.

Nottebohm, Gustav. *Beethovens Studien*. Leipzig, 1873.

Quantz, Johann Joachim. *Versuch einer Anweisung die Flöte traversiere zu spielen*. Berlin, 1752; rpt. Leipzig: Kahnt, 1906.

Rameau, Jean-Philippe. *Nouveau système de musique théorique*. Paris, 1726.

Richter, Ernst Friedrich. *Lehrbuch des einfachen und doppelten Contrapunkts*. Leipzig, 1872.

Riemann, Hugo. *Grosse Kompositionslehre*. Berlin and Stuttgart, 1902.

————. *Handbuch der Harmonielehre*. 3rd ed. Leipzig: Breitkopf und Härtel, 1898.

————. *Lehrbuch des einfachen, doppelten, und imitierenden Kontrapunkts*. Leipzig, 1888.